Breaking

Rhetorical Philosophy and Theory
A Series Edited by David Blakesley

Breaking Up [at] Totality
A Rhetoric of Laughter

D. Diane Davis

Southern Illinois University Press
Carbondale and Edwardsville

Library of Congress Cataloging-in-Publication Data

Davis, D. Diane (Debra Diane), 1963–

    Breaking up (at) totality : a rhetoric of laughter / D. Diane Davis.

       p.   cm. — (Rhetorical philosophy and theory)

    Includes bibliographical references and index.

    1. English language—Rhetoric—Study and teaching—Psychological aspects.

2. English language—Rhetoric—Study and teaching—Social aspects. 3. Report writing—

Study and teaching—Psychological aspects. 4. Report writing—Study and teaching—

Social aspects. 5. Laughter—Psychological aspects. 6. Laughter—Physiological aspects.

7. Laughter—Social aspects. 8. Feminist theory.

I. Title.   II. Series.

PE1404.D385   2000

808'.042'07—dc21

ISBN 0–8093–2228–5 (cloth : alk. paper)   99–32609

ISBN 0–8093–2229–3 (pbk. : alk. paper)   CIP

To Paul A. Mowery,

for the love, the lust, and the laughs

The "burst" of laughter is not a single burst, a detached fragment, nor is it the essence of a burst—it is the repetition of the bursting—and the bursting of the repetition. It is the multiplicity of meanings as multiplicity and not as meaning or intention of meaning. Intention is abolished in laughter, it explodes there, and the pieces into which it bursts are what laughter laughs—laughter, in which there is always more than one laugh.

—Jean-Luc Nancy, *The Birth to Presence*

Perhaps we should not seek a word or concept for it, but rather recognize in the thought of community a theoretical excess (or more precisely, an excess in relation to the theoretical) that would oblige us to adopt another praxis of disclosure and community.

—Jean-Luc Nancy, *The Inoperative Community*

[The university is] the place where writing loses its edge, knowledge its insomnia.

—Avital Ronell, "The Worst Neighborhoods of the Real"

Contents

Rhetorical Philosophy and Theory Series

The Rhetorical Philosophy and Theory Series aims to extend the subject of rhetoric beyond its traditional and historical bounds and thus to elaborate rhetoric's significance as a metaperspective in provocative ways. Rhetoric has become an epistemology in its own right, one marked by heightened consciousness of the symbolic act as always already contextual and ideological. Otherwise known as the rhetorical turn, this dialectic between rhetoric and philosophy may lead to views transcending the limits of each and thus help us better understand the ethical problems and possibilities of producing theory.

The Rhetorical Philosophy and Theory Series seeks quality scholarly works that examine the significance of rhetorical theory in philosophical, historical, cultural, and disciplinary contexts. Such works will typically bring rhetorical theory to bear on the theoretical statements that enfranchise disciplinary paradigms and practices across the human sciences, with emphasis on the fields of rhetoric, composition, philosophy, and critical theory.

Queries and submissions should be directed to David Blakesley, Editor, Rhetorical Philosophy and Theory, Department of English, Southern Illinois University at Carbondale, Carbondale, IL 62901–4503.

ACKNOWLEDGMENTS

It is with warm appreciation that I acknowledge this work's (not so) silent partners: the friends and colleagues who have generously offered their feedback and encouragement, the antagonists who have forced me to think more carefully through my positions, the graduate and under-graduate students in my classes who typically have taught me more about the issues discussed here than I have taught them, and the institutions that have offered their resources in support of this project. Without these partners, this text could not have been written.

I would like to thank those who advised me during the very early stages of this work, beginning with my dissertation committee at the University of Texas at Arlington—for, even after a considerable overhaul, this project remains a product of their influence and inspiration. Thanks, specifically, to Victor J. Vitanza, for his guidance and his friendship—I am deeply indebted to him for his irreverent scholarship, his unusual style, and his determination to attend to the exscribed; Luanne T. Frank for teaching me the importance of rigor and, quite literally, for teaching me how to read; Susan Hekman for engaging me in productive discus-sions and disagreements about the philosophies, politics, and feminisms discussed below; Carolyn Barros for her careful readings of my work; and Hans Kellner for asking difficult and thought-provoking questions. Thanks also to Michelle Ballif, Bob Cook, Cynthia Haynes, Rebecca Sabounchi, and Jo Suzuki—UTA's "Humanities Mafia"—for keeping me laughing, lunching, and thinking during my years at UTA and for enriching my life exponentially.

I would also like to thank those who have advised and supported me throughout the thorough reworking of this project over the last few years.

Special thanks go to my close friends and respected colleagues, Michelle Ballif, Cynthia Haynes, and Roxanne Mountford, for reading and responding to various chapters of this book—their friendship and feedback have been invaluable, their outrageous humor has kept me sane, and their own work has kept me intellectually invigorated. Thanks especially to Michelle, for convincing me that this project is a contribution to the field and for talking me through several sticky/tricky issues that arise in it. Thanks, also, to Bill Endres, a treasured friend and fabumundo poet, both for inspiration and for granting me permission to print here his poem, "A Short Discourse."

Thanks to the colleagues and friends with whom I worked and played during my two years at Old Dominion University, especially Juanita Comfort, David Metzger, and Joyce Magnotto for numerous conversations about teaching and writing; Janice Conard, Dana Heller, Ed Jacobs, Sujata Moorti, Manuela Mourão, Andrea Slane, and Jenny Terry for many helpful discussions about politics and gender studies (and for the beach bashes); Elaine Dawson for her desktop publishing wizardry; Jeff Richards, chair of the English Department, for allowing me to develop and teach courses that directly contributed to the development of this book; and the students in my *écriture féminine* seminar, especially Tammy Davis Bird, Jennifer Ciaccio, Mark Hiebert, Sarah Livingston, Josh Knutsen, Michelle Pifer, Melissa Range, and Tim Richardson, whose arresting insights and astonishingly *post*modern writing and thinking set me in motion again.

I also want to thank my new friends and colleagues at the University of Iowa for their advice, support, and/or disagreements with me as I worked through the last stages of this project. My special thanks to Eduardo Cadava, whose friendship, extraordinarily generous spirit, and unquestionable brilliance inspired several re-visions and re-thinkings. Thanks also to Fred Antczak, Barb Biesecker, Ralph Cintron, and Takis Poulakos, all of whom encouraged me, sometimes without knowing it, to think more carefully and more rhetorically about "community." And thanks to Monique Gross, my talented research assistant, for her dedicated searching and sifting on behalf of this project.

Thanks to the gifted SIUP crew—particularly former acquisitions editor Tracey Sobol-Hill and series editor David Blakesley—for taking a chance on this book. Thanks to David also for his insightful and often witty feedback.

And finally, I would like to thank my family for their love, their support, and their enormous capacity for laughter. Thanks to Gizmo Mowery Davis, my infamous Shih-Tzu, and Paul A. Mowery, my more-than-significant other, for forcing me into *play* breaks—pig fests, laugh-a-thons, and bad movies—and for their understanding when I could not play. They are "home" for me; they made this work possible. Thanks to my very hip parents, Guy and Jeanne McNeely, for urging me to take risks and offering me their unqualified acceptance. And thanks to my brother Kerry McNeely, for his love, his friendship, and his way-over-the-top sense of humor.

Breaking Up [at] Totality

PREAMBULATORY EMISSIONS:
A PREFATORY POST-SCRIPT ON
WHERE WE WILL HAVE GONE

[H]ow can we measure up to the universe if we content ourselves with the slumber of conventional knowledge?

—Bataille, *Accursed Share*

Without "chaos," no knowledge. Without a frequent dismissal of reason, no progress.

—Feyerabend, *Against Method*

The problem of the value of truth came before us—or was it we who came before the problem? Who of us is Oedipus here? Who the Sphinx? It is a rendezvous, it seems, of questions and question marks.

—Nietzsche, *Beyond Good and Evil*

In his preface to *The Order of Things*, Michel Foucault says that his book arose out of a passage in Borges, out of the "laughter that shattered," as he read, "all the familiar landmarks of [his] thought—our thought, the thought that bears the stamp of our age and our geography." The passage to which Foucault refers is from a Chinese encyclopedia in which "animals" are divided into such categories as: those "having just broken the water pitcher," "suckling pigs," "stray dogs," those that are "frenzied" or "fabulous," and those "drawn with a very fine camelhair brush." "In the wonderment of this taxonomy," Foucault says, "the thing we apprehend in one great leap," the thing that is "demonstrated as the charm of another system of thought, is the *limitation of our own*, the stark impossibility of thinking *that*" (xv). Not because it's wrong—categorizing

1

according to genus and species would not be *more correct*—but because it exposes an/other way seeing, an/other way of carving up "the world." It exposes the excess flying around, that overflow for which any one system of thought will have been unable to ac/count.

The "shattering laughter" sparked in this "wonder-filled" instant is not (only) the laughter that Aristotle attributes to Gorgias, the laughter that opposes meaninglessness to meaning (*On Rhetoric* 3.18). It's a laughter that shatters what Jacques Derrida calls the very "fabric of meaning" ("From Restricted" 259) through which the notion of meaninglessness becomes meaning*ful*, through which meaninglessness comes to operate as the dirty underside (the negated) of meaning (or, in Gorgias's case, vice versa). This book arose out of Foucault's tossing of this metaphor: laughter as an ex-plo-sion of the border zones of thought. Our categorical boundaries operate as artificial guardrails, protection against what Friedrich Nietzsche calls "the great sweep of life," which never ceases to overflow our categories and "to be on the side of the most unscrupulous polytropoi" (*Gay Science* 282).

It is negation/exclusion, via our categorical distinctions, that makes both "order" and cohesion possible. But what of the excluded? Judith Butler's answer is chilling: they constitute those "*populations erased from view*" ("Contingent" 13, my emphasis). And there it is, the terrifying potential for a(nother) Final Solution, what Victor J. Vitanza calls the "wreck" of the negative. The desire to postpone perpetually this "wreck" by steering anywhere and everywhere *else* is the primary motivation behind this project. A laughter that shatters would laugh with the "sweep," with what Hélène Cixous, in "The Laugh of the Medusa," calls the co(s)mic "rhythm that laughs you" (882). Laughter that shatters is an affirmative laughter, arising from the overflow, the excess, and capable of momentarily and instantaneously catapulting us out of negative dialectics by negating negation itself.

We-Westerners have a tendency not to laugh enough and not to *appreciate* laughter enough. A face (but also a text and/or a *techné*) contorted in laughter, Milan Kundera notes, has never been considered beautiful or sublime. "[A] beautiful face," he says, tends to be "imaginable only in its *immobility*" (*Immortality* 322), and it's beautiful inasmuch as it expresses "presence of thought" (323). If the Mona

We fear fluidity
We fffear fluidity
We fear ffffluidity

Lisa had been *cracking up*, in other words, the world may never have known her. What we find appreciable is the stability of the knowing smile and/or the controlled chuckle. The instability of irrepressible laughter is an affront to our humanist sensibilities: we do not want to *crack up*. And we don't want to deal with a world that is cracking up and that cracks *us* up—often without our consent. *Fluidity ssscares us*. But our *will* will not (and ought not) save us from the "great sweep of life." In some sense or another, we *are* breaking up, in every instant, whether we choose to affirm it or to deny it, whether we find it sublime or paltry. $^{Why}_{~~~do}$ $^{we}_{~~~fffear}$ $_{fluuuidity}$ $^{ffffluidity???}_{~~~fluidityyyy}$ This book is an invitation to break up with the force that breaks us up, to laugh with the Laughter that laughs language and technology and human beings, to explore another sensibility, another way of thinking (writing, reading), one that might steer clear of an/other *Final Solution*. What follows is an invitation to leap into the sweep . . . and to say

YES.

The Pronoun Thing

Though this book does indeed proceed with a certain re/present/ational intent, it also hopes, simultaneously, to perform what Georges Bataille and Maurice Blanchot call a "nocturnal communication," or even a nocturnal *emission*: a "communication which does not avow itself, which antedates itself and takes its authority from a nonexisting author," an author who is *breaking up* (Blanchot 20). Both author and audience are a problem for this project. The "I" and the "you" are never given, never stable: "we" are *breaking up*; it is beyond "our" control. "*I*," however, will not Shrink from the pronouns that necessarily will not have covered their territory fully enough—after all, what are "my" options? The "I" who writes and is written by this project, the "I-write," as Avital Ronell calls it, will not have been steady/solid or in complete command of the keyboard. Nietzsche said it: You were always a different person (*Gay Science* 246). "I" will not have been reducible, absolute, solid. And, therefore, this piece of writing will not/ought not/could not have been sssettled. It, necessarily, will have been both from "me" and from beyond "me." It will have exposed both more and less than "I" intended and will never have finished [itself off]. To get a "final tabulation," as Ronell suggests, "one [would have] to account for the incalculable and for the unexpected granting through which writing comes to pass" (*Finitude's Score* 1). *One would have to solidify.* "I" will not have been able to do that.

And those for whom I-write? This much has been dis/covered: The reader to whom the I-write owes its lives was always a *different* reader, dis/solving, shifting, changing hats in midsentence. And there will have been innumerable hats. As Blanchot, reading Bataille, who had been reading Nietzsche, points out: those for whom I-write are those whom "I" cannot know (23). And yet, it is inevitable: I-write *for*. The exigency of writing hails the I-write into existence(s). And those for whom I-write, the "we" this project arrogantly and tactically assumes, will have been those who have experienced an abandonment in(to) infinite finitude. For, as Blanchot suggests, there is "no end there where finitude reigns" (20). I-write *for* those who have found themselves trembling at an ecstatic limit of Being and have said (or are trying to say) *Yes*. I-write *for* those thinkers who are more interested in slow reflection than in "gaining time," who are more interested in ethical re-valuations than in "economic calculation."[1] I-write *for* those who, in spite of everything, will have appreciated breaking up, cracking up, busting up; those who will have appreciated (longed for?) a community, a pedagogy, and a politics that *begins* t/here, from a finite and disidentified fluidity that will have been "us," that will have been who "*we*" are.

Re-Tellings/Re-Spinnings

It is with a nod to our own fluidity and to the perspectival nature of any knowing that this book offers a re-reading of certain "established" histories. It seems necessary to refrain from positing a(ny) history as The History and, therefore, from simply referring to any version of history as the real thing, solid and certain. This project will be interested, then, in rereading/re-interpreting certain histories—of subjectivity, language, technology,[2] politics, and pedagogy, for instance. But these retellings/re-spinnings are not my attempt finally to get the story *straight*, to offer an objective and/or *corrective* History. *Why would I solidify?* Rather, they are an attempt to offer my own terribly interested take on an already over-

So you can never "know" your audience [handwritten marginal note] appropriated body of works. It seems necessary to spin out my versions of these histories, to make my way backwards through my own re-constructions, before getting on with a *writing toward futurity*, which will have been the aim of this book.

A word about style also seems necessary. This text may resist a swift reading. At times, it teases, refuses to come clean, to make crystal clear connections in the reader's time. It occasionally breaks with traditional *topoi*, pleading for a different approach . . . an/Other way of reading. Here, the desire is not to "argue well" but rather to *write differently*, to make an/other kind of sense.[3] This text will be less interested in proving a(ny) point[4] than in inviting unusual linkages, in calling for new idioms, in holding the space of

> EXPECT
> SOME
> LEAKSsss

questioning open. Ours will be "humble questions, which do not even ask for answers: they ask for life" (Cixous, "Coming to Writing" 138). In the name of writing, this book hopes to parody/pastiche, to crack up the language game of "exposition" wherever possible. It hopes to perform a juggling act; to get a scramble of ideas up into the air together and to invite the reader to hear the ssstatic-c-c created by the crisscrossings and sideswipings of those ideas. If it will have been up to "you," the reader, to hear the static, it will have been up to "me," the I-write, to have evoked something for you, to have *set you in mmmmmmmotion*.

A Word about Motivation

> In the dream as in the text, we go from one amazement to another. I imagine many texts are written completely differently, but I am only interested in *the texts that escape*.
>
> —Cixous, *Three Steps*

Though this text devotes itself to the field of "rhetoric and composition"—most specifically but not exclusively to the teaching of what goes by the name "writing"—it will not have been a "*how to*" book. Too much can slip by unquestioned in "how to" books, too many hidden assumptions can *remain* hidden. There is, of course, a time for that, for developing and promoting a particular approach and methodology. But here we will be interested in something else altogether, in a re-thinking, a re-viewing of what is called "writing" and what is called "teaching." Composition courses, even at the graduate level, tend to operate as service courses designed to help students master the "basic" language skills they need to succeed in other courses (conservative) and/or to help students become aware of ways in which these "basic skills" are ideologically invested (liberal). Either way, the writing in a typical comp course is conducted for something else, in the name of some greater aim or grander goal than *writing itself.*

Writing gets codified, disciplined, domesticated in the typical composition course; indeed, writing is often sacrificed *in the name of "composition,"* in the name of this "discipline's" service-oriented and pre-established requirements. As Lester Faigley notes in *Fragments of Rationality*, what passes for "good student writing" in the typical composition course is still the "modernist text," the linear and progressive narrative written in an authoritative voice and arising from accepted conceptual starting places (*topoi*) (15–16). The point here is not to suggest that there is no longer a place in this postmodern era for the "modernist text"; rather, our concern is that this very particular *style* of writing has been allowed (even encouraged) to masquerade as *writing itself.* Though we-teachers have attempted to incorporate postfoundational ways of knowing into our pedagogical strategies, as far as I can tell, we have not allowed what Lyotard calls "the postmodern condition" to radically refashion our pedagogical goals themselves. Though we have, for instance, begun to design writing courses that encourage collaborative learning, emphasize process, foreground rhetorical situation, and make room for personal experience, the motivation behind these surface-level revisions typically remains the same: to better help students produce *the same old modernist texts.* Our criteria for determining "good writing" and our motivation for "teaching writing" have remained virtually unaffected by these "updates" in pedagogical style.

Here, however, we will attempt to make a space for a composition pedagogy of an/Other kind, one that puts itself into the service of writing rather than the other way around. Refusing to beg the questions of "writing" and of "pedagogy," this slow reflection will scan for thinking's POWs (double entendre intended), for the unusual connections, illegitimate linkages, and illicit mixtures that have been left for dead beneath the "sound and fury" of official pedagogical imperatives.

Though I-write for my colleagues and students in the field of rhetoric and composition, this text will not police/protect the borders of what we like to call "our *discipline*"; indeed, in the name of writing, this text will challenge the boundaries of the home field. The goal is a "crack up"—we will attempt here to do for "composition" what Victor J. Vitanza does for "The" history of Rhetoric: to jimmy its libidinal lock, to shatter its boundaries by *inviting in everybody*.[5] We will, more specifically, break up what is called "composition" by engaging in third sophistic re-readings of the grounds upon which this "discipline" has been built.[6]

Might as well admit it: *it's time*. Even a handful of rhetoricians, traditionally proponents of composition instruction, have begun attempting to extract themselves from comp's lethal grip.[7] One of the latest and most direct attempts is an insightful essay by Roxanne Mountford and Nedra Reynolds called "Rhetoric and Graduate Studies: Teaching in a Postmodern Age." The authors note that when we study "rhetoric *only* on behalf of composition," rhetoric ends up getting the squeeze. Composition has a tendency to reduce the complexities of "rhetoric to a set of formulas," to water it down for the sake of easy teachability (199). In the hands of comp instruction, they suggest, rhetoric loses its rhetoricity.

H Y P E R B O L I C

R A N T

Calling for rhetoric courses that teach "rhetoricality" and the "transdisciplinary potential" of rhetorical studies, Mountford and Reynolds imply that if rhetoric ever hopes to grow up again and *become what it is*, it will first have to pry itself out from under comp's heavy thumb.

Certainly, "composition" has earned this public reprimand—it has been shortsighted and rigid, trusting in its own discourse of mastery and silencing and/or ignoring what it is incapable of appropriating. When the stable self exploded and the "universal foundation for knowledge" crumbled, when the discreet partnership between "knowledge" and power was exposed and the linguistic ground of "rationality" was dis/covered—composition instruction quietly continued *to do what it had always done*, as if its goals and motivations had not been tremendously problematized by what had been going on outside its own house. Through this extreme negligence, through its devotion to some assumed nonrhetorical foundation, composition instruction has effectively given not only rhetoric but even *writing* (*écriture*) the squeeze. Within the typical comp classroom, a writing toward futurity, an extremist writing that pushes the limits of knowing and explodes thinking's border zones is sacrificed for the sake of "teachability." *Composition*, it's time to admit, is a control freak. So, it is with a grateful nod to Mountford and Reynolds that we attempt here to up their proverbial ante, to suggest that not only rhetoric but *writing, too*, has good reason to consider cutting itself loose from the "discipline" of "composition," divorcing itself from this overbearing and old-fashioned stepparent. Yes, yes, yes—even *writing* either ought to find a way to leave home . . . or to make its home unhomey, uncanny, to b-r-e-a-k it up.

Here, we will be interested in the latter, in reconceiving what is called "rhetoric and composition," in opening up this beast's protective skin to let in "impurities," to let in that which it has fought to exclude in the name of identity, of politics, of truth . . . of knowledge. We'll be performing a transfusion of sorts, but an illicit and unsanitary one, one that the body of composition instruction will no doubt violently reject, one that will both kill off the beast *and* offer it the chance to come to life. The business of this text, it should be noted, is not to *produce* the serum—that's already available; the crisis in the legitimation of knowledge and representation is precisely the pharmakonic lifeblood this text will attempt to *let in*, little by little, drop by drop. The task of this text will have been to *mainline the fix*, to *shoot it up*, to make the connections, to link-link-link. We will scan for leakage and strive for linkage. We will let it all in, quoting obsessively—not to *prove points* (the language game of logic) but to plug ourselves in, to *function with*[8] those

There have been other transfusions, of course. This work owes its life(s) to their proponents, to those countertraditionalists in our field who have had the courage of "indecency," the courage to speak the Unspeakable. If there is anything of value in this text, "we" have "them" to thank for it. If nothing of value shows itself here, however, it will have been due to "my" inability to make it through the doors they have left open for me. A few [im]proper names are in order. I refer specifically to these (and other) exceptional rhetoricians, all of whom claim the field of rhetoric and composition as "home" but who also strive to make it Unhomey, to offer it some kind of transfusion: Michelle Ballif, Jim Berlin, Sharon Crowley, Lester Faigley, Cynthia Haynes, Susan Jarratt, Roxanne Mount-

texts that have been pumping out the "serum" for well over a century. "*We*" are way behind . **.   .   .   .**

.

It's a
good
day
to die.

ford, Geoff Sirc, Greg Ulmer, Victor Vitanza, and Lynn Worsham. If this/my text fails to offer you the ride you deserve, I refer you to these rhetors, each of whom has, at some point, given me the ride of my life(s).

Some More Words about Motivation

Make no mistake: this transfusion will be brutal. The "serum," after all, is explosive; its *job* is to detonate, to touch off tiny explosions at the limits of "the thinkable." What we're infusing into "rhetoric and composition" is a crisis, a "shattering laughter," and any alliance with laughter is a risky business. Mas'ud Zavarzadeh and Donald Morton, for instance, have argued that laughter is an irresponsible approach to a violent world, a position that says to the oppressed: oh well, just laugh about it (44–48). And in a sense, it is precisely the point of this project to issue a call to "*just* laugh." But here "just" would have the double *entendre* Jean-François Lyotard gave it in *Just Gaming*: it would connote both "merely" and "justly." Though I do hesitate, for obvious reasons, to say that this is a *serious* topic, I do not hesitate to say that it is a responsible, political, and ethical one. If it's risky, it's because b-r-e-a-k-i-n-g up necessarily involves risk—there is no way of knowing what will be left in the wake of a laughter that shatters "all the familiar landmarks of [our] thought."

There can be no doubt about it, this laughter is *destructive*: An impulse toward destruction (clearing away) is involved in any thinking of futurity. In *Finitude's Score*, Ronell defines

Just laughing . . .
Just *laughing* . . .
Just laughing **. . .**

destruction as "a decisive doing away with that which, already destroyed, is destructive in its contin uance. To the extent that it is possible only on the basis of a new and more radical affirmation, destruction, moreover, has pledged itself to the future" (xiii). Destruction, then, aligns itself with Nietzsche's call to "shed [one's] old bark," to "have done" with the old to make room for new sensations and new potential futures (*Gay Science* 331). Ronell notes that *devastation*, on the other hand, "holds no such contract with futurity." Devastation, rather, "has to do with a fundamental shutdown," a "pathological" drive toward "a telic finality or fulfillment or the accomplishment, once and for all, of a Goal." Life is devastated when it is not permitted the room to move, to sweep, to shed. *Solidity* = *death* .

but

This project is joyfully de-structive; it hopes, along with Hélène Cixous, to "break up the truth" with laughter, to take Nietzsche's hammer to anything passing itself off as solid/closed/finished . . . dead.

A Request

Some will raise an eyebrow right here, close the book, and think: *Ludic*. But the matter ought not be decided too quickly. This work *is* irreverent, blasphemous; it calls current pedagogical strategies and political programs (even those we like to think are "progressive") into question. But the request issued here is that this text be granted a temporary stay, that we agree to pause momentarily to give a hearing to what it will have said. "Might as well face it," Ronell says, "[s]ome hesitations are rigorous" (*Crack Wars* 58). And this one will definitely require rigor. An ear fine-tuned to a logical *logos* will miss this text's emissions completely. It will be necessary to listen with an ear that can strain past the merely epistemological. Not much that is immediately applicable to age-old philosophical programs or so-called progressive pedagogical imperatives will be offered here. And/but that ought not suggest that what is offered is *un*productive or *un*important.

"[T]hat which ought to be cannot be concluded from that which is, the 'ought' from the 'is.'" (Lyotard and Thebaud, *Just Gaming* 17)

"What is needed above all is an absolute skepticism toward all inherited concepts." (Nietzsche, *Will to Power* 221)

The request: *that this work not be judged across the very criteria it aims to call into question, that it not be called to the carpet for not consistently performing those very language games it finds suspect.*

We will be less interested in building an argument than in spotlighting that which shows up for politics and pedagogy in the suspension of argumentative discourse. We will be interested in what our faith in the language game of logic has cost us, as a field and as a society, and in what that game makes it impossible to think. "Reason" itself is on the stand in this text, and it will have been found

GUILTY.

Thinking (writing, reading)-styles, as Lyotard suggests in *The Differend*, have not changed much since Nazism supposedly ended. Though we like to believe we understand why Nazism could have happened, what mistakes in thinking allowed it to become, for some, a supportable ethics;

Hypotactic linking practices are complicit with a mode of thought that can be tied to the Nazi disaster. These conventions of linkage are after closure, totality, final truth, and they will be questioned in this text, as they are in Lyotard's.

and though we like to think, as Ronell puts it, that an "indisputable sense of justice" has since reinstalled itself, we still have no "philosophical proof or a rigorous guarantee of the intelligibility of the Nazi disaster" ("Differends" 255). In fact, inasmuch as our contemplations about this disaster begin with the assumption that it was *Ir*rational, that it was due to *mis-takes* in thinking or to an *in*authentic ethic, they remain entrenched precisely in what they critique   •

•

•

•

•

•

•

This is the whole show.

The book's buck stops here. In the face of our own continuing complicity, with the re-cognition that, as Ronell notes, "the gas has not been entirely turned off, but continues to leak and to spread its effects" (255). "It" is not over, and "we" are not innocent. In fact, to "teach" writing is to push a world view, a way of ordering "the world." When we require students to write *only* according to the criteria associated with

> It is not wrong to wrest nazism from the deceptively secure space of a restricted national spasm . . . [we] all fed the death machine—one, as we may soon learn, that was not . . . merely "irrational." It makes sense. Indeed, what needs to be considered is that the project of making sense or rather making one sense is implicated in history's breakup with itself.
> —Ronell, "Differends"

what Faigley calls "the modernist text," we become pushers of hypotactic linking/thinking strategies; we push not simply a writing style but a *value system* that privileges hierarchy, mastery, and (Final) closure. And we validate (encourage), as if it were *thinking itself,* a style of thinking that operates via negation—we teach students, as Vitanza puts it, "to think in terms of the negative . . . to say what something is by virtue of what this 'some-thing' is *not:* hence we have definition (meaning, rationality, community) by ill virtue of negation" ("Threes" 198). We have inclusion by ill virtue of exclusion. Or, à la Kenneth Burke: *congregation by segregation* ("The Rhetorical Situation" 268). We have, inherent in our discourses on writing, a rhetoric of totality.

Furthermore, when we-writing-teachers demand that writing begin from established conceptual starting places (*topoi,* common ground), that both the writer and the text, that is, *first* take their place within the "common" fund of circulating stories that bind a "community" (*mythos*), we demand that the Unthinkable remain unthinkable. There is supposedly nothing more common to the members of a "community" than the myths they share, the stories they tell each other about who they are (myths of identity), where they come from (myths of origin), and where they're headed (myths of progress). We might even say that myth and community define each other, and this, as Jean-Luc Nancy has pointed out, "motivates a reflection on community according to myth" (*Inoperative Community* 42). And yet, we also now recognize—after the horror of the Aryan myth—that the invention and perpetuation of communal mythology is always bound up with the staging and setting to work of a "Volk"; there is a discreet partnership between myth-production/perpetuation and the uses of its power (Nancy 42).

Any assumption of a "social essence" functions to deny both the infinite finitude (the unprecedented multiplicity) of singular beings and the radical differences among those singular beings. Even when it is downsized to the level of a "discourse community," as Faigley has observed, the myths of common-being serve to "suppress differences among members and exclude those who are labeled different" (231). Proponents of expressionist, feminist, and social epistemic rhetorics of composing typically deal with this problem by turning the pedagogical task toward myth *re-vision/re-production*. But, while reinscriptions are certainly not nothing (they are necessary), they also will not have been enough to effect a rigorous hesitation in the machinations of exclusion.

Such hesitations are sparked in the exposure of inscription's EXscriptions,[9] in a cranking up of excess's rustlings, which myth production is designed to reign in and/or cover over. The exscribed are what the *topoi* specifically *do not* invite. There is, of course, exscription in any inscription, so these inappropriable exteriorities inevitably crash inscribing's party,

> Blanchot on Bataille: How had he come to wish for the interruption of discourse? And not the legitimate pause that permits the give-and-take of conversations. . . . What he had wanted was something completely different, a cold interruption, the rupture of the circle. (in Nancy, *Birth* 333)

showing up anyway, in/as writing's openings, effecting tiny interruptions in the mythation process itself, petite ruptures in the myth of myth— ruptures that open toward unprecedented things, the singularities that the narrative demands of any myth necessarily will smother. *Writing: where the inscribed and the exscribed lock in an uncanny embrace.* But composition instruction fails community precisely inasmuch as it *ignores* the exscription involved in inscription, inasmuch as it promotes a *style* of writing that is allowed (or, really, *required*) to efface what it exscribes.

There are other styles. Some writing—*atopical* writing, *é(x)cri-ture*[10]—has the guts to attend to the exscribed, to respond to its call, for the sake of the *community* that the illusion of common-being conceals. Because what singular beings share is precisely that for which no myth can ac/count—their unsharable loose ends—community makes its debut (it outs itself) in writing that takes off from *anywhere* but "common ground," writing that pushes the limits of communal mythology, that even hushes it for an instant so that the finitude rustling beneath it might get a hearing and might, paradoxically, give community back to us (sans the "*myth* of community"), if only in flashes.

It's possible, of course, to continue teaching without considering which ways of being-with-one-another our pedagogies promote, to point a finger at another country or at the Neo-Nazi organizations within our own countries and to feel righteous, above it all. But the "reason" on which we base our innocence, that thinking-style that masquerades as thinking itself, that sends us scrambling to categorize, to separate the Self from the Other, the Same from the not-Same, the poison from the cure . . . reason is in deep. It can no longer be counted on to save us from disaster because it's *implicated* in too many disasters. Don't miss the significance of this: The Nazi Nightmare may not have been the result of "mis-takes" in thinking—it may rather have been the result of a thinking that was too logical, logical to the extreme. After all, the "project of making [One] sense" seems to have been hanging out at the scene of every massive crime against "humanity" recorded in our long and indecent histories—it presided over the holy wars, the Salem witch trials, and the Nazi massacres; it justified the storm of Desert Storm and the ethnic cleansing in Bosnia; in fact, it has been at the bottom of every hate crime but-tressed by presumed distinctions in race, sex, class, religion, sexual orientation . . . .

> From a strictly political point of view fascism and Nazism have not been over-come, and we still live under their sign.
> —Agamben, *The Coming Community*

ETC.

"Reason" seems always to have been there, camouflaging its alliance with particular communal myths, quietly founding and funding atrocity. It would be silly, of course, to argue instead for the IRrational. A simple negative deconstruction (privilege-flipping), in this case, would be absurd.[11] We're looking, rather, for lines of flight, for third positions outside the dichotomy altogether. This text hopes to make room for an/other sens/ibility, to make an/other sense, to *make sense proliferate*.[12] The request made here is that you/we consider precisely this before hastening to declare, by the old criteria, the following of *this* line of questioning to be ludic or irresponsible. We're after a new ethics of reading/writing/thinking here, one that does not leave us trapped within a fixed set of obligations: we hope to learn to read/write/think the unreadable/writable/thinkable.

The motivation for all of this destruction is the anticipation of an/other future, an/other way of being-with-one-another-in-the-world. Community is at issue here: we hope to find a way to approach reading/writing/thinking in the rhetoric and composition classroom that will not validate final solutions and that will find ways to steer clear of the "wreck" of the negative. De(con)struction is affirmative insofar as it hopes for a third way, out of logocentric meaning-making, out of the negation required for final closure. That is, it is through its No to nihilism that this destructive text comes to a genuine affirmation of life and of *writing*. It is in the midst of de(con)struction that momentary lines of flight[13] show up for us, lines out of the devastation of solidity and into the multiple tropings/turnings of "life," into the co(s)mic rhythm of playful laughter. This project will shoot for a thinking of fluidity and a fluidity of thinking. It will invite you to leap into the sweep and to look for ways to

say
Yessss.

Disclaimer on [My] Inevitable "Stupidity"

One thing about *any* thinking, though, is that it's always stalked by more thinking. Inasmuch as "thinking is trying to think the unthinkable," as Cixous puts it—because "thinking the thinkable is not worth the effort" (*Three Steps* 38)—it is both on the run from thinking and in hot pursuit of it. It is, on the one hand, vulnerable; having crossed the line, it makes itself a target without a shield. But it's also merciless; thinking past the thinkable involves crashing through it, exposing the limits it sets as erroneous, as the functions of an enormous blind spot or of . . . let's just say it: *ssstupidity*. Thinking always has a contract out on that which has already been thought. The instant a thinking text hits the streets, its days are numbered. The stupidity police *mobilize*. Ronell, in fact, devotes an entire essay, "The Uninterrogated Question of Stupidity," to what she says Gilles Deleuze, in the memoirs found after his death, had called "the transcendental principles of stupidity."

In a sense, though, one wonders who would be spared liability where stupidity is concerned. Is there not a suspicion, an anxiety, that you, a fugitive from stupidity, are on the verge of being caught (finally) by some smart bomb headed straight for your house?

—Ronell, "The Uninterrogated Question"

Acknowledging that it is "undoubtedly someone's responsibility to name that which is stupid," that "stupidity can and must be exposed," Ronell also observes that the project of exposure is inevitably infected with that which it hopes to expose. Working the limits of what goes by the name "stupidity," she operates as double agent, determined to ferret out and denounce stupidity and/but also to expose the "relatedness of stupidity to intelligence," to any pursuit that "seeks to establish itself and territorialize its findings." Including her own. "A total loser, stupidity is also that which rules," perpetually reproducing itself via the very cogitations employed to detect and correct it. Furthermore, though there is a certain intellectual courageousness associated with "being able to catch the other in the act, flashing onto stupidity," especially when it involves thinking past thought's border zones, Ronell cautions that there is also, simultaneously, "something altogether traditional about [making] such clear-cut determinations," about the will to zone off "the nonconsensual other into sites of stupidity" (1–2).

We'll take that as The Caution of cautions and admit up front that even as we attempt to cross limits and bust the stupidities that set them, we will not ourselves have escaped the bounds of "the stupid." Here, we will be in the business of exposing, among other things, the apparent *will to stupidity* that drives many composition curriculums, which demand, for instance, that students (and scholars) rush to judgment in the name of the Conclusion, that they simplify complexity in the name of clarity, and that they reign in their own multiplicitous sites of exploration in the name of *The* authoritative voice. And yet, it is necessary that we also acknowledge our own complicity in the processes of stupidity. Though we will be calling for that which does not reterritorialize, for that which does not seek to establish itself and that validates the space of indecision/hesitation, we will not have

> This is why, in a sense, tests such as those administered to children invariably belong to the realm of stupidity. To the extent that they demand an answer and instrumentalize the moment of the question, they escape the anguish of indecision, complication, or hypothetical redoubling that would characterize intelligence. In the instance of producing an answer, the intelligent examinee has to play stupid.
> —Ronell, "The Uninterrogated Question"

succeeded in fully *answering* that call. Borders will have been set here, too; the blind spots and stupidities driving this I-write will have been fully functional. "Stupidity," Ronell observes, "is everywhere." And neither her essay nor this book is exempt from that critique. Though it is typically the other who gets figured as stupid, Ronell suggests that, given the omnipresence of stupidity, the "only possible ethical position" would have to be: "I am stupid before the other" (13). The best we can do, it seems, is nod vigorously in agreement, take a deep breath, and . . . still . . . *get on with it.*

Trajectory of the T-t-text

This text has been divided into four chapters and a major excursus. The first two chapters and the excursus attempt to articulate a rhetoric of laughter, a rhetoric of "cracking up," across which we might reread our political and pedagogical strategies. This rhetoric of laughter hopes to offer not an/other topos but what Ronell calls "an ectopia of all proper places" (*Finitude's Score* 1–2), a breaking up of our accepted topoi, a shattering of what we tend to assume is common ground. Beginning from the notion that life, language, and Being are in motion and that we are not in charge of the flow, this rhetoric of laughter attempts to continue Nietzsche's revaluation of all values. Consider these first chapters prep for the transfusion—they are an articulation of that which our field has managed, for the most part, not to hear, not to attend to. In the last two chapters, the transfusion begins. These chapters offer a reading of feminist politics and composition pedagogy across the rhetoric of laughter "prepared" in the first half of the book. The third chapter breaks up and then redefines "feminist politics" as that which EXscribes itself from (phal)logocentric ordering systems, and the fourth chapter articulates a composition pedagogy based on this refashioned and post-gendered "feminist politics." This reading-across is an attempt to inject composition pedagogy with life's proliferating impulse, to invite the possibility for an/other politics and an/other pedagogy that would attend to the excess overflowing any binary opposition, that would attend to the excluded third that current composition pedagogy perpetually "erases from view."

The first chapter concerns itself with physiological laughter and the tendency of the laugher *to be laughed*. Human beings, chapter 1 suggests, are routinely caught in the co(s)mic "sweep," seized by outside forces, which manifest themselves, for instance, in bursts of irrepressible laughter. Because human reason is rendered powerless in the face of these polymorphously perverse "rhythms," which echo from the "noise" of *physis* (nonrational) rather than the melodies of *nomos* (rational), the (saving) power of rationality and, therefore, human agency have become suspect. To be possessed by this movement of energy, laughed by a co(s)mic Laughter, is to be thrown into a *petit mal* in which one's consciousness, one's capacity for meaning-making is suspended. And/but to fight with the sweep is to fight with *life*. An affirmative response to this posthumanist notion, on the other hand, would offer a burst of the laughter that *ssSHAT-T-TERS*—a simulation of the "sweep," which would point up the illusions of fixed identities and what we have thought of as human *agency*. In the moment that one laughs into the sweep, that one laughs with the Laughter that laughs her, s/he both laughs (functions as subject) and *is laughed* (functions as object); and that, as Georges Bataille says, is comedy (*Accursed Share* 1.70). At this moment, meaning/logic exceeds itself in a burst of laughter, and the boundaries of the ego crack up.

If we are periodically convulsed by a physiological manifestation of co(s)mic Laughter, we are also possessed by a *logos* that hails us into subject positions and speaks us. But the force of Laughter convulses language as well as bodies, giving the *logos* a Being of its own that is nonlogical and playful. Chapter 2 suggests that it is a laughing *logos* that hails us, a *logos* that is traversed by co(s)mic Laughter. The Laughter-in-language pro-

He has labeled what he's doing as laughter. Therefore categorizing it

Preambulatory Emissions 19

liferates meaning rather than fixating it; it has the tendency to disrupt any *techné* and to *seduce us as it tropes*.[14] To be spoken by a language contorted in laughter is to be spoken by *language on the loose*, a schizoid language, capable of hailing into being only sssplintered subjectivities. Affirmative responses to this Laughter-in-language would simulate it in an overperformance of its violations of semantic order. The aim would be to begin to hear this discursive form of laughter not across our desire for the "progress of the mind"[15] or the unity of the subject but other/ wise, with an/other ear, as an/other affirmation of the "sweep." An ethics of decision in a world that has lost its criteria for responsible action begins with straining to hear the excess that gets drowned out, sacrificed for the clarity of One voice, One call, One legitimate position. A posthumanist ethics ought not be about shutting down the flow but about opening it up, pulling back the stops.

In the excursus that follows chapter 2, the question concerning (laughter-in-)technology is addressed. If we are periodically seized by co(s)mic Laughter and hailed by a laughing logos, we are also "enframed," as Martin Heidegger says, by technology. However, against Heidegger, this excursus notes that even technology does not escape the reach of the "sweep": we are "enframed" by a *laughing techné*, which manifests itself in violations of the semiotic/symbolic order. The sacred borders/binaries that support (gendered) power relations, identity politics, and human production are unceremoniously transgressed in cyburbia, where interfaces (with the Other) are made *everywhere*. Donna Haraway's cyborg, for instance, is the metaphysical subject grazed by schizophrenia, broken up (and *breaking up*), displaced into what Ronell calls "splintering disidentifications" ("Activist" 299) without a substantial referential image. Cyborg subjectivity is the result of our encasement in a technological frame that is "breaking up." Affirmative responses to the hail of this laughing technology would engage in deliberate violations of the semiotic/symbolic order to spotlight the co(s)mic Laughter that convulses the technology that calls us.

Chapter 3, which is divided into two sections, offers an application of a rhetoric of laughter to pragmatic American feminist politics. Here, Teresa Ebert's distinction between "ludic" and "resistance" postmodernism, a distinction on which many American feminisms operate (even if they don't accept Ebert's terminology or her brand of materialist feminism), is questioned and a posthumanist, postidentity *politics* for feminism is sought. This chapter explores the potential for an/other "feminism," one that would be political *other/wise*, that would make its way out of oppositional politics and into a third and affirmative space. Crossing a rhetoric of laughter with what Ronell calls a "grim[acing] and humorless" oppositional feminist politics, chapter 3 locates a post-humanist "feminist" "politics" that takes off from a notion of community that is not tied to subjectivity—or rather, that is tied to subjects who are *breaking up*. This performative feminist politics devotes itself not to the polis but to *community*—and the distinction turns out to be critical both for feminism and for politics: this *feminist politics* devotes itself to the breaking up of totality, to the affirmative unraveling of the myth of common-being.

The final chapter offers a critique of composition's "progressive" pedagogies across Michel Foucault's notion of the "carceral city," and it suggests that, though radical (including feminist) composition pedagogies claim to be "empowering," they are often actually no less violent and no more "liberating" than the traditional pedagogies they aim to supplant. Pedagogical violence has simply been camouflaged in the move from one mode of "normalization" to another. Chapter 4 crosses a rhetoric of laughter with a serious-minded will to (critical/feminist composition) pedagogy in an attempt to explore the potential for a laughing pedagogy, which would celebrate performance, seduction, *and* resistance. Teaching writing, as Jim Berlin reminded us again and again, is a seriously political business. Given that, this chapter attempts to build a composition pedagogy un/founded on the redefined "feminist politics" discussed in chapter 3. The result is a postgendered "feminist" composition pedagogy that invites an/Other kind of writing, one that is interested at least as much in exscriptions as inscriptions, an *é(x)criture* that zooms in on what the will to "clarity" sheers off: on what is *laughable* and *laughing* in the language.

1

PHYSIOLOGICAL LAUGHTER: THE SUBJECT CONVULSED

We should consider every day lost on which we have not danced at least once. And we should call every truth false which was not accompanied by at least one laugh.

—Nietzsche, *Thus Spoke Zarathustra*

Living, there is no happiness in that. Living: carrying one's painful self through the world. But being, being is happiness. Being: becoming like a fountain, a fountain on which the universe falls like warm rain.

—Kundera, *Immortality*

Woe to those who, to the very end, insist on regulating the movement that exceeds them with the narrow mind of the mechanic who changes a tire.

—Bataille, *Accursed Share*

In one of my most vivid childhood memories, I am sitting in church, watching a tuft of hair—a twig—at the back of the minister's head bounce up and down as he speaks. I don't remember what he's saying, but I do remember how that twig seems to have a being of its own. The more animated the minister becomes, the more that twig comes to life, and the more I become amused. He obviously believes himself in complete control of his person, but I recognize that this twig is demanding its independence. I see, too, that it's exactly at the back of his head, just out of a frontal view in a morning mirror-check, and I realize that it has no doubt been *precisely* that mirror-check that has created his illusion of self-mastery in the first place. It's in this instant that my mind grasps the comical; it grasps the distance between that rebellious twig and the minister's illusion of self-unity. It grasps what I would now refer to as

21

Jean Baudrillard's notion of object strategies: the domination of the "sub-ject" by the "object."[1] And this realization prompts an amused smile to stretch across my face.

My amusement, however, doesn't last long. In the very next instant, and quite without warning, *my* subjectivity, too, is called into question. My body feels overwhelmed, intoxicated by an inexplicable force; I feel weak, out of control. My whole being wants desperately *not* to laugh, and yet it's clear to me that my will is not in control; something else has hold of me—I wonder if it's God. Despite my willpower, despite my squirming and my clenched teeth, I hear mySelf beginning to *lose it*; "I" am beginning to "crack up," both literally (the stability of the "I" is chal-lenged when it becomes the *object* of this laughter's force) and figurative-ly. I feel harsh eyes boring into me from all sides, and I fight desperately for control. But to no avail. My body has been *possessed* by the force of laughter: Despite my reason and my will, laughter bursts out. The battle is over: "I" have been conquered.

This was one of the most traumatic experiences of my young life. But a few years later, in one of my favorite episodes of *The Mary Tyler Moore Show*, I found comfort. In this episode, Chuckles the Clown pays the ultimate price for challenging the reality principle: he dresses up as a giant peanut in a parade and becomes lunch for a confused and hungry elephant. Mary and a somber newsroom crew pay their respects at the memorial service. But suddenly, out of the blue, Mary begins to lose it. The bizarre humor of Chuckles' ill-fated simulation hits her without warning, and when it does she flies into an irrepressible fit of laughter. Other mourners stare at her in disbelief and disgust, and she's mortified by her own irreverence. But Mary Richards is clearly not piloting this moment of her destiny. She's out of control, seized, overtaken.

I identified with Mary's struggle through every agonizing second. This kind of laughter is over-the-edge, excessive; it is irrepressible, ir-rational, and quite irreverent. I no longer believe it to be a manifestation of God, but I do think it may be the gods;[2] or, rather, it may be the powerful force of an intertwined *logos* and (Gorgian) *kairos*: what Hélène Cixous might call "the rhythm that *laughs you*" ("Laugh" 885). This present study is an exploration and an affirmation of that "rhythm," with which we are occasionally in touch, and of the (post)philosophical, post-humanist consequences of its nonrational seizures. This Laughter[3] is not human, not logical, yet is capable of overtaking human beings—of *laughing us* even when we choose not to laugh.

This book accepts the posthumanist notion that human beings are always already functions of other functions: not only are we frequently laughed more than we laugh, we are also spoken more than we speak and even *gestured* more than we gesture (Kundera, *Immortality* 7). Human agency is problematic indeed in the face of this realization: if human beings are routinely and unceremoniously possessed by outside forces or "rhythms" that have little to do with social norms (*nomos*), they can hardly fancy themselves in control either of their lives or of the course of human events. This is the posthumanist paradox: that we both make and/but are also (more so) *made by History*.

We get into the most trouble and become the most dangerous in the instant we believe we've found a way out of the paradox, the instant we believe we've found a way to usher in a new Eden. The Communist regimes of Central Europe, as Milan Kundera notes, "were made not by criminals but by enthusiasts convinced they had discovered the only road to paradise" (*Unbearable* 176). If human reason is rendered powerless in the face of polymorphously perverse "rhythms," which echo out of the "noise" of *physis* (non/rational) rather than the melodies of *nomos* (rational),[4] then the (saving) power of rationality and, therefore, human agency become suspect. Our subjecthood looms infinitesimal in the face of our overwhelming subjection, and it becomes necessary to determine once again what it

> It is only where, historically, finitude has been infinitized that endless damage has been done: the frightful hubris of metaphysical man.
> —Ronell, *Finitude's Score*

means to be human, "what," as Rosi Braidotti asks, "counts as human in a post-humanist world" (162).

That (post)modern question has, paradoxically, re/turned many to the premodern, the pre-Platonic (specifically, Heraclitean) notion of Being as Becoming. In "Nietzsche and the Obscurity of Heraclitus," Sarah Kofman notes that for Heraclitus, *physis* (Being) is bound up with *doxa* (appearance) and the endless ebb and flow of becoming. Kofman, reading Nietzsche, who is reading Heraclitus, notes that becoming is not "unruly or disorderly chaos" (47). Rather, for Heraclitus, Kofman says, the world:

is not dialectical but juridical and agonal, truly Greek: [the process of] becoming implies the splitting of a single force, such as fire, into two qualitatively different activities which, while they tend to merge, also fight each other without either one being capable of ultimately triumphing. (47)

Apparent stability should not be mis/understood as either side's ultimate victory; it only indicates the momentary advantage of one side over the other. Being, for Heraclitus (and, presumably, other pre-Socratics or—Nietzsche's term: "preplatonics"), is not stable but is rather what Martin Heidegger referred to as a wild and unruly storm of Becoming (*Early Greek* 78).

And/but if Being *is* Becoming, "we" lose our capacity to locate a sticking point for the "I," a solid foundation upon which to build our Selves and our world. If "nobody is self-made, least of all man," as Donna Haraway notes ("*Ecce Homo*" 86), and if even the "I" is a catachresis, a "necessary error," as Judith Butler suggests (*Bodies That Matter* 230), then identity becomes an unstable foundation for (traditional approaches to) politics and our notions of agency beg to be rethought. *The* subject is in crisis, and Butler's demystifications leave no room for hedging: "The subject as a self-identical entity," she says, emphatically, "is no more."

POTENTIAL RESPONSES TO THE PARADOX

But these postmodern-cum-premodern notions of subjectivity leave we-bi-products-of-modernist-political-agendas vulnerable, conflicted; they leave us standing on a ground that is crᵣru^m_m^{m}bling under our feet. It is from this precarious position that we are forced to respond to the post-humanist paradox and its challenge to our political hopes. Potential responses are few; in fact, for effect, we will stoo

oo

oop

to an either/or here: *either* there is affirmation of the noncenter, the non-foundation, *or* there is negation of it. Negation typically manifests itself in one of three ways: (a) as Idealism, or a blatant *refusal* to respond, which fights against the flow and says "No! I won't believe that there is

NO-THING there!"; (b) as Modernism, or an exceedingly hopeful attempt to (re)construct the foundation that has been *lost*, to build a Some-Thing (presence) out of No-Thing (absence); and (c) as what Peter Sloterdijk, in *The Critique of Cynical Reason*, calls cynicism, a hopeless and nihilistic experience of the noncenter as a *loss*, a No-thing where there had been hope/faith that there was Some-thing, or rather One Thing. The cynical response accepts its foundationless fate, but it does not do so happily. Rather, it becomes paralyzed by nostalgia and a sense of loss for everything in which it had once held faith.

An/Other, fourth, and (perhaps) less typical and less obviously negative response manifests itself in what Sloterdijk calls kynicism. The kynic, the cynic's uncivil opposite, leaps into the negative, the NoThing, *positively*, and therefore flips the privilege from the Some-Thing to the No-Thing, from the positive to the negative. The kynic *celebrates* the meaninglessness of the world. "Kynicism," Slojov Žižek tells us in his discussion of Sloterdijk, is the "plebeian rejection of the official culture by means of irony and sarcasm: the classical kynical procedure is to confront the pathetic phrases of the ruling official ideology . . . with everyday banality and to hold them up to ridicule, thus exposing behind the sublime *noblesse* of the ideological phrases the egotistical interests, the violence, the brutal claims to power" (*Sublime Object* 29). But the kynic's battles against meaning and order are fought without tears: the kynic's weapon is a devilish *laughter, which* cracks up, not only [at] the cynic's sorrow but also [at] the idealist's naïveté and the modernist's hopes.

Affirmative responses resemble the kynical response inasmuch as they also celebrate the posthumanist paradox; however, they do not do so by fighting against meaning. Rather, affirmative responses view the non-foundational state not as the loss of a foundation but as a space of overflow. The Some-Thing does not give way to a No-Thing; rather it is exploded into a radical excess. Where we thought there was only One Thing, there exists a wild multiplicity. Whereas kynicism aims to shift the privilege from one side of the binary to the other (which is not nothing), affirmative approaches *dis/solve* the Some-Thing/No-Thing dichotomy itself. They respond neither (1) positively (Some-Thing is present) nor (2)

> [T]he great sweep of life has actually shown itself to be on the side of the most unscrupulous polytropoi.
> —Nietzsche, *Gay Science*

negatively (Some-Thing is absent) but rather (3) with an affirmation of the nonpresence that is neither positive nor negative: Affirmative responses denegate the negative. As Derrida suggests in his discussion of Bataille, a kynic's devil laughter slips into an affirmation when it rips through the very fabric of meaning in which meaning and meaning-*less*ness are inscribed, when it "tears apart the negative side, that which makes it the reassuring *other* surface of the positive[,] and . . . exhibit[s] within the negative, in an instant, that which can no longer be called negative" ("From Restricted" 259). Of the utmost importance here is an emphasis on the instantaneous "nature" of this affirmative response. This book is not interested in a Final Solution to the problem of the negative. It only hopes to get a peek at the hysteria in which our "saneness" is inscribed, to witness a moment in which the boundaries of negation fail to hold steady.

This chapter is devoted to an exploration of each of these potential responses to the posthumanist paradox; however, we will not (and could not) proceed disinterestedly. Our examination of negative responses will be conducted across our *desire* to get to the possibility for an affirmative response. This project is driven by the urge to explore the potential for saying "yes" to a so-called "uni/verse," which reveals itself, in an instant, as (more so) a multi-verse, a poly-verse—unac/countable and unmaster-able. It is motivated by the desire to get in touch with the "rhythm that laughs [us]," a rhythm that this project will attempt to link with a particular notion of *kairos*, a notion that has been attributed to Gorgias's epistemology rather than to Plato's.

Gorgian *Kairos*

The most popular understanding of the notion of *kairos*, which James Kinneavy suggests is a "neglected" concept in rhetorical and critical theory, is a Platonic one. *Kairos*, as Plato says in the *Phaedrus*, is the "propriety of time," the capacity to say the right thing at the right moment to gain the desired persuasive effect. *Kairos* is, therefore, linked to *nomos*, to human social and cultural norms. Bernard Miller notes that time, for Plato, is *chronos* (linearity), and that *kairos* is simply a "special case of

chronos" (172). *Kairos*, here the opportune moment, exists
device of linear time, which the philosopher/speaker mu
for the sake of expediency. But this understanding of *kairos*, a.
suggests, implies a particular metaphysics of presence and an enormou.
faith in reason. It assumes that time can be reduced to a series of "nows"
and "seized in a concept; [that] it is at man's [*sic*] disposal, and his mastery of it therefore depends upon time as an abstraction" (172).

Miller, who interprets *kairos* across Martin Heidegger's notions of
time and Being, finds this approach highly problematic, and he suggests
that Gorgias's use of *kairos* as a concept differs considerably from Plato's.
Gorgias, he says, appears to fashion his notion of *kairos* after Heraclitean
rather than Platonic notions of time and *logos*. His trilemma—nothing
exists; if it exists, it can't be known; if it can be known, it can't be com-
municated (Sprague 42)—results, as Miller notes, in the "inevitable yield
of reason" (174). For Gorgias, according to Mario Untersteiner, *verba*
(the word) only ever represents *verba* and not *res* (the "thing"): there is
no metalinguistic foundation on which to base *logos*, so the decision between contrasting *logoi* cannot be "grounded" in logic. Gorgias's *Encomium of Helen* suggests that Helen was, no matter what the circumstances,
"caught in the net of fate"; she was not the master of her destiny, not the
author of her/story. It is not the subject/speaker who gets to do the seizing in Gorgias's epistemology; it is, rather, *kairos* that seizes time and
overrules human logic. The *kairotic* moment names that instant when
our meaning-making is, in a flash, exposed as an operation inscribed in
rather than opposed to play. Helen's decision was made for her by *kairos*,
an extralogical force that is, according to Miller's interpretations of
Gorgias, linked not to *nomos* but to *physis*. *Kairos*, in other words, is
linked to "divine law" (nonrational) rather than human law (rational). It
operates as a "rhythm" that arises not from negation (a process of reason)
but from excess (which is non- or extra-rational), from the free-play of an
unmasterable *physis*.

For Gorgias, Untersteiner says, *kairos* becomes "something living, a
prompting which continually by means of irrationality overcomes recurring opposites" (197). "If man, as happened for Helen," Untersteiner
writes, "comes into immediate contact with *logos*—that is, with the divine transformed into logical power—*logos* in its working splits into two

opposite directions which with their antithetical existence destroy the ideal of rationality to be recognized in all nature" (140–41). The force of *kairos* swooops in at the moment reason yields to a *dissoi logoi* to overcome the impasse by imposing *its own* decision (181). Helen was confronted with such an impasse, whether to stay or to go, and the decision was not, as Untersteiner suggests, "soluble by reason" (177). Rather, he says, "the act of cognition capable of being transformed into action cannot come from a rigorously logical law but from the persuasive force of *logos* which is *released* in the instant of the decision (*kairos*) which has as its object . . . the right thing at the right moment" (177, my emphasis).

Here, the *logos* is dispersed by *kairos*, a force, an atonal rhythm, Miller suggests, that is much more "mystical" for Gorgias than for Plato.[5] According to Miller, "*kairos* itself designates a 'spontaneity' in the generation of language that has discomforting similarities to processes of psychic intervention, poetic frenzy, and divine madness" (169). This *kairos* possesses the subject/speaker and wills its "decision," making the speaking subject (also) a spoken subject, that is, making the subject also an object (of *logos/kairos*). Victor Vitanza, who reads Gorgias across Nietzsche's notions of affirmative excess rather than Heideggerian ontology, suggests that Gorgias's epistemology makes both the *logos* and the "subject" "a function of *Kairos*" ("'Some More' Notes" 124) rather than the other way around. When *kairos* intervenes and "makes something new, irrational" (Untersteiner 161), Vitanza notes, "'things' fly apart. The binaries are exploded" (125).

The negative, which makes it possible for reason to operate, is de/negated in the *kairotic* moment with a bursting forth of *physis*, of the excess in which both the positive and the negative are inscribed. *Kairos* manages to explode the logocentric system by "denegat[ing] the negative informing, that is suppressing, repressing, politically oppressing *logos*" (Vitanza, "Taking A-Count" 184). For Vitanza and for this discussion, *kairos* is characterized as "affirmative desire; it is un/founded on a metaphysic of excess, not lack" (184). That is, for this book, *kairos* is tied to what Nietzsche called a wild and undistinguished "polymorphous perversity"; it is tied to a nonrational *physis* that is excessive and unmasterable.

KAIROTIC LAUGHTER

I would like to stretch this notion of *kairos* still further and suggest that it gets played out not only linguistically but also physiologically. The force of *kairos* can dance across the body, can instantaneously possess the subject and explode its boundaries/binaries of identity. This project suggests that these *kairotic* moments manifest themselves physiologically in spontaneous generations of laughter, which, by the way, are anything but situationally correct. By the standards of the local *nomoi*, this laughter is rather the most *absurd* response possible in any given situation. It respects no categorical distinctions and follows no social norms: it simply swoops in without warning, *sseizes* the body, and challenges the boundaries of the ego by taking it for a spin through everything that was negated for the sake of its formation. *Kairotic* laughter arises not so much from the (rational) realm of meaning-making as from the overriding (nonrational) realm of play, of excess, in which the phase of meaning-making is also situated. In Untersteiner's terms, this is "divine" rather than human laughter; it is not the laughter of *nomos* but of nonrational *physis*. It is born of the excess flying around, of the "most unscrupulous polytropoi," which always escapes human reason's categorizations; it is born of the remainder, which social norms hope to but never quite succeed at repressing or appropriating: this is not the controlled chuckle but the co(s)mic rhythm that laughs you.

I suggest, along with Milan Kundera, Hélène Cixous, and Georges Bataille, that our bodies are capable of being overtaken by the force of this Laughter, capable of being possessed, seized by this illogical rhythm that cannot be contained or repressed. The cosmos is laughing/playing, and it can and will sweep us into that laughter/play, perhaps when we least expect it. We cannot protect ourselves from the excess, from the play that will not recognize our categories, identities, or boundaries. Overflowing the bounds of time and will, the *kairotic* force of Laughter *laughs us* more than we laugh it.

Kundera and Bataille say this Laughter "convulses" us, momentarily dispensing with meaning and memory, demanding a purely bodily response; there may be thought/reason before but not in the midst of a laughing *fit* (Kundera, *Book of Laughter* 58 and *Immortality* 323; Bataille, *Guilty* 97). In the midst of this laughter, one experiences a moment of

what Ronell calls "hijacked existence," a moment of "motionless desti-
tution" (*Finitude's Score* 5). In Kundera's *Immortality*, a character named
Rubens asks himself if this can be true—isn't laughter itself, after all, "a
lightning *thought* that has just grasped the comical?" But, no; Kundera
assures us that

(schizoid
   f-f-fit)
in the instant that he grasps the comical, man [*sic*] does
not laugh; laughter follows *afterward* as a physical
reaction, as a convulsion no longer containing thought.
Laughter is a convulsion of the face, and a convulsed
person does not rule himself, he is ruled by something
that is neither will nor reason. (*Immortality* 323)

The minister's twig of hair, after all, had been forgotten by the time
my body convulsed with a laughter that I could not *will* back. Reason
could not/would not save "me." The rhythm that laughs us sends us into
a *petit mal* that assures us that we are, as Gorgias's Helen was, "caught in
the net of fate." Contra Descartes and Kant, the subject is not and cannot
be the author(ity) of his hi/stories nor the master of his destiny.[6] To be
convulsed by the force of Laughter is to be assured that we are both the
subject *and* (more so) the object of our stories; this Laughter serves as a
co(s)mic reminder that there is no way out of this posthumanist paradox.
The question of interest today is not so much *whether* we are done at
least as much as we do but rather how affirmatively we will accept that
recognition. And what hangs in the balance of our affirmation/negation
are (the slumbers of) humanism and reason themselves. Affirmation,
laughing with the Laughter, may be the way of an awakening; negation,
however, perpetuates the lullaby.[7]

IDEALISM—REFUSALS TO RESPOND

That twig of hair and the minister's illusion of self-unity/mastery may be
a good place to begin a discussion of the problem of idealism and the oppression inherent in its conception of the unified "individual," of "identity." I suggested that the minister's illusion of self-mastery had likely been
the result of a morning mirror-check, in which the unmasterable twig of
hair would not have been visible. The morning mirror-check is a daily

remystification of identity. It operates as a perpetual reaffirmation of the *mis-recognition*, the mis-identification experienced in what Jacques Lacan calls the mirror stage: that stage in which one comes to believe that the "Ideal-I" one sees reflected in the mirror constitutes one's Being in total and through which "the agency of the ego" is situated fictionally

> When we are thrust out into the world just as we are, we first have to identify with that particular throw of the dice, with that accident organized by the divine computer: to get over our surprise that precisely this (what we see facing us in the mirror) is our self. Without faith that our face expresses our self, without that basic illusion, that archillusion, we cannot live, or at least we cannot take life seriously.
> —Kundera, *Immortality*

(*Ecrits* 2). The illusion (*mésconnaissance*) that the mirror-check perpetuates is that the individual exists as a unified and constituting subject who can act, who is in control of his or her person and of his or her world. This mis-recognition perpetuates the idealistic notion that Being exists as pure and substantial presence. To operate on the illusion that the mirror-check offers, as the idealist does, is to (re)actively negate the post-humanist paradox, to refuse to respond to it by clinging to a naive belief in stable/solid identity.

Kundera, on the other hand, suggests that our faces are *not* expressions of "individual selves." A face, for Kundera, is no more than the "serial number of a human specimen": it is that "accidental and unrepeatable combination of features." The face, Kundera suggests, "reflects neither the character nor the soul, nor what we call the self" (*Immortality* 12). Still, the illusion of the mirror-check is a powerful one; to lose faith

> *The "serious" premises*: Every man [*sic*] possesses a central self, an irreducible identity. These selves combine into a single, homogeneously real society which constitutes a referent reality for the men [*sic*] living in it. This referent society is in turn contained in a physical nature, itself referential, standing "out there," independent of man [*sic*]. Man [*sic*] has invented language to communicate with his fellow man [*sic sic sic*K!].[8]
> —Lanham, *Motives of Eloquence*

in that illusion is to lose the ground upon which we build our "world." Idealists refuse to do that.

In *The Motives of Eloquence*, published in 1976, Richard Lanham refers to the idealist as "*homo seriosus*" (6), the serious soul working from *serious premises*, from supposedly solid foundations. These premises/foundations take the pure presence of Being as an *a priori*; they are built, in other words, upon the face-as-Self illusion, the morning mirror-check phenomenon. In an article entitled "Contingent Foundations: Feminism and the Question of 'Postmodernism,'" published in 1992, Judith Butler takes on the "serious" epistemological attitude that arises from these very same premises. Sixteen years after Lanham's critique, then, *homo seriosus* has not (been) budged and remains an object of significant critical attention. Butler notes that it is the tendency of the politically inclined to "shore up the primary premises, to establish in advance that any theory of politics requires a subject, needs from the start to presume its subject, the referentiality of language, the integrity of the institutional descriptions it provides." The preconception is that "politics is unthinkable without a foundation, without these premises" (3).

But Butler reconceives this pre/conception, suggesting that it is not that politics "is unthinkable without these prized premises" but that "a *specific version* of politics is shown in its contingency once those premises are problematically thematized" (4, my emphasis). A specific version of (humanist) politics does indeed require a stable identity: the only way to continue what Kundera, in *The Unbearable Lightness of Being*, calls the "Grand March" (of freedom, equality, etc.) is to continue to believe in the subject as a self-identical agent who is capable of changing the world. But Butler makes it clear that "to claim that politics [in general] requires a stable subject is to claim that there can be no political opposition to that claim. Indeed, that claim implies that a critique of the subject cannot be a politically informed critique but, rather, an act which puts into jeopardy politics as such" (4). Hence, critics of the unified subject are accused of being *apolitical*.

This accusation, however problematic, is a favorite of *homo seriosus* ("serious man"), or what Kundera, in *Immortality*, calls the "ideologue": the metaphysician of presence or sub/stance, adherent to a long line of philosophical Tradition, which believes unyieldingly in a sticking point, a foundation (God, transcendental signifier) on which to ground both knowledge and truth and on which to erect a universal political program. The ideologue belongs *mostly* to what Michel Foucault calls the Classical Episteme, which not only takes identity as given but also assumes that words have a one-to-one relationship with material things. These assumptions make it possible to concoct an objective "taxonomia," an "exhaustive ordering of the world" via a "tabulated space" created by the act of naming. This "table on which knowledge is displayed" (*Order of Things* 74), or rather *displays itself*, serves to pin things down, to "immobilize" them, to create a sense of stasis or sub/stance, so that "representation [might] render beings visible in their truth" (311), in their pure presence.

When laughter rings from the midst of these metaphysicians of presence, it is a laughter that celebrates meaning, order, and Truth; Kundera calls it "Angel laughter." *Homo seriosus* and the ideologues laugh a "serious laughter, laughter beyond joking" (*Immortality* 58), which "rejoice[s] in how rationally organized, well conceived, beautiful, good, and sensible everything on earth [is]" (62). There is no abandonment here—this is a heavily *invested* laughter. Lyotard says this laughter is the product of a joy that is "constructive, concentratory." Both he and Kundera characterize it as a floating circle dance, a form of self-righteous "elevation" (Lyotard, *Libidinal Economy* 41; Kundera, *Book of Laughter* 61–62), in which the laughers (knowers) celebrate their under/standing of the pure presence of the real world, of *the order of things*. This laughter laughs against what Nietzsche calls the "great sweep of life" (Nietzsche, *Gay Science* 282) against the impending threat of meaninglessness.

There is, however, a problem with the so-called "presence," the "foundation" or sub/stance upon which this order rests: it never actually appears. Even the "individual" never finally shows its sub/stantial self. As Kundera's Agnes says in *Immortality*, "your face is not you." In fact, what one is struck with when one is confronted with a mass of faces, side by side, is that "it's all just one face in many variations and that no such thing as an individual ever existed" (33). At some moment it becomes necessary that we stand in front of the mirror and ask ourselves: "Why did I want to identify with *this*? What do I care about this face? And at that moment," Kundera notes, "everything starts to crumble. Everything starts to crumble" (34). The "individual," the sub/stance, which supposedly grounds the order of things, is, at that

> [O]ur self is a mere illusion, ungraspable, indescribable, misty, while the only reality, all too easily graspable and describable, is our image in the eyes of others. And the worst thing about it is that you are not its master.
>
> —Kundera, *Immortality*

moment, *EXPOSED AS AN ILLUSION*. Presence itself here becomes suspect. Searching for final presence inevitably leads to what Jonathon Culler calls "nonoriginary origins" (96).

An examination of our notion of presence unconceals it as an absence: presence is perpetually deferred by a particular style of genus/species analytics, which does not nail down what something "is" but rather *what something is nnnot*. The mirror-check identifies us as individuals—I am me because I am not you. Even History, which ideologues hope to make human, to saddle and drive in a particular direction, is an *effect* of negation: it's an effect of absence/exclusion rather than presence. Vitanza notes that *The* History of Rhetoric, for instance, comes into being only through the exclusion from that History of those (hysterical) rhetorics that cannot be easily assimilated. Meaning is never finally present, and apparent presence is actually always already an apology for [its own] absence. Significantly, the apparent presence of identity is no exception: we have/master identity itself by "ill virtue" of exclusion/negation, by "ill virtue" of trimming off the "excess." The political/ethical implications of this are incredible, as Vitanza makes clear when he quotes Theodore Adorno, who suggests that our negative dialectics led us "quite logically to Auschwitz," to an unbelievable massacre of the negated/excluded, to "Genus-cide" (Vitanza, "Threes" 199).

It is negation that makes both the "order" and the cohesion of the humanist community possible; it is by virtue of exclusion that the "included" might join hands in a "magic" circle dance (Kundera, *Book of Laughter* 63, 65). The excluded, on the other hand, must be "deactivated" in some way, so that they cannot pose a threat to the closure of the O. Butler's description is chilling: "Subjects are constituted through exclusion, that is, through the creation of a domain of deauthorized subjects, pre-subjects, figures of abjection, *populations erased from view*" ("Contingent" 13, my emphasis). And there it is: the terror that the laughter of the Angels attempts to cover over. *Why do we f-f-fear fffluidity?* It is this, the terrifying potential of a Final Solution, which Vitanza calls the "wreck" of the negative ("Threes" 199), that will have inspired our critical attention to idealism's unchecked will to sub/stance and will have informed our discussion of the presence/absence of the "individual" in this chapter. The humanist community, which is

erasing the Other
erasing ~~the Other~~
erasing . . .

always after closure, is decidedly *not* the "community" we are after.

Ideologues posit their own *a priori* essence or "sub/stance," their pure presence as solid "individuals," in order to ground their identity-based politics; however, they neglect the political construction of the so-called individual itself. Here, we'll examine the negation/repression necessary for *the* individual to appear in the first place. Let us, as we go, allow the image of that rebellious twig of hair and its parodic performance atop the head of that unsuspecting minister to serve as a perpetual reminder of the illusion/delusion of self-mastery/unity. For this book accepts and promotes Butler's suggestion that critiques of *the* subject are not apolitical but rather lead to a politics that would

Be

Other/Wise.[9]

Herder's Critique of Pure Reason

The ideologue's notion of the central and fully-present Self as political launch pad typically includes the assumption that that Self is capable not only of making choices but also of using reason to learn to choose *correctly*. Faith in human reason is woven into a faith in the productive/progressive agency of the "individual"; therefore, pulling the thread of human reason may lead to an unraveling of idealism itself. But deconstructive critiques of reason, which have shed a suspicious light on the "purity" of the transcendental rationality that has grounded our humanist hopes since Descartes and Kant, are no/thing new. In his "Essay on the Origin of Language," for instance, Johann Gottfried Herder offers a radical critique of the Enlightenment Project's ideal of Pure Reason from *within* the very midst of that Project. All Enlightenment beliefs hinge upon the validity of the transcendent subject—the capability of the subject to transcend "his" situational and sensual elements to reach a state of disembodied, rational thought. And yet Herder, following Johann Georg Hamann, argues that pure abstraction of any kind is impossible: all abstractions are grounded on sensations, the soul's "forms of perception" (142). "[R]eason is not a separate and singly acting power but an orientation of all powers" (113). Long before Roland Barthes's *Pleasure of the Text*, Norman O. Brown's *Love's Body*, French Feminism's "writing the body," Deleuze and Guattari's "body without organs," and the general postmodern reaffirmation of "empirical worldly existence" (Derrida, *Speech and Phenomena* 35), Herder, in the 1770s, notes the impossibility of bracketing off into separate faculties what he refers to as the "total undivided soul" (111).

Contra Immanuel Kant, reasoning for Herder is "the unique positive power of thought . . . associated with a particular organization of the *body*" (110, my emphasis). Whereas Kant believed reason could be a way out of the body and its distortion of the Truth, Herder situated reason in the body too, made it as much a function of the body as of the mind. Rational thought, for Herder, must take place inside the "total arrangement of all human forces, the total economy of . . . [the] sensuous and [the] cognitive" (109–10). "Man's rationality," Herder says, is "the overall determination of his powers of thought within the total complex of his senses and of his drives" (111). An individual is not comprised of a mind and a body but is "a single thinking *sensorium commune*, touched from various sides" (139). Herder's theory of the unity of the "total individual soul" aims to mend the body/mind split carved out by the Enlightenment. His re-fusion prefigures a modern and postmodern return to the body and its senses as a *topos* for a counterethics that also challenges the notion of Pure Reason.

Nietzsche's Critique of the "Total Undivided Soul"

Nietzsche follows Herder's line of thought, to a certain extent. He affirms "the body and [its] physiology" as the appropriate "starting place" for thought (*Will to Power* 271), and he celebrates the reign of the passions, relegating reason to a tool, a weapon used to defend one's *affective* regime. The motivating force behind all reasoned arguments, then, is not the Truth but desire, passion, instinct: Nietzsche accuses philosophers of "the misunderstanding of passion and reason, as if the latter were an independent entity and not rather a system of relations between various passions and desires; and as if every passion did not possess its quantum of reason" (*Will to Power* 208).

However, Nietzsche's critique of the "individual" is much more radical than Herder's: what Herder refers to as "the individual soul" is, for Nietzsche, an abstraction of a multiplicity of passions. The so-called unified soul, the self reflected in the mirror, is what Nietzsche calls "the subject as multiplicity," "a kind of aristocracy of 'cells' in which dominion resides" (*Will to Power* 270). The apparent unity of the "individual" is for Nietzsche an abstraction of a multiplicitous selfhood, in which each passion, each instinct and drive, has its own capacity for reason and will to dominate. It is only the momentary ordering of this wildly protean conglomeration that can be abstracted to the level of a "soul" or an "individual." So-called rational thought performs in the service of the sensuous ruler of the moment, the ruling passion of the *kairotic* instant. Reason, then, is a function of the *body's* will. As Zarathustra says, "There is more reason in your body than in your best wisdom" (Nietzsche, *Thus Spoke* 34). The "individual," for Nietzsche, is not a self-unified soul but rather "the subject as multiplicity" (*Will to Power* 270), and "there is no [unified] '*being*' behind [its] *doing, effecting, becoming*; 'the doer' is merely a fiction added to the deed—the deed is everything" (*Genealogy of Morals* 45, my emphasis).

Butler's Nietzschean Critique
of Identity and the Body

This line of thought is picked up by several contemporary critics, including Butler, who takes it into gender theory to "trouble gender categories" and problematize our conceptions of anatomy as an *a priori* category. In *Gender Trouble*, for instance, Butler argues that the distinction gender theorists have made between sex (as "biological intractability") and gender (as social construction) is a false one. However, against the traditional notion that gender is the "natural" outward expression of anatomy's inner truth, Butler's radical proposition is that "sex is as socially constructed as gender" and that what masquerades as anatomy has always already been the construction of an/other construction: "anatomy" is an effect of *gender* (*Gender Trouble* 8). Butler spotlights a covert compulsory heterosexuality, which operates as a sort of sexing machine that abjectifies anything outside the established heterosexual boundaries. A thoroughly Nietzschean Butler notes that "there is no gender identity [sex] behind the expressions of that gender; that identity is performatively constituted by the very expressions that are said to be its results" (25). It is the "doing" that creates the illusion of "Being." The heterosexist regime of power *produces* both sex and gender by inscribing them upon a body; that body then establishes and maintains its identity through the perpetual performance of that sexed and gendered inscription.

Our exceptional performances of these inscriptions, Butler notes, "create the illusion of an interior and organizing gender core," which is then "discursively maintained for the purposes of the regulation of sexuality within the obligatory frame of reproductive heterosexuality." Butler's argument is compelling:

> The inner truth of gender is a fabrication and if a true gender is a fantasy instituted and inscribed on the surface of bodies, then it seems that genders can be neither true nor false, but are only produced as the truth effects of a discourse on primary and stable identity. (136)

Butler argues that what seems to be a self-identical subject, a unified individual is actually a politically oppressed/repressed/suppressed excess: it is a subject-as-multiplicity that has gone through political negation, abjection, inscription in order to fix it, to hold it steady. Along with Deleuze and Guattari (*Anti-Oedipus* 26), Butler argues that there is NO SUBJECTIVITY WITHOUT REPRESSION, no illusion of coherence without negation. "The subject," she says, "the speaking 'I,' is constituted by the force of exclusion and abjection" (*Bodies That Matter* 3). Butler, alongside Julia Kristeva (*Powers of Horror* 3), suggests that "the boundary of the body as well as the distinction between internal [me] and external [not me] is established through the ejection and transvaluation of something originally part of identity into a defiling otherness" (*Gender Trouble* 133). The expulsion and then repulsion of otherness operates to consolidate stable "identities" across stable notions of sex, race, and sexuality. But, Butler notes,

the whole show

> The boundary between inner and outer is confounded by those excremental passages in which the inner effectively becomes outer, this excreting function becomes, as it were, the model by which other forms of identity-differentiation are accomplished. In effect, this [negation] is the mode by which Others become shit. (133–34, my emphasis)

(We have been here before, at the site/cite/sight of negation, with Vitanza, and we will be here again and again and again.)

And yet, this "process" of expulsion and repulsion is not absolute; it cannot finally produce stable subjects because it cannot extinguish the remainder, the excess that it abjectifies. Even if it could produce a "seamless boundary of the subject," Butler suggests, "this enclosure would invariably be exploded by precisely that excremental filth that it fears." In fact, the notions of "inner" and "outer" are linguistic categories, which "make sense," she says, only "with reference to a mediating boundary that strives for stability" (134). The excess re/turns, perpetually, in the form, for instance, of an unruly twig of hair and/or an irrepressible burst of laughter, to keep "identity" shaken up, unfixable, uncontrollable. *rrrevenge of the object*

the object

objection!

.

.

.

If human reason is problematized by an inescapable affiliation with the materiality of the body, what becomes of it when the materiality of the body is itself problematized? What happens to it when even the body can no longer be assumed, as if it were a preexisting sub/stance, an ahistorical presence? Critics of *Gender Trouble* have attacked Butler for leaping into a *theory* of the body rather than dealing with the body *itself.* Butler, therefore, devotes *Bodies That Matter* to the "matter" of the body, to the question of the body's materiality. Significantly, however, that question gets immediately complicated when she asks how we might get at that materiality and why it is that some bodies end up mattering *more* than others.   o

o

o

f ! Butler's point is crucial to our discussion: *even matter has its own histories*, and those histories are "partly determined by the negotiation of sexual difference" (29). The sexed body is always already an effect of power; it is, Butler suggests alongside Luce Irigaray, produced by that very discourse that stabilizes itself by excluding "the feminine" (more on that later) all together. Even if there were such a thing as a "pre-symbolic" or "pre-discursive" body, it would not be available to us. Even the matter of the body is not *simply there*: its boundaries are politically/discursively constituted, and, in fact, the "body" itself exists only in and through the constraints of that political/discursive construction. There is, Butler says, no way to get

citing

BODILY

border

zones

outside these constraints to challenge/alter them: all subversive activities ("liberatory" politics) necessarily take place *within* the constraints of the established citational boundaries.

huh oh huh oh huh oh huh oh huh oh huh oh huh oh huh oh huh oh huh oh huh oh

This line of thought is terribly disturbing for *homo seriosus*, of course, who proceeds politically and ethically by taking the materiality of the body and the free-agency of the "individual" as unproblematic givens. Humanist politics demands a self-identified agent who has the freedom to effect change and the reason to determine what needs to be done. But if *the* "individual" is actually what Nietzsche calls "The subject as multiplicity" (*Will to Power* 270) and/or what Vitanza calls a "polyethoi (scattered subject positions)" ("Taking A-Count" 184; also "Concerning" and "Threes"); if the supposed unity of Being is always already an effect of power exercised to camouflage a wild and excessive process of Becoming, then identity politics and the humanist community take problematic turns—clOsure will certainly not be possible. If *the* individual is never really present in the first place and its so-called essence is something like a negatively projected hologram, *homo seriosus* is in some serious trouble.[10]

How many characters does it take to transform a body and alter our features, our expression? How many pregnancies to change a woman? How many orgasms to transform the first person singular?
—Nicole Brossard, "Only a Body"

MODERNISM—A TOO HOPEFUL RESPONSE

Indeed, it is in large part *homo seriosus's* "serious trouble" that inspires what Foucault calls the Modern Episteme. The perpetual deference of the presence of identity finally demands a re/conception of idealism's un-

questioned grounds, of its metaphysics of presence. The Modern Episteme becomes possible only after the "individual" has looked *suspiciously*
in the mirror and recognized that the face staring back offers no guarantee of identity: the Modern Episteme emerges after "everything begins
to crumble." The driving force of this Episteme manifests itself in a
relentless search for certainties and universals in a world that has lost its
ground, its sticking point. The conception of a potentially *knowing* subject, one who can transcend false consciousness (overcome the *méconnais-
sance* of the mirror-check), once again makes knowledge possible. "The
subject" gets injected underneath the Classical Episteme's crumbling
grounds to act as the substitute guarantor of truth and knowledge.

With the advent of the specifically human sciences, Foucault tells us,
"man appears in his ambiguous position as an object of knowledge and
as the subject who knows" (*Order of Things* 312). He begins to recognize
himself as not only the *orderer* of things but also as *ordered* by things.
Paradoxically, then, though Modernity balks at the possibility of representation through language (because there is no metalinguistic sticking
point), it nevertheless embraces a concept of the Self and the distinct possibility of self-representation. The unified "individual" is supplanted here
by the self-conscious "subject"; the illusion of self-unity necessary for the
former is demystified in the latter, who is, as Louis Althusser has suggested, "interpellated" or "hailed" into being by the language of the Law.
"The subject," then, exists inasmuch as it occupies the subject positions
into which it is called. This is obviously a significant turn of events.
Whereas the Classical Episteme is faithful to One, universal foundation
(the pure presence of its metalinguistic "table"), Modernity is postfoundational; it recognizes no metalinguistic foundation upon which to
stand. Modernists recognize a multiplicity of subject positions, and so a
multiplicity of meanings, a diversity of possibilities. Here, then, the neat
taxonomia of the Classical epoch f-l-i-e-s a-p-a-r-t.

Significantly, however, it does not fly very *far* apart. Foucault notes
that modernism refuses to let things remain unstructured; it has a propensity for unifying diversity, for huddling up multiplicities, systematiz-
ing them so that they might be master-able. The modernist project,
Foucault suggests, is a nostalgic drive for lost Oneness, for a "transformation without residuum, for a total reabsorption of all forms of discourse
within a single word" (305). Modernists re/cognize, in other words, that

there is no final foundation under their feet, but the typical modernist

H
E
R
E
W
E

response to that re/cognition is to attempt to *produce* the foundation that is thought to be lacking. *same song, second verse* And such a production/creation demands a knowing subject who can transcend false consciousness, determine what is "just," and act in the service of that knowledge of justice— i.e., to join in what Kundera calls the "Grand March" to usher in paradise.

GO AGAIN . . .

Metaphysics of Presence/Absence

The flipside of Idealism's metaphysics of presence or sub/stance, then, is modernism's metaphysics of absence: the former posits but defers the location of an *a priori* "some/thing" where there is actually no One thing. But the latter posits an *a priori* absence, a lack where once it had been assumed that there was a pure presence. The metaphysician of presence posits a foundation that is perpetually deferred and so is always already not there. The metaphysician of absence sees the nonpresence negatively, as a *lack* of presence. The "Real thing," the final foundation is, therefore, *impossible* rather than possible. But the modernist impulse is to (re)construct what appears to be missing. Vitanza notes that it works from the notion that out of the impossible comes the possible: "this impossibility, this absence/lack, creates the very conditions of possibilities for a newer affirmation. Modernists argue that we are no longer limited to what is (Realism/Idealism is dead!) but are now limited only by what we would imagine" ("On Negation" 2; see also "'Some More' Notes").

The metaphysician of absence sees the No/Thing as a blank space in which human beings might erect their structures, their hierarchies, their communities through local *nomoi*: out of the No/Thing comes Some/ Thing, comes Every/Thing. Modernism recognizes that the so-called presence is always already absent, but it hopes the big hope that, out of that absence, a presence, an essence, might be *constructed*—that the negative might be made a positive. Implicit in this hopeful approach is the faith that there is a substantial and knowable difference between a freedom fighter's revolution and a totalitarian's takeover. But it may be, as Kundera suggests, that no such distinction can be made: even the "fight for peace," he says, "ends with the destruction of everybody by everybody" (*Immortality* 89). When it comes down to it, totalitarianism and revolution are mirror images, both of which are bewitched by the notion that history is human, that human beings can know and act autonomously. The laughter of the hopeful modernist, then, is *also* an Angel laughter, a laughter that laughs with an air of certainty, of conviction that meaning can be made "correctly" and that the world can be set "right"— by "man." There is no abandonment here, either. This is *laughter with a fight*, community bound by the glue of a(n overwhelming) project.

Motivated by a nostalgic longing for a lost sense of presence, modernists strive "to confine the fragmented being of language once more within a perhaps impossible unity" (Foucault, *Order of Things* 305), a unity that often takes the form of a concentric circle drawn around "man" himself. Anthropology, the analytic of "man," is constitutive of the thought of all modernity: all of the human sciences find a point of unification across the anthropological question, "What is man?"[11] We are interested here, however, in the very thing that makes this question askable/thinkable in the first place, in that which is left unquestioned in this question. In what Foucault calls the "counter[-human] sciences," an answer is revealed: what is left unquestioned is the sub/stance of the subject/object dichotomy itself.

egocentrism

Counterhuman Sciences

The further evolution of psychology, anthropology, and literature (the human sciences) led to psychoanalysis, ethnography, and linguistics (the counterhuman sciences)—which, by exposing, for instance, the "unconscious and its historicity . . . threaten the very thing that made it possible for man to be known" (Foucault, *Order of Things* 381). They "do without the concept of man," and, in fact, "dissolve man," as both Foucault (379) and Lévi-Strauss (*Savage Mind* 247) suggest, because they always "address themselves to that which constitutes his outer limits" (Foucault 379). They do not ask the anthropological question, "What is man?";

rather, they direct their questions to what in man's culture and/or his psyche makes it possible for the abstraction "man" to appear. The question of autonomy is rendered irrelevant when the subject is exposed as the bi-product of cultural overdetermination, when its agency is exposed as the effect of a particular set of discursive practices. In short, the working through of the counterhuman sciences makes the idea of transcending false consciousness unthinkable—as there can be *no* consciousness beyond "false" consciousness. Modernism, it turns out, has not taken the subjectivity of the subject far enough. The illusion of agency produced by the very notion of a subject/object dichotomy conceals what the counterhuman sciences reveal: Even "the" subject is mostly a function of other functions, an object of other forces. Here, the "foundation" of human agency, once again, begins to $c\ r\ u\ \substack{m\\m}\ b\ l\ e$—and with it, modernism's political hopes.

Contemporary critiques of modernism's subject are both numerous and radically diverse, and yet a common element among many of them is a posthumanist approach, the assumption that there never was any autonomous

agency,

intention,

or will . . . not even within the subject positions into which we are called. Transcending false consciousness is not possible: the "subject" was always already more so an object, and the assumed subject/object dichotomy is one seductive trope among many. Of interest now is not so much the question of "man," a mere effect, but rather of what frontiers beyond the limits of "man" make it possible for him to show up for us in the first place.

A host of feminists/postfeminists, from Nancy Hartsock to Hélène Cixous, for instance, have exposed linguistic and social structures as androcentric; thus, man, "the subject," shows up as *gendered* "man." Jacques Derrida has exposed the Transcendental Signifiers that operate as the ground for what then functions as the "centered" subject. Foucault has exposed the discursive matrices of power that hail and so produce (docile, normalized) subjects. Gilles Deleuze and Felix Guattari have revealed the machinations of desire that must be repressed/negated in order for "the" subject to come into being. Judith Butler has exposed the "heterosexist" assumptions grounding the appearance of "the" subject as always already gendered. Jacques Lacan has explored the language of the unconscious, which he believes makes the subject and "consciousness" show up for us. And Jean Baudrillard has questioned even the *unconscious* as a final frontier, suggesting that we are in a state of perpetual simulation and that it should not be assumed that that simulation stops at the "unconscious" or that the realm of the unconscious is more "true" than the realm of consciousness.

> The point: the capacity even to consider these "new frontiers" spotlights the inadequacy of the old one— Man, the effect that masquerades as cause.

Indeed, it is the failure of foundations to hold solid for us, the failure of both idealism's individual and modernism's constituting subject fully to appear (as more than a hologram) that has prompted an enormous and *very serious* intellectual scramble; the goal: to *save* the subject. The unabashed drive to "rescue" and/or "discern" "the" subject stems from the hope that the notion of agency might be preserved in some capacity. What's at stake in this CPR for the subject is politics as we know it. The modernist subject has functioned as political *agent*; without agency, the "real" slides inescapably into what Baudrillard calls the "hyperreal," a realer-than-real state (*Selected Writings* 166; also *Simulations* 23) in which the real is produced according to its model and the referents of social theory simply disappear (*Forget Foucault* 90).

In other terms, without agency, ideology ssslips into what Kundera calls "imagology," which organizes a "peaceful alternation of its systems in lively seasonal rhythms. . . . [I]deology belonged to history, while imagology begins where history ends" (*Immortality* 116). Ideology believes in progress; imagology plays on that belief by assuming the *masks of progress.* The former, Kundera says, "was like a set of enormous wheels at the back of a stage, turning and setting in motion wars, revolutions, reforms." But the "wheels of imagology turn without having any effect upon history" (115). In the throes of imagology, "change," Kundera observes, takes on "a new meaning: it no longer means a new stage of development (as it was understood by Vico, Hegel, or Marx), but a shift from one side to another, from front to back, from the back to the left, from the left to the front (as understood by designers dreaming up the fashion for the next season)" (116). And this is a grrrrrim state of affairs for the idealist and the modernist, both of whom want to believe that the subject is an agent who has the power to effect change.

Between De- and Re-territorialization: Occupying the Space of the Hole

Ironically, Modernity's nostalgic drive to resuscitate the subject, as Lyotard suggests in *The Postmodern Condition*, must be preceded by the *post*modern recognition that the foundations tabled by the Classical Episteme have indeed collapsed. That is, it is the "death of man" that precedes the attempt to resuscitate him. It is what has been termed the *post*modern that manifests itself in that moment of foundationlessness, of nonidentity *before* the modern impulse charges in to lay foundations again (to save ideology from the grips of imagology). Paradoxically, *post*modernism must come first; it is, as Lyotard says, "undoubtedly a part of the modern" (*Postmodern Condition* 79). First the play of radical disunity, then the drive to reorder it. We are interested here in that postmodern moment, after deterritorializaion (no "community") but before reterritorialization (new "community"), when, in the flux of exploded identities, in the excess before re-distinction, the multiplicitous, splintered subject attempts to respond to her/his non- or rather poly-foundational multiverse.

Žižek opens *Tarrying with the Negative* with a description of one manifestation of this postmodern moment: the "violent overthrow of Ceausecu in Romania." Žižek describes a scene in which the "rebels [are] waving the national flag with the red star, the Communist symbol, cut out, so that instead of the symbol standing for the organizing principle of national life, there was nothing but a hole in the center" (1). This h●le indicates an "intermediate phase when the former Master-Signifier, although it has already lost the hegemonic power, has not yet been replaced by the new one." Deterritorialization has occurred and reterritorialization has not yet taken place. This "open" situation, what Žižek calls a state of passage from "one discourse (social link) to another," indicates a "hole in the big Other, the symbolic order." It is the "duty," Žižek says, "of the critical intellectual . . . to *occupy all the time*, even when the new order (the 'new harmony') stabilizes itself and again renders invisible the hole as such, *the place of this hole,* i.e., to maintain a critical distance toward every reigning Master-Signifier" (2).

Such a "duty" assumes that Master-Signifiers are, as Žižek says, "produced," constructed (2). And while the hopeful modernist recognizes this much, s/he tends to forget that they are also inherently *contingent,* that the star on the flag is arbitrary and that it might, at any moment, be cut out again. At that moment, the "community"—of the Self or of the social—which is bound together by its suddenly halted project, scatters like dust in the wind. If what it means to be human in a posthumanist world is to be a scattered and/or scatterable disidentity with no sub/stantial referential image, it is necessary that our question become: How will these disidentities share the world? In the face of Desert Storm, the wars in Bosnia, the Oklahoma City bombing, wilding, the Waco disaster, the epidemic of school violence, and the growing number of Neo-Nazi militia groups, this may be *the* question of our time. Potential answers may reveal themselves once we recognize that at least a part of our Being-as-becoming ought to continue to occupy the space of the h●le. It will be necessary that the hopeful modernist concede her/his faith in the potential production of a final foundation and so in the capacity to finally distinguish between a community bound by revolution and one bound by totalitarianism. Indeed, in the face of always already *contingent* foundations, nostalgic hopefulness is not an option: we may fly into laughter or into tears, into affirmation or into nihilism. The "cynic" flies into the latter.

CYNICISM—A NIHILISTIC RESPONSE

Sloterdijk notes the tendency of the posthumanist paradox to invite a nihilistic response, to lead us into the arms of cynicism: "an enlightened false consciousness" or "unhappy consciousness" that knows it has been duped but knows also, contra Karl Marx, that false consciousness cannot be transcended[12] (*Critique of Cynical Reason* 5). Žižek characterizes the cynic as one who "is quite aware of the distance between the ideological mask and the social reality," but who nevertheless "insists on the mask" (*Sublime Object* 28–29); the cynic, in other words, refuses to occupy the place of the "hole," even though s/he recognizes the hole as such. The cynical subject knows, as Luanne Frank has put it, that "[n]o sooner do you stop being this system's dummy than you're already that one's" (245). S/he knows that history, as Vitanza says, is "not human" ("Some Rudiments" 224), and that, as Kundera has suggested, the Grand Marches of totalitarianism and revolution are mirror images, each be-witched by the notion that human beings *make* history (*Unbearable Lightness*). The cynic is "enlightened" but paralyzed, full of regret and nostalgia for the hope that enlightenment humanism offered. It is rare that laughter of *any kind* will echo forth from the midst of cynical sub-jects. In fact, "behind the capable, collaborative, hard facade," Sloterdijk says, cynicism "covers up a mass of offensive unhappiness and the need to *cry*" (5, my emphasis).

Sloterdijk says that, though s/he smiles a "crooked smile" that as-sumes a "crooked superiority" (142), the cynic lives at the brink of tears. S/he is bitter, disappointed, and mistrustful. Cynics "cannot be tricked anymore. They know how things work" (143). Cynics have given up their interest in (humanist) community. They're too "enlightened" for it. But Sloterdijk warns that cynics can, nevertheless,

> easily make stupid mistakes once more when their bitterness causes them to also pass over what, after all those painful things, would do them good. Happiness will always look like a fraud and will seem much too cheap to be worth reaching for. Bound to past experience, the cynically bitter lips know only one thing: that ultimately every-thing is deception and that no one will ever again bring them to be soft and, blushing, surrender themselves to any temptation of the world's swindle. (143)

Cynics are metaphysicians of absence; that is, they have deter-mined that where they thought there was Some/Thing (God, foundation, presence, the "social"), there is actually No/Thing (absence, lack). But, unlike hopeful modernists, they recognize the impossibility of construct-ing that Some/Thing that has been lost. And that realization makes them unhappy, remorseful, nostalgic. Ludvik, the protagonist in Kundera's novel *The Joke*, is the cynic par excellence and thus an excellent example of Sloterdijk's point. In the preface to this novel, Kundera notes that when a man loses his future (as Ludvik does when he is forced to wear the black insignia), he clings to his past. Soon, the only link connecting him to a life continually slipping away through the crack called forgetting is a remorseful nostalgia that yearns to set things straight and to get even. Ludvik is at first an ideologue: he is a humanist who believes that human beings are in control, that history is human. Therefore, he believes particular, knowing subjects are responsible for his unhappy fate and that he has the capacity to return the favor. What Ludvik's pathetic attempt at revenge sets in motion, however, is out of his control from the very beginning: he is always already the butt of an intricate and all-encompassing co(s)mic joke.

When he writes the flippant postcard to get even with Marketa for her aloofness towards him in her letter, he becomes the butt of his *own joke* and gets sent off to a work camp by a humorless Communist authority that not only re/writes his past (his-story) but also snatches away his future. Ludvik's personal history with Marketa made him think his postcard could be read as a joke, but the spirit of the age (Zeitgeist) forced it to be read as a threat. Had he not assumed the mask of irreverent jokester (one of his many) with her, he would not have written the postcard in the first place. Had the historical backdrop been different, the postcard would not have been read as a threat. The point is that Ludvik was never in control of his destiny; he was always already a function of context and the bi-product of an infidelity of language, of the history that had constructed what masks he might wear, what he might say, and what he might desire.

Ludvik and other young Communists, Kundera says, let themselves be "bewitched" by history, by the possibility that they might saddle it and steer it in a particular direction. But Kundera notes that we can neither create history nor remain outside it, unaffected by it. In the end, when Ludvik's futile attempt to get revenge by sleeping with his perceived enemy's wife (Helena) ends in a disaster in the latrine, Ludvik finally recognizes that he has been more the object than the subject of his-story. He had been obsessed by a drive to correct what he thought were historical errors, but he is finally forced to realize that those "errors" have become the order of things rather than exceptions; they have become history itself.

It may even be, he thinks, that they were never errors at all, that they were merely manifestations of history's sense of humor. Sometimes history's all-embracing jokes might simply consist of making human beings powerless to revoke the little jokes they play. Ludvik's consciousness becomes enlightened but unhappy (he becomes a cynic) when he sees that his whole life has been involved in a joke much more all-encompassing and irrevocable than anything he could concoct himself, when he recognizes that history is not human. He also sees that there can be no correction, no rectification of history's "errors." No/thing, no "wrongs," no "mistakes" can be rectified—neither by vengeance nor forgiveness. Rather, it will all slip into oblivion and be forgotten. Where he thought there was Some/Thing, he now realizes there is No/Thing. And Ludvik is incapable of an affirmative response.

He feels his foundation brrrreaking up, and he can accept it, but he cannot affirm it; he can "savor" it, but he cannot stop feeling it as a loss because he is predisposed to experience the nonpresence as a *lack* of presence, the No/Thing as a *lack* of Some/Thing. Ludvik likens his nostalgia for presence, for foundation to a terrible feeling of homesickness. Listen to his despair:

> I felt the firm ground of my homeland sinking under my feet, felt myself falling, clarinet in hand, falling into the depths of years and centuries past, fathomless depths (where love is love and pain is pain), and I said to myself in amazement that my only real home was this descent, this searching, eager fall, and I gave myself up to it, savoring the sensuous vertigo. (265)

Ludvik's capacity to "savor" the vertigo cannot mask his enormous sense of loss nor his desire to go "home" again, to *recapture* what has been *lost*. In the end, Ludvik describes himself as "overwhelmed with grief" (266). When the corners of his mouth begin to quiver involuntarily because, as he says, "nervous tension lowers a person's resistance not only to tears but to laughter as well" (254), he does *not* find himself seized by that laughter. He does not abandon himself to his own abandonment. One ought not assume, however, that Ludvik has a sense of self-control that others do not. It may be, rather, that the cynic, who remains connected to his past by a "bond of vengeance" and nostalgic despair, is always already too close to tears to be possessed by the force of Laughter. Ludvik is devastated by the realization that he is not in control, that he has no real power over even his own (hi)story. He wants that power *back*, and it is, as Sloterdijk suggests, an "essential aspect of power that it only likes to laugh at its *own* jokes" (102; my emphasis). Ludvik is in no mood to laugh or to be laughed by a force that has made him the object of a cosmic chortle. His mouth, we can imagine, fits the description of Sloterdijk's cynic, "bitter and tight": "Lips that are pressed tightly together and narrowed to thin lines because of hardship," Sloterdijk says, "betray the worldly, experienced side of those who have been duped" (143) and who refuse to be duped again. Ludvik is quite consciously out of touch with the rhythm that laughs us.

Another of Kundera's characters, Stalin's son, Yakov, in *The Unbearable Lightness of Being*, stopped himself short of cynicism but not in an affirmative way. When the gestalt switch turned, he not only could not affirm what he saw; he could not *accept* it either. Unlike Ludvik, Yakov could not live the life of a cynic. He believed that he could protect his honor, that he had the power to set errors or accidents straight and to get even when he was "wronged." He believed in rectification. When he realized that human beings were not in control, that there was no universal sense of justice and/or honor, he could not live at all.

Having been reprimanded several times by British officers for leaving a "foul mess" in the latrine, Yakov demanded the intervention of the camp commander. But the commander refused to discuss the matter. Yakov could not accept that his humiliation would go unrectified, that it simply would be forgotten. He had been forced to undergo judgment not for his ideas or his beliefs but for "shit." Kundera reminds us that no one came closer at that time in history to being the Son of God than Yakov, the son of Stalin. And for the Son of God to be judged for something not in the highest realm of God and the Angels but in the lowest realm imaginable was more than he could take.

When the poles of opposition get blurred, when there is no recognized distinction between the sublime and the paltry, when the Son of God, in other words, can undergo judgment for sssshit, human existence loses its points of reference, its sense of justice, its foundational presence (Some/Thing). Yakov demanded that someone pay for the sin of blurring those distinctions. When it became apparent that there would be no rectification—that the soldiers would neither be punished nor be made to apologize—for this unholy joke, Yakov threw himself against the electrified fence. But Kundera assures us that Yakov in no way managed to rectify the matter by sacrificing himself for its principle; indeed, in dying for shit, Yakov managed to prove that his life was of no more significance than that shit he sought to rise above. Kundera says that if Yakov's body were placed on one side of the scales and shit were placed on the other, the scales would not move. This is the tragic knowledge of the cynic, who cannot affirm it as "what is" and who feels perpetually betrayed by a world that has suddenly *lost* all of its meaning and purpose, all of its hierarchical divisions, all of its capacity for (humanist) community. In the face of such a loss, the cynic cries bitter and nostalgic tears.

KYNICISM—AN/OTHER POSITIVE (CUM NEGATIVE) RESPONSE

Against the bitter tears of the cynic, Sloterdijk celebrates the laughter of the kynic. The kynic promotes a "cheeky" argumentation with which, "to the present day, respectable thinking does not know how to deal" (101). *Kynismos* is also a state of "enlightenment," but it is not an unhappy one. The kynic is not nostalgic or remorseful and does not consider his/her paradoxical situation to be the result of a loss. Rather, the kynic is happy to attain a distance from the tyranny of meaning, from the weight of Truth. Whereas Yakov could not live in a world where the sublime and the paltry were indiscernible, the kynic never recognizes that distinction to begin with. For the kynic, the "usual divisions are invalid; there is neither above nor below, neither dirty nor pure" (145).

> The age of tragedy can be ended only with a revolt of frivolity. . . . Tragedy will be driven from the world like a ludicrous old actress clutching her heart and declaiming in a hoarse voice. Frivolity is a radical diet for weight reduction. Things will lose ninety percent of their meaning and will become light. In such a weight-less environment fanaticism will disappear. War will become impossible.
>
> —Kundera, *Immortality*

Kynical reason culminates in the snubbing rather than the erection of "grand goals." The serious, philosophical mind sees this as a nihilistic response, but Sloterdijk says that "in this regard, we cannot be nihilistic enough": "Those who reject all so-called goals and values in a kynical sense break through the circle of instrumental reason, in which 'good' goals are pursued with 'bad' means" (194). When the consciousness becomes capable of letting go of the "good" as a goal and of simply embracing what is already there, Sloterdijk says, "a release is possible in which the piling up of means for imaginary, always receding goals automatically becomes superfluous" (194). According to Sloterdijk, cynicism can only be tempered by kynicism and not by morality: "Only a joyful kynicism of ends is ever tempted to forget that life has nothing to lose except itself" (194).

Kynismos is a rude, irreverent, blasphemous energy, at least by cynical/philosophical standards. Isn't it, for instance, just plain "crude and grotesque," Sloterdijk asks:

cheek
cheek
cheeky

to pick one's nose while Socrates exorcises his demon and speaks of the divine soul? Can it be called anything other than vulgar when Diogenes lets a fart fly against the Platonic theory of ideas . . . ? And what is it supposed to mean when this philosophizing town bum answers Plato's subtle theory of eros by masturbating in public? (101)

Well, crude or not, Sloterdijk notes that these "cheeky" argumentative strategies, these light-hearted, fun-loving blasphemies are next to impossible to counter with "serious" critique or "responsible" argument. They are animal; they are not ego-entities but id-entities, tied to the body and a playful impulse that appears to transcend the need for meaning-making. Reason struggles in vain to find a toe-hold in a kynical "argument."

The problem, Sloterdijk suggests, is that philosophers are interested in attempting to live what they say rather than in "*saying* what they live" (102, my emphasis). With the birth of "high theory" (à la Plato), argumentation gets severed from the body, materiality, and worldliness—from laughter. But that snobbish split is continuously dis/rupted by the emergence (à la Diogenes) of "a subversive variant of *low theory* that pantomimically and grotesquely carries practical embodiment to an extreme." If the cynic's enlightenment is "unhappy," the kynic's is "uncivil" (102). If cynicism covers over and represses nostalgic tears, kynicism explodes in excessive laughter, in a devilish buffoonery that *celebrates* the meaninglessness over which the cynic cries.

Whereas the cynic offers an illusionless "crooked smile" from the "heights of power," Sloterdijk says that it is characteristic of the kynic to laugh so loudly and unabashedly that refined people shake their heads. Kynical laughter comes from the intestines; it is grounded at the animal level and lets itself go without restraint . . . [in a] total, uncramping laughter that wipes away illusions and postures. (143)

Žižek calls the laughter of the kynic "totalitarian" laughter (*Sublime Object*),[13] and Nietzsche (*Gay Science, Beyond Good*), Sloterdijk (*Critique*), and Kundera (*Book of Laughter*) call it "devilish,"[14] a laughter that Sloterdijk says "has the energy of destruction within it with crashing crockery and collapsing walls, an evil laughter above the debris" (144). If Angel laughter is about meaning, Devilish laughter "point[s] up the meaninglessness of things" (Kundera, *Book of Laughter* 62). It is, as Lyotard suggests, the product of an "incredulous and insolent joy . . . the laughter of metamorphoses that awaits no one's recognition and enjoys only its ductility. It is a horizontal laugh without assent" (*Libidinal Economy* 42).

Sloterdijk imagines that Diogenes laughed in this way. And some laughing Buddhas also reveal a hint of this kind of animal laughter. Diogenes's weapon was not "so much analysis," Sloterdijk says, "as laughter." He strove for a "knowledge of free people; free also from the strictures of school, and with this he begins a series of names in which Montaigne, Voltaire, Nietzsche, Feyerabend, and others appear." A host of other names might be added as well, including Gorgias, Burke,[15] Kundera, Vitanza, and Sloterdijk himself. This "is a line of philosophizing that suspends the *espirit de sérieux*" (Sloterdijk 160), sparking a "motif of self-preservation in crisis-ridden times" (193). The idea is that the weight of meaning can only be countered with the lightness of an excessive laughter, and *not* with more meaning.[16] When things get too heavy, too saturated with meaning and wholes, the "force of gravity" becomes unbearable. Kynics respond to the overbearing weight of meaning with an overwhelming opposition to it. *Kynics do not fear fluidity.*

The cynic and the kynic offer two very different "enlightened" responses to the posthumanist paradox: one lives on the brink of tears; the other lives on the brink of buffoonery. One is too heavy, too saturated with meaning; the other is too light, too meaning*less*. Sloterdijk performs the latter so as to battle the almost unchecked reign of the former. The prescription for *kynismos* is not offered as a cure or as a final solution but as an *opposition* to cynicism and to both the idealism of the ideologue and the crypto-idealism of the hopeful modernist. If the serious cynic cries, the frivolous kynic laughs; if the (crypto)idealist celebrates presence, the "uncivil" kynic celebrates absence. Devil laughter is the negative deconstruction of Angel laughter—it flips [off] the site of privilege in a binary reversal of "absolute opposites" (Kundera, *Book of Laughter* 62). The kynic is a devil laugher out to "kill the spirit of gravity," not with "wrath" but, as Zarathustra suggests, with "laughter" (Nietzsche, *Thus Spoke* 41).

However, to fight *for* frivolity, *for* meaninglessness is to fight *against* meaning. Neither the key dichotomies nor the dichotomous structure itself are overcome in the kynical response. Kundera puts it this way:

the kynic
still holds
something
against
the Other

> To fight means to set one's will against the will of another, with the aim of defeating the opponent, to bring him to his knees, possibly to kill him. . . . [I]f you are in the habit of designating your striving with the word "fight," it means that your noble striving conceals the longing to knock someone to the ground. The fight *for* is always connected with the fight *against*, and the preposition "for" is always forgotten in the course of the fight in favor of the preposition "against." (*Immortality* 150)

The importance of this recognition ought not be missed: "War," as Ronell suggests, "is not natural but waged in the name of transcendental inscriptions—justice, God, truth, country, freedom, the white metaphysical subject's autonomy" ("Activist" 294). And, in the case of the kynic, one might well add another item to the list: meaninglessness. Because *Kynismos* is offered as an/other positive position—that is, because it, like modernism, flips the privilege of the same binary oppositions—it remains trapped in the negative: it offers a fight against cynicism, idealism, and modernism, but it (therefore) remains within the binary logic demanded by those negative and negative-cum-positive responses. *Kynismos* plays by the rules of the very game at which it laughs.

The kynical "community" would necessarily continue to take the form of an exclusive circle dance.[17] To fight for meaninglessness—and to stop there—is to make meaninglessness meaning*ful*. And yet, the kynical "community" would hardly be a humanist one. Indeed, inasmuch as its "project" is to fight for the meaninglessness of the world, the notion of

hold it!

a kynical "community" seems worthy of an arrested pause: in this *serious* commitment to *play*, there is no appreciable space for mourning the disappearance of the players of its game, no communal space for valuing the loss of a member to its *own brutal premises* (life is meaning*less*). Kynicism offers no traction on "the trace of the Other." And/but kynicism will not be ignored: the evidence of its devastating game makes headlines across the country every day—kynicism is *here*; its time is now.

AFFIRMATION—A COMEDIC RESPONSE

According to Sloterdijk, though, *Kynismos* occasionally slips into something beyond negation, beyond oppositional border zones. On these occasions, Diogenes and laughing Buddhas, for instance, evidence a laughter beyond the Devil's "crashing crockery," a laughter in which "the energy of perplexed affirmation is at play." It is here, in the course of battling against seriousness, that the ego doing the battling laughs *itself* "to death" (Sloterdijk 144). And, in that instant, something remarkable happens: the negative de(con)struction exceeds itself, bursting forth into an unchecked *affirmation* that is neither positive nor negative, but something totally other, something explosive, which up/sets binary logic from the inside.

It is necessary to re/cognize, however, that this is not a final exit from (phal)logocentrism—we are not after a final exit. What we are after here are moments, instances, glimpses, flashes. We are after an instantaneous gestalt switch rather than a long-term political program; we are after tactics rather than strategies. Because if, as Bataille says, "there is within us, running through the space we inhabit, a movement of energy [a rhythm, a force] that we use, but that is not reducible to its utility (which we are impelled by reason to seek), we can disregard it [idealism, modernism], *but we can also adapt our activity to its completion outside us*" (*Accursed Share* 1.69). Affirmative responses are tactical in this regard; they leap into the flow without reservation, without *limit*ationnnn.

Responding affirmatively requires not only that one recognize that the universe will forever overflow our superimposed categories and distinctions but also that one *celebrate* the unstructurable excess, the "polymorphous perversity" that is always already at play and in which we are always already caught up. As Lyotard points out in his "evil book," *Libidinal Economy*, the so-called perverse is "really simply diverse" and is "endlessly displaced from infancy over a surface without holes" (21). Deleuze and Guattari suggest that "anthropomorphic molar representation culminates in the very thing that founds it, the ideology of lack" (*Anti-Oedipus* 295). But lack theories are negations that assume h●les in the whOle; affirmative responses, on the other hand, assume a wild and overwhelming excess of "parts" that will never make a "whole": there can be no final One, no final Totalization, and therefore no lack. As the chicken commercial used to say, "parts is parts."

Deleuze and Guattari, then, have this to say of/to Freud:

```
E
X H         Castration, lack, substitution: a tale told by an over-con-
C O         scious idiot who has no understanding of multiplicities as
E L         formations of the unconscious. . . . It is not even suffi-
S E         cient to say that intense and moving particles pass
S S         through holes; a hole is just as much a particle as what
I           passes through it. Physicists say that holes are not the ab-
V           sence of particles but particles moving faster than the
E           speed of light. Flying anuses, speeding vaginas, there is no
            castration. (A Thousand Plateaus 32)
```

And an early Lyotard agrees: "There are no holes, only invaginations of surfaces"[18] (*Libidinal Economy* 21). Even desire, both Lyotard and Deleuze and Guattari suggest, lacks *nothing*. Desire is not a hole that longs to be filled: it does not lack even its so-called object (Deleuze and Guattari, *Anti-Oedipus* 26; Lyotard, *Libidinal Economy* 4). In fact, Lyotard assures us, it is not the Negative that creates our desire but rather, it is our (fascist) desire that creates the Negative (*Libidinal Economy* 11–12). Even the "I" is not a unified whole but is, as Nietzsche says, an abstraction based on faith in the grammatical structure, which posits a doer for every deed. Deleuze and Guattari suggest that Freud's analysis took a negative turn because he didn't see that the unconscious itself is "fundamentally a crowd" (*Anti-Oedipus* 29). What gets called "the subject" is a hoard of multiplicities, rhizomatic loose ends that will always overflow abstract categorizations. This does not mean that politics is no longer possible; it simply indicates that a certain kind of identity politics, as well as the so-called "communities" it fosters, may be counterproductive.

At first glance, positive responses (such as modernism's creations and the kynic's oppositional frivolity) would seem closely to resemble affirmative responses; however, the distinction between the two is critical for our purposes. Positive responses remain trapped within the positive/negative binary, within a "restrictive economy," in which the most radical subversion is limited to a *re*-action: flipping the privilege from one side of the existing dichotomy to the other. *solidity ffffetish* Affirmative responses, on the other hand, move out of reactive/binary logic by challenging or ignoring the limits it sets. Indeed, the distinction between positive and affirmative responses, as we will use them here, is analogous to the distinction between Hegel's lordship (positive position) and Bataille's sovereignty (affirmative position), as it is explicated by Derrida in "From Restricted to General Economy: A Hegelianism Without Reserve."

> What is real can be a trick of the human eye which sees what isn't there the moment that it sees. Magic, true metaphysics, teaches the boundaries of sight, that our eyes cannot be trusted any more than our words, that the nothingness which is claimed to be there before the coin rises from the hand or the dove from the ring of fire is the epistemology of saints. Heidegger once said the miracle is that "there is something rather than nothing." But the magician **creates the nothingness** out of which the bird of paradise sings. Oh ontological troubles! Is it as simple as Emerson said, "Genius adds"?
> —Bill Endres, "A Short Discourse"

> For that masculine subject of desire, trouble became a scandal with the sudden intrusion, the unanticipated agency, of a female "object" who inexplicably returns the glance, reverses the gaze, and contests the place and authority of the masculine position. The radical dependency of the masculine subject on the female "Other" suddenly exposes his autonomy as illusory.
> —Butler, *Gender Trouble*

The difference between the two, Derrida says, does not *make sense*, rather "it is the *difference of sense*, the *unique* interval which separates meaning from a certain non-meaning" (254). One accedes to lordship, Derrida says, when one manages to put life in the service of meaning-making, when one manages to make life work for the "constitution of self-consciousness." One becomes a master by risking one's own life in the negation of another's life: the master becomes master by denying the slave. (A subject is constituted by creating an object.) Lordship, then, makes the negative work in the service of the positive, the no/thing work in the service of the some/thing. Lordship, a modernist conception *par excellence*, uses the topos of the *Aufhebung*, "which conserves the stakes, remains in control of the play, limiting it and elaborating it by giving it form and meaning." But, Derrida says, "this economy of life restricts itself to conservation, to circulation and self-reproduction as the reproduction of meaning" (255–56). The master-slave dialectic locates the "truth of the master in the slave" (255). And it is here that "everything covered by the name of lordship *c*

ollapses into comedy."

For, "the independence of self-consciousness becomes laughable at the moment when it liberates itself by enslaving itself, when it starts to *work*, that is, when it enters into dialectics" (256). And Derrida notes that "laughter alone exceeds dialectics and the dialectician":

d   it bursts out only on the basis of an absolute renunciation
é   of meaning, an absolute risking of death, what Hegel calls
s   abstract negativity. A negativity that never takes place, that
    never presents itself, because in doing so it would start to
o   work again. A laughter that literally never appears, because
e   it exceeds phenomenality in general, the absolute possibil-
    ity of meaning. And the word "laughter" itself must be
u   read in a burst, as a nucleus of meaning bursts in the
v   direction of the *system* of the sovereign operation ("drunk-
r   enness, erotic effusion, sacrificial effusion, poetic effusion,
    heroic behavior, anger, absurdity," etc.). (256) [Derrida is
e   citing Bataille.]
ment

This, then, is Devil laughter *with a twist*. It might begin as a reaction, a fight against meaning, but it stops fighting in the instant that it stops recognizing the terms of the fight. In the bursting forth of this laughter, the conflict between meaning and meaninglessness is sidestepped. This laughter refuses to *work* in the service of that conflict. And it is here, in the burst of this laughter, that the distinction between lordship and sovereignty shows up for us. For sovereignty is not lordship,

Derrida observes, but "totally other. Bataille pulls it out of dialectics. He withdraws it from the horizon of meaning and knowledge" (256). Sovereignty does not fight with the negative; it simply refuses to take the negative seriously (256, 258). It laughs only, as Bataille says, in "the anticipation of a suspended, wonder-struck moment, a miraculous moment" in which it might catch a glimpse of life beyond "the circle of constraint" (*Accursed Share* 3.199–200). It bursts forth in anticipation of experiencing "the possibility of life without limit" (198).

It is also here that the distinction between Devil laughter and a third kind of laughter is revealed. Devil laughter remains tied to the negative (to a "restricted economy"—a binary economy); it *works* inasmuch as it remains tied to a fight against meaning, which is in itself a re/action and so a *kind of meaning-making.* Whereas the meaningful/ meaningless dichotomy remains intact in Devil laughter, this third laughter dis/solves the binary altogether by bursting through and then out of it, by treating "the seriousness of meaning" as "an abstraction inscribed in play."

> In discourse . . . negativity is always the underside and accomplice of positivity. Negativity cannot be spoken of, nor has it ever been except in this fabric of meaning. Now the sovereign operation, the point of nonreserve, is neither positive nor negative. It cannot be inscribed in discourse, except by crossing out predicates or by practicing a contradictory superimpression that then exceeds the logic of philosophy.
>
> —Derrida, "From Restricted . . . Economy"

Bataille's sovereign position, then, is not the negative: rather it *laughs* at the negative. And yet, neither is this laughter a return to the metaphysics of presence. The sovereign position is a third way, a third position outside the positive/negative dichotomy altogether. The laughter that constitutes sovereignty is neither the Angel's (absolute meaning) nor the Devil's (absolute meaninglessness) because it does not recognize the terms of that dichotomy. It is a third and affirmative laughter, which, nevertheless, grows out of, from the inside of Devil laughter. It grows from the clearing established by the work of devilish laughter. This third laughter is an affirmation of the nonpresence as excess rather than lack. Derrida hits it square on the head here:

> [Sovereignty tears] apart the negative side, that which makes it the reassuring *other* surface of the positive; and it [exhibits] within the

negative, in an instant [e.g., *in a burst of laughter!*], that which can no longer be called the negative. And can no longer be called the negative precisely because it has no reserved underside, because it can no longer permit itself to be converted into positivity, because it can no longer collaborate with the continuous linking-up of meaning, concept, time and truth in discourse; because it literally can no longer labor and let itself be interrogated as the "work of the negative." (259–60, my emphasis)

The sovereign position, therefore, begins inside a negation of meaning and then *breaks with that negation*, taking a third way, which de/negates the negative by exposing what Derrida calls reason's "unlimiting boundaries of non-sense" (261). Vitanza notes that the *"tendency to negate is the defining tendency of modernism"* and that "what is lost to modernism (what is lost to reality, realism!), however, is regained (spoken and heard) by ill-virtue of negation. (Here [Freud was right], *no* means *yes*.)" ("Taking A-Count" 185). Vitanza attempts to do for *The* History of Rhetoric what Bataille attempts to do for philosophy: that is, to affirm a "particular postmodern repositioning that would be a double negative—that is, a negating of the negative (a denegation) in dis/order to get to some nonsynthetic 'some more' [excess]" (185). Both Bataille (in philosophy) and Vitanza (in rhetoric) are after a way out of binary logic and into third positions, which are *nonpositively affirmative*. Bataille's sovereignty, which is constituted by a nonreactionary laughter, is one such position.

Nonpositive affirmation celebrates the parts, the excess, the playfulness, viewing the No/Thing not as a loss or lack of "Some/Thing" (*The* Thing). Rather, the excess is assumed to preexist the abstractions and categorizations that we have foisted upon it: there never was any lack but only and always an ominous and overflowing excess. *Fluidity.* In the face of this excess, the affirmer does not cry like the cynic: s/he laughs in what Nietzsche calls a "superhuman and new way" (*Beyond Good and Evil* 233). S/he laughs a third laughter, a laughter that endlessly "gives." But here, it is necessary that the term "give" be recognized as a double *entendre*: it stands in for both "to give way" and "to offer [itself] up." A giving laughter is a laughter that participates in and then moves beyond Bataille's (cum Mauss's) "potlach"—it gives itself up without respect for limits, and, in doing so, its limits end up giving

The inhabitants of limbo . . .
do not know that they are
deprived of the supreme good, or,
if they do know . . . they cannot
suffer from it more than a
reasonable person is pained by the
fact that he or she cannot fly. . . .
The greatest punishment—the
lack of the vision of God—thus
turns into a natural joy:
Irremediably lost, they persist
without pain in divine abandon.
God has not forgotten them, but
rather *they have always already
forgotten God*; and in the face of
their forgetfulness, God's
forgetting is impotent.

—Agamben, *The Coming Community*

way; the binary structure overflows, explodes in a burst of laughter. A giving laughter laughs its way out of the "circle of constraint" and into a *general* economy; it celebrates the play of the universe by *joining in its co(s)mic Laughter*.

A *giving* laughter, which is human, bursts forth as an affirmation of the irrepressible force of a *kairotic* Laughter that swoops in and takes us over. Giving laughter desires *kairotic* Laughter and simulates it, engaging it, putting forth a call to it, and inviting it to swwwwwweep us up. It is in the throes of a giving laughter, Bataille suggests, that human beings might "grasp what eludes [them]," that they might "combine the limitless movements of the universe with the limit that belongs to [them]" (*Accursed Share* 1.70). Indeed, this book suggests that to respond to the posthumanist paradox with a giving laughter that invites the "sweep" is not to be *apolitical* but to engage in an *affirmative* politics-cum-ethics. And it may be here, in the space of meaning-making's repose and reprieve, after a glimpse into the excess, that we might determine to occupy, as Žižek suggests, the "place of the hole." For it is in the place of the hole that there exists the potential for a less dangerous, postfascist community of shattered disidentities.

This giving laughter is not offered as a cure for the negative, as a final awakening from the double slumber; it is offered as a *pharmakon*, or what Vitanza calls a "paracure" ("Taking A-Count" 202; see also Vitanza's "On Negation"): both a momentary line of flight from the debilitating dis-ease of humanism and reason and also a joyful and explosive momentary metamorphosis of the fascist within. The future does not depend, Nietzsche suggests, on finding a way to react to a hostile external (positive/negative response); it depends upon one's becoming "incapable of taking one's enemies, one's accidents, even one's own misdeeds seriously for very long" (*Genealogy of Morals* 39) (affirmative response). It depends upon our capacity for c-c-comedy. Comedy alone challenges what Nietzsche calls "the force of gravity," the tyranny of meaning, because it doesn't take faith in The Truth (the negative) seriously anymore. A giving laughter says "yes!" to the eternal comedy of existence by simulating it, exploding with it.

Angel laughter is a kind of celebration of the limits of identity, which make possible the expulsion and then repulsion of otherness; it is a celebration of vomiting. But a giving laughter *bursts through* the restrictive economy's conceptual border zones. The butt of its joke is fascism in any form, and what it celebrates is the *expelling of expulsion itself.* A giving laughter, in other words, celebrates a kind of *meta*-vomiting, which doesn't vomit to negate but to negate negation, to denegate the negative by vomiting up vomiting. A giving laughter, then, serves to kick loose what Lyotard calls the "disjunctive bar" that separates the terms in a binary opposition. The bar stands as gatekeeper, as guardian of the binary order, signaling an "either this or not-this" mode of thought (*Libidinal Economy* 14). The disjunctive bar is the very foundation of rationality and identity, of (phal)logocentrism, and Lyotard notes that "every concept is therefore concomitant with negation, exteriorization" (14). That bar serves as the sticking point that allows philosophy to do reason's work. And yet, it also serves to cancel out a world of excesses, remainders that reside outside the terms of the "dichotomy" it holds in place. A giving laughter gives itself up in the face of this "seriousness," refuses to take the seriousness seriously, and knocks over the bar with its

gust of giving,

with its irrepressible overflow, leaving the scene in a free-flowing (excessive) dis/order.

Devil laughter acts as a negative deconstruction that breaks a path for an affirmative, third and nonreactionary laughter that leaps out of the binary, calling hopelessness into question without positing a new god/foundation/philosophy. If devilish laughter kills God (by mobilizing the encrusted site of privilege from meaning to meaninglessness, from presence to absence), a giving laughter performs an affirmative deconstruction by overflowing the limits of negation. When the kynic's laughter exceeds the limits of the binary, it slips into a nonpositively affirmative laughter, in which

> the energy of perplexed affirmation is at play; in spite of its wildness, it also sounds contemplative, celebratory. The Devil's energy is the energy that laughs until the others fall silent. [But i]n the laughter of Diogenes and Buddha [giving laughter], the ego itself, which had taken things so seriously, laughs itself to death. (Sloterdijk 144)

This third kind of laughter has no stake in control: it laughs so excessively and with such abandon that in the end there is "no ego left in the laughing, only a serene energy that celebrates itself" (144). In the throes of a giving laughter, the borders of the ego *give way*; we are hurled outside the "fabric of meaning," the restrictive economy, and into a general economy, what Nietzsche calls the "open sea" of excessive possibility. Here "the horizon appears free to us again, even if it should not be bright" and our "ships may venture out again . . . to face any danger" (*Gay Science* 280). In the bursting forth of this third laughter, an *instantaneous* and *momentary* invitation is issued: an invitation to "shed our old bark" so that we might "grow not in one place only but everywhere," so that we re/cognize that "we are no longer free to do only one particular thing, to *be* only one particular thing" (*Gay Science* 331).

This is a joyful, tactical laughter that operates as a negating of negation, reveling in an affirmation of "what is." Ludvik suffers from nostalgia for a lost sense of purpose and meaning in the world. He moves from being a metaphysician of presence (Some/Thing is Present) to being a metaphysician of absence (Some/Thing is Absent): where he once saw a founding order, he now sees the *lack* of it. But "the" "subject" engaged in an affirmative, giving laughter is engaged in a yes-saying that is so powerful, so excessive, that s/he does not experience the nonorder as a *lack* of order. Affirmative laughers laugh *with* the *kairotic* force of Laughter, celebrating the free-play of Being in an ecstatic denegation of negation itself.

At the moment this "laughter laughs," Derrida suggests, the Negative, the Impossible, the *Aufhebung* is *mediated* by an affirmation outside the positive/negative, SomeThing/NoThing binary, which manifests itself as this burst of laughter. This laughter is excessive; it overflows; it *bursts* in a way that does not contain itself. Though it offers no "hope" in the humanist sense, it is also not burdened by loss, remorse, or nostalgia. What it recognizes is what idealists, hopeful

To laugh at philosophy (at Hegelianism)— such, in effect, is the form of the awakening—henceforth calls for an entire "discipline," an entire "method of mediation" that acknowledges the philosopher's byways, understands his techniques, makes use of his ruses, manipulates his cards, lets him deploy his strategy, appropriates his texts. Then thanks to this work which has prepared it—and philosophy is work itself according to Bataille—but quickly, furtively, and unforeseeable breaking with it, as betrayal or as detachment, dryly, laughter bursts out.

—Derrida, "From Restricted . . . Economy"

modernists, cynics, and even kynics (most of the time) cannot recognize: that "the conscious suspension of play," in order to make meaning, "was itself a phase of play; play *includes* the work of meaning or the meaning of work" ("From Restricted . . . Economy" 266, my emphasis).

Meaning-making is just a tiny aspect of what Nietzsche called "the eternal comedy of existence"; meaning is not "not there"; meaning "happens," but it is always contingent and *embedded* in a laughing cosmos where expenditure exists as pure *waste* in the form of play. Where metaphysicians of absence posit a lack, affirmative laughers celebrate a wild and "polymorphously perverse," or rather "diverse," *excess*. Thus, when this laughter laughs, it gushes over the disjunctive bar, de-negating the Negative, the *idea* of the great No/Thing, and setting Nietzsche's hammer to the ground upon which philosophy does reason's work; for, reason feeds on the *Aufhebung*. In between the logocentric poles of opposition, this laughter points to an indiscriminate open sea.

AN AFFIRMATIVE ALLIANCE

To be swept into the co(s)mic force of Laughter, according to Bataille, is to be swept into "the absolute risk" of No/thingness. To be laughed by it is to be seized, possessed, to be thrown into a *little death* in which one's consciousness, one's capacity for meaning-making is suspended. When you are seized by Laughter, Bataille says, "a load of worry's off your shoulders: the frame explodes that gives order to action" (*Guilty* 95). A *giving* laughter, or what Derrida calls "minor laughter" aims to simulate this "major laughter" by consciously exposing "the seriousness of meaning" as "an abstraction inscribed in play." Derrida says that this "minor laughter" must "simulate, after a fashion, the absolute risk, and it must laugh at this simulacrum" ("From Restricted . . . Economy" 256). In the instant that a giving laughter meets with the co(s)mic force of Laughter, the laugher both laughs (subject) and *is laughed* (object), s/he is both limited and unlimited. The result, Bataille says, is "comedy" (*Accursed Share*

To
vanquish
the
impossible
each
day
and
have
always
a
yes
in
advance
on
chance.
—Cixous,
"*La*—The
(Feminine)"

1.70). And "in the comedy that [this simulacrum] thereby plays for itself," Derrida points out, "the burst of laughter is the almost-nothing into which [the very fabric of] meaning sinks, absolutely" ("From Restricted . . . Economy" 256). Whereas devilish laughter typically offers an escape route from one side of the binary to the other, it also, occasionally, exceeds itself in a burst of *this* laughter, and in that instant, it offers a successful line of flight from binary logic itself, an escape, for an instant, from (phal)logocentrism.

A defining difference between the cynic's crooked smile and the kynic's belly laughter is that the latter is occasionally swept away in an affirmative forgetting, whereas the former is motivated by the persistent and angry need to remember. Nietzsche wanted to "serve history only to the extent that history serves life" (*Untimely Meditations* 59), affirming not only the determination to re-remember what has been systematically dismissed, as Michel Foucault attempts to do in his production of countermemory, but also to then let it go, to "shed" it, to actively *forget* it again.[19] Forgetting, for Nietzsche, is a process of allowing oneself, as he says, to "shed [one's] old bark," to "have done" with the old to make room for new sensations and new potential futures (*Gay Science* 331). Active forgetting is described in *The Gay Science* as an active throwing off of stifling models and histories, a will to shed them and make room for something new.

Affirmation requires the capacity to let memory go; and when the invitation of a nonpositively affirmative laughter is answered by the *kairotic* force of Laughter, both meaning and memory are suspended in a convulsion of extrarational and extramoral affirmation. Kundera says this affirmative alliance "sweep[s] us off in unbounded effusion. Bursts of laughter, laughter rehashed, jostled laughter, laughter defleshed, magnificent laughter, sumptuous and wild" (*Book of Laughter* 56). And because philosophy knows "no other aim than knowledge," because it did not consider this laughter *first*, it is now incapable of successfully appropriating it. Hegel, Bataille says, "canceled out chance—and laughter" (*Guilty* 96).

To engage in a laughter that has no stake in control is to set one's feet upon momentary lines of flight from the tyranny of meaning and from the violence of a community held together by that tyranny. The hope involved in this political-cum-ethical mode of Being-in-the-world is not about (finally and for good) getting out of the negative; it is about, in a flash, experiencing the flow, the excess beyond our control, beyond our (violent) grasp.

The hope is that these glimpses beyond constraint will up/set or at least problematize our determination to create *systematic* exclusions, to devote ourselves more to our linguistic categories than to the Others that those categories create and then *flush*. The hope is that the experience of abandoning oneself to abandonment in this affirmative alliance will nudge our perceptions into a space where a different and post-humanist Being-with-others might be/come possible. Ronell, after Bataille, describes such a community as "without essence, without a substantial project (qualities which, for example, would underlie a fascist community), a community shattered and way past the mirror stage of self-recuperation." This community would be "infinitely divisible, yet sharing" (*Finitude's Score* 2). And that certainly would be worth laughing for.

First, though, it will be necessary that we move beyond our faith in logic and language, beyond our faith in paradise. An obscene kind of simplicity (complete with scapegoat) is fashionable today; we want a quick and simple fix to inequity and injustice. But the issues we face are far from simple and "it is now more necessary than ever," Ronell observes, "to resist being simplistic or hardened by oppositional logic and rude calculation" ("Activist" 297). Theoretical reflection will have been necessary. Space for an/Other('s) sensibility. . . .
. . . .
.

will

have been

imperative.

2

DISCURSIVE LAUGHTER: COMPOSITION C^ON^VU^LS^ED

My intellectualism told me problems had to be solved by thought. My dramatic propensities made me think hamming it up was better than going through an abstract argument.

         —Feyerabend, *Against Method*

The abyss appears when Nietzsche, Freud, Heidegger, Derrida lift the lid of the most familiar and comforting notions about the possibility of knowledge.

       —Spivak, preface to Derrida's *Of Grammatology*

The death of God does not restore us to a limited and positivistic world, but to a world exposed by the experience of its limits, made and unmade by that excess which transgresses it.

       —Foucault, "Preface to Transgression"

We do not start off saying to ourselves: there is someone or something that *speaks* to us, I must understand them. We hope rather to be set in motion. Consequently our passion would sooner be the dance, as Nietzsche wanted.

         —Lyotard, *Libidinal Economy*

Who is speaking when something is spoken?[1] The idealist, as Richard Lanham suggests, would answer, unproblematically, that the speaker speaks: "Man has invented language," according to *homo seriosus*'s serious premises, "to communicate with his fellow man" (*Motives* 6). Speech is equivalent to communication, and communication offers communion. For Descartes and company, "man" is the center of language, the master of his own speech, and that speech is an expression of man's consciousness. It is a

(Problem / No problem)

tool used to communicate and to commune with others. Language is not a problem for *homo seriosus*.

But if the subject is not in control, if the subject is more so an object, a function of other functions, an effect, language becomes highly problematic. What, for instance, are we to make of this "phantom's" speech? What is called the "author" in a posthumanist world? If it is not the "subject," then who/what speaks when something gets spoken? One answer to this question,[2] now frequently offered, dis/solves the author-slot by making the "author" the function of what gets said; it answers that *language* speaks. The so-called subject is spoken by language in much the same way that it is laughed by Co(s)mic Laughter. Here, human "consciousness," rather than being the origin of speech/writing, turns out to be its *effect*. Jacques Derrida puts it like this:

B-
B-
BIG
PROBLEM

> [W]hat was it that Saussure in particular reminded us of? That "language [which consists only of differences] is not a function of the speaking subject." This implies that the subject (self-identical or even conscious of self-identity, self-conscious) is inscribed in the language, that he is a "function" of the language. He becomes a *speaking* subject only by conforming his speech. ("Differance" 145)

Derrida continues these thoughts in "Eating Well," suggesting that language makes us, both turns us on and turns on us, and/but that it is only *because* it does that something like the "subject" can come into being (100). Our ethics, and so our politics, have been limited by what Heidegger called thinking's "enframement" within its own particular History or Tradition. There is a circle of constraint that frames our vision, forces us into what Bataille called a restricted economy. We can't think or speak just anything but only what is thinkable and speakable within that constraining frame. Heidegger and Paul Celan saw that human beings are enmeshed in language, hailed into Being by a language that speaks us more than we speak it. And there's no way to get out of this web, to separate Being from Being-in-language. As Judith Butler notes, with Derrida, we can be only by virtue of the fact that we are *called* into Being; human "agency" takes place only within our *reiteration of the reiterable* (see Butler's *Bodies*; also Derrida's "Eating Well").

The radical implications of such a suggestion ought not be overlooked. If there is no autonomous authorship—if it is not the "author" of a text but *language itself* doing the communicating, we ask:

What is called communication/communion/community?

If any "subject" and any writing-speaking "produced" by that "subject" always already operates as a kind of prosthesis for the *logos*, what of resistance? What of revolution? What can *justice* mean in a posthumanist world?

.   .   .   *pause for reflection*   .   .   .

If, when you write, as Avital Ronell observes, "there are certain things that force your hand," something "you owe before you think, understand, or give," a "historical compulsion" that "copilots your every move" (*Crack Wars* 57–58), then Tolstoy's question takes on a desperate dimension: "What then must we *do*?"[3] Can *we* do anything? If notions of responsibility can no longer be connected to conceptions of autonomous subjectivity, it is necessary to ask, with Jean-Luc Nancy, "Who [or what] comes after the subject?" ("Introduction" 5); or, with Foucault, What happens after we awake from our "anthropological sleep"? (*Order of Things* 340).

On the one hand, as Ronell suggests in *Finitude's Score*, *we may have gone too far*—that is, too far to backlash again into humanist reinterpretation. This time, there may be no CPR powerful enough to save the humanist subject or its epistemological appropriation of writing and speech. Human beings, we will suggest, are at least twice possessed: by co(s)mic Laughter and by the *Logos*. What is called "humanity" is on the line, articulating a quivvvver between agency and determinism, occupying a paradoxical space between doing and being done, speaking and being spoken. "Humanity" is an inmate in the "prison-house of language."[4] But there is still an/other hand.

On the other hand, the *logos* that hails us into Being is perpetually "stepping out" on itself; that is, the body of language is unfaithful to its own discursive injunctions, to the Law. The *kairotic* convulsions of co(s)-mic Laughter charge through language as well as bodies, giving the *Logos* a Being(-as-becoming) of its own that is illogical and playful, that is incapable of denoting without, at the same time, disseminating itself into discursive forms of laughter. If the "house of Being" is indeed a "prison-house," it is not a maximum security facility: there are plenty of un-guarded gaps, ruptures, escape routes—not out of *language* but out of (civil) *discourse.*

This chapter follows Norman O. Brown, among others, in his sug-gestion that "language is an operational superstructure on an *erotic* [laughing] base" (*Life Against Death* 69). I suggest, along with Nietzsche and his line of countertraditionalists, that it is a schizoid *logos* that hails us into subject positions, a *logos* traversed by an erotic and *kairotic* Laugh-ter, which proliferates rather than fixates meaning. Because our category systems, our genders and genres, are linguistic constructions, and lan-guage is anything but stable, Being and truth, as Heraclitus observed, are always already infused with the rowdy force of becoming. Language may indeed be what Heidegger calls the "house of Being," or at least the "house of becoming," but any house that perpetually shakes with laughter seems to be less a "prisonhouse" than a "funhouse" (Derrida, "Eating Well").

funhausfunhausfunhausfunhausfunhausfunhausfunhausfunhausfunhaus

And here, we will be after a bit of fun in the House; we will inten-tionally transgress the rules and "play" indoors, *hoping* to b-r-r-reak something. Indeed, in our efforts to dis/cover what Ronell calls a post-humanist "ethics of decision," we will attempt to laugh with the Laugh-ter-in-language, to sssShake with the House. Here, we are looking for a way of Being-in-language that will open the door to an/Other politics and an/Other ethics. Humanism will be called to the carpet for in-decency in this text, for just going on as if its terrifying notions of justice were still valid—after, for instance, Auschwitz. We'll be pushing the envelope here, searching for another future, an/other sense of justice, one that begins with a radical ssshedding, Nietzsche-style.

We're not talking about a simple subversion or surface revision. We're talking about an extreme re-visioning, a fundamental rup-turing/shedding that breaks with the humanist program altogether. We're talking about the antici-pation of and projection into a future not tethered by the bonds of reaction, an active decision to *let memory go.*

The task of extremist writing is to put through a call for a justice of the future. Henceforth, Justice can no longer permit itself to be merely backward looking or bound in servility to sclerotic models and their modifications (their "future"). A jus-tice of the future would show the will to rupture.

—Ronell, *Crack Wars*

We will be after ways we might free ourselves from the "cowardliness pressing upon social convictions of the present, subjugated as they are to reactive, mimetic, and regressive posturings" (Ronell, *Crack Wars* 21). That is, we wish to locate ourselves on the way to what has not yet (and may not ever) come into discourse, on the way to a different and *post-humanist* sensibility. We are after an/Other ethics of decision here, and we will seek/chase it in a tripartite move: firstly, by locating our subjectivity *within* the House of language; secondly, by recognizing the instability of language, the foundationless foundation of our House; and thirdly, by finding a way to both celebrate the Laughter-in-language and to reformulate a sense of "responsibility" and "community" within that celebration.

BESPEAKING THE SPEAKER: AGENCY AND AUTHORSHIP RE/VISITED

[**Excursus**: "*Being*-on-Drugs." In *Crack Wars: Literature, Addiction, Mania*, Ronell cranks up "the communication systems with the question concerning addiction" (33), announcing that "addiction will be our question: a certain type of 'Being-on-drugs' that has everything to do with the bad conscience of our era" (3). For now, we are here to listen, to open lines of communication, to make connections. Ronell begins by generalizing our notion of "drugs," suggesting that we have been duped by and about them, in part, because we have expected them to operate within a "restricted economy." We have assumed that one is either on drugs or not on drugs and that Being is good but that Being-on-drugs is bad. We have assumed an either/or structure and, therefore, the capacity to make an easy and clear distinction between the two. This logocentric formulation of "the drug problem," Ronell suggests, has led us into an ugly war-on-drugs, which quickly proved itself to be unwinnable.

Suggesting instead that we may have waged war with a structure (Being-on-drugs) that operates as a fundamental tenant of our existence, she asks: What if "drugs" were not simply "one technological extension among others, one legal struggle, or one form of cultural aberration?" What if, instead, " 'drugs' named a special mode of addiction . . . or the structure that is philosophically and metaphysically at the basis of our culture?" (13). In other words, what if we are always already "drugged"? What if *there are no drug-free zones*? What if Being itself is, by definition,

> "Being
>
> -on
>
> -drugs"?[5]

Hear her out. "Drugs," she observes, "are excentric. They are animated by an outside already inside" (29). Endorphins, she reminds us, "relate internal secretion to the external chemical" (29). The human body operates, it seems, as threshold, as a limit where outside and inside touch. Suggesting a connection between language and drugs, Ronell points out that when we borrow the words of others to make ourselves understood, we enter the realm of what we could call "Being-on-*language*." When Benjamin quotes Baudelaire to explain what he feels when hashish first begins to take effect in his own body, he "takes an injection of a foreign body (Baudelaire's *Les Paradis artificiels*) in order to express his inner experience." Language: an outside inside. And Ronell reminds us that this "is by no means an atypical gesture. To locate 'his' ownmost subjectivity, Thomas De Quincey cited Wordsworth. These texts," Ronell observes, "are on each other. A textual communication based on tropium" (29).

Opium and "tropium," Ronell suggests, are both drugs, both mind-altering, and both addicting. What Ronell calls "tropium" is close to what Derrida calls "grafting": the need for every text (and every *identity*) to graft itself onto something else, some other text (or identity-as-text) to *become who or what it is*. And here, the easy binary between Being authentically and Being-*on-drugs* breaks down/up. We have to be *under the influence* (of language, of technology, of History/Tradition) to Be at all. If drugs are "mind-altering" or "frame-setting" substances, we are high or low on them all the time. Being-on-drugs indicates, Ronell says, that "a structure is already in place, prior to the production of that materiality we call drugs, including virtual reality or cyberprojections" (33). "Drugs," she says, "are crucially related to the question of freedom" (59): What can freedom be if to Be at all is to be hooked, to be an addict? Liberation, it seems, must be re/thought. "Drugs do not," Ronell observes, "close forces with an external enemy (the easy way out) but have a secret communications network with the internalized demon. Something is beaming out signals, calling drugs home" (51).[6]

what are we before or we're the drug

To be a human-Being is to be dependent for one's very life on something that is *not human* but that *brings the human into Being*. There is no Being that is not possessed, thrown, animated by one "drug" or another. There are "good and bad addictions, and anything," as Ronell says, "can serve the function of a drug" (53). The "bad conscience of our era" is the result of our blind drive to find a more authentic mode of Being than "drugs" can offer, to separate the self from the Other, the poison from the cure. This chapter will have been an attempt to explore the "drug" we call language and to let it Be, to answer its pharmakonic call.]

The House of Being

Martin Heidegger begins the essay "Language" with the phrase "Man speaks." This is hardly a revolutionary notion. However, one page later, he displaces "man," the subject/speaker, when he tosses out the phrase "language speaks" just as easily and with at least as much conviction. Heidegger says that to dis/cover the nature of language, he will *listen* to it speak; he will be/come-audience in an attempt to "leave the speaking to language" (191). This is problematic for all kinds of reasons, of course, but what's important to us here is Heidegger's recognition that language is always speaking when something gets spoken. It is also important to note that this is not an unhappy realization for Heidegger.

> We have to cease to think if we refuse to do it in the prison-house of language; for we cannot reach further than the doubt which asks whether the limit we see is really a limit.
>
> —Nietzsche, *Will to Power*

He cites a letter written by Hamann to Herder in 1784 in which Hamann expresses his agony over the realization that "reason is language," that there is no metalinguistic rationality, no space for logic to operate that is not shot through with language. Listen to Hamann's despair:

> If I were as eloquent as Demosthenes I would yet have to do nothing more than repeat a single word three times: reason is language, *logos*. I gnaw at this marrow bone and will gnaw myself to death over it. There still remains a darkness, always, over this depth for me; I am still waiting for an apocalyptic angel with a key to this abyss. (191)

Hamann was forced to turn to language to define reason; "[h]is glance," Heidegger notes, "aimed at reason, [fell] into the depths of an abyss," a linguistic abyss, a fluid gulf with no sticking points.

But what was agonizing for Hamann appears to be exciting for Heidegger. Heidegger says we use the name "abyss" when we speak of a place "where the ground falls away and a ground is lacking to us, where we seek the ground and set out to arrive at a ground, to get at the bottom of something" (191). And there it is: What makes the abyss agonizing is one's unanswered desire to hit bottom so that one might start building one's way back up and out. Heidegger, however, appears to enjoy the vertigo of the ffff

a

G
N P
I U   ll. Here's his response to Hamann's despair:
L
L   Language speaks. If we let ourselves fall into the abyss
             denoted by this sentence, we do not go tumbling into
A   emptiness. We fall upward to a height. Its loftiness opens up
             a depth. . . . To reflect on language means—to reach the
F   speaking of language in such a way that this speaking takes
             place as that which grants an abode for the being of mortals.
             ("Language" 192)

The "abyss" of language, Heidegger observes, is where we *are*, where we *live*: it is the "abode," the dwelling place, the home of human beings, even if we do not *feel* "at home" t/here. Even if we are always hoping to find a way back out. Heidegger's overarching project, however, invites us to enjoy our stay, to explore and celebrate the House of (our) Being, which *is* language.

Speaking tends to be viewed as a human activity, the simple outward expression of "something internal"; and language tends to be viewed as an unproblematic tool used to utter that expression. But Heidegger suggests that language "first brings man about, brings him into existence." For Heidegger, it is language that makes Being possible: "Understood in

[I]f human speech is taken simply to be the voicing of the inner man, if speech so conceived is regarded as language itself, then the nature of language can never appear as anything but an expression and activity of man. But human speech . . . is not self-subsistent. . . . *Mortal speech must first of all have listened to the command.*

—Heidegger, "Language"

this way, man would be bespoken by language" (192). Here Heidegger, in an aftershadowing of Gorgias and Nietzsche, offers a *fore*shadowing of Jean-Francois Lyotard's pagan politics, Jacques Derrida's citational politics, and Judith Butler's performative politics, to name only a few. Heidegger writes: "Mortals speak insofar as they listen" (209); and then: "Man speaks in that he responds to language" (210). S/he speaks in that s/he responds, then, to the *call*, to the *hail* that language issues. In fact, s/he *exists* (only) in that s/he responds to the hail. As Heidegger notes elsewhere, language "is the foundation of human being" (*On the Way to Language* 112). Language is the web in which we *are*, in which we *Be/come*; we come into Being by virtue of the fact that "language itself has woven us into the [its] speaking" (112). Paul Celan, who published *Language-Mesh* the same year (1959) that Heidegger published *On the Way to Language*, suggests, similarly, that we are enmeshed in language, caught in its network, and that we were always already with language before anything else. Eduardo Cadava, in "Toward an Ethics of Decision," notes that both Celan and Heidegger, despite their differences, indicated that this "network, this mesh or web" was the "proper matter of language" (4). Indeed, what's "at stake," for both Heidegger and Celan, "is the possibility of tracing a bond that, traversing the web that language is, and in a way that remains strange and unreadable, works to unbind and deliver language to itself. This bond would form relations without relation, would unbind by binding" (4). Lyotard would, perhaps, say that it would "just link," link according to a game plan that would be dis/covered *after* the linking rather than before it. The point would be, as Heidegger says, "to experience the unbinding bond within the mesh of language" (*On the Way* 113).

Our finitude is tied to our enmeshedness in language—we may not leave language to study it or ourselves from some other place, some metalinguistic spot. And, as Cadava notes: "In order to be who we are, we are obliged to remain faithful to this experience of our finitude," of our situatedness within the web of language (5). The science of linguistics faces its major hurdle here, in the recognition that we may study language only insofar as it already has hold of us, insofar as it already "regards us, already appropriates us to itself" (5). But Cadava goes further: "To say that who we are is interlaced with language is to say that we are constituted from out of language, that we are in control of neither language nor ourselves.] We do not possess language. On the contrary, it is in language that we are *dis*possessed" (5, my emphasis). Language, then, which is not human but is, according to Celan, "turned toward the human," leads/hails us *away* from ourselves, *dispossesses us*, like any other drug. And, as Cadava suggests, with Ronell, this leads us now to ask new questions about responsibility and community that are not tied to "egological forms of subjectivity" (5), questions that celebrate Being-on-drugs.

The Hail

Philosophical notions of "agency" and "authorship" are invited to take a rhetorical turn after Heidegger and Celan, a turn Louis Althusser[7] takes in his explications of the ideological interpellation of subjects. The self-proclaimed "central thesis" of Althusser's "Ideology and Ideological State Apparatuses" is that ideology interpellates individuals as subjects (170). Subjects have always already been hailed by ideology; Althusser's subject is both a proponent and also (more so) a function of that hail—the subject owes its Being, in part, to the "drug" he calls "ideology." Here's Althusser:

> The category of the subject is constitutive of all ideology, but at the same time and immediately I add that *the category of the subject is only constitutive of all ideology insofar as all ideology has the function (which defines it) of "constituting" concrete individuals as subjects*. In the inter-action of this double constitution exists the functioning of all ideology, ideology being nothing but its functioning in the material forms of existence of that functioning. (171, his emphasis)

If Althusser's "ideology" seems strangely reminiscent of Heidegger's "Being," it is, perhaps, because language houses them both. If language is the "house of Being" for Heidegger, it's the house of "ideology" for Althusser. His "ideology" is a linguistic structuration, and he follows Freud and Lacan when he observes that "everything depend[s] on language" ("Freud and Lacan" 207). Grammatical structure creates the category "subject," and "*all ideology hails or interpellates concrete individuals as concrete subjects*, by the functioning of the category of the subject" (173, his emphasis). Ideology, Althusser suggests, "recruits

Language Is the House of Ideology

subjects among the individuals (it recruits them all), or 'transforms' the individuals into subjects (it transforms them all)" (174) through the operation of "interpellation."

Althusser's primary example of this operation is the hail of the police: "Hey, you there!" When the addressee (the individual-who-is-not-yet-[a]-subject) turns around, Althusser says, "by this one-hundred-and-eighty-degree physical conversion, he becomes a subject" (174). Once the "individual" recognizes (or mis-recognizes [méconnaissance], just as in the mirror-check) her/himself as having been addressed, s/he has answered the call (in)to subjectivity. According to Althusser, then, the subject is socially constituted through the hail; in this example, through the hail of the police. Police officers represent the law, and their address/reprimand ("Hey you!") extends that law to the one who is hailed. Before the address/reprimand, the addressee is not, according to Althusser, fully a social subject. The reprimand not only controls the social subject, Althusser says; it also brings the subject into being by calling the individual into a subject position. Ideology operates as a pharmakonic drug: it is *both a poison and a cure*.

H E Y Y O U !!

For Althusser, this hailing or "interpellation" not only compels obedience through fear but also offers recognition; it offers *subjecthood*. The police officer's hail, or *any* hail, plucks the not-yet-One from pre-symbolic obscurity and deposits her into the discursive domain of the subject. Theoretically, it turns the not-yet-One into One: through the hail of language, the individual is called into a subject position s/he then denotes with the identity-term "I." Therefore, when that "I" speaks, s/he necessarily speaks from the position into which language has always-already called her/him. Echoes of Heidegger: Human beings speak only inasmuch as they "respond to" or are *ssspoken by* language.

Performing the Hail

Judith Butler begins chapter 4 of *Bodies That Matter*, "Gender Is Burning: Questions of Appropriation and Subversion," with Althusser's notions of subject "interpellation," noting that the "call" of language "is formative, if not *per*formative, precisely because it initiates the individual into the subjected status of the subject" (121). Butler's notion of performative politics begins with Althusser's notions of the subjected subject, who is hailed into Being as a subject by language. It is language, Butler says, that hails us into subjectivity and calls us to perform a particular sexed and gendered subject position. Both gender and sex, she says, are linguistically constructed positions that we are hailed into and then called to perform.

Butler's notion of performativity, however, ought not be mis/taken as an insidiously humanist enterprise—one must have been injected with language to engage performativity. It is not, Butler suggests, the "function of an originating will" (13). Performativity is a form of constructivism for Butler, but "it would be a mistake," she says, "to associate 'constructivism' with 'the freedom of a subject to form her/his sexuality as s/he pleases'" (94). The misunderstanding here arises from the notion that constructivism and determinism are mutually exclusive. It arises from the notion that one can Be without Being-*on*-something.

Butler's reconfiguration dis/solves the constructivism/determinism dichotomy by making constraint "the very condition of performativity," by making Being a function of the "drug" we call language. Performance is "precisely the re-iteration of norms" (94), a kind of "dissimulated citationality" (13) in which the repetition is not performed *by* a subject but is rather

> The reading of "performativity" as willful and arbitrary choice misses the point that the historicity of discourse and, in particular, the historicity of norms (the "chains" of iteration invoked and dissimulated in the imperative utterance) constitute the power of discourse to enact what it names.
>
> —Butler, *Bodies That Matter*

what *enables* a subject to come into being at all (95). And this will have been a major point, both for Butler and for us. It's the posthumanist paradox again: that we both speak and/but are also always already spoken. Vitanza, too, notes that even as we speak for free-flowing desire-in-language, *it speaks us*. Even as we speak our desires, we are always already subject to the desires of that speech. It is to that extent that we both are and are not a function of language ("Concerning"). It's not an either/or choice; it is, rather, a both/and, a

crooked

truth.

"Performativity," Butler says,
"is construed as that power of discourse to
produce effects through reiteration" (20), to
"produce what it declares" (107).
Performativity, however, is only possible *within*
the constraints of "iterability." We are spoken more
than we speak, done more than we do; therefore, we
are constrained "by what remains radically
unthinkable," and, in the area of sexuality, by
"the radical unthinkability of desiring
otherwise" (94). Inhabiting a sexed
position, then, always
involves engaging citational practices,
"citing the law" (107) "under and through the
force of prohibition and taboo, with the threat
of ostracism and even death controlling and
compelling the shape of production" but
without fully pre-determining it (95). "Agency,"
then, according to Butler's
*re*configuration, is always "on
drugs." It is always under the
influence of language and can only take
place within our reiteration of the
reiterable.

THE HAIL BREAKS DOWN/UP; OR,
ADDING A *PARA* TO THE *DISSOI LOGOI*

To stop here would be to leave Butler's performative politics heralding
an "agency" bound by the long arm of the Law; if Being is Being-on-
drugs, it is also Being-in-shackles. This was Althusser's point. But what
was not said and wants to be said—and here we will part company with
Althusser—is that the shackles are far from secure. Neither language nor
the Law, in other words, is stable; there are gaps, rup-tures, un-hing-ings,
escape routes. Because laws and conventions only get their authority
through "an echo-chain of their own reinvocation" (*Bodies That Matter*

107), the Law itself, Butler notes, "perpetually reinstitutes the possibility of its own failure" (108). Within the space of the "slippage between discursive command and its appropriated effect," there exists the potential for distortion, for hyperbole, for flight. In the space of that slippage, she says, "a radical resignification of the symbolic domain" might be achieved through *deviations* in the "citational chain" (21–22). Butler, then, introduces Nietzsche's concept of the "eternal return" to linguistic structure (the iterable), and what results is not the return of the "*same*"; it is not the eternal *rerun*. The reiteration of the reiterable becomes, rather, the return of difference/differance.

Butler "recast[s]" performativity as "a specific modality of power as discourse," suggesting that for "discourse to materialize a set of effects 'discourse' itself must be understood as complex and convergent chains in which 'effects' are vectors of power. In this case, what is const-ituted in discourse is not fixed in or by discourse, but becomes the condition and occasion for a further action" (187). According to Butler, subjects/bodies materialize as *effects* of a discursive injunction. But "this 'materialization,' while far from artificial, is not fully stable." Identity terms, "I-slots," do not fully hold steady and are not "exhaustive." They mean to "establish a coherent identity" but are perpetually "troubled by [the] failure of discursive performativity to finally and fully establish the identity to which it refers." Indeed, the "constitutive outside means that identity always requires precisely that which it cannot abide" (188).

> [R]esistance is present even in obedience.
> —Nietzsche, *Will to Power*

Because the bodies that materialize as effects of injunction are not fully stable (187) and because identity is always locked in a hostile embrace with exactly what it "cannot abide" (188), the Law can be made to create "more than it ever meant to, signifying in excess of any intended referent" (122). According to Butler, then, language, the "house of Being," is not necessarily a stable structure. Language, and therefore Being, can exceed the structure (of discourse), overflow the boundaries, transgress the limit(s), break

the

Law. What Butler suggests is that the *logos* that hails us into Being is perpetually "stepping out" on itself. The body of language is unfaithful to its own discursive injunctions. It breaks down/up, Butler says, and overflowsss the structures of discourse. This would indicate that it is not going to be possible to master language by mastering its structures; it is, therefore, not going to be possible for human beings to own their own discourse or their own Being.

A Look at the (Fun)"House"—
Structuralism and Its Dis/Contents

Butler obviously butts heads here with the structuralist icons, from Plato to Althusser and Saussure. Her notions of performative agency raise all sorts of questions about the structurality of language, questions that others, too, have raised. In "Structure, Sign, and Play" Derrida links structuralism to a typically Western blindness to the structurality of structure. He suggests that, from the dawning of Western philosophy, the concept of structure has been connected to a center, a reference point, a fixed origin that serves to freeze the free-play of the structure. But Derrida de-centers the concept of the center, leaving a "rupture" in structure's history, and leaving us with a dynamic structuration that is uncontrollable and unmasterable, that is in a state of perpetual becoming. What Derrida does in this essay, among other things, is focus our attention on the structuralist/poststructuralist duel, on its developmental sequence, a sequence that can be traced back to ancient Greece.

Some Prototypes

In "Nietzsche and the Obscurity of Heraclitus," Sarah Kofman notes that both Plato and Aristotle accused Heraclitus of being obscure, of (intentionally or not) concealing his ideas behind his un/clear, im/mature, "mythic discourse," a discourse that proved impossible to reconcile with their own. Because it was contradictory and incomplete, it could not "submit to questioning," to "dialectical examination." It was labeled "irresponsible" because it proved impossible for them to stuff into any structural schemata without a vast remainder, a vast excess of unconforming individualities/singularities with which neither Plato nor Aristotle knew what to do (41, 43).

For Heraclitus, according to Martin Heidegger, *logos* puts us in the presence of undifferentiated Beingness (*ouisa*): it is not "reason," but language as a "collecting," a "gathering," that puts subject and object in such proximity that they exist undivided (*Early Greek Thinking* 60). But for Plato, *logos* is *reason*, and reason demands the firm division between subject and object. Language must be mastered as a tool for reason to work, and through its lens poetic/mythic language becomes a "word magic" that has no/thing to do with "reality." Plato and Aristotle assume that the world is naturally orderly, and, like good protostructuralists, they go about fitting everything into their (obsessive-compulsive) structural schemes—what can't be fit in gets erased.

But perhaps the major distinction between the dynamic structurations of the pre-Platonics and the fixed structures of Plato and his children (including us) is that the former is based on a system of *co*-ordination and the latter is based on a system of *sub*-ordination. With subordination (hierarchy), it becomes possible to locate some concept/term (transcendental signifier) at the base of an architectonic structure to keep it stable, unmoving. Heraclitus did not appear to have such a term/standard; for him, the oppositional structure appears to have been dynamic and unstable. Within this structure, one had no way to formulate logically: both language and Being were caught in a wild and untamable storm.

Plato and Aristotle strove to calm the storm, to drive it away by taking the becoming out of it so that it could be stabilized, structured. But Heidegger notes that "this calm is no tranquillity. It is only anesthesia: more precisely, the narcotization of anxiety in the face of thinking" (*Early Greek Thinking* 78). Nietzsche would say it's *against life* because every attempt to stop the flow represses singularities, chance, *kairos,* all that will not or cannot fit into an *invariant, universal mold* (*Untimely Meditations* 66–67). The anesthetic is purchased at the expense of free-play, positing a structural center (transcendental signifier), which functions as its anchor. For Plato, that anchor is Being; for Aristotle, it is sub/stance. And now we have come back around (with a bow to the circular temporality of Nietzsche and Heidegger) to Derrida, who would decenter the center and

              ooo   -ooo   -w   us
         rrr   back
    thr   i
                                             n
                                             t
                                             o
                              the sssstorm.

That's what poststructuralism does: it attempts to shake loose the structures that cage us in and put thinking to sleep. Bernard Miller suggests that Gorgias, who responded to his day's rampant structuring of thought with blatant contradictions and a celebration of the yield of reason, may have been the first poststructuralist critic. What's important here is that it's probably not productive to view structuralism and poststructuralism in terms of opposition. Obviously, poststructuralism is parasitic on structuralism; and/but, more interestingly, structuralism is also parasitic on poststructuralism, scrambling to construct a system of meaning in a world that has been radically "de/constructed." Lyotard, in *The Postmodern Condition*, suggests that *post*modernism precedes modernism and that it is inevitably a *part* of the modern. Similarly, poststructuralism is a part of structuralism; it is a honing in on and a charging through the gaps and openings left unsecure in any discursive structuration. Structures are constructed, and then they are de/constructed; or, à la Deleuze and Guattari, we territorialize, deterritorialize, and *re*territorialize *all over again*. The dueling banjos will not have stopped: there will have been no winner here.

Structuralism Proper

The modern structuralist revolution, (up) against which poststructuralists like Butler and Derrida write, devotes itself to the scientific search for stable and centered structurality. Structuralism has developed a system of holistic analysis that begins with the notion that all phenomena can be analyzed in terms of parts and wholes *and* that the structure itself is a function of the interrelation of the parts within a common system. Structuralism searches for stable and universal structures, underlying systems that organize individual phenomena into coherent and cohesive units. With Immanuel Kant, structuralism aims to purge itself of subjective valuations, to attain disinterested objectivity and, therefore, *scientific status*. Seemingly against Kant and with Butler and Derrida, however, structuralism proper's critique of modernism/liberalism also offers a radical rejection of humanism, the very foundation of the human sciences since Kant. Structuralism abandons the notion of autonomous subjectivity and posits the notion of the subject as constituted by the very structures s/he aims to study. It tends to forget, however, that not even those who wish to analyze those structures can get out of them to offer

It's interesting how English Co-opted neo Philosophy

an objective analysis. Derrida's insight in this arena is profound.

Structuralism proper arrived on the American scene sometime in the mid-1960s and immediately took a linguistic turn. The application of Saussure's structural linguistics to the human sciences marked the scramble to accommodate an increasingly potent scientific impulse in the humanities; the result was a radically different concept of language, reality, and human-Being. Saussure's *Course in General Linguistics* takes a semiotic approach to the study of language and suggests that this approach be applied to the study of all social and cultural phenomena. His call has been answered with the application of linguistic/semiotic principles to anthropology (Lévi-Strauss), psychoanalysis (Lacan, Kristeva, Irigaray), Marxism (Althusser), fashion (Barthes), and art (Mukarovsky, Uspenski, and Lotman), to name only a few.

For Saussure, the linguistic sign consists of a signifier (sound image) and a signified (the mental image or concept that the sound image conjures up), which have no natural bond and no connection to an extra-linguistic referent. Each individual speech act (*parole*) is capable of producing meaning only inasmuch as it can be located within a larger and underpinning *system* of language (*langue*). Meaning can arise only within this underpinning system and only differentially: words acquire meaning only by reference to what they are *not*. In other words, linguistic structure is a closed system of signification: the sign has two sides (signifier and signified), each deriving its meaning and its value from the other.

Claude Lévi-Strauss's appropriation of Saussurean structural linguistics results in a shift in focus for anthropological analysis: the subjects of a culture become less important to the ethnographer than the *mythology* of that culture. Lévi-Strauss analyzes a culture's mythology in the way that linguists analyze sentences, directing his attention to the texts cultures produce and scanning for the cross-cultural systems that organize those texts. His dis/covery of what he believes are stable structural elements of mythology across several cultures offers a mighty swipe at humanism. The subject, for Lévi-Strauss, becomes an overdetermined effect/function of cultural coding . . . and anthropology mutates into a counterhuman science.

In *Structural Anthropology*, he offers a structuralist critique of Russian Formalism, which assumes that the form (concrete) is intelligible but that the content (abstract) is arbitrary. Lévi-Strauss argues that this form/

```
        F   A
        L   L
  N     U   L
  o     I   O
  o     D   W
  o     I   E
  o     T   D
        Y
```

content opposition is an illusion; structural analysis illuminates *both* form and content because both get their meaning from the underpinning system itself. Form and content can be analyzed as *parole*, and the underpinning structure can be analyzed as *langue*. What's important here is the gigantic scope of structuralism's mastery: through its lens, every human experience becomes a *rational* one, a scientifically definable one. There is no excess that cannot be pinned down, under/stood; there is no potential for rupture, no lines of flight. Structuralism operates as if it has all its bases covered. *it assumes solidity . . .*

Juri Lotman's *Structure of the Artistic Text* follows both Saussure and Lévi-Strauss in his application of structural linguistics to the artistic text. With Lévi-Strauss, Lotman suggests that there can be no formalist division of form and content because the meaning arises out of the overall structure, which absorbs both form and content. According to Lotman, the artistic text functions as a model of the universe, a reflection of the infinite in the finite. But this is possible only because it is assumed that both art and the world are manifestations of stable structures of under-standing, structures that are available to the objective observer. Using Saussure's distinction between *parole* and *langue*, Lotman differentiates between the message (of the particular artistic text) and the code (under-pinning system of meaning). In order to receive the message transmitted by an artistic text, we have to learn its language, master its code. Infor-mation transmitted by an artistic structure is meaning*less* outside that structure: you can't destroy the structure without irreparably distorting the message.

The Poststructuralist Turn

It's not difficult to imagine what *post*structuralist thought will do with this. If structuralism wants to master the world by mastering its signs, poststructuralism "decon-structs" the scientific pretensions of structuralism, refusing to take them seri-assly. Poststructuralists

"You spirit of gravity . . . do not make things too easy for yourself!"
　—Nietzsche, *Thus Spoke Zarathustra*

echo Nietzsche's Zarathustra, who cautions the dwarf against making things "too easy" for himself. Lévi-Strauss's "objective" pretensions get this very response from Derrida, who dismisses them as unfounded (*Of Grammatology*), since it would be impossible for Lévi-Strauss to step outside the structure he's examining. Structuralism ignores the excess, the *lllleakage* of the structure, and therefore makes things "*too easy*," too simple.

A "scientific" examination of culture would require that one step to a place outside of the structures that drive it and look in, but, as Heidegger noted, after Nietzsche but way before Derrida, there is no so such place outside Tradition or outside History. Structural analysis necessarily takes place *within* the structures it's trying to describe; there can be no "objective" examination of a structure and so no *science* of structuralism. To think structuralism can be objective and scientific is to not be suspicious enough of the rational, unified, autonomous subject that structuralism claims to displace. And what's at stake in this lack of suspicion is the continued capacity for *system/atic exclusion-extermination*, for stamping out all singularities (difference/differance) that will not or cannot stay/play within the lines.

In a playing through of the assumptions of structural linguistics, poststructuralism discovers something Saussure did not: signification is unstable. The sign unit Saussure describes, the one upon which Lévi-Strauss and company build a science, doesn't operate as a fixed entity, a closed system; rather, it operates as a momentary connection between two *protean* "layers" of meaning. The dictionary confirms the endless mutability of the sign: every signified is also a signifier. If structuralism confines the play of language within closed structures of oppositions, poststructuralism celebrates the *floating* signifier, the dynamic and independent linguistic machine, and the radical instability of meaning. If structuralism would box up language neatly, poststructuralism would bust it loose and invite *it* to "bust up." "Dissemination" is the term Derrida gives this endless and independent production of signification, which resists imposed structural constraints.

Derrida's critique of Lévi-Strauss in "Structure, Sign, and Play" and in *Of Grammatology* is ultimately a deconstruction of structuralism's encasement of a wild and unruly storm of differences (differance) within a simple binary opposition. Lévi-Strauss privileged a nature/culture binary, which, Derrida shows, cannot hold up in an examination of the incest-taboo because that taboo partakes of *both* nature and culture, a realization that breaks down/up the binary itself. Tacking a second phase onto Heidegger's *destruktion*, Derrida makes his de(con)struction a two-part process: first, it disrupts the stability of the "Tradition" (Heidegger) or, more precisely, the apparent stability of the logocentric system of binaries that orders the text; and second, it searches for third terms (but this has nothing to do with Hegelian synthesis) outside of those binaries, disruptive terms like hymen, for instance, that cannot locate themselves neatly on one side or the other. It searches for the remainder, the excess, the "stormy" overflow that cannot be contained or ac/counted for in a binary structure (which, as Vitanza suggests, can only count to two, or One-cum-two, but never to *three*).

Poststructuralist Applications

Several styles of deconstruction have followed Derrida's lead, directly or indirectly dis/rupting and/or expanding the Saussurean model of structural linguistics that has been so instrumental in the development of structuralism proper in this century. Emile Benveniste's poststructuralist linguistics begins with Saussure and his ancestors, as does Derrida's grammatology, Jacques Lacan's psychoanalysis, Luce Irigaray's critique of Lacan's psychoanalysis, and (less directly) Michel Foucault's critique of disciplinary matrices of power, to name just a few.

Benveniste notes that pronouns illustrate an important problem for structural linguistics. They are subject-slots, subject *positions*, into which language calls us. Communication depends upon our acceptance of these *reversible* linguistic slots, but in the space between two communicative instances, pronouns completely lose their value. They are valuable only during specific discursive encounters. If Heidegger points out that we cannot separate thought from its History or Tradition, Benveniste notes the impossibility of separating *langue* from *parole*, even for the sake of analysis (*Problems in General Linguistics* 223–30). Benveniste also suggests the impossibility of isolating language from subjectivity: the former creates the latter through pronouns that function

> There is no concept "I" that incorporates all the *I*'s that are uttered at every moment. . . . [W]hat does *I* refer to? To something very peculiar which is exclusively linguistic: *I* refers to the act of individual discourse in which it is pronounced, and by that it designates the speaker.
>
> —Benveniste, *Problems in General Linguistics*

as subject-slots. But the "individual" and the "enunciating" subject slot, into which an individual steps, are two different spaces—we've been here with Nietzsche. The apparent unity of "the" subject is an illusion created by our faith in the "grammatical habit" of locating a doer for every deed (Nietzsche, *Beyond Good and Evil* 24; see also *Will to Power* 268).

Poststructuralist thought is after an exploration of the space between the "individual" (or, rather, the singular being) and the subject-slot from which it speaks. Both structuralism and poststructuralism look beyond the humanist subject, but poststructuralism is more suspicious, more anxious to explore how singularities are constituted as subjects and hailed into particular subject positions. Foucault locates the construction of the subject in the discursive and disciplinary practices of the subject's own historical epistemic space (e.g., *The Order of Things, Madness and Civilization*, and *Discipline and Punish*). For Foucault, the subject is hailed by various discursively produced matrices of power, which dictate what that subject can know, think, and even desire. This subject is radically situated within a particular epistemic domain that dictates her/his conditions of conceptual possibility.

Foucault describes discontinuous surfaces of disciplinary discourses that cannot be viewed as causally linked (hypotaxis) but can be viewed as coordinatively linked (parataxis) across broad epistemic domains. In *The Order of Things*, he attempts to identify the conditions of possibility for knowledge, the system of rules of formation that operate beneath the level of intention within each of these epistemes. But, for Foucault, not even these epistemic structurations are stable, progressive, or rational. They are historically changing and specific to given discursive domains. Furthermore, he recognizes that he can only anachronistically reconceive/redescribe previous epistemes across the one in which he is presently involved. When he attempts to describe the Contemporary Episteme, he becomes lost in a web of signification that makes him (and us) dizzy with possiblisms. He acknowledges that he cannot get out of the structure he describes.

In *Madness and Civilization* and *Discipline and Punish*, Foucault is explicitly interested in spotlighting what has been excluded and or subjugated by the discourses of exclusion and institutions of confinement that would draw a distinct division between self and other. The visible, branded existence of "madness" and "delinquency" serves to sustain the distinction between the sane and the insane, good citizens and criminals. But Foucault's archaeologies suggest that the distinction is illusory, *created* by the very discourses enlisted to study the "insane" and to control the "delinquents." The disciplinary structure makes the extra- or non-structured storm of being seem structured and orderly by silencing those who would disrupt it, much the way Plato and Aristotle silenced Heraclitus by declaring him "obscure."

Jacques Lacan restates Freudian psychoanalysis in Saussurean terms but with a crucial distinction: the unconscious processes are identified with the *unstable* signifier. For Lacan, the signifier floats, leaving a perpetual gap between it and the signified, which is analogous to the space left between the I-slot and the individual who steps into it, between the specular image in the mirror and the protean pre-linguistic "self" who looks. The floating nature of the signifier is manifested, according to Lacan (*Ecrits*), in any kind of psychic distortion—and for Lacan, signifiers are *always* distorted. The unconscious (the repressed force of desire), which is structured like a language, constructs the subject and speaks the subject more than the subject speaks, much the way *langue* speaks through *parole*. The unconscious also continually manifests what is repressed there; it shows up in typos, sssslips of the tongue, lapses. It manifests itself in that excess, the ooooverflowwww between what the "speaking subject" intends to say and that (irrepressible) remainder that slips out accidentally. What's important here is that gaps, differences, and the dissemination of meaning are celebrated over cl$O$sure and tOtalization.

Luce Irigaray's critique of Lacan's psychoanalysis points up the ways in which it remains as phallogocentric as Freud's and argues that it's not suspicious enough of the phallocratic tradition in which it has its roots. Irigaray's project is to locate and disrupt that tradition, to examine and critique the theoretical concept, the theoretical machine, which completely excludes the feminine. She advocates a deconstructive project she calls "mimicry," which operates within theoretical discourse and overperforms it in order to draw attention to what has been excluded from it. What she's after is a "jamming [of] the theoretical machinery itself" by examining its grammar, by exploring its linguistic style in order to get at what is left unsaid, unthought in it (*This Sex* 78).

Butler's performative politics begins with Irigaray's mimicry, and it could not become thinkable without a poststructuralist critique of linguistic structurations, without its recognition of the potential ssslippage between the signifier and the signified. As long as the two practice fidelity, no performativity is possible. But once language steps out on its *own* discursive structure, once it engages in infidelity against its own discursive injunctions—once it begins to *laugh*—Butler's performative politics becomes thinkable and both "agency" and "ethics" get re/fashioned; they get a fashion update. And this time, old notions of autonomy and pure presence are going to Goodwill.

Chasing a Language on the Loose

Heidegger's *destruktion* and Derrida's deCONstruction of what he calls "the metaphysics of presence" spotlight the dependence of meaning (including "the" meaning of identity) upon an always already *absent* foundation. The pure presence of meaning is continuously deferred in what Derrida calls the "trace" (*Of Grammatology, Dissemination*) and Heidegger calls the "tracks of the dead gods" ("What Are Poets For?"). But neither the trace nor the tracks are substantive. Both are non-existent, the residue of a metaphysical longing, a metaphysical *expectation* of pure presence. It is the trace/track that reveals meaning and truth as always already not there. Jasper Neel puts it this way:

> Speaking, in short, like writing, remains forever incomplete because what it would present if it could actually present what it *re*presents becomes "gone" only when speaking or writing appear on the scene to stand for the "thing" that can be recognized as "gone" now that a symbol appears to stand in its absent place. (117)

Faith in language is faith in the pure presence that it promises, faith in our ability to finally catch up with the "meaning," the "truth" that left the tracks/trace   .

.

.

.

.

.

•
•

But language proves ultimately incapable of producing the meaning it promises; following the tracks/trace leads us on an endless chase into what Baudrillard calls an "abyss of linguistic seduction, a radically different operation that absorbs rather than produces meaning" (*Seduction* 57). "The" meaning is perpetually deferred as signifiers engage in dissemination rather than denotation, proliferating potentialities and engaging differance. "The signified," Derrida says, "is originarily and essentially . . . trace," that is, "it is always already in the position of the signifier, is the apparently innocent proposition within which the metaphysics of the logos . . . must reflect upon writing as its death and its resource" (*Of Grammatology* 73).

Derrida follows Saussure in the notion that there are only differences within a system of language. But he also notes that these differences are "themselves *effects*":

> What we note as *differance* will thus be the movement of play that "produces" (and not by something that is simply an activity) these differences, these effects of difference. This is before them in a simple and in itself unmodified and indifferent present. Differance is the non-full, nonsimple "origin"; it is the structured and differing origin of differences. ("Differance" 141)

Derrida, then, suggests that difference is the effect of differance and not of a pure presence or a "being that is somewhere present and itself escapes the play of difference" (141). Both God and the subject/author are dead here, and we are left with differance. It works, Derrida says, because we're duped by a metaphysical longing for pure presence. We agree to chase the "trace," the "tracks" of the presence we are after in language without recognizing that the trace/track is also an effect of the play of absence and presence that constitutes language. The presence that supposedly left the trace/track was always already not there, a mere function of the play by which it is constituted.

Differance: "the movement by which language, or any code, any system of reference in general, becomes 'historically' constituted as a fabric of differences."
—Derrida, "Differance"

Even the presence of Being, Derrida says, "can be called the play of traces." Being is "a trace that no longer belongs to the horizon of Being but one whose sense of Being is borne and bound by this play; it is a play of traces or differance that has no sense and is not, a play that does not belong" (154, my emphasis). In case we're still a bit fuzzy on this, Derrida makes things, as Vitanza might say, *unclearly clear* for us: "There is no support to be found and no depth to be had for this bottomless chessboard where being is set in play" (154). Being itself is getting re/conceived here.

> Being: an *effect* of the play of language,
> of a dissemination that
> *never finally lands/stops*

•

Julia Kristeva calls this continual deferral of One meaning "revolution in language" or "desire-in-language"; Vitanza calls it the "anti-body rhetoric" ("Critical Sub/Versions") or "*dissoi paralogoi*" ("Threes"; "Concerning") or "libidinalized language" ("Threes"); Hélène Cixous and Luce Irigaray call it "*écriture féminine*." While these (anti)theories are far from conflatable, they do each refer to a *Laughing*-in-language that will not and cannot be suppressed. "The repression of writing," Derrida suggests, is the "repression of that which threatens presence" ("Freud" 196). Indeed, *the* entire history of philosophy and philosophical approaches to rhetoric can be read as the attempt to find a way to suppress the *kairotic* force of Laughter-in-language, to suppress its tendency to go organic and overflow our intentions.

But, as Nietzsche suggests in the *Genealogy of Morals* and Derrida repeats in *Speech and Phenomena*, the attempt is not successful: not only is One meaning perpetually deferred, we are also perpetually deferred. Language is finally incapable of *habeas corpus*; it cannot produce a stable, unified subject. Our faith in agency, Nietzsche says, is based on our faith in grammatical structure, which requires that every deed have a doer, that every action have an agent. Our faith in *the* subject is based on our faith that neither we nor the language that speaks us gets laughed. But Nietzsche has no such faith. Nor does Vitanza, who suggests that the *logos* that hails us does not simply speak either "yes" or "no"; it speaks both "nes" and "yo" ("Octalog" 30, 44). If the subject is spoken by a schizoid *logos* that *seduces* even as it appears to produce, that *proliferates* even as it appears to fixate, then *the* subject cannot *Be* at all; *the* subject, as Nietzsche, Deleuze and Guattari, and Vitanza suggest, is actually what Vitanza calls a "polyethoi" or "scattered subject positions" ("Taking A-Count" 184; also "Concerning," "Threes"). Nietzsche calls it the "subject as *multiplicity*" (*Will to Power* 270), a community-of-the-self that is always already and only a site of competing instincts and dueling drives in the midst of be-coming.

Because there is no way to finally suppress for good the force of Laughter that traverses the *logos*, there may no way for language to save us (usher in paradise): not through dialectic and not through logic or reason. If even philosophic language is incapable of suppressing its laughter, then it may not be capable of founding the "Grand March" of liberalism or freedom or equality. A laughing language is capable of founding no/thing. It can't be anchored; it is, rather, bound to disrupt, disperse, disseminate. It can have no vendetta and no regret; it can offer no "justice." Indeed, it can have *no subjects* in the humanist sense; those subjects are the result of a repression (Deleuze and Guattari, *A Thousand Plateaus*) a laughing language knows no/thing about. To be spoken by a language contorted in laughter is to be spoken by *language on the loose*: no/thing is excluded, censored, or negated, and every attempt to reduce difference to sameness is dispersed by more "c|u|t|t|i|n|g up."

Safe Text? Or,
Philosophy Breaks Down/Up

And yet, the philosophical impulse is relentless in its efforts to censor, to negate, to still the roaring laughter-in-language so that it might build its epistemologies and establish its ethics. It is relentless . . . but *unsuccessful*. In her essay entitled "The Worst Neighborhoods of the Real: Philosophy-Telephone-Contamination," Ronell illustrates the problem. She takes on both the Bernsteinian[8] celebration and the Derridean *critique* of the language of Michel Foucault. The charge against which she plays defense attorney is that Foucault uses what we could call word-condoms, that he produces "safe text," text that avoids "deviance" and stays put, signifying clearly.

The "charge" is that, though Foucault writes *about* madness in *Histoire de la folie*, his writing is free from it. In "On Foucault," Michael

Bernstein celebrates Foucault's writing for exactly that reason, arguing that Foucault's language is, thankfully, clear and precise rather than "deviant." For Derrida, however, this is nothing to celebrate. In "Cogito and the History of Madness," Derrida's gripe with Foucault is that "everything [in *Histoire de la folie*] transpires as if Foucault *knew* what madness means" (41). But Derrida notes that language is always *reason's* tool and that Foucault's language is no exception—any attempt to speak *for* madness will simply rearticulate the *reason* that silenced it in the first place. This seems particularly antirhetorical and an odd critique for *Derrida* (of all people) to make, at least without his also offering the flipside—that is, if language is indeed reason's tool, it also always exceeds reason in a *non*-sane, hypertextual overflow.

Ronell takes this position and counters the charge against Foucault with the suggestion that if Foucault's language were self-cleaning enough to successfully avoid "deviance," it would indicate that he were speaking

> from the other side of the barricades—this side, perhaps, of institutional safety zones; he would be speaking in order to maintain deviance in its exteriority, to gag it once again, to incarcerate and protect language from the contamination of poisoned otherness, from the contagion of linguistic misbehavior, that is, from madness's contagion. ("Worst Neighborhoods" 220)

But, as Ronell notes, Foucault said nothing if not that philosophical discourse simply cannot avoid "contamination." Any discourse is always already infused with language's *madness*; it cannot "create for itself a zone of radical immunity": the barricades are never powerful enough, and discourse always runs the "risk of exposure." There is a slippery gap, continuously transgressed, between the "body of language" and its "antibodies," between what Ronell calls "the language of deviance and that of prescriptive normativism" (220). (We have been here with Butler—it is in the space of the gap that we find our re/fashioned "liberation" and "agency.")

Foucault discusses this transgression at length in an essay called "Language to Infinity." There, he describes his encounter with the dis-eased language of Sade, his rendezvous with an excessively multiplicitous language that won't rest, that "drives itself out of any possible resting place" (65). This dis-eased language, he says, cannot/will not denote without disseminating; it is a language of excess that suffers a "deficiency," never being free from what he calls the "wound of the double." Foucault deserves to be quoted at length here:

> [This terrifying language] can no longer avoid multiplying itself—as if struck from within by a disease of proliferation; it is always beyond the limit in relation to itself; it speaks only as a supplement starting from a displacement such that the language from which it separates itself and which it recovers is the one that appears useless and excessive, and that deserves to be expunged; but as a result of that same shift, it sheds, in turn, all ontological weight; it is at this point excessive and of so little density that it is fated to extend itself to infinity without ever acquiring the weight that might immobilize it. (65)

This multiplicitous language is an obsessive weight watcher, singularly driven to shed its ontological poundage, to the point of disease. And Foucault's texts are as infected with this language as Sade's. Indeed, when any reading of Foucault's texts does "not produce the effect of a scandal," Ronell notes, it indicates that "his discourse . . . [has] been submitted to the sanitation department—neutralized and expulsed from the *filth* and the *aberration* which it *wanted to let speak*" (220, my emphasis). In "Nietzsche, Freud, and Marx," Foucault indicates as much, noting that, though this infectious language is "malevolent" and "violent," to stop the violence and opt for clarity is to bring on a "reign of terror" (65, 67).

And this will have been our point: whenever the dust is made to settle around Foucault's texts, around *any* text, one can be fairly certain that a highly skilled cleanup crew has been at work behind the scenes, domesticating and processing the language, determined, in the name of Knowledge and/or Truth, to give *writing* the squeeze. Not only composition courses but the UniVersity itself is implicated in this charge. The kind of thinking and writing that pushes the limits of the knowable and the writable, that challenges established bodies of "knowledge" and disciplinary boundaries, is rarely welcome in the academy. Typically, academia is not about *learning* at all but about teaching, about reciting over and over again what we already "know." It's about protecting what has already been established, codified, and made "teachable" from anything that might call it all into question. No doubt about it, academia is guilty of getting "writing" in a choke-hold and lulling "knowledge" to sleep. But any discourse is vulnerable to the body of language it attempts to reign in, vulnerable to its breakouts, its dis-ease, its obsession with *shedding*. And the academy's philosophical discourse is no exception. "Philosophy" must scramble constantly to hold it all together . . . has been scrambling for more than two millennia.

We've suspected for quite some time, at least since Heidegger and Paul de Man,[9] that, though philosophy puts on the ritz from the "transcendental heights" of its Ivory Towers, it also hangs out at the grungiest of scenes—it was hanging out at Auschwitz, at Vietnam and Desert Storm. It was hanging out at the Salem Witch Trials and on the battlefields of Bosnia. "Philosophy," as Ronell suggests, "was always exposed"; it was never "not starting trouble or beyond contamination" ("Worst Neighborhoods" 223). "Reason," Hamann says, "is language." And language is not *only* "reason's tool." Rather, reason also *gets used* by a wildly infectious language, and even the toughest, thickest prophylactic is no match for it.

The will to Truth, however, is tenacious in this regard—philosophy has not given up its scramble to find and shut down leaks, to anticipate and contain potential "carceral breakouts." It continues to engage itself in a "general movement to close things off . . . to detect and bind official openings, the still festering wounds or cuts from which uncontrollable utterances might be stopped" (Ronell, "Worst Neighborhoods" 223). The aim is to whip language into submission, to pin it down, to make it masterable so that we might, as Wittgenstein put it, "battle against the bewitchment of our intelligence by means of language" (*Philosophical Investigations* 47). The philosophical enterprise, it seems, requires a clean-up crew that is nothing short of *enormous*.

However, lest an Us/Them dichotomy threaten to take form here, let us note up front that *we are all*, at some level, moved by the philosophical/epistemological impulse. We are all, to some extent, believers in logic, in the *logos* as savior. And to the extent that we operate on this belief, we engage ourselves in a collective dream to "shut down the flow," to stop the "contagion," to put the body of language "to sleep." To the extent that we participate, we attempt to protect ourselves against the contagion of a *language on the loose*, a language that refuses to *work* for us, to remain faithful to our progressive aspirations and our will to Truth.

But we have been and continuously will be unsuccessful. What Derrida himself says about the AIDS virus could as easily be said of the infectious body of language: it "may *always already* have broken into any 'intersubjective' space" ("Rhetoric of Drugs" 20). Even when we have thought we were on this side of the "institutional safety zones," we have actually been wide open to contamination. Even in the ivory towers, there has always been a "secretly cycling poison" oozing in from un-detected leaks in the shield. And now, after what Ronell calls some intense "applications of hyperdetection and a new examination of the shit we keep on walking into" ("Worst Neighborhoods" 223), it is clear that the (word)condom had a h●le in it: Hamann was right; "reason is language," and philosophy has offered us a defective shield against the infection of linguistic missss-behavior.

Indeed, philosophy has always been infected *and infectious*. It has al-ways, as Ronell says, "cruised the streets, moved in gangs, or as a solitary punk [in the form of, say, Socrates] looking for a dose of trouble and aporia" (223). Philosophy was never safe in its ethereal "home." Rather, it was "hanging out in the worst neighbor- hoods of the real," and it was always packing big guns equipped with high- tech silencers. What it quietly blows away is not "Falsity" and/ or "Heresy" but the excess that cannot be easily ac/counted for, that can be neither absorbed nor opposed by the particular Regime of Truth *packing the pistols*. Again, however, philo-sophy is never finally tough enough.

> This sounds very remote in-deed from the lofty peaks that you felt philosophy was scal-ing. You were wrong. You didn't read close enough, with your nose to the ground.
> —Ronell, "Worst Neighborhoods"

What we typically teach in composition classrooms and analyze in rhetoric classrooms is "philosophical rhetoric," rhetoric that has been roughed up by philosophy's body guards. We teach and study what Ronell, in "Namely, Eckerman," calls "hy-gienic writing," the "self-cleaning text," designed to crack down on

> Each thinking text, to the extent that it develops strategies of protection against outside interference or parasitism, is run by an immunological drive. Perhaps every text can be shown to be phantasmatically producing antibodies against the auto-immune community it has established within itself (a within that is constantly leaking, running an exscription machine, exposed precisely to a contaminating "outside").
> —Ronell, "Namely, Eckerman"

"impurities," to fend off "carceral breakouts" (159). This is the writing that composition teachers applaud for its "clarity," its "precision." And, yet, even hygienic writing is perpetually bombarded by contaminants and doomed to run a never-ending mop-up job: the work of the self-cleaning text is never done. The strategies of linguistic protection we teach students in comp courses—those strategies designed to maintain a text's integrity against "outside interference or parasitism"—do battle perpetually with any text's own propensity to *crack up.*

And so, we philosophers, we academes, we limbs and organs of the body politic are called to offer even the self-cleaning text some outside hygienic protection. We are called into the vocation of cleanup crew for the sanitation department of the philosophical enterprise. "Whether it is a matter," Ronell says, "of the house of being or the prison house of language, people get paid for keeping it clean" (160). And, indeed, even when the most profoundly *unhygienic*, the most profoundly infected texts (such as Nietzsche's or Cixous's or Bataille's) get run through the sanitation department of most universities, they do appear to "come out clean, like laundered money and safe text. They are made digestible by the huge garbage disposal systems which uni[-]versities sometimes are" (160).

And yet, what's important to us here is that even the most effective cleanup crew isn't perfect. Even after a text has been sanitized, the most suspicious of snoots will detect a lingering odor. Interestingly enough, the cleanup crew itself, which necessarily, as Ronell notes, "retains traces of [the] filth" it is hired to purify, becomes infected and so is *infectious* (160). And at the moment the cleanup crew gets infected and starts infecting, philosophy is exposed as the product of *sophistry*, the prophylactic is revealed as a symptom of the *infection*, and Truth is unconcealed as a phase of the linguistic *mis/behavior* from which it *desperately tries to disassociate itself.*

[● ● ● ARRESTED PAUSE ● ● ●]

"Enlightened" cleaners work the night shift, Ronell says, and busy themselves with those underground "hyperdetections," sometimes called "deconstructions," which unconceal the dis-ease with which even self-cleaning texts are *thoroughly infected*. There is no prophylactic strong enough, no cleanup crew fast enough to fully protect or even steer clear of a *language on the loose*, a

time
to
rigorously
hesitate

body of language convulsed in laughter and determined to mis/behave, determined to engage in what could be called a linguistic form of   w-
w-
.gnidliw

Language Affirmatively Loosed

Could be. But perhaps an/other rigorous hesitation is in order. If philosophic rhetoric has been "exposed," "infected" from the start, if there never was any safe text or effective word-condom, perhaps a redescription would be helpful. Though it is, as Richard Lanham notes, "generally assumed that language originally tried to be clear and only later degenerated into self-pleasing rituals," we may well ask, with Lanham, "why not the other way around—*pleasure* first?" (*Motives* 21, my emphasis). What if we assume that "health" lies in the flow of language rather than in those structures designed to plug it up? That "the bad conscience of our era" grows out of our unfulfilled and poisonous desire to stop the flow, to stop what Nietzsche has called "the great sweep of life"? This is a question of atypical starting points, of starting points that would be Other/Wise, of *a*topoi out to *celebrate Being-on-drugs*. If we've been situating "antibodies" on the side of "prescriptive normativism" and have been charging them with fighting off the infection spread by the body of language, Victor J. Vitanza, in "Critical Sub/Versions," suggests that it is "prescriptive normativism" that has "*infected* Rhetoric" and writing (46).

For Vitanza, it is philosophy's dream of an ultimately transparent language, of a discourse finally *cleansed* and *stopped*, that has gone about poisoning an otherwise healthy flow. It's the "dream of the triumph of the language of truth over the language of error [*doxa*]" (47) that ssss-p-r-e-a-d-s the infection. Philosophical rhetoric, Vitanza says, is often "fostered by a fear of *excess* and an ignorance of *lack*." Proponents of a fully cleansed and transparent language fear "the proliferation of meaning in discourse" (47). *They fear fff-l-u-i-d-i-t-y.* But Vitanza, like Ronell, notes that language simply cannot be cleaned up, purged of its irrepressibly playful element.

He suggests that there is "no Reason . . . to worry about the priggish onto-theological nightmare" because there is also "a counter-sub/version, a counter-infection, in the form of a competing and contradictory, though theoretically complementary, Rhetoric" in operation, what he calls the "Antibody Rhetoric" (48). This " 'nondisciplinary Rhetoric' and its antibodies" are perpetually counterattacking, Vitanza says. "Even when they are under the *influenza* of the Dream of Reason," he continues,

> [they] dream a perverse dream that is the hope for a language of not just numerous competing glosses, but also of endless de-bunking counter-interpretations. Its sole *telos* is to debunk the ideology of "techne" or of "consensus" as they are variously espoused from Aristotle to Habermas. . . . What The Antibody Rhetoric dreams of, then, in its struggle against author/ity, is to enhance our abilities to tolerate the incommensurabilities that make up what cultural critics are calling post-modern knowledge. (49)

The Antibody Rhetoric, Vitanza says, "dreams of being in a 'festive' mood, being nondisciplinary, nonlogical, f[l]avoring 'category mistakes,' whether or not they be what philosophical-serious types call 'dissembling' metaphors or ironies" (49). Alongside Foucault's description of a multiplicitous language, Vitanza gives us a description of a language with the "ability to suspend, counter-balance readings interminably." Echoing Nietzsche, he describes language as a "mobile army of counter-sub/versions composed *not* of, but constituted by, the differences that shuttle between metaphor and irony (and what is irony but the epitome of The Antibody Rhetoric, that is, language putting a question to itself that it cannot answer?)" (49–50). "A totally serious, referential use of language," Lanham suggests, "never lasts long. It becomes stylized, turns playful." Even "bureaucratic jargons," which hope to be "purely denotative, strictly business," always "end up as games of euphemism, of obfuscation, of plain verbal nonsense." "Language," Lanham says, "cannot last long without returning to its rich resources of play" (31).

Che Vuoi?

This antibody rhetoric, this Laughter-in-language, this schizoid *logos* is what we could call the language of desire. It wants to want, and because its desire cannot be fulfilled, it never stops, never finally sticks. As Slovoj Žižek has suggested, its answer to our sacrificial offerings (to each *objet petit a* we offer up) is always "this is *not* it" (*Sublime Object* 91). Žižek notes that it always "becomes evident that the finally found real object is not the reference of desire even though it possesses all the required properties" (91). *Coke* is certainly *not* the "real thing." No/thing will finally satisfy the demand within, the language of desire that desires desire itself, that desires perpetual dissemination and will not simply denote.

This is also, as Vitanza notes, the language that hails Gorgias's Helen and Kazanzakis's Christ in *The Last Temptation of Christ*. Both Helen and Christ are called by this schizoid logos, but to do what? They cannot be sure; no matter how carefully they listen, what is wanted is never clear. It's never clear because, as Vitanza says, this *logos* is "not always rational or trustworthy" ("Taking A-Count" 183). And it's not just that it says both "Yes" and "No" at the same time; Vitanza doesn't stop at the level of the *Dissoi Logoi*. Rather it is, as Vitanza says, that it says both "Nes" and "Yo"; this *logos* "dis/engage[s] in *dissoi* para*logoi*" (184).[10] It speaks no logical course of action; it gives us no rational answers. But it does, nevertheless, urge us to *act* in our uncertainty.

What is "crucial" here, Vitanza says, is "the revival of the ambivalence/confusion of (or even deception [apate] inherent in) *logos*" (184). It's the early Greek realization that there is no separating the *logos* from *doxa*. Vitanza quotes Heidegger: "For the Greeks appearing belonged to being, or more precisely . . . the essence of being lay *partly* in appearing" (Heidegger, *Introduction to Metaphysics* 103; Vitanza, "Taking A-Count" 184). If we follow Vitanza here, what Ronell calls the "bad conscious of our era" would have to have begun way before *our* era. For Vitanza, it began when Plato and Aristotle re/fashioned *logos*, when they separated *physis* from *doxa*, privileging the former and making the latter mere "supplement" (182). It began when it stopped being in vogue to re/cognize the *logos* as the confusion of *physis* and *doxa*, when language and truth began to be viewed as separable and the former became a supplement for the latter. It began when we decided that Being authentically was fundamentally opposed to Being-on-drugs. The reign of terror begins there, with the determination to categorize, hierarchicalize, and prioritize, with the determination to stabilize language and get to the bottom of things.

Breaking Up [with] Language; Or, Toward an Ethics of Decision for the "Polyethoi"

Language's propensity to bust loose from any structuration and to refuse to make present what it promises has called the epistemic-philo-sophic attitude to red alert for more than two and a half millennia. The solution is always to try to re-contain, to "reterritorialize" what will not be held down and to force into presence what can only ever Be trace. "Turned towards the lost or impossible presence of the absent origin," Derrida says, the epistemic attitude feels "saddened, *negative*, nostalgic, *guilty*," and tries to reestablish the "immediacy," the "pure presence" that the play of language dis/rupts ("Structure" 292). And when it does, it engages a terrifying and contagious *ressentimental* politics—a politics of *horror*.

Those possessed by/of another sensibility, on the other hand, who interpret interpretation, structure, and play other/wise, have a tendency to celebrate the untamable aspect of language, to encourage it to play, to release its flow from the logocentric territorializations that attempt to strangle it. And their motivations for such a celebration are clear. Lyotard warns in *The Postmodern Condition* that "the price to pay" for the tran-scendental illusion of the ultimate totalization of language games is "terror"—

s
y   genocide
s
t   genus-cide
e
m   gynocide
a.
tic exclusion/extermination.

An all-out attack on metanarratives is an attack on a politics of hor-ror that has led us around by the nose since way before the Third Reich and has not let go of us since. Lyotard argues that the "nineteenth and twentieth centuries have given us as much terror as we can take. We have paid a high enough price for the nostalgia of the whole and the one," he says, "of the transparent and the communicable experience" (*Postmodern Condition* 81–82). Lyotard suggests that a necessary course of "action" is to "wage war on totality," to "be witnesses to the unrepresentable," to "activate the differences and save the honor of the name" (82).

This is a dangerous course of "action," as *language on the loose* is wild, uncivil. It doesn't play by any rules; it just perpetually plays. But, as Heidegger notes in "What are Poets For?" living itself may be an unshielded turning toward the "Open," the abyss, the unmarked territory that is unrestricted possibility (which is probably also the Nothing for Heidegger, but it is a de-negated "open sea" for Nietzsche, Derrida, Butler, and Vitanza, for instance). "Shielding" is equivalent to all of the category restrictions that provide for us a safe haven of meaning. Poets, Heidegger says, are those willing to shed their protection and venture into the Open *unshielded*. In "Structure, Sign, and Play," Derrida suggests that this unshielded state is cause for joy rather than sorrow or fear.

For those capable of such a Nietzschean affirmation, the so-called war against totality has taken the form of a playful spotlighting of what Derrida calls the "adventure[s] of the trace" ("Structure" 292). That is, a discursive form of giving laughter, which laughs in resistance to totality but also in affirmation of perpetual play, has, for these comedians, become a powerful weapon against the tyranny of One meaning—against the horror of "making *one* sense." The *performance* of semantic/syntactic violations (minor laughter) offers

> [T]he Nietzschean affirmation[—]that is the joyous affirmation of the play of the world and of the innocence of becoming, the affirmation of a world of signs without fault, without truth, without origin which is offered to an active interpretation. *This affirmation then determines the noncenter otherwise than as loss of center.* And it plays without security.
>
> —Derrida, "Structure, Sign, and Play"

a simulation of the *kairotic* Laughter-in-language (major laughter); it is a laughing *with* the force of Laughter, an embracing of the Nietzschean affirmation to which Derrida alludes.

It is not, of course, that any text needs any help or encouragement to play. It is rather that *we* have been so well trained to read for *the* meaning that the play of language tends to escape us. We have for so long seen *through* reason's conceptual grid that it has become for us less a *form* of thought than the whole of thought itself. It is we who need the help to notice the Laughter-in-language, to notice its playfulness. Theoretical/philosophical discourse demands a linear, authoritative, progressive mode of presentation, a structured and orderly *use* of language. But, as Lyotard suggests in *The Differend*: "Perhaps writing ought to be understood, or rather presented, *otherwise*" (113). Our course of "action" is again a simulation of *kairotic* Laughter, one that overperforms its violations of discursive structure and semantic order in a way that calls attention to them.

The Postmodern Turn

One way to accomplish this, to laugh with the Laughter-in-language, is to engage a radical *redescription* of "the world" through metaphors of heterogeneity and multiplicity: metaphors of *excesss* and over*ffflow*. If poststructuralism is a radical critique of structuralism and its modernist/liberalist tendency to huddle up multiplicities, then the space it creates through that critique for new ways of thinking, writing, and "seeing" are taken up by postmodernism. It seems, according to this distinction, that Derrida's first phase of deconstruction is poststructural, as it is a radical de/construction of modernism's constructions. But the second (affirmative) phase is postmodern, as it is a productive search for new metaphors, re/descriptions of the world that turn on a third term that cannot be located within the standard binary divisions.

Ecriture Féminine

Luce Irigaray's mimicry might be considered a poststructural discourse, but *écriture féminine*,[11] for which mimicry acts as a pathbreaker, is a postmodern discourse. Like Derridean affirmative deconstruction, *écriture féminine* offers a new inscription of the world. It's not, though, an inscription of a specific content so much as it is an inscription of heterogeneity itself, an/other way of being that affirms radically dynamic and *multiple* sexual voices. Suggesting that structuralist theories of language form a link between rationality and a mechanics of solids (unmoving structures), Irigaray links *écriture féminine* to a mechanics of *fluids*, given to excess, overflow, and the blurring of boundaries (*This Sex*). With *écriture féminine*, Irigaray redescribes and reinscribes the world as protean, unruly, "stormy," *fluid*.

Hélène Cixous also champions *écriture féminine* as a postmodern discourse and refuses to theorize or conceptualize it, refuses to make it a reinscription of a specific content. *Ecriture féminine*, for Cixous, is a force *inside* language (like Vitanza's antibody rhetoric and Kristeva's desire-in-language) that creates a perpetual and irrepressible revolution in language itself. It "will never be able to be theorized, enclosed, coded," Cixous says, "which doesn't mean that it does not exist" (*Newly Born* 92). This writing *exceeds* "the discourse governing the phallocentric system," and, Cixous notes: "It will not let itself think except through subjects that break automatic functions, border runners never subjugated by any authority." There is and will be no way to codify this multigrooved writing—pardon the phallic metaphor, but *that* would be *the point*. "But one can," nevertheless, Cixous says, "begin to speak . . . to point out some effects" (92).

In "Laugh of the Medusa," Cixous makes Medusa her muse because she's beautiful and she's *laughing*: for Cixous, *écriture féminine* is a form of discursive laughter that keeps things shaken up, refuses to let them settle and be made into ideology. Laughter is a powerful force that seizes time and momentarily dispenses with meaning. And *écriture féminine* is an explicitly laughing language, a language transgressed by a Laughter that releases the desire, the excess, the overflow that is covered over and suppressed in the structurations of theoretical discourse. This laughing language has no boundaries, makes no distinction between the object and the subject, as Cixous notes in "Castration or Decapitation?" when she says that this language is infused with a laughter directed at *herself*. Cixous's language frees itself, through laughter, from the tyranny of the signified and celebrates the dissemination of meaning, the proliferation of potentialities. *It celebrates* ^fluidity fluidity fluidity^. This writing must, Cixous says:

> make up the unimpeded tongue that bursts partitions, classes, and rhetorics, orders and codes, must inundate, run through, go beyond the discourse with its last reserves, including the one of laughing off the word "silence" that has to be said, the one that, aiming for the impossible, stops dead before the word "impossible" and writes it as "end." ("Sorties" 94–95)

Cixous wants to "blow up the Law," and she insists that this "explosion" is not only "possible" but is also "inescapable . . . from now on." Her demand is that we "let it happen, right now, in language" ("Sorties" 95). She's asking us to celebrate a language that invites the nondiscursive underside of "discourse" to speak, shine, unconceal itself. Cixous says it *will* happen because when " '*The* Repressed' of their culture and their

society come back, it is an explosive return, which is absolutely shattering, staggering, overturning, with a force never let loose before, on the
scale of the most tremendous repressions" (95).

This attempt to laugh with the Laughter-in-language is nothing
more or less than an attempt to "make another way of knowing circulate." It is, as Cixous says, "[a]nother way of producing, of communicating, where each one is always far more than one" ("Sorties" 96). It is not
tied up in what Ronell called "the *project of making sense* or rather making
one sense" ("Differends" 256). We're talking about "stealing into
language and making it fly," about finding pleasure in "scr[-r-r]ambling
spatial order, disorienting it, moving furniture, things, and values
around, breaking in [and up], emptying structures, turning the selfsame,
the proper upside down" (Cixous, 96). Laughing with the Laughter-in-
language cannot, Cixous says, "be more subversive"; it's a "volcanic
heaving of the old 'real' property crust" (97).

Pagan Pragmatics—*Just* Linking

What's at stake in this postmodern turn is l-l-l-i-n-k-a-g-e. The language game of reason, of knowledge, of theoretical discourse, produces
results through *hypotactic* linkage. One phrase is linked to another phrase
in a pattern of subordination. One phrase is subordinated to another,
called as supplement to another. In this way, major concepts are born
and the structure of discourse is laid down over the nondiscursive body
of language. But, as Lyotard suggests, "phrases can obey regimens other
than the logical and the cognitive" (*Differend* 65). There are language
games, in other words, that do not rely on hypotaxis; they operate on
"paratactic" linkage, on a pattern of connection based on coordination
rather than subordination. Here's Lyotard:

> Conjoined by *and*, phrases or events follow each other, but their
> succession does not obey a categorical order (because; if, then; in order
> to; although . . .). Joined to the preceding one by *and*, a phrase arises
> out of nothingness to link up with it. Paratax thus connotes the abyss
> of Not-Being which opens between phrases, it stresses the surprise that
> something begins when what is said is said. (66)

Paratactic linkage is one more way to point up the Laughter-in-
language, to laugh with it rather than to suppress it. "*And*," Lyotard says,

"is the conjunction that most allows the constitutive discontinuity (or oblivion) of time to threaten, while defying it through its equally constitutive continuity (or retention)." But a simple comma "or nothing," Lyotard says, will also "assure the same paratactic function" (66). What's important here, in this call for *just* linking, Lyotard suggests, is that there is always already the phrase and the call to link.

We have been here in different terms with Heidegger: our linking procedures have been guided by the "enframement" of our thought. We can only think/speak what is thinkable/iterable within our constituting frame. We are *seduced* into linking point A to point B; and once seduced, we perpetuate that convention and call it *logical*, necessary. However, what paratactic linkages do for us is point at the wide open spaces between phrases, at the phrases that are not being uttered. Lyotard reminds us that "everything has not been said," and that, inasmuch as anything so far unspeakable "is unable to be phrased in the common idioms, it is [nevertheless] already phrased, as *feeling*" (80). Once a silent phrase is experienced, the "vigil for an occurrence, the anxiety and the joy of an unknown idiom, has begun." And what is at stake in this "vigil," as we will discuss below, is a new ethics of decision, an ethics that demands a special *hearing*, in both the physiological and the legal aspects of the term.

> For there to be no phrase is impossible, for there to be And a phrase is necessary. It is necessary to make linkage. . . . To link is necessary, but how to link is not.
>
> —Lyotard, *Differend*

"A Light Manipulation of Appearances"

In *Seduction*, Jean Baudrillard asks, "How can one oppose seduction? The only thing truly at stake is mastery of the strategy of appearances, against the force of being and reality. There is no need to play being against being or truth against truth; why become stuck undermining foundations, when *a light manipulation of appearances will do*" (10, my emphasis). And, indeed, a "light manipulation" of the surface of discourse, a *light* tactical maneuver involving its re/present/ation is another way to laugh with the Laughter-in-language, to attend to inscription's exscriptions.

Avital Ronell's *Telephone Book*

Ronell's *The Telephone Book: Technology, Schizophrenia, Electric Speech* offers a good example of the "light manipulation" we're after. This book is at least as much a *performance* as a re/present/ation. It both presents and *enacts* a theorization of the techno-logical challenge posed by the telephone for metaphysics, epistemology, and psychoanalysis. By manipulating the surface appearance, that is, by engaging in formatting *illegalities*, Ronell invites the body of language to *show through* from underneath her discursive, re/present/ative lines.

In the section about the ways in which the telephone has become "an organ without a body," *w/holes* are the point. Ronell wants to spotlight especially bodily (w)holes but also political and ethical openings of all kinds into which technology has broken. She doesn't simply offer a discursive representation of that notion, however; rather, Ronell offers both a discursive and a *non*discursive one. Here is a taste of what goes on between pages 109 and 111:

> The withdrawal int**o** a b**o**dy-with**o**ut-**o**rgans . . . d**o**es n**o**t make schiz**o**phrenia the clean-cut **o**ther **o**f the n**o**rmally c**o**nstituted subject, h**o**wever. The c**o**ncept itself **o**f a "n**o**rmally functi**o**ning human being"—**o**ne equipped, s**o** t**o** speak, with pr**o**per sh**o**ck abs**o**rbers f**o**r enduring interrupti**o**n and pain—and *c**o**nversely, within this norma-tivity, the c**o**ncept **o**f breakd**o**wn,* dem**o**nstrate the effects **o**f wiring systems. (110)

To illustrate the nondiscursive ways in which language also points to (w)holes—that is, some of the ways it points without *saying so*—Ronell highlights every "**o**" in this section. For a little more than two pages, every "**o**" is bolded, but she doesn't discuss it. She doesn't bring that nondiscursive *performance* of (w)holes into discursive representation. She amplifies it by calling our attention to what language is *doing* along with what it is *saying*, to what's going on in language that has no/thing to do with discourse.

The entire book engages the same sort of light manipulation of the surface of discourse to illustrate the nondiscursive laughter "supporting" it from below. In her "User's Manual" for the book, she warns us of this typo-graph-ical play and clues us in on its significance:

We have attempted to install a switchboard which, vibrating a continuous current of electricity, also replicates the effects of scrambling.
At first you may find the way the book runs to be disturbing, but we
had to *break up [! crack up!]* its logic typographically. . . . To crack
open the closural sovereignty of the Book, we have feigned silence and
disconnection, suspending the tranquil cadencing of paragraphs and
conventional divisions. . . . *The Telephone Book* releases the effect of an
electronic-libidinal flow using typography to mark the initiation of
utterances. ("A User's Manual" xv, my emphasis)

Victor J. Vitanza's "Theatricks"

Vitanza's performative texts[12] also engage in a light manipulation of
appearances, a manipulation he calls "theatricks," which he says has its
rhizomatic roots in Joyce's *Finnigans Wake* and Lyotard's "paganism."
Theatricks, Vitanza says, "wages war against The Truth and against
Author/ity" ("An After/word" 250). Here's Vitanza: "Whereas *sentences*
deal in truth claims and whereas *utterances* deal in authorial-perfor-
matives, theatricks (*theos*—tricks, 'sounddance,' farce) wage perpetual-
pagan war (on sentences and utterances) through sophistic trickery and
ruse after ruse" (250, my emphasis).

Vitanza's prose is performative in much the same way Ronell's is. It
enacts language in a way that exposes the hypertextual playfulness beneath the discursive imperative. In other words, while progressing forward, it also proceeds to "steal and fly," seemingly everywhere, in all
directions at once. By a light manipulation, in the form of unusual or
"illegal" diacritical marks and a joyful skewing of grammatical/mechani-
cal injunctions, Vitanza manages to carve out a space for language to
show off its perpetual mis/behavior. Here's a classic example of Vitanza's
theatricks:

I am who I ham. And I ham who I am. (I h/am, among the various
"I's," [cum-schizo "they's"] a Zuni clown.) The primary language
game, then, not being the language game of knowledge, *is* the language
game of avant-garde art. The language game of the future (post)
anterior (modo). . . . An hysterian and a schizo—after all is said and
un/done—know that s/he *can* (Finnigans) wake up from the nightmare of history, and, therefore, desire a desire to trotsky (farsycally
dance) through it. (251)[13]

Vitanza and Ronell, among others, of course, are out to give nondiscursive language a showing. They are out to offer a glimpse of excess, of linguistic overflow that no amount of restrictions can finally expel or sop up. In this way, they manage to laugh with the Laughter-in-language, to offer a discursive form of giving laughter that resituates us, both ethically and politically, in a nonhumanist location. A location that is not only "beyond good and evil" but also, therefore, beyond humanism and logocentrism.

DECIDING FOR/WITH LAUGHTER— A POSTHUMANIST ETHICS

> Don't delude yourself. Being is yours only to the extent that you cannot shirk this responsibility; it is your duty, you are nothing before being. Hence your immoderately obliging assignment. Being, finally, is *nothing other* than this duty that calls you, possesses and debits you, guiltifies you from the moment you are—you, the Unique, the Called.
> —Ronell, *The Telephone Book*. . . . .

. . . Ronell, reading Mikkel Borch-Jacobsen, who is reading Heidegger, reminds us that we are not One, not whole, not free: "You are stretched out between you and yourself," she observes; you are stretched, as Nietzsche might say, between your creator and your created self. And "about the death that you have been owing since your birth," Ronell continues, "you'll never be able to realize, effect, or present it." Why? Because "there is no 'ethics,' no 'morals,' of finitude. But even as it is endless, and so much the more demanding, there is the *call* of finitude . . ." (*Telephone Book* 72). In a world where territories are perpetually deterritorialized, where structures are perpetually deconstructed, in short, where the postfoundational thought has been thought, ethics become terribly problematic. And yet, we are *called* (we *hear* it), by the voice of our finitude, into an ethics of decision.[14]

Heidegger says it is the voice of conscience that calls us, that directs our responsibility to ourselves and others; Freud says it is the voice of the superego. Either way, however, in a postfoundational world, as Ronell observes, any/every "ethics demands a hearing" (105). The double *en-tendre* here is intended: it is necessary that the call of an ethics be both *listened to* and, in a pseudolegalistic sense, *judged.* What we ought not forget is that both Heidegger and Freud, for all their good faith, answered calls that led them into some of the most *unethical* and *irresponsible* territory possible, into an ethics too capable of sacrificing the Other.[15] What needs to be said here is that "*the* voice," *the* frequency into which I tune, which "comes from me and from beyond me can be a *phony* one, it can miss the point, performing and inducing fraud" (Ronell, *Telephone Book* 45).

Nevertheless, *the* call calls. It says *decide*; it says *it's very simple.*

> [B]efore anything is said . . . the punitive voice or the voice of con-
> science . . . appears to make ethically clear statements to the subject.
> These statements may not be attached to a signified. They come in the
> form of a demand or ethical posture. There is no call that does not call
> forth responsible responsiveness. (Ronell, *Telephone Book* 106)

But we have lost our criteria for "responsible" action. Today, promoting an ethics of responsibility based on a knowing and autonomous subject is anything but responsible. The question, then, is what can responsibility and decision now be if "they must be thought in terms of our relation to language?" (Cadava, "Toward" 5), if they must be thought in terms of our Being-on-the-drug-of-language, of our addiction to "tropium"? What can responsibility, an ethics of decision, amount to if "*the* call" is actually a scramble of calls, a *dissoi paralogoi*, a schizoid hail that remains unattached to a *clear* and *present* signified?

Ronell suggests that we may find an answer, some answers, to that question if we learn to read with our ears and to "tune [our] ears to noise frequencies, to anticoding, to the inflated reserves of random indeterminateness—in a word, [we] are expected to stay open to the static and interference that will occupy [all] lines" (*Telephone Book* xv). The formulation of an ethics of decision in a postfoundational world may require simply this: that we learn to hear the noise,
the excess
that gets sacrificed
for the clarity of the One.

A posthumanist ethics ought not be about shutting down the flow but about opening it up, pulling back the stops. An ethics for our time may require that we learn to hear the Laughter-in-language, that we affirm it, and that we join in with it: that we laugh with the Laughter that is laughing language . . . before we "hasten to decide" anything, anytime.

What's at stake in our capacity to hear this laughter, to tune into its frequencies and laugh along, is what Lyotard terms the "differend." The "differend" can be defined, loosely, as the differences, unresolvable through litigation, between two parties who do not share the same rules of cognition. The differend manifests itself as a chasm between interlocutors, a gap where the lines of communication are not *down* so much as they are not direct, not clear. There is an obnoxious static, a fuzzy noise that *invites* the *refusal* to connect at any level.

But a determination to tune into the static on the line, a capacity to affirm it may well send us beyond the *differend* proper. Beyond it. It may well send us into what Ronell, in "The Differends of Man," calls the "affirmative differend." Ronell says this one "strains beyond the politics of *ressentimental* phrasing," it "talks and negotiates; it listens and articulates itself responsibly rather than reactively" (262). Indeed, inasmuch as it "explores the limits of the *differend* in the mode of positivity, it is questionable whether it constitutes the differend as such, or whether the differend can indeed guarantee the conditions of colegitimacy that it promises" (262). This is what we will have been after, this is what will have been worth laughing for.

An affirmative differend would introduce a third term/position from which to break down/up [at] the oppositionality constituting the *differend* proper.

"Let's talk,"

Ronell says, "at once invokes a posturing of the differend *Dasein* while it challenges the unbridgeable gap imputed to the post-differend condition." "Let's talk" means, she says, *"Let's listen,"* . . . which implies the "irreducible presence of the Other to the self" (265). And from here, from a position that says "let's talk" *and* "let's listen," to the *noise*, to the *static*, to the *laughter*, we will have found ourselves on the way to an/other "responsibility," an/other ethics and an/other community that is not bound to metaphysical longing or fascist/liberal programs/pogroms.

From here, we will have found ourselves in the midst of differend after differend, which, however, will not necessarily lead us into a delegitimation—a negation—of the other. Learning to laugh with the Laughter-in-language may well be as responsible a response to the terror as we will have been capable of offering. Any decision issued forth from a Being-with-the-noise/laughter/static will have been under no illusion of totality. It will not have performed itself as the final word but as one sssspasm in the perpetual convulsion, one defining and yet "drugged" moment, always tentative and up for more "talking" and "listening," more "negotiations" designed to open the flow rather than shut it down. If there is a telos, it will have been to further complicate any matter rather than to "make things too easy" for ourselves. We hope not to land but to be sssset in motionnnn. A posthumanist ethics of decision will have been about, as Ronell says, "suspension, a hiatus in meaning, reopened each time in the here and now, disappearing as it opens, exposing itself to something so unexpected and possibly new that it persistently eludes its own grasp" (*Finitude's Score* 4). Decisions arising from this ethic will have enacted themselves according to the rules of Homer's contest—they will never have been final; the matter will never have (been) settled;

the laughter
will never
have (been) stopped

•

•

•

•

•

•

EXCURSUS

BEING-HARD/WIRED:
CYBURBIAN CONVULSIONS

KANT (1724–1804): German philosopher; big time humanist; got off on the notion of disinterested reason.

Random House: "SNEEZE, to emit air or breath suddenly, forcibly, and audibly through the nose and mouth by involuntary spasmodic action."

Sneezing, then, is something like a seizure of the nose . . . we might call it a *SNEEZURE.*

IMMANUEL KANT spent his life, his secretary says, engaging a "permanent vigilance, very strict rules for living—not to sweat, not to cough, not to sneeze" (Agacinski 17). And no big surprise that Kant couldn't tolerate any sort of bodily spasm. Certainly, the autonomy of a sneezing subject is severely compromised. And one suspects that a certain kind of irrepressible laughter would be right up there with sneezing on Kant's s/hit-list. A subject who can, in an instant, be/come the *object* of a *spasm's will* can hardly claim to be master of her/his own house. But, as Sylviane Agacinski suggests, mastery over the body is a central concern for the philosophical subject, whose creed includes "making the first move, getting ahead of the body, programming it oneself, being in command" (17). The capacity to suppress a "SNEEZE" (and/or a giggle fit), to *just say no*, becomes, after Kant, a philosophical statement.

If this unabashed drive for mastery seems harmless and a bit amusing at the level of the sneeze, however, notice how much the ante is upped when it sets its sights beyond one's *own* body. It is what Foucault calls "the fascism in us all" (*Anti-Oedipus* xxiii) that buttresses this indecent humanism, that demands we take control, that we get a choke-hold

116

on all manifestations of the flow of life. At some level, most of us acknowledge that human beings are not in control and that to just say no to the demands made *on us*, for instance, by language, by technology, and, as Kant discovered, by the sneeze is simply not a viable option. We do still tend, however, like ZARATHUSTRA's dwarf, to "make things too easy" for ourselves. We do still tend, unproblematically, to place ourselves (the "human") at the center of our contemplations and descriptions of the world(s), and when we do, our vision is distinctly weakened.

MARTIN HEIDEGGER recognized early on the significance of the "question concerning technology" and the importance of a posthumanist approach to it. By now, this question has established itself as one of *the* critical questions of our time, and some of the world's most prominent thinkers are grappling with a nonhumanist redescription of it. The vast majority of conversations about this issue, however, continue to take a humanist slant. Whether we celebrate technology as the road to human(ist) "progress" and "empowerment" or denounce it as a threat to human(ist) autonomy, technology gets relegated to an outside (Other) that perfects or endangers the inside (Self). In other words, whether we love it or hate it, modern technology is, for the most part, described and defined across humanist hopefulness. This excursus, however, will be after a redescription of the relationship among language, technology, and (human) Being. If, as we suggested in chapter 2, we must Be-on-*some/thing*, if we can never Be-on-*no/thing*, then both our celebrations of and our paranoia about technology, as one such some/thing, are exposed as dangerously shortsighted. This excursus will be after a nonhumanist interpretation of technology,

ZARATHUSTRA: Mr. Gay Scientist himself. Protagonist of Nietzsche's *Thus Spoke Zarathustra*. The dwarf has the tendency to not think things through rigorously enough. Zarathustra sets him straight/crooked.

HEIDEGGER (1889–1976): German philosopher into hermeneutics and the question of Being; wrote *Being and Time*; held the university rectorship 1933–34.

"The 'Heidegger question' did not seem to me to be 'Is he a bit of a Nazi?' (obviously, obviously) but 'What was his role in this new injection of history of philosophy?'" (Delueze, *Dialogues* 12).

an interpretation that links it both to language and to drugs and that *just* says *YES[!]* to the inevitable laughter-in-*techné*.

BEING-*ON-LANGUAGE*, AGAIN

Heidegger showed us that language is the very "foundation of human being" (*On the Way* 112), the web in which we *are*, in which we *Be/come*. With that in mind, Eduardo Cadava reminds us that "We do not possess language. On the contrary," and here's the point, "it is in language that we are dispossessed" (5). Language, then, which is not human, **HAILS** us *away* from ourselves, dispossesses us, like any other "drug." Heidegger celebrated Being-on-language, called language the House of Being, and offered us a "fix" of it without the slightest hint of "bad conscience." Heidegger, however, is no indiscriminate pusher; he clearly privileges what Ronell called "tropium" over opium and, more to the point here, over the technological tranquilizer. If language gets to be the cozy House that brings Being into existence in Heideggerian ontology, technology is relegated to a makeshift enframement that keeps authentic Being from itself, that lulls Being to sleep.

BEING-*ON-TECHNOLOGY*

Heidegger suggests that the call of technology encases thought, "en-frames" it within the mode of an ordering-forth, a "challenging" and mastering of revealing. The danger of this enframing is that "all revealing will be consumed in ordering and that everything will present itself only in the

HAIL: To interpellate.

INTERPELLATE: To hail; also to interrupt, intercept, cut off, or prevent. Louis Althusser's theory of subjectivity suggests that ideology turns individuals into subjects by hailing or interpellating them. When the individual answers the hail, s/he has assumed a subject position.[1]

unconcealedness of standing-reserve." And Heidegger says that "human activity can never directly
counter this danger. Human achievement alone
can never banish it" ("Question" 33). What Heidegger sees, against the grain of modern enthu-
siasm, is that human Being has become a function
of technology; it has been *turned on*, gotten hooked
on the technological tranquilizer. And *this* addiction does not please Heidegger; he remains determined to locate a more authentic relation to Being
than technology can offer ("Question" 28; cf. also
Ronell, *Telephone Book* 16). **HEIDEGGER HOPES**
that a fundamental difference establishes itself between "technical" and "natural" worlds, between
techné and *physis*. Though language (*logos*) belongs
to an "original revealing," his idea of *techné*, as
Ronell puts it, "stands mostly under the shadow
of the negative" ("Worst Neighborhoods" 227).
He sizes it up as a bad drug, a call from the They,
which *covers over* a more authentic call into Being.

And this is understandable to a certain extent.
Techné, after all, plays into the hands of humanism;
it calls us to production over seduction, to method
over chance. Ruling out play and excess, it hails us
as masters. No doubt about it, modern technology
prompts a God-complex. Technocratic hope is a
metaphysical after-spasm, a rallying cry for those
still holding out for humanism's comeback. In an
interview in *Mondo 2000*, for instance, Virtual
Reality wizard Jaron Lanier celebrates what Ronell
calls the "ego-building prowess of VR designs"
("Activist" 299). Suggesting that Virtual Reality
should have been called "*Intentional* Reality,"
Lanier notes that "ultimately everything is done by
people and technology is just a little game we play"
(Barlow 49). Retrofitting "the technological prosthesis to a metaphysical subject," Lanier locates

HEIDEGGER'S
HOPE: "The threat
to man does not
come in the first
instance from the
potentially lethal
machines and
apparatus of tech-
nology. The actual
threat has already
affected man in his
essence. The rule of
Enframing
threatens man with
the possibility that
it could be denied
to him to enter into
a *more original
revealing* and hence
to experience *the
call to a more
primal truth*"
("Question" 28,
my emphasis).

virtual reality smack dab in the middle of "the control rooms of his majesty the *ego*" (Ronell, "Activist" 299). Ed Regis, author of *Great Mambo Chicken and the Transhuman Condition: Science Slightly over the Edge*, notes, similarly, that "the desire for perfect knowledge, and total power" is *the* motivation for technological advancement. "The goal [is] complete omnipotence: the power to re-make humanity, earth, the universe at large" (7). Here, technology gets demoted to a prosthetic extension of the sovereign subject, serving to amplify and intensify the mastery of his majesty.

This understanding of technology, however, assumes something that Heidegger does not: that TECHNOLOGY WILL NOT "SLIP FROM HUMAN CONTROL" ("Question" 9). In fact, Heidegger notes that an "anthropological definition" of technology conceals more than it reveals. What Heidegger sees here is not visible through humanism's lens—the de/con/structed Self has no solid stump on which to slip a prosthesis of any kind. Indeed, Heidegger sees that human-Being has begun to *Be-on-technology*, that we do not *possess* technology; on the contrary, it is in modern technology that we are *dis*possessed. Human Being is possessed by *technology* inasmuch as technology has begun to bring the human into Being. If technology would not be Heidegger's drug of choice, he does, nevertheless, recognize its capacity *as a drug* and our addiction to it.

Thus far, then, we are three times possessed: by a *kairotic* Laughter, by a laughing *logos*, and by *TECHNÉ*. But it is the point of this excursus to suggest that even *techné* (method) does not escape the reach of *kairos* and its jolting manifestations. We are not, in other words, enframed by an *unpossessed techné*; we are enframed by a *techné* convulsed in

Anthropologist Edmund Carpenter on CONTROLLING TECHNOLOGY: "[Technologies] permit little experimentation and only a person of enormous power and sophistication is capable of escaping their binding power" (*Oh, What a Blow That Phantom Gave Me!* 188).

TECHNÉ: art, skill, method. Often opposed to *tuché* (chance).

kairotic Laughter, a *laughing techné* that, as Donna Haraway has noted, takes "pleasure in the confusion of boundaries" ("Manifesto" 191). What's important at this point is that a *desire* precedes its technical installation. Heidegger worried about that; he recognized that technology is not an original call. It is, rather, a response itself, an answer to another call. Something is beaming out signals, again, calling the drug-of-technology home. And here, we are attempting to put a trace on that call. If we're addicted to technology and other "drugs," it's only because addiction is necessary for Being to Be—*dis*possession is required, and the homing-signals can be traced back to us, to what is human (unconscious), in order to guarantee Being (consciousness). Indeed, it appears to be "the call of addiction" itself—a manifestation of the will to power—that calls *techné* home.

But as Heidegger noted, **ADDICTION** is always addicted to itself first (*Being and Time* 240);[2] the temporary stand-ins that it chooses are incidental and also countless. Technology, in other words, is never the only pill we're popping. A reexamination of "the question concerning technology" suggests that Heidegger may have worried unnecessarily. Just as civil discourse floats tenuously atop a rowdy body of language, *techné* is always situated within the wild excesses of a nonrational *physis*. If, as Derrida says, "the work of meaning or the meaning of work" is simply one of the many phases of play ("From Restricted . . . Economy" 266), it seems fair to suggest that *techné* is simply one of the phases of *physis*. *Techné*, that is, turns out to be "a little game" *physis* plays. And technology has not managed, as Heidegger feared it would, to shut down Being; it has, rather, worked up against other drugs to yield new forms of Being—some are exciting;

Heidegger on **ADDICTION:** "What one is addicted 'towards' is to let oneself be drawn by the sort of thing for which the addiction hankers" (*Being and Time* 240).

Ronell on **ADDICTION:** The structure of addiction, and even drug addiction in particular, is anterior to any empirical availability of crack, ice, or street stuff. . . . A quiver in the history of madness (to which no prescription of reason can be simply and rigorously opposed), the chemical prosthesis, the mushroom or plant, respond to a fundamental structure, and not the other way around. Of course, one can be hooked following initiation and exposure but even this presupposes a prior disposition to *admitting the injectable phallus*" (*Crack Wars*).

Ronell on ENEMY BODIES: "If we refuse to recognize and acknowledge the Other as fragile, destitute, mortal, and finite—that's when we start bombing the shit out of them!" ("Interview" 142).

some are frightening. But then, with drugs, it's always a matter of dosage. Dosage and mixture.

BEING-*IN*-CYBURBIA

We might as well admit it up front that virtual space operates on a number of metaphysical cravings: the desire to transcend the body, for instance, is aligned with a nasty history of the denial of human finitude. Heidegger's fears are understandable when we remember that giant corporations, the mafia, and the military are jacked into cyberspace. And inasmuch as Being is hooked on this technology, it gets jacked around with it. As Donna Haraway so eloquently and pointedly puts it, "Modern war is a cyborg orgy" ("Manifesto" 191). Wars, Paul Virilio reminds us, can now be waged in the blink of an eye—time needed for reflection has been *virtually* eliminated (*Speed and Politics* 143). Perhaps the best recent illustration of this danger zone is the seemingly bloodless Gulf War, fought and viewed as a high-tech head game that offered roughly zero contact with THE *BODY* OF THE "ENEMY."[3] At a more personal level, the drive to transcend the body by leaping into virtual space, by slipping on the "technological prosthesis," Virilio suggests, ends up turning "the overequipped, healthy (or 'valid') individual into the virtual equivalent of the well-equipped invalid" ("The Third Interval" 4–5). And yet, we're *all* still heavily invested in metaphysical cravings, so we might as well allow VR its own stash of them.

It may be more important that, despite our irresistible and irrepressibly humanist appropriations, these cravings often get played out differently in the spaces of cyburbia because technology often manages to "slip from human control." If Heidegger understandably feared the demotion of human Being to a technological prosthesis, he also never got a glimpse of the modern "CYBORG," a human-machine hybrid that extends Being beyond itself, that makes connections between the self and the techno-body, which leave both undeniably and profoundly altered. In its liberation of "the location of being to non-substantial spaces," Ronell says, cyberspace is trying to "reconfigure the possibilities for sharing the world" ("Activist" 299). It makes little sense at this point to refer to virtual reality as *fake* reality—inasmuch as virtual reality offers another inflection of Being, it demands validation as simply *an/other* reality. And when any supposedly unified subject or telos jacks in, it exposes itself to a shakedown (or a *crack up*[!]), a sneak attack on its unity. Technological forms of *kairotic* laughter manifest themselves in involuntary violations of the semiotic/symbolic order.

CYBORG: A cybernetic organism, both human and machine, both "natural" and "artificial." But you don't have to have an artificial ticker or log hours a day in VR to be a cyborg. If you drive a car, talk on the phone, get e-mail, pop any kind of medication, and/or pace your life around a clock, you're a cyborg. Welcome to your Self.

It's not only that our machines, as Haraway suggests, have become "disturbingly lively" ("Manifesto" 194); it is rather that *their* liveliness has dispersed *us*. Much to humanism's chagrin, Being goes rhizomatic in the cyburbs. Egos get shattered. "To a certain extent," Ronell says, "the metaphysical subject *is broken up* and displaced into routes of splintering disidentification" without "a substantial [referential] image" ("Activist" 299, my emphasis). In virtual space, there are few either/or restrictions. Coded boundaries like male/female, Self/Other, and subject/object, which support notions of (gendered) power relations, identity politics, and human production, are unceremoniously transgressed in "cyburbia," where we can be everywhere at once and take on any number of "identities" wherever we go. Indeed, here "hierarchical dichotomies that

Cyburbia[n]
Leaks
e
a
k
a
g
e

have ordered discourse since Aristotle," Haraway says, are "techno-digested" ("Manifesto" 205) by an order of microelectronic simulation that makes interfaces (with the Other) *everywhere*. "No objects, spaces, or bodies are sacred in themselves," she says; "any component can be interfaced with any other if the proper standard, the proper code, can be constructed for processing signals in a common language" (205). *Cyburbia fluidifies.*

Haraway notes that the metaphysical subject has been replaced by the cyborg: *we*, the illegitimate and so, as Haraway says, *unfaithful* offspring of war-machines, are human-animals perpetually *jacked in* to technology's machinations. And our very existence as such testifies to the breakdown of what Haraway calls "three crucial boundar[ies]," boundaries that make the notion of a fixed identity possible: human vs. animal, human-animal vs. machine, and physical vs. nonphysical (or, via Baudrillard, real vs. "**HYPERREAL**"). The border wars fought to keep organism and machine rigidly separate were, as Haraway says, all about "the territories of production, reproduction, and imagination." But the cyborg, she says, takes "pleasure in the *confusion* of boundaries" (191, my emphasis). *Cyburbia ffffluidifies.*

HYPERREAL: Jean Baudrillard's term for a more real than real state in which the so-called referent is replaced by its representation. See below.

Cyberspace has problematized our specular image and spawned new forms of subjectivity. The cyborg is the metaphysical/specular/*memorized* subject grazed by schizophrenia, broken up and *breaking up*(!). The cyborg is not limited by nor faithful to the reflection it offers itself in the mirror. If, under the influence of technology, we are seduced to produce and commanded to master, we are also invited—more covertly—to let go, to unhinge, to *crack up*. This technology takes an unexpected and irrepressible swipe at metaphysics. Even as the subject's desire for mastery leads it to the cyburbs, cyburbia is busy splintering off the subject who would master. Heidegger need not have worried quite so much: *techné* was always only one mode of *physis*, one little turn in what Nietzsche calls "the most unscrupulous polytropoi" (*Gay Science* 282; also Baudrillard, *Seduction* 34). We don't own this game board; we've just been tossed (or, à la Heidegger, "thrown") out here to play on it.

Contra Heidegger, this excursus suggests that technology is not a bad drug; but, with Heidegger, it would also suggest that, depending upon the ontological mixture, it can offer a horrifyingly *bad trip*. Perhaps we can agree, for instance, that one particular intersection of humanism and technology—an intersection that promised a Final Solution—stands as the *worst moment in the history of both*.[4] The point here is not to suggest that we dig in and refuse technology's hail; we will go with the **BORG** instead of Heidegger on this one: "resistance is futile." For, as Ronell suggests in *Finitude's Score*, we've gone too far to turn back. We're hooked, and "there is no technology that will not be tested" ("Activist" 297). Here, we are only interested in spotlighting the *laughter-in-technology*, the tenuous position of *techné* within the great sweep. Technology cannot harness the rowdy body of "nature" any more than civil discourse can harness the rowdy body of language.

The **BORG**: a particularly menacing and almost all-powerful cyborgian structure in the *Star Trek: The Next Generation* series. Its mantra, which it announces to any race that refuses to be immediately absorbed is: "Resistance is futile. You will be assimilated."

CYBURBIAN POWER STRUGGLES

Modern technology offers a great deal to the projects already underway today. But Heidegger warned that we are delivered over to technology in "the worst possible way when we regard it as something neutral" ("Question" 4). And Jean-Luc

CYNTHIA HAYNES:
Contemporary
techno-rhetorician
and coadministra-
tor (with Jan Rune
Holmevik) of
Lingua MOO, an
educational MOO
devoted to rhetoric,
composition, and
contemporary
critical theory.

Nancy reminds us that to consider "technologies as means in the service of ends" is to be dangerously shortsighted ("War" 41). When we opened up to technology, when we allowed it to bring us into Being (which is not to suggest that we ever had a choice), we invited it to redefine what Being can be. And we invited, as **CYNTHIA HAYNES** has suggested, the re/production of "new *genres* (such as hypertext), new *tropes* (such as speed), [and] new *morphings* of identity (such as agents or emissaries)" ("prosthetic_rhetorics" 88). Make no mis/take, taking a full hit of modern technology has significantly affected who "we" are and what we think is possible. We're not talking about surface re-visions; we're talking about a radical rupture, an epistemological shift in what we thought was possible. And we are in control of neither its direction nor its impact.

To laugh with the laughter-in-technology would be to voluntarily go *with* its violations in the semiotic/symbolic order, with its cyburbian giggles; it would be to allow cyberspace to bring us into Being *differently* and to re/cognize that the *realities* we experience t/here overflow even Lanier's *intentions*. In virtual space, for instance, it may be necessary to wholly re/fashion what we call "politics." Things are moving too fast to attempt to shut down "offending" voices or to hold anyone accountable for them. Indeed, nomadic cyber-surfers often have no traceable address. They cannot, therefore, be hauled in and commanded to produce their identity papers. Old notions of "justice" and "agency" get a new twist here.

In cyburbia, there
are a lot of fake
IDs.

Consider, also, the new brainstorm in Artificial Intelligence (AI): the development of software that generates "agents" or "emissaries" that *learn* a user's habits and interests so that they can program themselves to emulate that user's patterns. Reva Basch, a "cybarian" whom *WIRED* magazine dubbed "the ultimate intelligence agent," calls these emissaries "knowbots" (Whalen 153). While the user takes a walk or a nap, her "knowbot" may be busily collecting data, arranging information, or making connections with other "agents" in her behalf. In the April 1995 issue of *WIRED*, Pattie Maes discusses the development of these "agents," suggesting that they will become our "alter egos" inasmuch as they will understand our interests and help us manage the info-glut by "monitor[ing] databases and parts of networks" for us (Berkun 117). Basch says these "personifying agents" learn to map and then emulate their user's point of view.[5] So, it is not only that *we* can be everywhere at once and take on any number of "identities" wherever we go; it is also that we can enlist "knowbots" to exponentially multiply and enhance our own proliferation.[6] Furthermore, these "agents" are *designed to learn*, and they are capable, based on what they learn, of overriding some of the commands given by the user. They may, then, in addition to gathering the information needed for our work, also be spewing "**OFFENSIVE**" cyber-chat over the net-waves *in our names*.

The question here is: Who will be responsible for *these* "offending" voices?[7] The users they emulate (but also *overflow*)? The software companies that design the "knowbots"? It is necessary that the distinction between RL (Real Life) and VR (Virtual Reality) as well as our traditional (humanist) notions of "justice" be rethought in the face of cyburbian "agency." It may be that the only way to "act justly" in a posthumanist, hyper-technological age (or perhaps it has always already been this way?) is to *just act*, to jump into the middle of those voices

[UN]HOLY PROLIFERATIONS! [UN]HOLY RHIZOMATICS!

OFFENSIVE: —syn: displeasing, vexatious, vexing, unpleasant. See "hateful."

and to speak our large or small truths there, without authority, in the midst of the noisy network that Haraway has called "the belly of the monster" ("The Actors Are Cyborg" 6).

It is almost reflex to want to join those modern revolutionaries (feminists, Marxists, liberals, etc.) who necessarily want to concentrate on violence in the *real* world. But such a preconception would, once again, posit a fundamental difference between technical and natural worlds, a more original relation to Being than technology can offer. It would be to refuse, idealistically, to recognize that our subjectivities have already been produced *through* technologies, that the self and the techno-body affect each other profoundly, that "real life" cannot protect itself from what's going on in the cyburbs. Ronell illustrates this point well with the simple instance of the ringing telephone (which, for Ronell, operates as a synecdoche for technology): it rings and we become immediately ANSWERABLE to it, dropping everything to answer its call. "We" created the technology of the telephone, and now it has remade *us*, who we can be and what we can envision. And this is only the beginning. So-called RL often manifests itself as a *function* of VR.

Edmund Carpenter on BEING-ANSWERABLE: "I copied down the numbers of several phones in Grand Central Station and Kennedy Airport, and called these numbers. Almost always someone answered. When I asked why they had answered, they said, 'Because it rang.'" (*Oh, What a Blow That Phantom Gave Me!* 4)

HyperReality

In fact, Jean Baudrillard argues that "reality" itself has collapsed, much to Plato's chagrin, into the "third order" of representation, the order of "shams, of reflections, and shadows" (Pefanis 59). Plato cautions us against this third order of poets and painters not only because it is twice removed from *essential reality* (the Forms) but also because its simulations are not a function of reason: this is the realm of *seduction* rather than production. But

Baudrillard reminds us that production is always already one of the modes of *re*production, of seduction, of the so-called sham world (64). In the electronic age, there is no "real world" that is unmediated and unaffected by the so-called sham world, no production that is not already a reproduction. The significance of this re/cognition becomes evident when the theoretical reflections of Foucault (which are revolutionary in their own right but which are focused on politics in the "real" world) are considered in conjunction with Baudrillard's.

Power and Knowledge in the "Real World." In *Discipline and Punish*, Michel Foucault describes the historical formulation of the subject within various disciplinary matrices of power, which operate not only in prisons but also in all major societal institutions: military forces, schoolhouses, universities, hospitals, psychiatric wards, and families. Foucault reinterprets the individual not only as a discursive construct but also as an effect of political technologies through which its very identity is constituted. The final goal and effect of discipline—which Foucault says "makes" individuals (170)—is normalization, the production/construction of useful and docile subjects. Our bodies and desires, he tells us, are formulated by various disciplines and operate as functions of those disciplines. In *The History of Sexuality*, Foucault unveils sexuality as one more political construction; he exposes sex—that agency that "appears to dominate us," that "seems to underlie all that we are"—as "the most speculative, most ideal, and most internal element in a deployment of sexuality organized by power in its grip on bodies and their materiality, their forces, energies, sensations, and pleasures" (155).

P
O
W
E
R

I
S

E
V
E
R
Y
W
H
E
R
E

Sex, too, is a function of power; it is "historically subordinate to sexuality" (157), which is "an especially dense transfer point for relations of power" (103). So Foucault advises that, if we hope to "counter the grips of power with the claims of bodies, pleasures, and knowledges, in their multiplicities and their possibilities for resistance," we must in fact *break away* from "the agency of sex" (157). It follows that we have been wrong to assume that power operates through the repression of sex; instead, it operates through a discursive production of sexuality, of subjects who have *been given* a "sexual nature," which can be held within acceptable perimeters by a network of normalizing powers. Through an "anatomo-politics of the human body" and a "bio-power" exercised at every level of the social body, an extensive "ordering of human multiplicities" (*Discipline* 218) has been attained, and both pleasure and knowledge have been defined and controlled.

For Foucault, power can no longer be viewed unilaterally, as a one-sided domination that could be reversed by an organized coalition of the dominated masses. Rather, power must now be viewed as a "multiple and mobile field of force relations where far-reaching, but never completely stable effects of domination are produced" (*History* 102). Power is functional; it is not "an institution, and not a structure"; neither is it an attribute; it is rather "a complex and strategical situation, . . . a multiplicity of force relations." Power is "distributional" (93), operating through relays and transmissions. There is no source or center of power to contest, nor are there any subjects endowed with it, so there can be "no single locus of great Refusal, no soul of revolt," no universal "source of all rebellions." There can be only "mobile and transitory

p-power is
everywhere
everywhere
everywhere

points of resistance" (96), because "power is everywhere" (93).

Forget Foucault—"Reality" Goes Hyper-Active.

However, it is precisely this omnipresent notion of power that makes Jean Baudrillard suspicious. Foucault, as Baudrillard points out, attempts to illuminate the power struggles of our own era by unpacking the machinations of power in the *nineteenth century*. This is a problem for Baudrillard, who recognizes that we have seen significant developments in power distribution in our own era. His own discussion of this "moment" posits a new age of radically disembodied semiotic power, a "hyperreality," in which models of simulation have replaced their referents. Contemporary subjects are bombarded by a steady flow of information, via technological communication systems (including the so-called information superhighway) that invite signs to take on a life of their own, to constitute a new social order structured by models, codes, and signs. In the process, the distinction between the model and the original, between the real and the unreal, is dissolved. And we are not free to *just say no*: it's "happening,"[8] whether we *choose* to jack in or not.

Baudrillard's term "hyperreality" signifies a more-real-than-real state, in which the real is produced *according to its model*. When an original (for instance, a landscape) is artificially (re)produced as real (for instance, a simulated environment on a film set or at a MUD/MOO site), it becomes not unreal but more real than real, refurbished in "hallucinatory resemblance" with itself (*Simulations* 23). The model, simulated reality, before long becomes the criterion for the real itself, and the boundary between hyperreality and reality is erased.

So it is
nowhere
nowhere
nowhere

P
o
w
e
r

I
s

N
o
w
h
e
r
e

P
o
w
e
r

I

s

D
e
a
d

In *Forget Foucault*, Baudrillard proposes that Foucault's theory of power is "magisterial but obsolete" in a postmodern era of simulation, where the referents of social theory have disappeared (into simulacra) (90). We are no longer subjects but hyper-subjectivities. While Baudrillard applauds Foucault's recognition that power is relational and pluralized, he argues that Foucault failed to recognize that in this age of techno-digestion, power has become completely abstract. For Baudrillard, power is no longer disciplinary; it has become a simulacrum, a sign invented on the basis of other signs. Foucault's fundamental mistake was to accept unproblematically the presumed reality of power, to base his radical reformulations on traditional definitions of the object. Foucault, in other words, forgot that even human (re)productions often end up *(re)producing the "human."*

Baudrillard suggests that power is "dead[.] Not merely impossible to locate because of dissemination, but dissolved purely and simply in a manner that still escapes us, dissolved by reversal, cancellation, or made hyperreal through simulation" (88). Baudrillard's criticism is that power in Foucault is still "turned toward a reality principle and a very strong truth principle" (88). Both sex and power have become dominant catchwords: everything is sexual and power is everywhere. But for Baudrillard, when a phenomenon takes on the illusion of omnipresence, it is very likely in a state of crisis, in the process of redoubling, of implosion into an undifferentiated flux of simulacra. "Things," he says, "have found a way to elude the dialectic of meaning, a dialectic which bored them: they did this by infinite proliferation, by potentializing themselves, by outmatching their essence, by going to extremes" ("Fatal Strategies" 185).

Sexuality, for instance, survived "sublimation, repression and morality," but it vanished in the "hypersexual" (188), in the proliferation of the sexual: there is no sex, for instance, in Madonna's *SEX* or in pornography. If it seems as if "everything is sexual," it is because sex has disappeared as a reality, it has curved in upon itself to (re)produce its simulacrum. There is no longer a border between sex and hypersex, between the model and the original. Power, Baudrillard suggests, is well on its way to the same end. But Foucault "does not see that power is dying . . . that it is not just pulverized but pulverulent, that it is undermined by a reversal and tormented by a reversibility and a death which cannot appear in the genealogical process alone" (*Forget Foucault* 100). What Foucault does not see is that "power is never *there*" (101, my emphasis). It is "executed according to a reversible cycle of seduction, challenge, and ruse" (102), and it is nearing its end in its own redoubled simulation. The secret of power's lack of existence is shared by "the great bankers, who know that money is nothing, that money does not exist"; and it is shared by "the great theologians and inquisitors who knew that God does not exist, that God is dead" (109). It is useless, Baudrillard says, to "run after power . . . since from now on it partakes of the sacred horizon of appearances." According to Baudrillard, the joke is on us: the "other side of the cycle" has begun, and power has reverted "into its own simulacrum"; power, as such, no longer exists (105).

SEX: A collection of erotic/erratic photos of Madonna (the pop star, not the Virgin) and a series of partners; sold a bunch of copies @ 50 bucks a pop; consists of typical bourgeois fantasies; a reproduction of the same old reproductions.

DEADLY SIMULATIONS—CYBORG WRITING

This, of course, is not to say that a simulation of power doesn't *operate*. It obviously does. And, interestingly, its operations are no less deadly. The cyborg, as Haraway notes, "is not subject to Foucault's biopolitics: the cyborg simulates politics." And she suggests that this simulation is "a *much more potent* field of operations" ("Manifesto" 205, my emphasis). But, though we surely agree with Haraway that these simulations of power and politics are "no joke," it also seems, by now, safe to suggest that they do at times effect a *gleeful snort*—at and with the out-of-control violations of traditional semiotic/symbolic *order*. And in the moment of that dis-placing laughter, there may be the sense of an/other hope, or rather, hope of an/other kind: that "we can learn from our fusions with animals and machines," as Haraway puts it, "how not to be Man, the embodiment of Western Logos" (215). It may also be possible, from here, to imagine a community that would not be based on the humanist nightmare, to imagine a subjectless community of disidentified cyborgs who re-cognize that the very basis for community is our finitude.

Laughing with the Laughter-in-technology manifests itself, for instance, in cyborg writing. "Writing," Haraway says, "is preeminently the technology of cyborgs, etched surfaces of the late twentieth century" (218). And the writing engaged by cyborgs turns out to be an ethical/political business. What gets celebrated in CYBORG WRITING is the always already troublesome notion of pure boundaries and border zones. What gets celebrated is the cyborg-self itself, or what Haraway calls the "transgenic": the commingling of the organic and machinic, of the Self and the techno-body. "Inside the stories where [cyborgian monsters] circulate," Haraway says, "they trouble kind and force a re-thinking of kin. Gender, that is, the generic, is askew in the transgenic." Cyborgs, she continues,

Haraway on CYBORG WRITING: "Cyborg politics is the struggle for language and the struggle against perfect communication, against the one code that translates all meaning perfectly, the central dogma of phallogocentrism. That is why "do not rest in the semantic coffins of finished categories but rise in the ambiguous hours to trouble the virginal, coherent, and natural sleepers" (*Modest Witness* 119). Cyborg writing interrupts what Foucault calls our "confused [anthropological] sleep" ("Preface" 29). It laughs with the Laughter-in-technology by celebrating the ways in which the technology that *enframes us* also provides its own lines of flight at those rupture sites where the Laughter-in-technology *sssssshakes loose* the frame.

cyborg politics insist on noise and advocate pollution, rejoicing in the illegitimate fusions of animal and machine" ("Manifesto" 218).

3

A RHETORIC OF LAUGHTER
FOR FEMINIST POLITICS

—Section 1: The Back-Spin—

> If action is to be our key term, then drama. . . . But if drama, then conflict. And if conflict, then victimage. Dramatism is always on the edge of this vexing problem, that comes to a culmination in tragedy, the song of the scapegoat.
>
> —Kenneth Burke, *Language as Symbolic Action*

> If we become too obsessed with the Good and with a corresponding hate for the secular, our obsession with Good may itself turn into a force of Evil, a form of destructive hatred for all that fails to correspond to our idea of Good.
>
> —Slojov Žižek, *Sublime Object of Ideology*

It's little wonder that the phallus, as Jacques Lacan suggests, is our "privileged signifier," the favored child of our *logos*-centric affections. The phallus marks, he says, that space in which "the role of the logos is joined with the advent of desire" (*Ecrits* 287); it's the prime mover, the yardstick for the good, the true, and the beautiful. It's no accident that the term "Proper" denotes the concept "upstanding." Anything unified and erected fills the bill. As unification and erection personified, the phallus exemplifies perfectly the three primary laws of reason and logic—that is, the three primary logocentrisms: the law of identity, the law of the excluded middle, and the law of the excluded third. Taken together, they demand that any statement be either true or false, but never both, never neither, and never a third option. Even *we* must either be wholly male (the signifier is present) or wholly female (the signifier is absent);

logically, there are no other options.[1] The phallus represents well this Oneness, this hegemony that is privileged by the Logos: One truth, One meaning, One libido.

Feminists, of course, have protested this discreet partnership, coined "phallogocentrism," because it defines woman as lack, that hole (absence) against which the "whole" (presence) of male identity sustains itself. It comes down to presence/activity vs. absence/passivity, and "male" identity is always associated with the former. But female identity? Toril Moi notes that "anything that is not shaped on the pattern of the phallus is defined as chaotic, fragmented, negative or non-existent" (67). "Women" are by definition not proper, not "up-standing"; Cixous says that to be Woman is to "make trouble" ("Laugh" 876). And Moi reminds us that the "terrifying chaos of the female genitals" leaves "women" in the margins of a fascist, phallogocentric society that valorizes the One. "There has been a long history," Cixous says, "of gynocide" (888).

It is in response to this ghastly situation that feminists have made a move that has been coined "gynocentric" (there are other moves, of course), inverting the privilege of the established binary and arguing for "the superiority of values embodied in traditionally female experience" (Young 173). And this has been somewhat successful as a negative deconstruction—a strategy that sets the privilege in motion, that keeps it shuffling back and forth. But the success of this negotiation is limited because flipping the privilege only perpetuates the logocentric structure itself, which remains faithful to the unity and totality symbolized by the Phallus. Ironically, gyno*logo*centrism may be no less phallic than phal*logo*centrism. It's the either/or structure itself that promotes phallocracy: because binaries are only monads *masquerading* as dyads, there may be no separating the *Logos* (as logic and reason) from the Phallus. Negative deconstructions—even those designed for "women"—remain faithful to the phallogocentric structure that "disenfranchised" them in the first place. This is why Luanne Frank, in her essay on Baubô, suggests that "feminism as we know it seems, if not exclusively, then characteristically inscribed *within* phallocracy" (246).

Here, we will be shooting for something more; we will attempt to run an exscription machine, to locate a "feminist politics" that is "feminist" precisely because it remains ex-scribed from what we know as mainstream feminist politics,[2] because it opens lines of flight from reactionary mode, if only in momentary flashes. In an interview with Avital Ronell in a cutting-edge publication called *Re/search: Angry Women*, Andrea Juno asks: "What's 'wrong' with feminism today?" And Ronell's answer runs a parallel course with our own: "It's dependent upon what *man* does. Feminism today has a parasitical, secondary territoriality, and if you respond to present conditions, you're subject to reactive, mimetic and regressive posturings" (Ronell, "Interview" 127). Lines of flight are what we're after, "*sorties*," ways out of this reactionary feminism. But, as Ronell says, "the problem is: *how can you free yourself?* How can you not be *reactive* to what already exists as powerful and dominating? How can you avoid a *ressentimental* politics? Is it possible to have a feminism that is joyous, relentless, outrageous, libidinally charged[?]" (127).

Teresa Ebert would no doubt answer Ronell's inquiry affirmatively but with a grimace; this "libidinal" feminism, this *laughing* feminism that we seek, along with Ronell, is the product of what Ebert calls a "ludic politics," which she finds utterly "ineffective for feminism" ("Ludic Feminism" 5). For Ebert, postmodern politics is divided into two factions: ludic and resistance. The latter, which she champions, embraces a transformative politics in the form of a critique that "marks the transformability of existing social arrangements and the possibility of a different social organization—an organization free from exploitation" (9).[3] The former, which she disdains, is, she says, "postpolitical," making politics a "language-effect, a mode of rhetoric aimed at changing cultural *representations*." Ebert finds this approach both dangerously playful and neo-conservative. "After Lyotard, Jacques Derrida, Michel Foucault, and such ludic feminists as Luce Irigaray, Alice Jardine, Susan Suleiman, and Donna Haraway," Ebert quips, "emancipation—the collective social struggle to end exploitation—becomes simply a metaphysical project: a metanarrative" (6). She reiterates this charge in her book, *Ludic Feminism and After*, arguing that "not only the possibility but the very issue of emancipation has been occluded in ludic feminism: dismissed as itself a totalizing (read totalitarian) metanarrative" (xi).

And Ebert would be correct about that.[4] The question, however, is why this would be so disturbing for her. Fortunately, she answers that question for us herself, and in her answer, it becomes unclearly clear what she is protecting:

> This ludic valorization of "pleasure" as liberation, the affirmation of existing social differences, and the fetishization of the "local" and the specific raise serious problems for feminist and oppositional culture critique. . . . [I *insist*] on a transformative emancipatory politics in postmodernism and on the necessity of critique for an oppositional culture studies. ("Ludic Feminism" 8–9, her emphasis)

Because Ronell wants to escape precisely what Ebert wants to protect (oppositional/"ressentimental" politics), they speak at cross purposes. Ebert champions pragmatic feminisms dedicated to establishing *equality* between the sexes,[5] typically by constructing a critical theoretical framework based on "women's experience." And, certainly, this has proven a powerful course of action. It is a form of "negative deconstruction," a sophistic tactic designed to make the weaker side the stronger and, thus, to keep the privilege shaken up. And yet, while this is a valuable tactic and cannot/ought not be dismissed, it is also necessary to remember, as Ronell does, that stopping there leaves feminism trapped within the "masculinist" theoretical framework against which it labors: "The feminine becomes a kind of answering machine to the [already reactionary] call of the male metaphysical subject" ("Interview" 128). What's wrong with many feminisms today is that they exist as a . . .

reaction

to a

reaction.

If the mood of postmodernism can be defined, with Lyotard in *The Postmodern Condition*, as an incredulity toward metanarratives (antifoundational) and the mood of modernism can be defined as the longing for unmoving grounds (foundational), it is possible to suggest that feminism (as we know it) can only ever be a *modernist* enterprise. This is not (only) because it is historically linked to liberal humanism,[6] but because it is always already a reactionary position: "*feminist* politics" is, by definition, a reaction against "politics as usual." *Action* is precluded by the reactive imperative, voiced, for instance, in the dream of "liberation," which, even when loosed from the *grand* narrative of emancipation, is nevertheless "grounded" by phallogocentric notions of gender and women. Most feminisms today have one eye on infinity (metaphysical descriptions) and the other on "what was." But this limits feminism's triumphs, Ronell says, to the reproduction of "*what is* with tiny reversals" ("Interview" 128), gynocentric reversals.

Ronell wants a different game entirely, a way out of the old stories, out of Oedipal subjectivity, out of the logocentric system itself—what she wants is not "post-political" but politics that would *Be* Other/Wise, politics of an/Other kind. And Ronell is not alone. Hélène Cixous and Julia Kristeva, for instance, flatly refuse the label "feminist," a term they both associate with (mostly American) women's bourgeois fight for equal power. Cixous is not interested in participating in logocentric politics: if she has a battle cry, it's more like *let's get out of here!!*[7] This chapter examines the potential for a "feminist" "politics" that is not parasitic up-on the status quo and that does not participate in what Donna Haraway calls "the manic compulsion to *name the Enemy*" ("Manifesto" 193, my emphasis). Rather this feminist politics will have had one eye on *finitude* and the other on *futurity*.

Crossing what Ronell calls a "grim[acing] and humorless" pragmatic American feminist politics with the posthumanist paradox, we will ex-plore the potential for an/other "feminism," a postfeminist *femi-nism*, capable not only of what Foucault calls "counter-memory" but also of what Nietzsche calls "af-firmative forgetting." It is in the space of this forgetting, in the space of the repose and reprieve that it offers, that there exists the potential for an/Other "feminism"

> [I]f identities were no longer fixed as the premises of a political syllogism, and poli-tics were no longer understood as a set of practices derived from the alleged interests that belong to a set of ready-made sub-jects, a new configuration of politics would surely emerge from the ruins of the old.
>
> —Butler, *Gender Trouble*

and an/Other "politics," which is less interested in "what was" than in what *will have been*, and which can laugh, even—or rather, *especially*—at itself.

PREFATORY REMARKS ON
FEMINIST POLITICS AND NEGATIVE DECONSTRUCTIONS

It seems important to stop, before we get started, to acknowledge this work's debt to feminist thought of all flavors. This book, while it hopes to push the limits of what typically calls itself *feminist politics*, does not and could not assume an *anti*-feminist posture. In fact, this chapter could not have been written if it were not for the work already accomplished by pragmatic feminisms, if not for their down-and-dirty performance at the barricades, their struggle to keep the privilege shuffling back and forth. It has been in that very shuffle that tiny ruptures have begun to appear, ruptures from which an/other sensibility has begun to spring, from which a third way, beyond the either/or choice, has begun to shimmer on the political horizon. If first- and second-wave feminisms are necessarily parasitic on the phallocratic system against which they battle, it is nevertheless their work that (if you'll pardon the occulocentric trope) makes light the path *out* of the old battle altogether. If, in this chapter, we hope to point our feet elsewhere, we do so with the realization that a long history of pragmatic and theoretical feminisms hold the candle for us. This thought does not occur in a vacuum . . . it is only one potential re-iteration of the always already reiterable. Cixous expresses the aims of this project nicely:

> The future must no longer be determined by the past. I do not deny that the effects of the past are still with us. But I refuse to strengthen them by repeating them, to confer upon them an irremovability the equivalent of destiny, to confuse the biological and the cultural. Anticipation is imperative. ("Laugh" 875)

This book is not about dismissing the work of feminism; it's about re-defining its limits by giving voice to an/Other vision that would not have been possible without that work.[8] Cixous's project has two goals: "to break up, to destroy; and to foresee the unforeseeable, to project" (875). This chapter is interested in participating in that projection, in anticipating it, thinking it, feeling it; it's about facing Cixous's challenge to "bring about something new" (876), not by getting angry or by getting even . . . but by *b-b-breaking up*.

(SELF) RE/PRESENTATION, TAKE ONE— THE FIGHT FOR SUBJECTIVITY

Over the last several decades, masculinist and misogynistic representations of women in the media, in textbooks, and in conversation have been exposed as overwhelmingly inadequate, and several studies have noted the extent of the problem. Frank and Ashen's *Language and the Sexes*, for instance, attempts to expose the mechanism of language itself as a weapon of oppression against women. The authors note that in school textbooks, references to men outnumber references to women by seven to one, that so-called neutral nouns are often marked in some way when they refer to women (poet-*ess*, for example), that verbs are sex-differentiated (women *shriek* or *scream*, for instance, and men *bellow*), and that the "generic" he is, way more often than not, actually gendered (a host of others have pointed this out, as well: Julia Stanley, Robin Lakoff, Ann Bodine, Cate Poynton, Cixous, Irigaray, etc.). Robin Lakoff notes that several adjectives take on sexual overtones when applied to women but not when they are applied to men: note the difference, for instance, between "he is a professional" and "she is a professional" (i.e., prostitute). There is a similar problem with greetings in business letters: "Dear Sir" versus "Dear *Madam*."

Furthermore, the seemingly innocuous habit of calling a woman a "girl" masks the larger problem with which Carol Gilligan has dealt: the assumption that women are incapable of moral maturity. The seemingly polite habit of calling a woman a "lady" not only suggests that she is passive, proper, and obedient but also validates the existence of the supposed "opposite" of that socially acceptable position: a ssslut (who just *asks for it*). And, as feminists from Kate Millett to Mary Daly have argued, the very definition of "sexual intercourse" as "the act of penetration" assigns to women, by default, the passive role in sex—why not, for instance, "envagination" or "engulfment" or even "circumfusion"? What's important here is that these linguistic representations participate in and set up women for abuse that is not constrained to text on a page. Linguistic representation not only reflects but also shapes perception. It is impossible to deny that our language usage supports the grisly state of affairs that bell hooks has so unabashedly noted: men "fuck" and women "*get fucked over*," in life and in language (57).[9]

Equal Re/Presentation

This unconscionable situation has led feminists on both sides of the Atlantic to join in the debate about the possibility of women's representation and of representation in general. On this side, a "battle" has emerged, an understandable fight to win the right for women to represent themselves. With a gaze that is fixed on a traditional notion of liberation, many pragmatic American feminists (there are, of course, other American feminisms) aim to create a female subject position, to get women speaking so that *the* female experience might be wholly represented. The assumption here is that there is a category of women with which feminists identify and for which they seek liberation. And both of those assumptions are built on another one: that a feminist (or anyone else) can *know the truth* about "women" and then re-present that truth adequately and honestly. Mainstream feminist politics has traditionally taken off from this set of assumptions.

Cate Poynton's *Language and Gender: Making the Difference*, for instance, spotlights the ideological reasons for language practices that keep women alienated from power. Because only what we can name can be discussed and because what we say becomes what we see, obtaining the power to name one's own reality is critical. Elaine Showalter echoes Poynton, suggesting that (a phallocratic) language structure is *not* the problem; the problem is getting the "full resources of language" to women so that they might begin to alter language *usage* as they speak themselves into it (255). So they might, in other words, "foster the political visibility of women" by representing them "fully and adequately" (Butler, *Gender Trouble* 1). Much important feminist work has been accomplished with this goal in mind.

Deconstruction/reconstruction is the plan most often enacted to achieve this goal: first expose the androcentric assumptions buttressing the Occidental intellectual tradition and then reconstruct the same basic setup with the added benefit of women's concrete experience. Seyla Benhabib and Drucilla Cornell map out this plan in their introduction to *Feminism as Critique*. The plethora of works dedicated to such an effort evidences the extent to which American feminists have attempted to fill in the (feminine) gaps left by Western thought/representation. Nancy Chodorow, for instance, develops a *feminine* ego-psychology based on connectedness rather than autonomy; Carol Gilligan develops a *feminine* theory of moral development based on feminine gender coding; Iris Young develops the notion of a "gynocentric" feminism that questions humanist epistemology; Gisela Ecker defines a *feminist* aesthetics based on a *feminine* utopian vision; and Sandra Harding and Nancy Hartsock develop a *feminist* standpoint theory from which to critique and resist dominant ideology. Liberation means (full) representation to many pragmatic American feminists, and adequate representation can only be attained when women represent themselves, when they speak of and for themselves. If women ever hope to attain liberation, Jean Elshtain suggests, feminism must devote itself to "a project of rational discourse"; such a project, she says, "can be one emancipatory window into the future" (129).

Susan Bordo's *The Flight to Objectivity* is a brilliant exemplification of the deconstruction/reconstruction feminist strategy. Bordo argues that Cartesian rationalism is a flight not to the Truth but *from the feminine*, and she notes that Descartes' celebration of abstract rationality is a celebration of the escape from the organic to the cerebral, from the body to the mind, which functions in Cartesian philosophy as the mirror of nature (106). Bordo then attempts, with a powerful swipe at the likes of Descartes and his children, to reconstruct a "feminine" foundation for knowledge based not on objectivity but on "empathy" and interconnectedness (112), a move that takes us back to the body, into women's concrete experience.

Chodorow, Gilligan, and Belenky (et al.) also offer deconstruction-reconstruction approaches to the validation of a female speaking subject, and all three are worthy of brief mention. Chodorow's *Reproduction of Mothering* takes on Freudian psychology and its metanarrative of oedipalization. Her work offers a compelling explanation of gender acquisition, minus the penis envy: little boys have to separate from what they are not—the (m)other. Little girls, on the other hand, are encouraged to remain connected to the mother because she represents what they are to become. So little boys begin to value individuality, autonomy, disinterested deliberation. But little girls value interpersonal connection—they are always who they are by virtue of context, relational possibilities. Chodorow's approach exposes the unwarranted nature of masculine privilege; it kicks the privilege loose and sets it in motion.

Gilligan uses Chodorow's work to lay out an alternate moral code of development based on interpersonal relations, interconnection, and interested, contextual deliberation. Gilligan manages to disrupt the hegemony of the definition of moral maturity advanced by Kant and followed by Kohlberg by taking on the very foundation of this morality, questioning the history behind it, the context in which it works, the interests it serves, and the oppression that results from it. What she comes up with is the validation of another ("feminine") moral code, another set of stages for moral development that she argues are as valid, as scientific, as undeniable as the one Kohlberg sets up. By challenging the hegemonic ideal of moral development and moral action, Gilligan makes it possible to recognize its contingency, its historicity and, again, leaves both sides of the binary validated.[10]

Belenky and her coauthors (*Women's Ways of Knowing*) use Gilligan's study to challenge what Paulo Freire has called the "banking system of education" (*Pedagogy of the Oppressed*), that traditional model of learning that posits a knower charged with depositing information and a learner charged with sucking it up. Belenky et al. suggest that women are more comfortable with different, more connected and dialogical learning styles. Women tend to learn better through equal dialectical exchange than through the "sponge syndrome." And the authors affirm those alternate styles as legitimate and productive. In fact, *Women's Ways* celebrates a wide spectrum of learning styles, which the authors present as equally important and equally valid.

Privilege Flipping

Other approaches, such as radical, spiritual, and eco-feminist movements,[11] are interested less in equity than in finding ways to flip the binary privilege. These feminisms offer women a sense of inclusion as women by inverting the masculine/feminine binary so that the "feminine" comes out on top (so to speak). They are not interested in proving that women can participate in abstract rationality as well as men or that, à la Gilligan, thinking-through-connection is equally as valuable; instead, they advocate a total reconception of the world based on women's experience, a way of seeing the world across interconnection and re/pro/creation—"sisterhood." Most spiritual and eco-feminist movements allow "men" into

> We cannot simply turn the Emperor's coat inside out, for in fact he wears no clothes.
>
> —Jardine, *Gynesis*

their circle-dance, but only inasmuch as those "men" are capable of becoming "sisters." Men are validated as speaking subjects, in other words, only by becoming like women—an interesting turn of the (gender) trope.

Recovering the important women who have been ignored in traditional histories is generally important to these feminisms. Refashioning history so that it takes an ac/count of women's oppression and women's contributions makes it easier to envision a women-centered future. Gerda Lerner's *Creation of Patriarchy*, Elinor Gadon's *Once and Future Goddess*, Merlin Stone's *When God Was a Woman*, Riane Eisler's *The Chalice and the Blade: Our History, Our Future*, and Elaine Pagels' *The Gnostic Gospels* are all examples of the attempt to re/construct and/or re/capture a women-centered past to establish the basis for a women-centered future.

Retrieving the symbol of the ancient Goddess, for instance, appeals to feminists because She affirms a golden age in which female wisdom, power, and sexuality were celebrated; and by doing so, She legitimizes a much sought after woman-as-subject position. The Goddess validates a hierarchy that is antithetical to the traditionally accepted order of things: it focuses on immanence, the earth, and the body rather than transcendence, heaven, and the mind (Gadon xii). Truth is not the result of abstract reasoning so much as it is a social and linguistic construction, woven out of a series of interconnections; this is a setup that makes women's ways of knowing, speaking, and deliberating *the* ways to know, speak, and deliberate.

Eisler says the Goddess is associated with a feminine model of social relations based on "power-as-linking" (28), on partnership. Ancient societies of Goddess-worshipers, she posits, were gentle, egalitarian, and peaceful before violent, sky-god worshipers from the Asiatic north (who have flourished ever since) wiped them out. Her point: if this peaceful and egalitarian model of social relations worked once, it could work again. Starhawk, a Wiccan High Priestess, advocates a return to that golden age by supplanting "masculine" metaphors of war and domination with "feminine" metaphors of birth and regeneration, connection and nurturing, because feminine metaphors allow us to view the world as interconnected and unified (174).

"Dead Men Don't Rape"—
Feminism and/as CounterViolence

For many feminists, however, this seems no time to sit around dreaming about a "return" to a "golden age." Women are being hurt; women are being killed—right here, right now. Indeed, running concurrent with the well-documented backlash against feminism[12] in the last few decades is a less documented call to arms among pragmatic American feminists. So much for the "partnership model": This is a call for women to return violence for violence in the "war zone" we call society. Andrea Dworkin is one of the most vocal contemporary proponents of this call. Listen to how she characterizes this (obviously horrific) situation—men attacking women—and to what she is calling feminists to do:

> We are in a *war*. We have not been fighting back to win this war. We are in need of political resistance. . . . I am asking you to organize political support for women who kill men who have been hurting them. . . . I'm asking you to *stop* men who beat women. Get them jailed or *get them killed*. . . . I am asking you to look at every single political possibility for *fighting back*. (37–42, my emphasis)

This is no isolated plea, nor is it a new one. Valerie Solanas's *SCUM [Society for Cutting Up Men] Manifesto* certainly leaps to mind as a forerunner, an early advocation of violence first and last: "SCUM will not picket, demonstrate, march, or strike," Solanas writes. "Such tactics are for nice, genteel ladies. If SCUM ever strikes . . . it will be in the dark with a six-inch blade." Significantly, this is not a call for random but for *rational* murder. Solanas, apparently attempting to offer assurance to the skeptic, asserts that "both destruction and killing" in the name of SCUM "will be selective and discriminate." "SCUM," she says, "is against half-crazed, indiscriminate riots, with no clear objective in mind and in which many of your own kind are picked off. . . . SCUM will coolly, furtively, stalk its prey and quietly move in for the kill."

For those of us who feel less than assuaged by Solanas's distinction between "selective" and "half-crazed" killings, Dianne Chisholm, in "Violence Against Violence Against Women," reminds us that this is not at all a new direction for feminism. Solanas may have been the one and only member of SCUM, but she was not/is not the only feminist advocating murder in the name of counterviolence. In fact, the *SCUM Manifesto* enjoys wide contemporary appeal.[13] And despite what Chisholm calls a "weakening conservatism which believes that violence is not feminine and contrary to a prevailing liberalism which places faith in humanist institutions governed primarily by men," feminism has a long history of promoting counterviolence (30). Chisholm cites Grant McCracken, head of the Institute of Contemporary Culture at the Royal Ontario Museum, who says he finds feminist counterviolence "inevitable," and he suggests that the local sidewalk graffiti, which reads "dead men don't rape," is only one manifestation of women's determination to start fighting back en masse (A16).

Chisholm notes that the entire October–November 1992 issue of the Canadian periodical, *This Magazine*, was devoted to an update on women and violence. Articles, including "Fighting Back," "If Boys Will Be Boys, Girls Will Now Take Action," and "Revenge Becomes Her," Chisholm says, break "the silence with a gesture of vociferous militancy." And she adds: "Perhaps the period of mourning is passing . . ." (48). Moira Farr, author of "Revenge Becomes Her," notes with satisfaction that there has been a resurgence of women's "revenge fantasies" in literature and theater. Here's Chisholm on Farr's *own* fantasies:

> Moira Farr fantasizes the arrival of Clara Kent, "mild mannered reporter by day and amazing fembo at night," and of "Dirty Harriet," the little girl who wanted to be an engineer but who became a mobster instead. Farr also reports the arrival of "Comix Bitch," creation of Seattle artist Roberta Gregory; apparently "next to her Thelma and Louise look like Lucy and Ethel." (49)

Another barometer of the cultural climate in this arena is the public's response to the Lorena and John Wayne Bobbitt affair. Indeed, Lorena ascended to near demi-god(dess) status almost overnight in many feminist circles, including rhet/comp feminist circles. She was alluded to with celebration and admiration at a feminist workshop at the 1994 Conference on College Composition and Communication (4Cs) in Nashville, Tennessee (where, incidentally, one of the speakers proposed an antipluralist feminist political strategy and echoed Farr's exultation of feminist revenge fantasies). The rampant celebration of a woman for having had the nerve to mutilate her attacker is symptomatic of the spirit of an age that has seen too much unanswered violence against women. Too much abuse has been endured, too many men have gotten away with it, too many women have suffered alone. While men around the country very likely shuddered at this syndicated story, public sympathy appeared to be overwhelmingly directed toward Lorena. And yet it is necessary to consider this apparent public support for women's counterviolence carefully before declaring it any more than a hollow "victory" for

women
in the
war zone

●
●
●

Take Two—Forget
Re/Presentation and the "Fight"

These pragmatic feminist movements and theories, diverse as they are, find a significant point of unification across their production of what Foucault calls a "counter-memory." Too much *unproblematic* forgetting and systematic *exclusion* has left us where we are today. And the task we set for ourselves when we engage any of these pragmatic feminisms and feminist theories is a productive re-thinking of the past, a digging up of forgotten/excluded texts, ideas, statements, about what *else* might have happened and what *else* might have been. It is from this creative re-thinking of the past, this production of a countermemory, that feminists of all flavors have made it possible to recreate a new potential for this present existence. And the value of this move has crossed gender lines into the arenas of race, class, sexual orientation, and physical ableness. It is crucial to this project that a critical distinction be maintained between *unproblematic* forgetting ("just forgetting," which invites systematic exclusion) and forgetting *justly*, or affirmatively forgetting. Before we can ask for the latter, and we will definitely do that, it will be necessary, as Ronell says, to gain "some understanding of what it was we were supposed to forget" ("Activist" 296). This is an important point: we are dismissing neither these diverse pragmatic feminist efforts nor the significance of counter-memory here. Countermemory will have been our starting point, our springboard.

On the other hand, it is not enough simply to produce counter-memories in the hope that providing evidence of past injustices will stop the "war." The question, then, is where to go from here. It seems neces-sary to note that, while these (American) feminist approaches to women's oppression spin off in various directions, they begin their spin atop many of the same basic assumptions: that re/presentation, in general, is pos-sible; that a female-subject position is desirable; and that an important aim for feminism(s) should be to speak (for) the silenced *flip-side* of a cer-tain metaphysical structure in which "women" have already been im-printed. To get where we want to go in this chapter, it will be necessary first to back-spin a bit, to break up [at] the ground supporting so many (American) feminist projects.

The re/presentation question is an important one. When feminists push for women's right to represent themselves, they/we have a tendency to speak as if they/we know who "women" are and as if the task were simply to gain, for "women," the right to express that knowledge. How-ever, within the last several years, even that basic assumption has been challenged, from *within* feminist discourses, on two counts. First, the category "women" never covers its territory fully enough; the term itself tends to signify white, upwardly mobile, heterosexual, thirty/forty-some-thing females. And, as Butler notes, with her usual directness: even "the theories of feminist identity that elaborate predicates of color, sexuality, ethnicity, class, and able-bodiness invariably close with an embarrassed 'etc.'" (*Gender Trouble* 143). At issue here is the *leftover*. "It is," she says, "*the supplément*, the excess that necessarily accompanies any effort to posit identity once and for all" (143). Donna Haraway agrees, noting that:

> There is nothing about being "female" that naturally binds women. There is not even such a state as "being" female, itself a highly complex category constructed in contested scientific discourses and other social practices. Gender, race, or class consciousness is an achievement forced on us by the terrible historical experience of the contradictory social realities of patriarchy, colonialism, racism, and capitalism. ("Mani-festo" 197)

Indeed, she continues, "painful fragmentation among feminists (not to mention among women) along every possible fault line has made the concept of woman elusive, an excuse for the matrix of women's domina-tions of *each other*" (197, my emphasis). The sexed body, Butler reminds us, is always already an effect of power; it is *produced* by that discourse, as Irigaray has noted, that stabilizes itself by excluding "the feminine" all together. Sexual materiality, therefore, ought to continue to be an object of feminist inquiry, but, Butler argues (against Irigaray), it ought not be invoked as its *ground* (*Bodies That Matter* 49).

Similarly, though Irigaray claims that sexual difference is *the* question to which we must address ourselves, and though many psychoanalytic feminists claim that sexual difference is *the* fundamental difference among differences,[14] Butler argues that "women" do not "monopolize the sphere of the excluded" (*Bodies That Matter* 48). That realm of abject bodies is peopled/populated by innumerable other Others. In fact, Butler apologizes for her own previous privileging of gender "as the identifica-tory site of political mobilization" (116). She insists, for instance, that there is no relationship of "sexual difference" that is "unmarked by race" (181).

And secondly, even the notion that we might know *ourselves* so that we might represent *ourselves* more accurately has become suspect since the subject itself has come under fire recently in both feminist and post-structuralist theory. If even self-mastery is an illusion (based on the re-flection we offer ourselves in the mirror) and if even our own discourses cannot operate representationally (too much slippage), the goal of (even self) representation seems misguided. Indeed, the drive to re/present even ourselves accurately is a manifestation of the idealistic refusal to acknowl-edge the posthumanist paradox, an unchallenged faith in the morning mirror-check. The (feminist) community in which this idealism invests is still a humanist one. There can be no self-knowledge without a *stable, knowing subject* and no self-re-presentation without self-knowledge.

Furthermore, it would seem that, contra Showalter and company, the *inherently* phallocratic structure of civil discourse is *precisely* the prob-lem. The logocentric linguistic structure that many American feminists uphold in their struggle is a phallocentric one that will continually mis-fire for "women" *because* it demands that one be either male or female, active or passive, subject or object. Women have been posited as the object to men's subject, the hole to men's whole. And yet, none of this is to say that the Phallus does not *get around* to women—indeed, women can and do operate as subjects. According to Luce Irigaray, women *exist* (take on the role of subject) precisely inasmuch as they can be "transformed by phallocratism" (*This Sex* 111). The insert page of Eva Keuls's *The Reign of the Phallus* illustrates the problem: it sports a naked, matronly figure, running, and clutching an enormous penis; that is, the woman is *making off* with the power of the Other. The caption reads: "caricature of female phallic aggression."[15] It could as easily have read:

Dressing for success
in the Western World . . .

It's not that women are not representable in the linguistic structure; it's rather that they are *only* representable as men's Other, as men's opposite. Women have done a good job of inhabiting that subject position—of being transformed by phallocratism. What is completely *unrepresentable* in discursive structure, what is linguistically absent and unthinkable, is not "women" but another sensibility entirely,

> The feminist dream of a common language, like all dreams for a perfectly true language, of a perfectly faithful naming of experience, is a totalizing and imperialist one.
>
> —Haraway, "Manifesto"

outside the dichotomy, outside phallogocentric thought/language. Some have called this radical other in itself "the feminine," but this is not the feminine as opposed to the masculine. It is something else entirely, something that exceeds the structure, that leakssss and is not ac/count/able. For Irigaray, both the subject (male) and its Other (female) are masculine manifestations of a closed signifying economy that excludes the "feminine" altogether. Paradoxically, if one of Freud's glaringly sexist blind spots was his assumption that language signifies for only One sex/libido—and that is the masculine—one of Irigaray's great insights has been her confirmation of that assumption. To get the full resources of *this* language to "women" would hardly be productive.

It will not be nearly enough simply to develop strategies for getting women more fully represented in discourse and so in politics. That is, it is not enough simply to hope to make women *stronger* subjects, more active and present subjects. What's needed at this point is not so much a celebration of the category "women" but an inquiry into how that category has already been constructed by the very structures of power feminism aims to defeat. As Butler suggests, "the domains of political and linguistic 'representation' set out in advance the criterion by which subjects themselves are formed." And when feminists enter a campaign to represent "women," they engage themselves in a vicious circle: "representation is extended only to what can be acknowledged as a subject," that is, you have to be a subject *before* "representation can be extended" to you (*Gender Trouble* 1–2). "Women" end up the creation/production of the very discourses assigned to study and, subsequently, to *represent* them. The "feminist subject," for which feminists have been fighting for years, "turns out," as Butler notes, "to be discursively constituted [determined] by the very political system that is supposed to facilitate its emancipation" (2): *feminist* politics. *This*

is

a

problem.

And it has not gone unnoticed. Indeed, it has led to what has been termed a "post-feminist" moment, a moment of political hesitation in which, as Butler says, feminists have begun to "reflect from within a feminist perspective on the injunction to construct a subject of feminism" (*Gender Trouble* 5). This reflection engages a radical rethinking of identity and representation that hopes to "free feminist theory from the necessity of having to construct a single or abiding [and necessarily exclusionary] ground" for itself (5). The drive to fill the woman-as-subject position, which is necessarily a masculine position, simply perpetuates a naive gender relation, which, Butler notes, is "precisely contrary to feminist aims" (5). And "what sense does it make" anyway, she asks, "to extend representation to subjects who are constructed through the exclusion of those who fail to conform to unspoken normative requirements of the subject?" (5–6). Perhaps Butler is correct when she suggests that "'representation' will be shown to make sense for feminism only when the subject of 'women' is nowhere to be presumed" (6).

A politics that upholds an essentialistic view of men and women, that calls for a fight *in the name of women* and female subjectivity, upholds rather than displaces (phal)logocentric notions of language and ethics. With respect to the Bobbitt "affair," for instance, it seems that to take *out* the "big Dick" is not necessarily to take *on* phallocentrism. It can be, rather, to *strap it on*, to participate in it, in the name of "female phallic aggression." It is naive, Irigaray suggests, to believe (as many radical, eco-, and spiritual feminists do) that one need only be a "woman" to "remain outside phallic power" (*This Sex* 81). Trading one totality for another, the fascist feminist for the fascist masculinist, for instance, amounts "to the same thing in the end" (68); it amounts, as Irigaray suggests, "to sameness, to phallocentrism" (33). A feminist who negates the Other by means of mutilation and a misogynist who negates the Other by means of rape are playing the same phallocratic game: stamping out difference in the name of the Self-Same. There's no/thing new here.

It's not nothing that Lorena left the scene of the counterattack with the top third of the Transcendental Signifier itself clinched tightly in her fist. The desire to finally *have* it rather than always having to *be* it is seductive indeed.[16] But this mainstream feminist desire for an appropriation of phallic power will not get Lorena (or us) very far. To want only to have our own little "pocket signifier," as Cixous calls it ("Laugh" 890), to want only our fair share of the very thing that has oppressed us, the power of the Other, is not to want nearly enough. Feminists who aim for a simple "change in the distribution of power, leaving intact the power structure itself . . . are resubjecting themselves, deliberately or not," Irigaray says, "to a phallocratic order" (81). It should not go without notice that what Keuls calls the "scepter of sovereignty" (2) was quickly returned to its "rightful" owner—reattached in a matter of hours.[17] No/thing new here, either.

As long as the game is binary (i.e. absence vs. presence) women will be the absence, the lack, the hole. "Opposition, hierarchizing exchange, the struggle for mastery which can end only in at least one death," Cixous reminds us, "all [of] that comes from a period of time governed by phallocentric values" ("Laugh" 893). This game (logocentrism) cannot be won by anyone but the One. The cards were always already stacked so that the phallus could not lose. These feminisms are, as Luanne Frank

> If we keep on speaking the same language together, we're going to reproduce the same history. Begin the same stories all over again. . . . The same discussions, the same arguments, the same scenes. The same attractions and separations. The same difficulties, the same impossibility of making connections. The same. . . . Same. . . . Always the same.
>
> —Irigaray, "When Our Lips"

suggests, inscribed *within* phallocracy. They owe their lives to exactly what they set out to kill/cut off.

Until there is an explosion of the structure itself, there will be no dis-location of the system that leaves us floundering in an either/or mental-ity, a mentality that must have an enemy, a bound and gagged other who is systematically excluded. Women have been fairly successful in appro-priating phallic power, but surely we're after more than this. As Haraway has noted, feminist claims to "innocence," and the corollary insistence on victimhood as the "Only ground for insight, has done enough damage" ("Manifesto" 199). God and Goddess come down to the Same simple dichotomy, a closed system of signification in which each term gets its meaning through the exclusion/negation of the other. It is this closed structure itself that needs to be rethought. As Haraway reminds us, "It's not just that 'god' is dead; so is the 'goddess'" (204).

And finally, the kind of counterterrorism advocated by Dworkin and company, no matter how understandable and seductive within its inheri-ted logic, operates on an idealistic notion of identity and a naive view of power. Chisholm, on the other hand, recognizes that there is no way to "deploy an effective counter-violence when violence has been discovered at the very center of the machinery of this age of post-structuralism, and to be endemic to the machinery that operates the entire social system" (32). She argues that the only "reasonable" attack for feminists to launch in a postmodern age is an attack "on the notion of the humanist subject itself." Women's "counter-terrorism" is, at best, she says, a "pseudo-insurrection." But there is another option: "destroy the very construct 'subject.'" Not just the male subject but the female one as well, "and the entire humanist culture from which it arose" (32–33). Now we're on our way.

It seems necessary, finally, to admit, as Chisholm does, that "men's" violence against "women" is an "*effect of*" rather than "a *cause for* the intervention of the (father's) law."[18] If it is indeed time for "women" to get violent, they/we ought to go for the BIG picture, take out the "whole social order" by going for the jugular: the symbolic order. They/we ought to "master a pen that will blow a nation of swords to smither-eens" (Chisholm 33). In Irigaray's language, this would read: "jam the theoretical machinery" (*This Sex* 78). Such a jamming would invite an/other game entirely, an/other feminism: it would hope not to "win" a *fuller* inscription within the phallocratic structure but, rather, to inhabit an exscripted space, to be written *out* of the "battle" altogether, if only for instants, moments, hijacked flashes.

FEMINISM(S) AND/IN POSTMODERNISM(S)

What's at stake in this vision for *an/Other* "feminism," of course, may be what we know as *feminism* itself. And those stakes are too high for many feminists. That is, it is more appealing to Be in the phallocracy, where the lines of the fight seem quite clear, than to allow oneself to inhabit a fundamentally different, exscripted space where things could be worse and the "enemy" might not be quite so easily spotted. This is a significant point. The concern about neoconservatism, about landing ourselves right back at a prefeminist starting point, warrants a hearing. Sabina Lovibond has articulated this position eloquently in her article "Feminism and Postmodernism," and I believe that she is worth quoting at length here:

> I think we have reason to be wary, not only of the unqualified Nietzschean vision of an end of legitimation, but also of the suggestion that it would somehow be "better" if legitimation exercises were carried out in a self-consciously parochial spirit. For if feminism aspires to be something more than a reformist movement, then it is bound sooner or later to find itself calling the parish boundaries into question.
> . . .
> So postmodernism seems to face a dilemma: either it can concede the necessity, in terms of the aims of feminism, of "turning the world upside down" in the way just outlined—thereby opening a door once again to the Enlightenment idea of a total reconstruction of society on rational lines; or it can dogmatically reaffirm the arguments already marshalled against that idea—thereby licensing the cynical thought that, here as elsewhere, "who will do what to whom" under the new pluralism is depressingly predictable. (22)

Many feminist descriptions of "postmodernism" evidence a struggle with this particularly difficult dilemma. Jane Flax, for instance, in *Thinking Fragments: Psychoanalysis, Feminism, and Postmodernism in the*

Contemporary West, suggests that postmodernism can be characterized as a belief in and celebration of the *death* of philosophy's holy Trinity: the death of Man, of History, and of Metaphysics. In "Feminism and Postmodernism: An Uneasy Alliance," Seyla Benhabib discusses and, for the most part, applauds Flax's characterization (or caricature) of what they both call "*the* postmodern position." Their unproblematic use of the definite article in this characterization is, as Heidegger likes to say, not nothing; it implies, paradoxically, that postmodernism is unified and settled, that it exists as one more totalizing metanarrative engaged in a fight for primacy. It is, therefore, more easily dismissed. Flax's language, which Benhabib quotes without comment, is also telling. Here's Flax's characterization, for instance, of *the* postmodern critique of the unified subject of History:

> Postmodernists wish to *destroy* all essentialist conceptions of human being and nature. . . . In fact Man is a social, historical, linguistic *artifact*, not a noumenal or transcendental Being. . . . Man is forever *caught* in the web of fictive meaning, in *chains* of signification, in which the subject is *merely* another position in language. (Flax 32; Benhabib 18, my emphasis)

This pejorative language exposes certain assumptions that it will be necessary to examine. Flax, Benhabib, Ebert, and a large number of mainstream American feminists evidence a sense of paranoia about nonfoundational thought, a paranoia (or xenophobia?) that proceeds (phal)-logocentrically: *either* we are concrete subjects *or* we are "merely" fictions "caught" in the "chains" of language; *either* we support the political fight for "liberation" *or* we lapse into nihilism; *either* we support "feminist politics" *or* we, consciously or not, support the status quo. There is an exhausting lack of (re)vision apparent here, a relentless dependence upon binary distinctions, a persistent fixation on "what was." And this unimaginative reaction against "postmodernism" is by no means atypical; in fact, it runs amok in mainstream feminist political theory.

Nancy Hartsock, for instance, finds it "suspicious" that the concept of the subject would become problematic just at the moment when "marginalized" groups have begun to demand to be heard (163).[19] Bordo argues that postmodernism is dangerous to feminism, suggesting that "most of our institutions have barely begun to absorb the message of modernist social criticism; surely, it's too soon to let them off the hook via postmodern heterogeneity and instability" ("Feminism" 153). Christine Di Stefano fears that postmodern critiques of the subject promote a "postfeminist tendency, an inclination which is fostered by a refusal to systematically document or privilege any particular form of difference or identity against the hegemonic mainstream" (73). Di Stefano, along with Harding, Bordo, Flax, Hartsock and others fear that postmodern critiques of the subject will return us to the days of prefeminist thought, to an/other humanism that would once again invite us to forget and to silence women.

Linda Alcoff specifically takes on Derrida's deconstructive method, which takes on the binary system itself: logocentrism. According to Derrida, Alcoff suggests, the only way for women to break out of the oppressive system is to refuse to be located within that system, which means to refuse to use or even to define a category "woman." Ignoring deconstruction's affirmative endeavors, she argues that following Foucault and Derrida, feminism could only be a wholly negative enterprise, continually deconstructing everything but never constructing anything (420). Bordo agrees, arguing that deconstruction leaves feminism with a wholly theoretical perspective that allows no room for generalizations and so no political potential ("Feminism" 142–43).

Michel Foucault is the object of Hartsock's attacks in "Foucault on Power: A Theory for Women?" for many reasons. Hartsock argues that he is complicit with the oppressive power structure because he ultimately "fails to provide an epistemology which is usable for the task of revolutionizing, creating, and constructing" (164). She argues that he writes from "the position of the dominator" (165), that his "imagination of power is 'with' rather than 'against' power" (167). She dismisses Foucault as a part of the problem because he was, after all, a white, male academic whose conception of power as a "multiplicity of force relations" has made it impossible to find someone to blame for the wrongs women have suffered. He fails to provide an epistemology that makes revolution possible. Both the enemy and the "woman" must be *stable subjects*, it seems, for feminism to be a viable political enterprise. If this subject is "abandoned"[20] and there is no way to privilege one social set up over another, there will be no way for a feminist politics to proceed.

In "Toward a New Nomadism," Rosi Braidotti offers an insightful explication of the work of Gilles Deleuze and Felix Guattari, suggesting that their nomadic metaphors (like the schizo, the rhizome, and the nomad) may offer women a way out of phallogocentric modes of thought and into an/other sensibility. Significantly, however, what she hopes to gain from that "other" sensibility turns out to be more of the same. What she's after is an angle "through which women can gain access to a nonlogocentric mode of representation of the *female feminist subject*" (Braidotti 160, my emphasis). She also notes, quite correctly if also unfortunately, that "feminism is about ac*count*ability; it is about *grounding* a new epistemology and a situated ethics; it is about *foundations*" (162, my emphasis). These aims are hardly "nonlogocentric"; in fact, they look disturbingly familiar.

Braidotti also argues that "feminist theory, far from being a reactive thought, expresses women's ontological desire, women's structural need to posit themselves as female subjects" (161).[21] What is not getting said here is that this "ontological desire" is *already* reactionary; it is inscribed within an already phallocratic hope. If that's not clear yet, perhaps Braidotti's own words, which echo Hartsock,[22] will drive this point home:

> One cannot deconstruct a subjectivity one has never been fully granted control over; one cannot diffuse a sexuality that has historically been defined as dark and mysterious. In order to announce the death of the subject, one must first have gained the right to speak as one. (169)

The demand that women be *granted* the right to *enjoy* their subjecthood before the problematic construction of that subjecthood is called into question . . . reeeeeeks of *bad faith* for at least three reasons: (1) it implies that being "fully granted control over" one's own subjectivity is a right that someone somewhere already enjoys, that it is possible to get out of the posthumanist paradox (one wonders, among other things, who would do the granting); (2) it evidences a desire to get hold of the very thing that has oppressed women—the power of the other—to get it and make use of it before it is called into question; and (3) it assumes that women have *not* been speaking as subjects already (without having full control over that subjectivity)—it assumes that women have remained outside phallic power, as if everyone has not always already been hailed into subjectivity. More important than any of that, however, is this: to say that subjectivity is not stable, that the rhizomatic potentialities of Being will remain unexhausted by any interpellation into subjecthood, is not to suggest that "we" need to deconstruct it. "The" subject needs no help from us to de/construct—it is happening, it is crumbling *on its own*. And that crumbling leaves us not with *no subject* but with a *multiplicity* of subject positions, none of which will fully cover the metamorphic potential of humans-Being.

What comes into focus in this (way too) brief survey of negative feminist responses to postmodernism is that "feminist politics" often goes unquestioned in mainstream feminist theory; we-feminists tend to be reluctant to admit that feminism itself often operates as a metanarrative grounded in the notions of gender and woman(-as-man's-Other). Even most calls for feminist "coalitional politics," which try not to "assume in advance what the content of the category 'women' will be," as Butler observes, are still foundational and end up making promises about a future unity and solidarity under the name (*Gender Trouble* 14). Feminist "coalitional politics," Butler notes, still tends to operate on the notion that "there is a category 'women' that simply needs to be filled in with various components of race, class, age, ethnicity, and sexuality to become *complete*" (15, my emphasis). Descriptions and redescriptions of "the" power structure and "the" world are deemed acceptable or not according to whether they make a space for a viable "feminist politics" to keep
fighting
the
good
fight.
. . .

Though, as Benhabib points out, feminisms offer their own gendered critiques of (male) subjectivity, hi/story, and metaphysics, they have an overwhelming tendency to stop short of exposing "feminist politics" to the same critiques. Few feminists are willing to say, with postmodernists, that "the" subject has always been a function of other functions, an effect of linguistic structure, or that there is no place for the *knowing* subject in postmodern discourses and so no place for a knowing *female* subject. Mainstream feminisms in this country tend to be wary of radical redefinitions of key feminist terms (such as "women" and "politics"), of visions that would celebrate an/Other feminism and an/Other feminist politics, which would not require the "unity" of "women" to be effective.

Many feminists, then, have necessarily gone to great pains to distinguish between feminism and postmodernism.[23] Benhabib says that though "feminism and postmodernism have emerged as two leading currents of our time," both of which are invested in the "struggle against the grand narratives of Western Enlightenment and modernity," the two cannot be conflated. One must still ask: "feminism *or* postmodernism[?]" (17, my emphasis). Benhabib characterizes the distinction in terms of extremity of argument, noting that feminists can go with the "weak versions" of the three primary theses of postmodernism (the death of Man, History, and Metaphysics) but not with the "strong versions" (20–26). "Weak" versions leave *the good fight* unproblematized; they stop short of interrogating the *grounds* for "feminist politics." Ebert's distinction is much the same. Though she classifies both ludic and resistance feminisms as postmodern discourses, the former, she says, is too extreme.[24] While "resistance" feminisms would protect feminist/oppositional politics at (seemingly) any cost, "ludic" feminisms would put feminist politics on the chopping block with everything else—they would feel free to break up, even [at] *this* metanarrative. If "postmodernism" celebrates the *death* of Man, History, and Metaphysics (as we have experienced them), many feminisms celebrate, at the most, the *subversion* of them: these feminisms are after a revision but not a radical *re-visioning*. I am reminded here of Alice Jardine's by now overquoted wake-up call in *Gynesis*: "There is, after all, a difference between really attempting to think differently and thinking the same through the manipulation of difference" (17). In the next section of this chapter, we will have been after more than that.

—Section 2: A Thinking of Futurity—

[T]oo little joy . . . is our original sin. And learning better to feel joy, we learn best how not to hurt others or to plan hurts for them.
—Nietzsche, *Thus Spoke Zarathustra*

To escape from a pure and simple reversal of the masculine position means in any case not to forget to laugh.
—Luce Irigaray, *This Sex Which Is Not One*

It seems necessary to rethink this hardheaded determination to continue, for the "good" of *anyone*, our tendency toward oppositional/reactionary "politics." If it is difficult anymore to talk about "revolution" without a cynical gri[n]/mace, it is because in the arena of revolutionary success stories, we still have *zip*. Nothing seems to have worked—in fact, we would be hard-pressed to deny that history has been kicking our collective butt. What Kundera calls the "Grand March" has not changed the world any more than an education in "the humanities" made the Nazis more "humane." "Even the so-called Sexual Revolution," Ronell reminds us, "largely ended up fucking with women" ("Interview" 129).[25] And the problem has *not* been the refusal or the inability to mobilize "forces"; it has not been a problem of splintered factions that have not been able to unite and take action. Rather, in the last century, we have proved ourselves to be *hyper*[re]active. *We* (and "we-women" are not excused from this identity-term) have been *over*anxious to band together and mobilize—in the name of all sorts of atrocities: Final Solutions, lynchings, world wars, cold wars, and drug wars. "Take a look around you," Ronell says. "Haven't we, as a culture, been *too* active, *too* action filled?" ("Activist" 300). Thinking backwards—in the name of "justice" (or, à la Nietzsche: *revenge*)—has gotten us nothing but more suffering, more injustice.

What we will have been after here is a thinking of futurity . . . we will have been after precisely what has been missing in much (American) feminist politics, which has a tendency to relentlessly perpetuate

"what is" by fixing a
Oppositional politics
vampirized us, eco-
tionally. It can no
ethical to *fight the*
mobilizations are
banner of the Good.
that "[e]ven for the
were not mobilized
mobilized to be on a
Everyone," she notes,

> Humanity (a term which ac-
> quired the prestige of its con-
> temporary usage at the Nurem-
> berg trials) will certainly have
> to rethink the projects and pro-
> jections that have, despite
> everything, traced out a history
> of indecency—a history which
> compromises the very possi-
> bility of a thinking of futurity.
> —Ronell, *Finitude's Score*

gaze on "what was."
of every flavor have
nomically and emo-
longer be considered
good fight because *all*
activated under the
Ronell reminds us
Gulf War, people
to *murder*, they were
Mission from God.
"from Madonna to

Bush is on a mission from God" ("Interview" 150).

And that will have been our point: responsible responsiveness (ethical politics) will not have been possible in the name of a(ny) god/foundation/metanarrative. It will be necessary to engage a rigorous hesitation with respect to the political imperative driving many pragmatic feminisms. And the scramble to save *the* subject (male *and* female), in the name of (any) political action, also ought to be rethought. This scramble, which asserts an assault on "passivity," is, after all, typically prompted by the humanist impulse to "take charge." But the active/passive binary, as Ronell puts it, "proffers a deluded equation" ("Activist" 300).[26] The posthumanist paradox is that we both do and/but are also (more so) done. Furthermore, to remain convinced that "*the* call of conscience" or *the* voice of the superego that prompts us to action cannot be a "phony"[27] one, an incomplete one, is to continue to be contorted in a humanist afterspasm. It is to allow our "questioning" to remain a function of the "humanist arrogance of man," which, Ronell reminds us, "has effectively destroyed the world" (*Finitude's Score* 3–4). Here we will be after a questioning that would Be other/wise and a "politics" that Jean-Francois Lyotard, in "Lessons in Paganism," describes as "both godless and just" (135).[28]

"What would it mean," we ask with Ronell, "to follow a politics of radical nonclosure, leaving time as well as borders open to the absolute otherness that must accompany genuine futurity?" ("Support Our" 284; cf. also, Lyotard, *Just Gaming* and "Lessons"). What would it mean, in other words, to follow a politics that would "locate a passivity beyond passivity—a space of repose and reflection, a space that would let the other come"? (Ronell, "Activist" 300). What if our politics were about blurring lines of distinction rather than drawing lines in the sand? What if politics signified an invitation to *tremble at the edge of the sensible/ thinkable* rather than a battle *within* the border zones of thought? These questions ask not for final solutions but for perpetual negotiations. They lead us not to more arrogant missions but to a kind of passivity that is anything but inactive. Here, with these questions as our backdrop, we'll be after a *just* "feminist" "politics" that nevertheless recognizes, as Tomas does in Kundera's *Unbearable Lightness*, that "missions are stupid" (313); we'll be after a feminism that *thinks the unthinkable* and a politics that celebrates the *death of God and His missions*.

THE QUESTION CONCERNING SUBVERSION

For this, however, it will be necessary to imagine a feminism that moves beyond a desire for mere subversion. Subversion is a problem because it remains inscribed within the same binary structure it aims to dethrone. To subvert is to play by the rules of the system to be subverted. It traps feminism within a circle of re-action; a circle without futurity. "Feminist critique," as Butler suggests, "ought to explore the totalizing claims of a masculinist signifying economy, but also remain self-critical with respect to the totalizing gestures of feminism" itself (*Gender Trouble* 13). She argues that "the effort to identify the enemy as singular in form is a reverse-discourse [a negative deconstruction] that uncritically mimics the strategy of the oppressor instead of offering a different set of terms" (13). A "different set of terms" . . . or perhaps a radical reworking (working over) of existing terms. We will set our sights on the latter.

The binary machine is at the very base of dialectical representations, and it smothers difference in the name of the self-same.[29] Butler notes that the "language of appropriation, instrumentality, and distanciation germane to the epistemological mode also belong[s] to a strategy of domination that pits the 'I' against the 'Other.'" But, she says, the "epistemological point of departure is *in no sense* inevitable" (144, my emphasis). Deleuze, in fact, marks the assumption that it *is* inevitable as a crucial error in Hegelian thought: Hegel didn't see that *both* the master *and* the slave, as Nietzsche noted, are oblivious to the notion of difference/

[The epistemological point of departure] is an investment in a given system of thought—the West's long dominant one. . . . It's a bet on a horse carrying the labeler's colors. It's also an attempt by this rhetoric here to silence that over there . . . by misrepresenting its opponents, so that we cease to hear what it says. Doing our thinking for us, this rhetoric would have us not need (and not able) to look hard, for ourselves, from its terms to what it would describe.

—Luanne Frank, "Uncovering"

differance. That is, dialectic makes *everyone* a slave, a slave of a particular sizing up of the "great sweep of life." In the place of difference/ differance, the dialectic offers oppositions and their reactive imperative.

From here, there's not much chance of thinking the unthinkable. A feminist politics that does not find a line of escape from dialectics cannot be "liberatory" in any sense of the term. What is necessary for an affirmative "feminist" politics is a thinking beyond dialectics, a thinking that is not reactive, that is affirmative without sinking into the "negativity of the positive" (Deleuze, *Nietzsche* 180). What is necessary is an affirmation that differs from negation without opposing it—a *nonpositive affirmation*.

With that in mind, Ronell's question is this: "Is there a way to produce a force or an intensity that isn't merely a reaction (and a very bad allergic reaction) to *what is*? In other words, could feminism be a pointer toward a *future of justice* that isn't merely reproducing *what is*, with small reversals?" ("Interview" 128). A tentative but hopeful answer to this question is Yes, but it *will not* and *could not* happen in the name of the metaphysical category "women." Identity politics will not have been a line of flight for us. A feminism that points toward futurity, that does not get weighed down by reactive posturings, will not have emerged until "women" come to embrace the "death of man" as *also* the "death of woman-as-man's-Other." It will take some gender-sliding, some affirmative forgetting, and a healthy shedding of traditional "feminist politics" to get back to the future.

THINKING THE UNTHINKABLE— "LET'S GET OUT OF HERE!"

In 1975, Hélène Cixous, noting the "solidarity" between logocentrism and phallocentrism, asked the following:

> What would happen to logocentrism, to the great philosophical sys-
> tems, to the order of the world in general if the rock upon which they
> founded this church should crumble? . . . If some fine day it suddenly
> came out that the logocentric plan had always, inadmissibly, been to
> create a foundation for (to found and fund) phallocentrism, to guaran-
> tee the masculine order a rationale equal to history itself. (*Newly Born*
> 65)

It seems safe by now to say that the word *is out*, and that this realization
issues an as of yet unequaled challenge to feminist thought. Once it is no
longer acceptable to simply use the logocentric structure against itself,
that is, either to even out the privilege or simply flip it from one side of
the binary (masculine) to the Other (feminine-as-masculine's-Other),
then it will no longer be possible to advance a "feminist politics" in the
name of "women." This is a dangerous thought; an *irresistible* thought.
It's the death of God again: There is something about the dis/co-
vering and radical shedding (affirmative forgetting) of past/present foundations that leaves one wide open to previously unthought potentialities.
Cixous says that to think this thought, this thought that *shatters*, will
mean that "all the stories would be there to retell differently; the future
would be incalculable; the historic forces would and will change hands
and change body—another thought which is *yet unthinkable*—will transform the functioning of all society" (65, my emphasis). The struggle now
is to think the unthinkable, to engage a radical redescription of the world
in terms of heterogeneity and multiplicity, and to do this without regret
or falling again into nostalgia for a solid ground.

OVERFLOWING GOD—
A LIQUIDATION OF SOLIDIFICATIONS

In *This Sex Which Is Not One*, Luce Irigaray begins such a redescription
by leaping out of a "mechanics of solids" and into a description of
fluidity. Fluids evidence, she says, a "physical reality that continues to
resist adequate symbolization and/or that signifies the powerlessness of
logic to incorporate in its writing all the characteristic features of nature"
(106–7). Fluids are leaky; they do not stay put; they cannot be fixed in
an appropriation. This, of course, calls the epistemological attitude to red

alert and sends it scrambling to "minimize certain of these features . . . so as to keep it/them from jamming the works of the theoretical machine" (107) that we call "logic." "Real fluids" get *theorized* in a way that makes them acceptable, appropriable, workable. But what is at stake in the repression of a "mechanics of *real* fluids" is (phal)logocentrism's whole show; to leave the "economy of [*real*] fluids" uninterpreted, Irigaray says, is to hand "the real back to God" (109), to *keep* the unthinkable unthinkable.

Irigaray suggests that psychoanalysis is guilty of perpetuating exactly this when it "grants precedence to solids" by organizing every "psychic economy . . . around the [solidly present] phallus (or Phallus)" (110). Judith Butler echoes this criticism in *Bodies That Matter*, charging Freud with continually referring to the lesbian phallus as a "spectral representation of a masculine original" without then questioning the "the spectral *production* of the putative 'originality' of the *masculine*" (63, my emphasis). It is Freud himself, in *The Ego and the Id*, who recognizes that the so-called material body comes into being phantasmatically through particular prohibitions on love, that the very *notion* of a fixed anatomy is *produced* through negation and abjection. After Freud, it is "no longer possible," Butler says, "to take anatomy as a stable referent," a preexisting given. And inasmuch as Freud is guilty of precisely *this* when he posits a masculinist original, Butler suggests that there is something "clearly awry in Freud's analysis from the start" (63).[30] Butler's question, then, becomes: What is it that must be "*excluded* from the body for the body's boundaries to form?" (65, my emphasis). What exclusions or negations, in other words, must have already taken place for the so-called material body to appear, and to appear with originality tied to the masculine? (Irigaray whispers an answer to Butler and to us:

> what gets excluded/negated
>
> is the *fluid "feminine."*)

Butler poses basically the same question to Lacan. She likes Lacan and freely acknowledges her debt to him and his understanding of the body as a "psychically invested projection" (73). However, she also notes that Lacan's theory becomes phallogocentric at the moment he allows man's specular image to become "the principle of every unity he perceives in objects" (Lacan, *Seminar, Book II* 166; Butler, *Bodies That Matter* 77). "At this point," Butler says, despite Lacan's protestations, the phallus looks an awfully lot like the penis, and "the organs are installed as a 'privileged signifier'" (77). She makes a decisive break with Lacan when she argues that even this so-called privileged signifier is not the origin of signification but a *symptom*: "the effect of a signifying chain summarily suppressed" (81).

Irigaray's point, with which Butler appears to agree, is that "an economy of fluids" is excluded/negated for the material body to appear as it does, with its emphasis focused on presence and solidity. This, Irigaray says, is simply one more example of the "reabsorption of fluid in a solidified form" (*This Sex* 110). The excess/remainder continues to be dismissed, ignored, negated, and/or absorbed in the name of the solid structure—in the name of the poles of a fixed dichotomy. Penis over clitoris. Presence over absence. What's missing is what's in the fluid middle/muddle. The question is, *What would happen if the excesssss got its say?* What if the unac/countable overflow were spotlighted and celebrated? What if the mechanics of solids founding our oppositional politics were suddenly dis/solved into a ffffluid and uncontainable mmmmmotion?

OF DRAG QUEENS AND HERMAPHRODITES— THE JOYS OF GENDER-SLIDING

It would force us to find another way to look at gender, for one thing. It would force us to *re/cognize* the gender-thing as a function of a logic of solids, of the illusion logocentrism produces about biology: You must be either male or female but never both and never neither. Two sexes are presented as poles of opposition. But from a third (mobile) position, what comes into view is an overflowing excess lurking *between* and *beyond* the two terms. Dichotomies, including male/female and subject/object, exclude way too much in order to marshal in what Nietzsche calls that "mighty effect" of totality. What gets excluded continues to stir, to dance between/beyond the poles, and to show up sporadically, demanding to be heard. The binary system itself can't finally dispose of those whose very existence would explode it, can't eternally repress those exiles who would continue to return.

Butler's work in gender theory attempts to make those poles waver, to forefront the excess that is silenced by the dichotomous structure. She problematizes the masculine/feminine binary, noting that "drag queens," for instance, mock the notion of a true gender identity; their performances cannot but point up the "radical contingency" between sex and gender (*Gender Trouble*). The drag queen offers a kind of parody of femininity; but it is more complicated than that. In the performance of this "femininity," the supposed "masculine" core is also called into question. The drag queen actually performs a *pastiche* rather than a parody, becoming a copy of a copy, without an original.[31] The drag ball queen overperforms femininity and, as Butler says, "out-woman[s] women" as s/he rearticulates the terms of that subject position (*Bodies That Matter* 132).

Paris Is Burning's drag queen, Venus Xtravanganza, for instance, takes femininity into what Baudrillard would call the "hyperreal" and, simply by being who s/he is, forces the signifiers "woman" and "feminine" to signify in excess of their intended referents. Gender turns out to be something we *do*, something we perform, rather than an essential quality attached to biology. Butler says it's a "repeated stylization of the body" (*Gender Trouble* 33) that gives the appearance of "sub/stance"— but she agrees with Nietzsche that "there is no being behind [this] doing" (*Genealogy of Morals* 45). Victor Vitanza celebrates Butler's work in gender theory for "moving beyond a molar/capitalistic male and female" and for calling attention to the fact that both gender and sex operate as "simulation/simulacrum without reference or circumference, that is, without 'reality' or genus" ("Threes" 210–11).

Anne Fausto-Sterling's empirical studies also charge for that disjunctive bar between "male" and "female," this time kicking it loose by engaging subjugated sexualities, specifically those individuals she refers to as "intersexuals": those who literally embody *both* sexes and, therefore, challenge "traditional beliefs about sexual difference" by displaying "the irritating ability to live sometimes as one sex and sometimes the other" (24, my emphasis). An estimated four percent of the population, Fausto-Sterling says, inhabits a sexual space that cannot be reduced to an either/or choice (21). "Hermaphrodites have unruly bodies," she notes. "They do not fall naturally into a binary classification, and only a surgical shoehorn can put them there" (24). Hermaphrodites, "merms," and "ferms" are aberrations by logocentric standards, and some variation of hormone therapy and/or surgical intervention is almost always called upon to "cure" these sexes between the sexes, to make them "normal," to hold that bar in place by getting rid of or appropriating those whose very existence would cause it to *waver*.

The assumption that there are only two sexes and that anything beyond/between those two poles is an "accident of birth" (23), a mis-creation, a "deformity," is what Fausto-Sterling questions. She notes that by the time Christopher J. Dewhurst and Ronald R. Gordon's *The Intersexual Disorders* was published in 1969, "medical and surgical approaches to intersexuality" had adopted a "rigid conformity" (23). The plan was to stop these dreaded "accidents of birth" before the *victims* or the victims' families suffered beyond what they could bear. In fact, the very notion that such "deformities" existed prompted what Fausto-Sterling calls a "near-hysterical tone" in that book and others like it that followed (23).

Here's the point: What's at stake in the drive to *cure* "intersexuals" is the very notion of stable sexuality, the terrifying reassertion of that sexual excess that phallogocentrism MUST silence to reproduce itself. The intersexual in a phallogocentric economy operates like a pun at the edge of truth's closure, the appearance of which suddenly punctuates the *entire enterprise* with a question mark. The value of truth is compromised when it's discovered to be directly related to—or even the offspring of—a shameless rec-reational linguistics. The play of the pun, which is a burst of discursive laughter, infects even the most scientific "truths" with what Foucault called "the disease of proliferation" ("Language" 65). And the intersexual's capacity to inhabit both sides of the supposed dichotomy exposes phallogocentric order to the same disease. If sex is not clear-cut in *some* cases, doubt begins to haunt *every* case. The intersexual, like the pun, interferes with meaning-making's determination to wrap things up. If the pun exposes the loose ends of language, the intersexual exposes the loose ends of sexuality. So much for stable identity ● ● ●

But what would happen if we admitted that it is our own (phallogo-centric) "standards," rather than the people they classify, that ought to be revised and re-visioned? If we admitted that it's not even as simple as expanding our rigid categories to five: males, females, *merms, ferms,* and *herms*? Fausto-Sterling, after all, is not suggesting that there are five sexes; she is suggesting that she has counted five and is *still* counting. "The varieties are so diverse," she says, "that it is possible to know which parts

[W]hy should we care if a "woman," defined as one who has breasts, a vagina, a uterus and ovaries and who menstruates, also has a clitoris large enough to penetrate the vagina of another woman? Why should we care if there are people whose biological equipment enables them to have sex "naturally" with both men and women? The answers seem to lie in a cultural need to maintain clear distinctions between the sexes. *Society mandates the control of intersexual bodies because they blur and bridge the great divide.*

—Fausto-Sterling, "The Five Sexes"

are present and what is attached to what only after exploratory surgery" (22). If sex (and so gender) were viewed as a multiplicity of spaces along a line of continuum rather than a simple opposition, it could proliferate indefinitely, there could be as many sexes as there are individuals (Fausto-Sterling; Butler, *Gender Trouble*, 18; Deleuze and Guattari, *A Thousand Plateaus* 18). Sex and gender, like race, could then be seen to be political rather than biological categories.

It is naive, however, to believe that we can simply start to "celebrate our differences." If we can pin them down, we will hierarchicalize them: we have proven our will to hierarchy. This is why Deleuze and Guattari say it is time to "*make* the multiple"[32] (*A Thousand Plateaus* 6), to learn to "see" pluralistically rather than binaristically. It seems necessary that we begin to affirm the uncontrollable multiplicity and continuous multiplying of our differences so that it will no longer be possible to reduce them to a few (exclusionary) categories. There can be no stable "identity politics" if identity is a state of perpetual becoming. A politics based on the identity-term "women" will only trap those it is supposed to re/present within a reactive cycle without futurity.

OF HYMENS AND HESITATIONS— EVOKING "WOMAN" OTHER/WISE

The "laughing man" would be forever frozen in his grimace, whose range runs from the comic to the ironic and sardonic. But a woman would be the presence of a burst of laughter, the presence of laughter in peals.

—Jean-Luc Nancy, *The Birth to Presence*

We are after a "feminist politics" that will have broken out of that cycle, a politics turned away from the *fight* and toward what is yet unthinkable. A rigorous hesitation is in order—a slamming to a screeeeeeching halt of all the psychical, emotional, and physical motors driving this fight. A hesitation that, as Ronell suggests, "own[s] up to the fact that no decision is strictly possible without the experience of the *undecidable*. To the extent that one may no longer be simply guided—by Truth, by light or *logos*—decisions have to be made" (*Crack Wars* 58, my emphasis). And it's time, this chapter suggests, to *decide* to leave unanswered one of the questions that drives a good bit of feminist politics: How can we get "women" the right to full re/presentation and equal subjecthood? This problem cannot/ought not be *solved*; it is, rather, necessary to let it *dis/*solve. A more appropriate question for the new millennium may be

How can we evoke an ethical sensibility that will have been *beyond* "the" sexual difference? It is in that non-reactionary evocation that we might open a space that could be called "truly" feminist because it will no longer have been inscribed within phallogocentric thought. This evocation would activate the sites of *ex*scription— "the feminine," differance—which have never had a place within the phallocracy. Given that every conceivable *ground* for what we have known as feminism and feminist politics has been problematized, it may be time to regroup (or, really, to un/group): a new ethics may need to precede the demand for any reinscription of "politics." It may be, in other words, that the condition of possibility for a "truly feminist" politics will have been a radical ethics of self-overcoming.

With Cixous and Ronell, we're suggesting that a "re-valuation" of *ethics* is in order—an *affirmative forgetting* of the inherited value structure that has been "burned in" to our memories by techniques of punishment inherent in our social coding (Nietzsche calls these techniques the "*mnemotechnics*" of pain).[33] Significantly, Ronell looks to Nietzsche for inspiration in this *feminist/"feminine"* endeavor. She reminds us of Nietzsche's question: "How do we overcome our nausea about 'man'?" And she notes that his answer was to vomit "him" up[34]—to affirmatively forget him. Here's Ronell:

> For Nietzsche, vomiting represented a *reversal* of assimilation by the digestive system. . . . [I]t was: "No, I won't assimilate this; I'm going to reject this. I want to puke out all the poison I've been fed by philosophy, by history, by patriarchy." This is why Nietzsche tried to invent what is falsely translated as "Superman": the "Übermensch" is not necessarily a man—it's *trans-human.* And I submit that the gender

is *not clear*. . . . When Nietzsche was puking out Woman, he was puking out *Woman as invented by Man* (weakened therefore, and ravaged by resentment), and pinning his hopes on a *trans-human* that would have overcome misogynist inscriptions of woman. ("Interview" 151)

What Ronell recognizes here is something that many feminists have not recognized: that Nietzsche's attacks on women, and there are some harsh ones, are roughly equivalent to his attacks on men. If Nietzsche was guilty of misogyny, he was also guilty of misandry. He was not nearly so interested in the war between the sexes as he was in inviting the trans-human condition, the bridge to the future. And if he had a special distaste for the "feminists" of his day, women voicing "with medical explicitness what woman *wants* from man, first and last" (*Beyond Good* 163), it was because he recognized that they were moving in a pointless direction. They were not moving toward the *Übermensch* but only toward the "man" who already made him nauseous. What Nietzsche was after was a third (fluid) position, beyond good and evil, beyond male and female, beyond logocentric thought altogether.

Here, I'd like to follow the advice of Sarah Kofman and not "hasten to 'decide' whether or not to declare Nietzsche a misogynist" (in Jardine 199). Along with Gayatri Spivak, I'd like to "negotiate" with Nietzsche's texts and take "the risk of saying 'yes,'" for the moment, to his concept-metaphor "woman" ("Feminism" 112). For, this catachrestic, third position is fluid, *hymeneal*: it's a space of productive indecision, a *"feminine"* space. I'd like to examine his use of this catachresis, "Woman," across the context of his understanding of "truth," both of which are veiled by the quotation mark,[35] in an attempt to detach "woman" from women and to perceive Nietzsche other/wise, to hear him with an/other ear, an ear open to the *unhearable*. It is from here, in this evocation of "woman" Other/Wise, that we might find ourselves tossed into what Heidegger calls "the Open" and experience a nonreactionary "trembling on the edge of Being."[36]

Background—Nietzsche on Appearances

Nietzsche calls our attention to something that Occidental society has been reluctant to acknowledge: that "there is no 'reality' for us . . . what things are called is incomparably more important than what they are"

(*Gay Science* 121). He argues that it is no longer acceptable to "believe that truth remains true when the veils are withdrawn . . . today [it should be considered] a matter of decency not to wish to see everything naked" (38). He praises the Greeks for knowing how to "stop courageously at the surface, . . . to adore . . . the whole Olympus of appearance." "Those Greeks," he says, "were superficial out of profundity" (38). In a move that prefigures Jean Baudrillard's critique of depth theories and Judith Butler's notion of gender performances, Nietzsche attacks those tragedians who insist that "there is something behind life, beneath it" (74). The irony of Nietzsche's "eternal comedy of existence" is that, in fact, "there is no such substratum; there is no 'being' behind doing" (*Genealogy* 45). We have only surfaces, appearances, veils, and their simulation of truth. "Appearance," for Nietzsche, is "not the opposite of some essence: what could I say," he asks, "about any essence except to name the attributes of its appearance!" And yet appearance must "go so far in its self-mockery" that it propagates its common denotation as a "dance of spirits and nothing more" (*Gay Science* 116). "Knowers" are artists adept at manipulating appearances and capable, like the Greeks, of "stopping courageously at the surface," recognizing without remorse that, as Baudrillard says, "there is no God behind the images, and [that] the very nothingness they conceal must remain a secret" (*Seduction* 94). "Truth" is appearance, surface.

> [T]he blushing movement of that truth which is not suspended in quotation marks casts a modest veil over such a surface. And only through such a veil which thus falls over it could "truth" become truth, profound, indecent, desirable. But should that veil be suspended, or even fall a bit differently, there would no longer be any truth, only "truth"—written in quotation marks.
>
> —Derrida, *Spurs*

"Woman" as the Non-Truth of Truth

In his prefaces to *The Gay Science* and *Beyond Good and Evil,* Nietzsche proposes that truth is a woman. He has "woman," that is, stand in as the *non-truth* of truth, the "truth" modestly veiled by the quotation mark. "Truth" is a woman who has not been won, laid bare, by the "gruesome seriousness" of dogmatic philosophers. She has eluded their grasp. "What is certain," Nietzsche says, "is that she has not allowed herself to be won—today every kind of dogmatism is left standing despirited and discouraged. *If* it is left standing at all!" (*Beyond Good* 1). "Truth"/"Woman" will not, cannot, be pinned down by truth. Derrida makes the point more pointed(ly): "That which will not be pinned down by truth is, in truth—*feminine.*" But Derrida immediately offers a caution, one that is crucial to our efforts here:

> This should not, however, be hastily mistaken for a woman's femininity, for female sexuality, or for any other of those essentializing fetishes which might still tantalize the dogmatic philosopher, the impotent artist or the inexperienced seducer who has not yet escaped his foolish hopes of capture. (*Spurs* 55)

"Woman," the *feminine*, in this context, is not a reductive conception of the diversity of women; it is a catachresis that inhabits a linguistic space analogous to the one inhabited by Donna Haraway's cyborg: they are both "post-gendered" and "committed to partiality, irony, intimacy, and perversity" ("Manifesto" 191, 192). Both perform the non-truth of truth. For, it is necessary to remember, as both Spivak and Derrida have, that Nietzsche understood, before many feminists, that there is, historically, no *one* woman. "There is no such thing [in Nietzsche's texts]," Derrida says, "as *the* truth of woman" (*Spurs* 51, my emphasis). It is, therefore, as Spivak notes, "a certain *kind* of woman" that is "a model for the 'no truth.' Woman is thus [only] 'one name for that non-truth of truth'" ("Feminism and Deconstruction" 112).[37] (Differance and *écriture*, for instance, are others.) This is not the feminine as opposed to the masculine but something else altogether. Baudrillard, after Nietzsche, and after Derrida's reading of Nietzsche (in *Spurs*), calls femininity the "principle of uncertainty," "pure appearance denuded of meaning" (*Seduction* 94). The feminine is "not the pole opposed to masculinity, but what abolishes the differential opposition" (12). "It is not," he says, "that the feminine as surface is opposed to the masculine as depth, but the feminine as indistinctness of surface and depth." "In the feminine, the very distinction between authenticity and artifice is without foundation" (10–11). This is not woman-as-man's-Other; this "woman" is a "reversible space" that can cause "the sexual poles to waver" (12). And Baudrillard says that this "woman," as reversibility, "prevails secretly over the dominant form" (17).

Echoing Nietzsche, Baudrillard cautions feminists against "erecting a feminine depth" (10), against creating a "female phallocracy" (12), against legitimating the "phallic fable reversed" (16).[38] For Nietzsche, as for Baudrillard, it is in women's fight for equal rights that "*woman is retrogressing*" (*Beyond Good* 168). "Woman," for Nietzsche and Baudrillard, is a third position, beyond male and female, which operates as a rigorous hesitation, a postgendered reversible space. There is no way to effect communication between "woman" as the pause of indecision, who prevails by seductive indistinction, and literal women engaged in a *fight* for equal power. What is on the line here is "woman's" capacity to seduce and "refer man, the lord and master of sexual *reality*, to his transparency as an *imaginary* subject" (Baudrillard, *Seduction* 15). "One sees," Baudrillard says, "how ridiculous it is to want to 'liberate' the one in order that it accede to the fragility of the other's 'power'" (16).

For Baudrillard, "there is no need to lament the wrongs suffered, to want to rectify them. No need to play the lover of justice for the weaker sex . . . the game was played with a full deck . . . [a]nd men did not win, not at all" (19). Neither, of course, did women—though, according to Baudrillard, women had a better opportunity all along to win than men did. Now, however, "it is women who are about to lose," he says, and "precisely under the sign of sexual pleasure." The feminist drive to gain equality, sexual and otherwise, to become-man, is a drive in an unfortunate direction. For, while literal women have engaged themselves in a "battle of the sexes," on terms already set by the phallocracy, Baudrillard says, "woman," the "feminine," the postgendered and reversible nontruth of truth has been *winning* because she remains *exscribed from the battle*. To become-man or more fully to become woman-as-man's-other is to become a loser *again*. The call here is to become-"woman."

Truth as Woman as Baubô— Spinning Out the Übermensch

Nietzsche has "woman" stand in for "truth," suggesting that her name might be Baubô, that "primitive and obscene female demon,"[39] that goddess of unveiling *par excellence*. Baubô, then, stands in as Nietzsche's concept-metaphor "woman," which is standing in for his concept-metaphor "truth," as the dance of appearance and self-mockery Nietzsche applauds. Baubô, "gleefully anticipating her laughter, her mockery of man" (Derrida, *Spurs* 61), parodies philosophy's dream of dis/covery, its attempt to "lay bare" *the* truth. Indeed, what Baubô un/covers *is* "truth," what

Nietzsche calls "truth": a simulation, an appearance, an unsettling pause in the spinning of the veils. When Baubô *flashes* Demeter, she reveals "truth" (still covered) rather than *Aletheia* (final Truth *unveiled*). She reveals that "nudity," as Baudrillard suggests, "will never abolish seduction" (*Seduction* 43), and that "woman," the artist, as Nietzsche says, always "puts on something" even when she "take[s] off everything" (*Gay Science* 317). What Baubô reveals is *concealment* in an/other form. There is no/thing behind the veil; the veils are everything.

Baubô's parody of dis/covery is arresting in the way a drag queen's parody of gender is: both mock the supposed *original truth* in a way that destabilizes it, that denaturalizes it. Baubô and the drag queen perform a *pastiche* or a *simulation* (a copy of a copy) rather than a parody (a copy of an original). Butler says that in the performance of the drag queen, the original itself "is revealed to be a copy, and an inevitably failed one, an ideal that no one *can* embody" (*Gender Trouble* 139). And if Baubô gets roaring laughter from Demeter for her own performance, it is because she, too, exposes the non-truth of truth, the non-originality of the original, the hyper-reality of reality. It is in this way that "truth is like a woman." "Truth," Derrida says, "resembles the veiled movement of feminine modesty" (*Spurs* 51). The stripping of the veils—the strip*tease* toward final truth *can never be more than a tease*.

Operating as simulacrum, "woman" (the untruth of truth) is a "swirl of veils" (Jardine 194), a superficiality unconcerned with what Nietzsche calls the will-to-truth. She is a floating signifier: for her, as for truth, there is no adequate literal referent. For if "woman" is "truth," Derrida says, "she at least knows that there is no truth. . . . And she is woman precisely because she does not believe in what she is, in what she is believed to be, in what she thus is not" (*Spurs* 53). Willing appearance, willing artifice, willing chance, she easily seduces those seekers of the truth that she simulates. Operating as that *hymeneal* space between truth and the non-truth of truth, she dismantles the Truth/Dissimulation opposition, propagates the "continuation of the dream" (Nietzsche, *Gay Science* 116), and affirms a game of seduction that depends upon that dream.

[Excursus: "Putting the Name of Woman On."

So, for Nietzsche, there are man and woman, both of whom make him nauseous, and then there is "woman"; there are masculinity and femininity, both of which are "essentializing fetishes," and then there is the "feminine." The third position in each case "names" that reversible, unwinnable space from which the pause of indecision—*productive* indecision—is experienced. Though some feminists have protested the naming of this space "woman," others have used the name to stretch its signification, to make it "steal" and "fly" (Cixous, "Laugh" 887).[40] The latter seems necessary at this point. It engages what Butler calls a "complex reconfiguration and redeployment" of terms that is analogous to "taking up the tools where they lie, where the very 'taking up' is enabled by the tool lying there" (*Gender Trouble* 145). To leave *these* terms/tools, "woman" and "feminine," *where they lie*, silent and silenced, would seem a gross oversight. A resignification/reappropriation of these terms invites a negative and an affirmative deconstruction at once. It is not a call to leap from one side of the unproblematized binary to the Other but to problematize the traditional setup *as we leap*, so that where we land is in an/other (fluid) space entirely. Butler's problematizing of the heterosexual/homosexual dichotomy, for instance, makes it possible for her to re/claim the identity-term "queer," to stretch its signification potential and, in that way, finally allow this silenced and abject term/tool to have its say and make a new way, to speak the previously unspeakable.

Cixous offers another precedent for this approach. Following Derrida, she *steals* idioms from theoretical discourse and reinscribes them so as to make them *fly* out of the logocentric structure—in fact, she steals them *from* Derrida. He thieves the term *écriture* from the theoretical lexicon and makes it fly in the face of the structure that that lexicon supports. And Cixous, very much in the Derridean countertradition of the trickster, *steals* the Derridean notion of "*écriture*" ("writing-as-feminine-locus") and turns it into "*écriture féminine*." This engages a subtle distinction: "the feminine," though a postgendered space, remains, for Cixous, a space that females have an easier access to than males, precisely because of their gender coding.[41] Feminine writing, unlike "writing-as-feminine-locus," *begins* with an examination of the place of *women* in Western theoretical discourse, with an *examination* of the discursive practices that make them the Other.

The aim is not, however, to facilitate a fuller appropriation of a female subject position; Cixous is never interested (any more than Derrida) in simply flipping the binary privilege and so remaining encased in a phallogocentric structure. She is interested in continuously bringing to light the violent nature of subjectivity itself. Both Derrida's *écriture* and Cixous's *écriture féminine*, effect a reinscription of phallogocentric language by "taking up" the term/tool "feminine" and infusing it with an/other signification: the "feminine" is no longer simply the opposite of the "masculine" but a space of free-flowing elements, which simply cannot be codified and confined within the traditional setup. There is for Cixous, as for Derrida, a crucial distinction to be made between literal women fighting for equal power (a re/validation of the traditional setup, a refusal to *have done* with phallogocentric orderings) and "woman" as catachresis, that space of productive indecision, a space of *unworking (dés-oeuvrement)*,[42] into which both women and men are called. The former seeks a thoroughly modern subjecthood (a dubious *objet petit autre*); the latter is a *post*modern and affirmative space, outside the system of dichotomies, a space that denegates logocentrism's negations and opens up an/other sensibility, an/other "world." *This* is where we want to Be(come).]

• • •

OF "WOMAN" AND POLITICS—
COMMUNITY OF AN/OTHER KIND

[T]opos, is determined by the negative (i.e., species, genus, differentiae). . . . *E/utopos* is not finally different from topos; . . . *Atopos* is boundless, it is undetermined or overdetermined. It either finds itself . . . denegating the negative for a starting place of total excess; or better, it finds itself as without any lack whatsoever, as therefore affirmation or excess.

   —Vitanza, *Negation, Subjectivity, and the History of Rhetoric*

A.

Was I ill? Have I got well? Who was my doctor? Can you tell? Oh, my memory is rotten!

B.

Only now you're truly well. Those are well who have forgotten.

   —Nietzsche, "Dialogue"

"The gravest and most painful testimony of the modern world," says Jean-Luc Nancy in the opening pages of *The Inoperative Community*, "is the testimony of the dissolution, the dislocation, or the conflagration of community" (1). The deaths of God (transcendence) and Man (immanence) have abandoned us to our own isolation and left us no way to commune the Other. And no "politics," no political program will have been capable of giving communion or community back to us. A politics of "activism," of Grand Marching, is a humanist politics, one that puts its money on immanent individuals who become acting-subjects capable of "fighting the good fight"; but there is no community in subjecthood, or among subjecthoods. Community reveals itself in the pause of inde-cision, in the instant that one gives oneself over to a between-space, the between of the *you* and the *I*—not in the *solid*ification of identity but in the *fluid*ification of it. Community exposes itself in the *un*working of established linkages and chasms, in that active back-spin where finite Being co-appears (Nancy says "compears [*com-paraît*]"). Community does not take place in political activism; it is not in the common struggle among "individuals" or subjects that what Nancy calls "being-in-com-mon" is exposed. And yet, community, this being-in-common, is pre-cisely what revolutionary politics aims to produce and to protect.

Inasmuch as our notions of community are typically guided by an arrogant humanism, which assumes that we might *make* community happen, *produce* it, and/or *build* it,[43] we assume that we might found and fund a political program to facilitate those ends. And, proceeding from here, what gets founded and funded is a "community" *built* by the union of preexisting and self-determining subjects consenting to enter into a "social contract." Or, in a slightly different setup, it is a "community" that operates on an ideal of mutual indebtedness, a *body* politic that, as Georges Van Den Abbeele, in his introduction to *Community at Loose Ends* suggests, "thinks the communal only at the risk of positing the state as subject" (xi). The continuation of the humanist (and so phallocratic) nightmare is propagated by both of these notions of community, the first of which "strategically forgets the differences between subjects" and the second of which invites a "concomitant reduction of social differences" to the point of "fascism" (xi). Inclusion within these so-called communi-ties operates as an effect of exclusion: the apparent cohesion among their members is the result of a negation of difference/differance. Humanist notions of community are constituted through the production of an ab-ject realm, a domain of excluded sensibilities and excluded Others, both of which would threaten the closure of the "community's" circle. What we're suggesting here is that there is no *community* in these "communities."

E/utopian notions of a "feminist community," a communion of pre-existing "women" (whether *born* or *made*) bound together in a common struggle against the status quo, ought not be exempt from this critique. There is a familiar essentialism in this communal longing, an essentialism that covertly bolsters the humanist, self-determining subject all over again.[44] This notion of community works out of the negative, stabilizing and celebrating one group and one inflection of Being at the expense/negation of all others. But in a posthumanist era, any sense of community linked either to human immanence or communal transcendence is problematic. If all our communal models (Christianity, Communism, "the family," etc.) have failed miserably, it is because these models are founded on identity poly-ticks of one flavor or another (being-Christian, being-Communist, being-Mother or Father or son or daughter); it has been due, as Giorgio Agamben irreverently and insightfully notes, to an unproblematized faith in "set theory" (9).

[handwritten margin note: scripted space]

And it has been due to our inability to find a line of flight from our own humanist appropriations: that community is happening does not necessarily suggest that "we" have *made* it happen, that we could ever make it happen. In the face of the posthumanist paradox, it is not enough to simply relocate our humanist hopes from the individual to the communal, from the subject to "the social." A feminism that cannot think the posthumanist thought will not have found a way out of a phallocratic notion of community nor will it have engaged a *liberatory politics*. A radical rethinking of what is called "community" is in order here, a radical rethinking of human-Being and its modes of being-with-one-another in the world. Our question is this: What can "community" be *after* the "death of Wo/Man"? If there is no self-identified subjectivity, no reducible Self that can simply Be-authentically, what can it mean to Be-with-one-another?

The Question Concerning Consensus/Dissensus

As it has become more and more impossible, both theoretically and practically, to ground a politics on the moral imperative of the rational subject, to mobilize forces on the basis of individual identity, a fundamental shift in grounding has occurred, from *physis* to *nomos*, from philosophy to rhetoric: "truth" is often determined and "justice" is often

carried through in the name of *collective consent*. If the "self-identical subject" is a farce and, therefore, the validity of identity politics is on its way
out the window with Man and God, coalitional politics has become a
postidentity substitute. Coalitional groups, ideally, do not demand identity papers before extending membership and do not base the experience
of community they offer on a notion of preexisting identities.[45] Instead,
they base it on a unified aim. It is hoped that community will be experienced as a result of working together for a common goal, that "together-
ness" will be prompted by participation in a grand project. But locking
arms together in any Grand March will not have produced community;
what it will have produced is a certain
kind of
terror[ism].

The nature of this terror[ism] is unconcealed in a reading of consensus across Lyotard's explanations of the differend in his book by the
same name. Here's Lyotard's definition of that term:

> As distinguished from the litigation, a differend [*différend*] would be
> a case of conflict, between (at least) two parties, that cannot be
> equitably resolved for lack of a rule of judgment applicable to both
> arguments. One side's legitimacy does not imply the other's lack of
> legitimacy. However, applying a single rule of judgment to both in
> order to settle their differend as though it were merely a litigation
> would wrong (at least) one of them (and both of them if neither side
> admits this rule). . . . A wrong results from the fact that the rules of the
> genre of discourse by which one judges are not those of the judged
> genre or genres of discourse. (*Differend* xi)

Abbeele offers a definition in slightly different terms: "The differend is
a disagreement so structured that its resolution in the idiom of one of the
two parties (or even the idiom of some third party) necessarily wrongs the
other party" (xviii). It is the differend that gets silenced in any push for
consensus; what's at stake in a differend is an unthinkable sensibility,
which is kept unthinkable by the act of litigation. Consensus, Lyotard
says, always leaves a "residue beyond its control" ("A l'insu" 47), and that
residue is what we're trying to remember here today. This is what's on
the line in consensus-based politics: the unpresentable, those sensibilities

that have not (yet) come into discourse, that do not (yet) have idioms of expression.

Consensus, as Lyotard says, does "violence to the heterogeneity of language games" (*Postmodern* xxv); it cancels out difference in the name of the One, exposing a nostalgia for Oneness, for the Proper, for the very phallic standard from which feminists would do well to exscribe themselves. After all, erecting the "big solution," even if *together*, still valorizes the Big Erection. And the creation of any "collective" or totality produces not one but two: Self and Other, included and excluded. Consensus is attained, as Michel Serres points out, by supposing a third position and seeking to exclude it. "Dialectic makes the two interlocutors play on the same side; they do battle together [against the third position] to produce a truth on which they can agree" (67). And their agreement is the result of their standing together, on "common ground," and recognizing that what does not stand with them stands against them.

The loser in any consensus-based politics is that which cannot be co-opted by the collective, cannot be appropriated, *made* legitimate, *made* Proper. And it is against this loser that the winners claim victory, gain "liberation," and achieve consolidation. "Consensus, commensurability, communication," Lynn Worsham notes, "are old dreams of . . . the philosopher and the phallocrat. They are motivated by one desire: the desire for the same mind, the same meaning, the same standard, and the same language. They promise enlightenment, emancipation, and empowerment" ("Writing Against Writing" 99). What they deliver, however, is the legitimation of exclusion. What gets excluded in the production of any collective agency is that which is *not* shaped on the pattern of the Phallus. It is that which has been declared insoluble, inappropriate, un-True, that which has no proper name, no propriety, no property: again, it is "the feminine"; not women, who have been "transformed by phallocracy," but "woman," who "lacks" the Proper (equipment).[46] This is why Lyotard says that it is not consensus but "dissension that must be emphasized" (*Postmodern* 61).

Lyotard calls for an experience of community that does not necessitate the silencing of the differend, for a collective commitment to invent new idioms through which the differend might be phrased. Against consensus, Lyotard, echoing Cixous, asks that we strain to hear the as of yet unspeakable, that we "listen," Abbeele says, "to what as yet remains inaudible beneath the sound and the fury of official politics" (xix). That we cannot/do not hear it does not necessarily suggest that it is not *happening*; it may only suggest that our ears are too finely tuned to that which is accountable. It will have been necessary to sprout an/other (third) ear to tune into the rustling of the unaccountable.

Finitude's Infinity—
The Loose Ends of Community

In his essay in *Community at Loose Ends*, "A l'insu (Unbeknownst)," Lyotard speaks pointedly about the relationship between the unspeakable (the "unbeknownst") and the *polis*. Suggesting that all politics is a "politics of [unproblematic] forgetting," Lyotard notes that what gets forgotten is "that the community remains intractable (intraitable) to the treatment of political unity" (43). Here's Lyotard:

> What cannot be treated, what is not manageable [traitable] once and for all, and what is forgotten by political treatment in its constitution of a "commonality" of humans by dint of their belonging to the same polis, is the very thing that is not shareable among them, what is not communicable or communal or common at all. Call it birth and/or death, or even singularity. (43)

What gets forgotten, because it must be forgotten for the state to hold together across humanist notions of consensus-as-community, is our "finitude," what Jean-Luc Nancy calls the "being-in-common" (which is not at all the same thing as a common-Being) among "singularities." What must be forgotten in the *production* of any "community" is the finitude that locates *that* sense of community as always already *out* of our reach.

To follow Nancy and Lyotard here, it will be necessary to re/think the simple opposition typically accepted between infinity and finitude. Humanism goes meta-physical to avoid the fluidity of the finite; it theorizes ^{up} so that finitude can be made presentable, accountable, logical. By subjugating the finite to the infinite, humanism bets on the immanence of humankind, on a picture of finitude in which the loose ends are connected. But the relationship between infinity and finitude is much more complicated than a dichotomy would suggest. Indeed, infinity is *inherent in* finitude. Finitude is not about absolute limits or uncrossable boundaries; it doesn't signify the [ac]countable but rather the *Un*[ac]-countable. The finite has everything to do with unprecedented instances of being, instances that can't be theorized or categorized. Finitude is an *infinity of loose ends*, a fluidity that will not have been under our control. As such, it is all but totally covered over in Enlightenment dreams of liberation, which require that we zoom in and *take charge*.

Finitude is not about "teleological accomplishment," Ronell notes; it is about "a suspension, a hiatus in meaning, reopened each time in the here and now, disappearing as it opens, exposing itself to something so unexpected and possibly new that it persistently eludes its own grasp" (*Finitude's Score* 5). Finitude exposes itself in those moments of time that can't be measured out in a series of tick-tocks; it exposes itself in "dead zones, hollow times, times of futile effort, the empty interval and bad timing"; it exposes itself in "leisure time, the musical tempo, the meanwhile, the time you went out for a walk" (5). It exposes itself in the "hijacked" moments of the daydream, the laughing fit, and the *sneezure*. What's important here is "finitude's excessive nature," the infinite "inappropriability of its meaning . . . its refusal to disclose itself fully" (5–6). There never was any human immanence.[47] Our finite existence leaves us with (rhizomatic) *loose ends* sprouting out/up/down everywhere. Because infinity is inscribed within finitude, because finitude will always already be churning out an inappropriable overflow, self-mastery will be perpetually beyond our grasp. And this is a problem for any teleological impulse, any political endeavor requiring overall consensus and offering *promises* about redeeming the past sometime in the future. Nancy, following Georges Bataille, celebrates an/Other community, connected precisely through the copresentation of its finitude, which is what we have *in-common* but that is, nevertheless, *not* communicable as such. Being-in-common is exposed precisely in the play of differences, the experience of loose ends that cannot (and *ought not*) be tied together: it is exposed in the commonality of our *differences*, the commonality of our experience of Being as *différance*.

But any politics must necessarily and unproblematically forget the loose ends that define our finitude. And it is not helpful to instigate a counter*politics* that would attempt to approach what the politics of the status quo represses. In other words, it is not helpful to found a revolutionary *politics* that aims to expose the loose ends and make the community more faithful to them. Even a revolutionary fidelity to "the thing" (as Lyotard calls it, in psychoanalytic terms), to finitude, is also an infidelity or betrayal of it because any approach to it would necessarily need to domesticate and codify it so as to make it manageable, even thinkable—the mechanics of solids, *again*. Even revolutionary politics would necessarily theorize what is fluid and leaky into a form that might be accountable and appropriable. "Politics," Lyotard says, whether in the form of totalitarianism or revolution, "never ceases calling for union, for solidarity" ("A l'insu" 43) for *solidification*, and at the expense of that which has not and will not make its way into discourse. Politics as we know it infinitizes finitude, forcing it into transcendence or immanence; politics exists at the expense of the loose ends of finite being. In the name of politics, "one strives to become a realist, an activist, either stupidly or intelligently," Lyotard says. And by "intelligently," he means having a Machiavellian savvy that is "at least aware that politics cannot avoid betraying *the thing*. In any case," Lyotard reiterates, "realism requires amnesia" (45), unproblematically forgetting "the thing" that cannot be named or made accountable. Don't miss this: *Realism is NOT faithful to* (finite) *"reality."*

The question now, he says, is: "Are there other politics—other than revolutionary—that would make it possible not to be unfaithful to the thing [the intractable] that inhabits the polis unconsciously?" (46). Is there, in other words, a way to reinscribe politics as nonreactionary and nonphallocratic—as "feminine/feminist"? Politics as we know it is devoted to "the scene of representation from which the unpresentable presumably must be eliminated"; for a politics to protect the unpresentable (for it to be/come what we will call a "feminist" politics), it would, Lyotard decides, have to "risk *losing the polis*" (46, my emphasis). Put another way: the *"polis"* would have to experience itself as "inoperative" (Nancy, *Inoperative*), as "unavowable" (Blanchot), as broken up and *breaking up* (us); it would have to experience its *dissensus* as the *a priori* ground[lessness] of the community itself. It would have to recognize that its "subjects" will always already have been "possessed" by an "immemorial dependency" (Lyotard, "A l'insu" 46) on *finitude* and know that even human rights *resist* the finite: "you can't escape this aporia by adding [counter]memory to the list of human rights" (46).

Back to Ethics; Or, Politics Inverted—
Community as an Exposition of Singularity

This Other politics would have to affirm the posthumanist paradox, that humans-Being are always already indebted to their finitude and that finitude is *leak-leak-leakyyyy*. Human reason is no match for finite being. Neither is subjecthood. As Lyotard puts it, "The mind will have been dispossessed 'before' being able to certify or act as a subject" (46). Subjectivity is not the ground-zero upon which community is based; subjectivity is a *function* of this dispossession that "we" already share. To protect the unpresentable, our being-in-common, it would be necessary that a "politics" engage "a scrupulous fidelity to a state of *dependency* [Being-on-the-*thing*] more immanent to the mind than its state of mind" (47, my emphasis).

> Being, finally, is nothing other than this duty that calls you, possesses and debits you, guiltifies you from the moment that you are—you, the Unique, the Called.
> —Ronell, *Telephone Book*

The task at hand is to imagine a community that does not take the "subject" as its organizing principle, a community that is not comprised of "beings producing . . . their own essence as their work, and furthermore producing precisely this essence *as* community" (Nancy, *Inoperative* 2). The task is to re/cognize that "community" is "bound" neither by an abstract moral obligation nor by some common project; in fact, it may be time to consider that it isn't *bound* at all. Perhaps the communal relation is not the *result* of separate subjects pulling together; perhaps the communal relation is the "inaugural condition for the very subjectivities that claim to speak for it" (Abbeele xii). Such an intrinsic encroachment of singular beings on/in one another would indicate that sharing . . . *happens* . . . that it happens before any identity politicking, before any projected telos, before any scramble for control.[48]

We'll be interested in tracing the outline of this inaugural community, this nonhumanist community consisting of finite singularities who are infinitely divisible *yet sharing*. What we'll suggest is that "singular beings" *cannot not* share and that it is in this uncontainable sharing, this irrepressible communication, that an ethics of community announces itself.[49] But notice that the "singular being" is not the "subject." Even when the qualifier "postmodern" is attached to it, the notion of the "sub ject" continues to call up the possibility of immanence, of regrouping, of pulling itself together; that is, of conceiving of its Self as first of all out-side community. We will have inhabited subject positions—it is perhaps a necessity of Being. But subject-slots, no matter how determined they are, will not have led *toward* the community that always already is.

A singular being is more akin to what Martin Heidegger called Dasein (being-there) than to any notion of subjectivity. Whereas the subject resolves the question of the other within itself and not *with* the other, Dasein's *a priori* mode of existence is "being-there-with-others" in con-cernful solicitude. However, Dasein, for all its immersion in coexistence, doesn't finally break with a certain kind of (dangerous) humanist hope. Though perhaps no one had thought through "being-with-others" more thoroughly than Heidegger had in his lifetime, his fundamental ontology nevertheless wound up subordinating a relation with the Other to a rela-tion with Being. We will need to hone in on that element in Heidegger's work before we move into a consideration of what Jean-Luc Nancy calls "finite singularities"[50] and the kind of community that might (be) com-prise(d) (of) those singularities.

A disclaimer, though, before we begin. We won't be hoping to weave another ontology here—not unless we radically redefine "ontology" in terms of rhetoric. We won't be pretending to present the truth about truth but only to offer an/other rhetoric on Being, a rhetoric of *finitude* and of the finite community that would be associated with it. What we're looking for is simply a discourse on being-with-others that doesn't simultaneously demand the exclusion/execution of the Other.

Being-there

Dasein and the "They." To a certain degree, Heideggerian ontology adopts and refashions Freudian ego-psychology, turning the superego into a "voice of conscience." Here, we won't be interested in questioning the existence of this "voice." It's no surprise that Heidegger took it seri-ously—by the time he got to it, Freud had already established its connec-tion to all sorts of physical maladies, from constipation to hysterical blindness. So we'll be interested here only in what Heidegger makes of this "voice," in his interpretation of it. As Heidegger would have it, at criti-cal moments in my lostness in what he calls the "they," that is, in my small talk with others, a punitive voice will blast through my internal loud-speakers, issuing ethical demands to me. These demands are issued in the form of an appeal, a "call" (*Being and Time* 314), summoning "me" against "my" will from the "they-self" (or, inauthentic Being) back to *my* Self, which is authentic, what he calls my "ownmost potentiality-for-Being." Placing this call to me, ringing me up in my average-everyday-chatter, is my authentic Self itself, the me that is not lost in the "they." This call, then, comes in both from "me" and from beyond "me" (cf. 320).[51]

Heidegger explains the distinctions in *Being and Time*, and we'd do well to listen in very carefully:

> Dasein . . . can *listen* to Others. [In fact,] it fails to hear its own Self in listening [away] to the "they-self." . . . [but] this listening-away gets broken off by *the call* if that call, . . . arouses another kind of hearing, which, in relationship to the hearing that is lost, has a character in every way opposite. If in this lost hearing, one has been fascinated with the "hubbub" of the manifold ambiguity which idle talk possesses in its everyday "newness," then *the* call must do its calling without any hubbub and ambiguity. *That which, by calling in this manner, gives us to understand, is the call of conscience.* (315–16, my emphasis)

This passage ought to leave you shaking in your boots. What is going down here? This call claims to be *authentic, unified*—coming in as big thought, it announces itself as the absolute opposite of small talk. "Dispensing with any kind of utterance," this call "does not put itself into words"; yet, Heidegger assures us that "what the call discloses is unequivocal" (318). It is not a communication but a hail, a *summons* issued to me in my average-everyday Being-with-Others—my *they*self—to bring me "back" to authentic Selfhood. The awesome jurisdiction of the voice of conscience ought not be underestimated—it's clearly calling the shots, commanding my listening to Others to be "broken off" (315) so that I might listen all the more intently to my "Self."

Dasein, at the outset, Heidegger says, is *no one*; it is, rather, a neutral "They," from which it will have to extract itself before it will be able to accept responsibility for its life and its decisions.[52] To that end, Heidegger posits the call of conscience as that which summons Dasein forth and forward "to its ownmost-potentiality-for-Being-itself" (318). As for the fate of the "they" from which Dasein is summoned, Heidegger is clear: "the 'they' collapses" (317).

•
•
•

I'm merely trying to establish a backdrop for Heidegger's compromise with National Socialism. His ontology turns Being into a listening device—but one that values a certain frequency over all others. The very anticipation of a priority call prompts a hasty determination to answer the call of conscience without considering the possibility that it—like any other call—might be a prank, "performing and inducing fraud" (Ronell, *Telephone Book* 45). Indeed, *any* call that announces itself as *The* Call, as unambiguous and without "hubbub," deserves, as Nietzsche argued, all of our suspicion.

Heidegger, in his more-than-ten-year devotion to Nietzsche's texts, would have done well to take Nietzsche's advice on this one.[53] Though Dasein begins with-others, it also assumes that there is a more authentic relation to Being than being-with-others can offer and that the moment of authenticity is the instant of individuation marked by the COllapse of Others in Dasein's field of hearing. So no big surprise that the so-called voice of conscience got reread in Heideggerian phenomenology as the voice of authenticity itself, as the sign/al of sign/al/s. Despite Heidegger's insistence that being is always and only being-with, when it comes down to it, there's not much sense of *Mitsein* in Heidegger's descriptions of *authentic* Being; Christopher Fynsk, in fact, traces out what he calls Heidegger's "evasion of the question of the other" in *Being and Time* ("The Self and Its Witness" 185).

Beyond Dasein—Being-There-In-Common. And yet, the reconception of subjectivity as *Dasein* obviously broke through what had been some fairly impenetrable philosophical ground. There can be no doubt about it: Nancy owes a big one to Heidegger. Dasein's being-with is Nancy's starting point, his springboard. Nancy sticks close to Heidegger, rereading his work in much the way Lyotard rereads Kant's and Lacan rereads Freud's: generously. Perhaps, at times, *over*-generously, "doing" Heidegger more rigorously and more posthumanistically than Heidegger did himself. In *The Inoperative Community*, Nancy begins with and then pushes beyond Dasein, describing the "singular being" or the "singularity" (27) as a finite alternative both to the transcendent/immanent subject and even to Heidegger's not quite finite enough Dasein. Defining finitude as "the infinite lack of infinite identity" (xxxvii), Nancy notes that singular beings, because they are finite, are excessive, extended— never self-present, always overflowing, always exposed to an outside (29).

A finite community, composed of finite singularities, is not out to transcend the finite but to expose it, to expose, that is, what we do share: our unsharable loose ends. This community is not the product of subjects bound together by a common project; indeed, this community reveals itself precisely in the moment of "unwork" or what Nancy, after Maurice Blanchot, calls the "*dés-oeuvre.*" It exists as what is *in*-common *before* any projected *telos*. The members of a posthumanist community find their being-in-common across the exposition (exposing) of finitude: the sharing of an unsharable finitude, rather than an affinity of infinity or a communion of immanence, becomes the very condition for commonality in a posthumanist world. What we share, what we *cannot not* share, is finite Being, an uncontrollable and irrepressible finitude. Finitude is what— and *all*—we share. "[F]initude alone is communitarian" (Nancy, *Inoperative* 27).

In his essay "Of Being-in-Common," Nancy suggests that Heidegger's *Mitsein* (being-with) and *Mit-da-sein* (being-there-with) ought not be "added in a secondary and extrinsic way to being-oneself or being-in-solitude." To think being-with in this way, Nancy says, is not to think it "out as radically or as decisively as it should be" (2). The *mit* ought not be thought of as modifying the *sein* nor qualifying the *Dasein*. To think the *mit* in this way is to assume that "being could already sustain itself in some way, as if being *were itself*; that is, as if being *were* or *existed absolutely.*" The *mit*, Nancy says, is not a modifier but rather what "constitutes" the *Dasein* "essentially." The "with" is "itself a modality" *through which* being-there and being-the-there come into being. There is no Being that is not being-with. Here's Heidegger: "Not only is Being towards Others an autonomous, irreducible relationship of Being: this relationship, as Being-with, is one which, with Dasein's Being, already is" (*Being and Time* 162). This is Heidegger at his best.

By using the term "being-in-common," Nancy is trying "to indicate, at its limit, an experience—not perhaps, an experience that we have, *but an experience that makes us be*" (*Inoperative* 26, his emphasis). Nancy is very much with Heidegger when he says that the "there" of *Dasein's* "being-there" is "not the grounding for existence, but rather its taking *place*, its arrival, its coming—which also means its difference, its withdrawal, its excess, its 'exscription'" (2, my emphasis). (We could not be further from community-as-consensus here.) A finite community, composed of finite beings, cannot offer a higher level of Being than the finitude of any one singularity—a finite community doesn't offer a transcendence of the finite; it offers a sharing-out of it.

"Sharing," Nancy says, "comes down to this: what community reveals to me, in presenting to me my birth and my death, is my existence outside myself" (26). Sharing is the exposition of finite being, the exposure of an in-common (but unsharable) mortality and singularity that are not communicable but that are irrepressibly exposed/shared. In the face of this "originary" sharing, the illusion of interior existence is shattered. This is key: Finitude is what singular beings share prior to what Heidegger calls "the voice of conscience" and prior to any "prelinguistic interpretation."[54] This is an inaugural connection; it is what makes Being possible, and it means that the Other has always already closed in on you: no extraction will be possible. Whereas Heidegger's main concern is the individuation sparked by the call of conscience as it bursts through and knocks down the "they," Nancy's main concern is the fact that what divides "us" is precisely what "we" share: finitude, the "infinite lack of an infinite identity." Nancy traces the call of finitude straight to the Other-*that-shares*-Me, and his push beyond Heidegger is, in fact, a more rigorous carrying through of what Heidegger had begun but let go of much too quickly.[55]

Unlike Dasein, the singular being does not emerge against the backdrop of an undifferentiated "theyself." In fact, the "singular being *appears*, as finitude itself" in the instant of contact with "the skin (or the heart) of another singular being" (Nancy, *Inoperative* 28). The being of any singularity *comes into being* in its coappearance with other singularities (58). It is the call of finitude (being-in-common) that interrupts the singular being's illusion of interiority, the illusion of the possibility for extraction. In the call of finitude, it is not that the "they" collapses but that the fantasy/myth of common-being is exposed as such. What exposes itself in the withdrawal of the myth of communion, is *community itself*, being-in-common. Indeed, contra Heidegger, Nancy argues that community is what the singular being is called toward; a certain kind of community is the future for finite singularities (71). (This twist takes Nancy's posthumanism light years beyond Heidegger's.)

It's necessary to stress that though finitude is not communicable, it never stops *communicating*. In fact, finitude "*exists* as communication" (28). Because Being is always already being-in-common, "finitude co-appears or compears (*com-paraît*) and can only *compear*": "finite being always presents itself 'together'" (28). Finitude from the start implies community. What presents itself as a roadblock to this community that always already *is* turns out to be precisely what we set up, politically, to establish or protect it; for, it is precisely in our intended establishment and/or protection of "community" that we are bound to *forget* it, in the name of feminism, Marxism, Communism, Christianity, and/or any *unified* coalition.

The "essence" of community/communication in a posthumanist world is the exposition of finitude and *not a bond*, which is always already *bondage*, always already at work silencing the differance of our finitude—the very thing that makes community possible. The compearance of finitude exposes itself in a "formula," which Nancy asks us to learn to read in all possible ways: "'you (are/and/is) (entirely other than) I' (*'toi [e(s)t] [tout autre que] moi'*). Or, again, more simply: *you shares me* ('*toi partage moi*')" (29, my emphasis). The master/slave dialectic is not simply negated here; it is exploded in a nonpositive affirmation, which is signaled by a paratactic *and*. In a master/slave dialectic, there is no community (the Self exists at the expense of the Other); in compearance, however, communication always already *is*. Singular beings are not contained or unified; they are always already exposed to/open toward an outside, an outside *that they share.*

> [C]ompearance . . . does not set itself up, it does not establish itself, it does not emerge among already given subjects (objects). It consists in the appearance of the *between* as such: you *and* I (between us)—a formula in which the *and* does not imply a juxtaposition, but exposition.
>
> —Nancy, *Inoperative*

The "with" of "being-with" "is the singular logic of an inside-outside"—inside and outside merge, naming "what is between two, or several, belonging to all and to none" (Nancy, "Of Being-in-Common" 6). To be exposed is to be riding the limit where, simultaneously, you are inside and outside. The singular being as *Klein Jar or möbius strip.* This communication—the sharing of the "betweenus"[56] space—gives rise to a mutual interpellation of singularities *before* any address in language. In fact, this inaugural communication exists as the condition of possibility for any linguistic interpellation.

The irreduciblity of being-with is exposed, Nancy says, in "the banal phenomenology of unorganized groups of people." His example: passengers sharing the same train compartment. "Simply seated next to each other in an accidental, arbitrary" way, "they are not linked." And yet they "are also quite together inasmuch as they are travelers on the same train." Straddling a limit between the "*dis*integration of the crowd and the *aggre*gation of the group," our passengers are suspended in a "relation without a relation" (7). Resist the temptation, however, to imagine these passengers as unified "individuals" or self-identified subjects. They/we are singular beings, and even in its solitude, the singular being is never interior to itself, never not multiplicitous, extended, exposed—never not with-others.

Don't get me wrong, when it comes down to it, *you are all alone*, finite, mortal, abandoned; and yet, even in your solitude you are heavily populated, extended beyond yourself, exposed in your being-with to a finitude that never stops working you over, making "you" possible. Alone but *over*populated, always already functioning as "threshold," you are constantly exposed to an in-common outside and so are constantly communicating, polyethoi to polyethoi, by virtue of that exposure, by virtue of an involuntary . . . *touch* . . . an involuntary inhabiting of a betweenus space. There is no escaping community.

But resist imagining this community as "communion," as fusion, as the kind of melting together exemplified by Star Trek's Vulcan mindmeld. Communion names the final culmination of sharing, the *end* of sharing—it is a desire for closure, for finality, for the "completed identity of all in one" (Nancy, "Myth Interrupted" 66). (A Phallic Phantasy.) But what community shares is not the "annulment of sharing"; what it shares is *sharing* itself. Don't miss this: There is no communion. There is the exposure, the touch—the givens of finite being—and in this *community* that always already is, there is perpetual communication.

This communication does not happen *as a result* of the common pain of finite existence, the common experience of what Bataille calls "lacerations."[57] Communication does not *result from* the "triple mourning I must go through: that of the death of the other, that of my birth, and that of my death" (Nancy, *Inoperative* 30). Community exists in the very exposition of that "triple mourning." And it is not the singular being that gets lacerated by it; "on the contrary," Nancy says, "this is where the singular being compears," at the site of these lacerations (30), right there where the so-called "fabric" of common-being, the veil of "communion," rrrrrips enough to expose the finitude it is designed to cover.

We feel the rip, acutely—it's that sudden sensation of being torn from another, that devastating recognition of an uncrossable chasm between singularities. We feel it when we speak at cross-purposes, when we can't reach anything resembling an understanding. We feel it when we or someone else is swept into an irrepressible fit of laughter . . . or tears, both of which expose the separation, the alienation of the one b-r-o-k-e-n ^{up}. We feel it when a lover dies or a friend betrays us, whenever we experience the sensation of being severed from another. But what we feel is a phantom pain—"the social" is no less a linguistic construction than "the individual." This fabric never really exists, the lacerations, Nancy says, "do not happen *to* anything": "there is no tissue, no flesh, no subject or substance of common being, and consequently there is no [real] laceration of this being" (*Inoperative* 30). There's only a "*sharing out*" of it.

> Decisive here is the idea of an inessential commonality, a solidarity that in no way concerns essence. Taking-place, the communication of singularities in the attribute of extension, does not unite them in essence, but scatters them in existence.
> —Agamben, *Coming Community*

But it is necessary to qualify this "sharing out": speaking is not a *means* of communication or sharing. Communication is not about sharing *information* and expressing a *bond*; rather, speaking is "communication itself, an exposure" (Nancy, *Inoperative* 31).

Here, we return to a lesson from Freud: when we write/speak, we inevitably say both more and less than we intended. When the singular being writes/speaks, it inevitably exposes itself as not in control, as not unified; it exposes itself as differance, as (an) alterity, and its "initial plenitude," as Agacinski puts it, "is already shared" (13). Communication is not "understanding." Rather, communication communicates the withdrawal of understanding and the opening of another kind of sharing (Nancy, "Speaking" 314–15). This communication, then, is not what makes community possible—this communication is possible only because community, the originary sharing of finite being, always already is.

Community is not a product; it cannot be built or produced.

One *experiences* community, or rather, one is "constituted by it as the experience of finitude" (Nancy, *Inoperative* 31). To assume that community can be produced is to fall again into a humanist arrogance. It is to presuppose a knowing subject who exists autonomously and *decides* to build it. But the operations that get built in the name of community (feminism, for instance), no matter how much consensus they have, as Nancy puts it, "have no more communitarian existence than the plaster busts of Marianne" (31).[58]

It is not in the work but in   .   .   the "unworking" that community is exposed, *not in the*   .   s   *pulling together but in*
the brrreaking up. The un-   .   u   working, the *désoeuvre*, Nancy
says, is "that which, before or   .   s   beyond the work, withdraws
from the work, and which no   .   p   longer having to do either with
production or with comple-   .   e   tion, encounters interruption,
fragmentation, ...   n   . . . . . Community, being-in-
common, compears here, as   i   .   the "interruption of singularities"; or, rather it is made of   o   .   precisely "the suspension that
singular beings *are*." This is   n"   .   why my burst of laughter in
the middle of that church ser-   (31). .   vice offered a better glimpse of

community than the service itself ever could. And Mary Richards's burst of laughter in the midst of Chuckles' memorial service did, too. Both services, after all, were serious attempts to mend the "communal fabric" ripped to shreds by the death of the Other.[59] The spectacle of Mary and me in the throes of a laughing fit asserted an interruption in the meaning-making process, a challenge to the very "order of things" the services were trying to re-establish. In the midst of this pulling together, our break-ups exposed the loose ends of finite Being; they exposed precisely what we do share, which is no more human immanence than it is divine transcendence.

The leap from God to Man, from *physis* to *nomos*, is a compelling negative deconstruction that doesn't go nearly far enough. The excess that is our finitude gets trimmed off, either way. Nietzsche was frustrated with us because when we finally admitted the death of god, we then preceded to make the same mis/take again: we assumed that the fall of the Big Cheese restored us to what Foucault called a "limited and positivistic world," a world of logical continuity, rather than freeing us to "a world exposed by the experience of its limits, made and unmade by that excess [that] transgresses it" ("Preface" 32).

What's exposed in the irrepressible burst of laughter is a crisis in immanence—a laughing fit is not the result of some external force driving in but is rather the exposition of fractal interiorities. And when *one* body exposes its ownmost Being as a community-of-the-self, as a "polyethoi," as Vitanza calls it, *every body* is on the line. These crack uP^s crack dow$_n$ on our anthropological arrogance, hurling us into a nondialectical space, what Foucault calls the "space of the mad philosopher," our face-to-face encounter with that excess that transgresses us. In a burst of laughter, we find ourselves scootching in next to the hermaphrodite, riding side by side with the pun, infected with the dis/ease of proliferation, electrified by what Ronell calls an "atonal symphony of random noise" (*Telephone Book* 259). This noise is an exposition of the excess that we are, the excess that meaning-making must silence or appropriate by "rushing in a supply of semantic cover" (259). But the point is that it's never quite in time. It only takes an instant of exposure to become aware, as Foucault has noted, that "we are not everything," that even we-rhetors don't "inhabit the whole of language like a secret and perfectly fluent god" ("Preface" 42).

The burst of laughter does more to expose us to our being-in-common than any collective mission possibly could. "Pulling together" doesn't produce community, but c-r-r-r-a-c-king up exposes it. Singular beings exist as their loose ends,[60] as a fluidity that cannot be solidified. And communication among these disidentified fluidities is not the result of something having been expressed; communication exists as the *dés-oeuvrement* of the political work ("social, economic, technical, and institutional") that attempts—however subtly—to solidify the fluidity that we are (Nancy, *Inoperative* 31). We cannot *lose* community—no matter how arrogantly we engage work that will not have *produced* it. "Only the fascist masses," Nancy says, "tend to annihilate community in the delirium of an incarnated communion" (35). But even then being-in-common resists this smothering—community operates as a resistance to immanence. Community is a given of being; as Nancy says, "[w]e *cannot not* compear" (35, my emphasis).

COMMUNITY IN SPASMS—
A RHETORIC OF LAUGHTER FOR FEMINIST POLITICS

Laughter blesses where God curses. Unlike God, humanity isn't condemned to condemn. Laughter can be filled with wonder if that is what humanity wants it to be—it can be light and it *itself* can bless. What if I laugh at myself?

—Bataille, *On Nietzsche*

I am moved from nameless horror to mindless laughter. Beyond laughter there is death, desire (love), fainting, and the ecstasy associated with horror, a horror transfigured. In this beyond, laughter stops, though I retain my awareness of it. Attempts to continue with this and pry open the beyond would make laughter something "intended" and so ring false from lack of simplicity.

—Bataille, *On Nietzsche*

It will be necessary to radically refashion what is called "politics" if the term is to be of any use to us from here. If politics is to facilitate rather than hinder the exposition of being-in-common, and therefore freedom,[61] it will need, as Nancy says, to "inscribe the sharing of community" (*Inoperative* 40). Lyotard was right: it will have been necessary for politics to lose the *polis*. A politics of finitude necessarily would be a politics of the *self(s)*; it would proceed from a revaluation of *ethics*, which is perhaps the reason Nancy says that the "outline of singularity would be political—as would the outline of communication and its ecstasy" (40). Because the singular being is always already touching, sharing, a politics of the self-as-finite-being would already be a politics of community. An ethical politics would signify a "community ordering itself to the unworking of its communication, or destined to this unworking: a community consciously undergoing the experience of its sharing" (40). And here, "community" begins with the community-of-the-self, the "subject-as-multiplicity" (Nietzsche), the "poly-ethoi" (Vitanza).[62]

Feminist politics might take on a radically different appeal from here. If being is always already being-in-common, if *you already shares me*, the public/private dichotomy cannot hold; it dis/solves—the personal is, indeed, the political, and in ways we may never have imagined. If the term "feminist" can signify that (fluidity) which exscribes itself from phallogocentric orderings; and if the term "politics" can signify a devotion to *désoeuvrement*, a devotion, that is, to breaking up, to *Becoming-Woman*, then feminist politics would be about a *self*-overcoming, a conscious turning of what Nietzsche calls the "value-positing eye" (*Genealogy* 36) inward rather than outward. Feminist politics could operate as a critical *unworking* of re-actionism that would function as an exposition of sharing—not through production but through an *affirmative* unraveling, an affirmative *resistance to closure*.

Driving for closure is one of our most devastating and yet most seductive habits. In *The Genealogy of Morals*, Nietzsche suggests that "the paradoxical task that nature has set itself in the case of man" is to "breed an animal *with the right to make promises*" (57, his emphasis): to set a goal, attain it, and *wrap it up*. Promises are about hoping for closure, planning for closure in advance. But Nietzsche notes that this is "the real problem regarding man." Making promises involves an "active desire *not* to rid oneself" of the past, "a desire for the continuance of something desired once, a real *memory of the will*" (58). But Nietzsche warns that to "ordain the future in advance" requires that we locate ourselves outside our own finitude: it requires that we "become *calculable regular, necessary*" (58, his emphasis). It requires that we go meta-physical and solidify in closure. In making promises, Nietzsche says, we assert a faith in our own capacity to "distinguish necessary events from chance ones," to determine "with certainty" what we want and how to get it, and in general, "to be able to calculate and compute" (58). We also assume the virtue of cogitating across causal links and anticipating future potential (only) according to present circumstances. All (logocentric) political movements make promises about the future. But, again, *to make promises is to solidify the fluidity of the experience of our finitude*. We are after a politics that invites the experience of radical non-closure. Nietzsche's notion of the *Übermensch* and Butler's notion of "parodic inhabiting" will be instructive here.

Artifice as Politics

What *Homo Sapien* imagines, [s]he may slowly convert [her/]himself to.
—Saul Bellow, *Henderson the Rain King*

Nietzsche notes that a metaphysics of substance/presence has been "burned in" to our memories and that we operate on it unconsciously. What is not commensurable with it (the differance of our finitude, for instance) is unproblematically forgotten. To overcome the need for closure that this metaphysic dictates, Nietzsche recommends effecting a pathos of distance by recreating one's Self as a work of art. The distance is between the *creating* self (branded by a "burned-in" memory) and the *created* self (in touch with the loose ends of finitude), and Nietzsche says the two ought not be confused. In *The Gay Science*, he celebrates the art of viewing ourselves "from a distance . . . the art of staging and watching ourselves" (133), overcoming ourselves by a *performance* of that overcoming. What will help us overcome an "honesty" of selfhood, which "would lead to nausea and suicide," Nietzsche says, is *art*—"art as the *good* will to appearance" (163). But Nietzsche is not promoting artifice *over* "reality"; he is calling for the recognition that even our "corporeality" itself, which we tend to take for granted, is always already a work of art—this artwork, however, was a *gift* rather than a self-creation. As Butler notes in *Bodies That Matter*, bodies themselves have their own histories; they, too, are *creations, effects* of, in this case, the "*mnemotechnics*" of pain.

Such bodies are heavy, weighed down with meaning and (humanist) morals. Nietzsche says that it is because we are "at bottom grave and serious human beings—really more weights than human beings" that "nothing does us as much good as a fool's cap" (*Gay Science* 164). In "Nietzsche and the Pathos of Distance," Rosalyn Diprose notes that Nietzsche's "self as a work of art" is about the realization that "you are never identical to yourself" (6). Your finitude, in other words, always will have overflowed the borders of the subject positions into which you are hailed. And this is a "liberating" realization. For, if the artist *were* what s/he aimed to "represent, conceive, and express," Nietzsche says, then s/he "would *not* represent, conceive, and express it" (*Genealogy* 101, my emphasis). The created self is never equal to the creator self. But, as Diprose notes, this is "not because the self as artist is the true or essential self in contrast to a false, unique, extra-social image projected. Rather, the image which the artist self creates is a moment beyond the present self which creates it" (6). "Beyond" is the key here: *self-overcoming*. Nietzsche

> At times we need a rest from ourselves by looking upon, by looking down upon, ourselves and, from an artistic distance, laughing over ourselves or weeping over ourselves. . . . we need all exhuberant, floating, dancing, mocking, childish, and blissful art. . . . We should be able also to stand above morality . . . to float above it and play.
>
> —Nietzsche, *Gay Science*

calls it the bridge to the future, a way to begin to think the unthinkable. Once we have managed to forget (in tiny bits) the burned-in memory of unified and fully present selfhood, we will have been capable of re-configuring (re-membering differently) the past and our relation to it.

Much pragmatic feminist politics (though, certainly not all), however, tends to be less interested in an artistry of self-overcoming than in what Ronell calls a "politics of demasking or denuding," a drive to get at "a *Puritan* core" ("Interview" 128). In the interview with Andrea Juno, for instance, Ronell notes that the "ban on makeup" was about a "politics of self-presentation" that didn't "consider current thinking about: artifice, technicity, and so on" (128). The notion that there is an essential

[O]ne of my mentors, the French feminist writer Hélène Cixous, came to America years ago, and one of her first gestures (which horrified American feminists) was to point out what ugly shoes they wore. And this completely scandalized everyone! Hélène is an incredibly beautiful Egyptian lioness—she is splendidly dressed. Somehow the lines between pragmatic American feminism . . . and French theoretical feminism were drawn along eyeliner marks: artifice, seduction.
—Ronell, "Interview"

actor behind the act, and that an ethical politics would have to get at *that* first, tends to motivate much American feminist politics. Creation and artifice, therefore, are not valued—in fact, they are *demonized*. To modern feminist

French feminists, Ronell says, continue to explore "seduction as the power to create distance, to *dis-identify* with one's self, to mask and play around, and to perform different versions of oneself" (128). Pragmatic American feminisms (Dworkin is named in this interview as a good example of a "pragmatic American feminist"), on the other hand, tend to evidence a desire, "a totally *male* desire," according to Ronell, to get at the final foundation, the Being behind the mask. If French feminists tend to accept Nietzsche's re-valuation of artifice as "a playful honoring of life's multiplicity," that is, of the loose ends of finitude, many pragmatic American feminists are still after "absolute self-presentation without artifice" (128). There is no way to build a "bridge" to the future from here, no way to begin to overcome one's Self and think an/Other thought or an/Other "feminism." This is why Ronell says, "For me, feminism, as a perturbing *intervention* into *what is*, has to be very suspicious of *anything* that coincides with American ideology" (129). The appeal to "sincerity" and "honesty," she suggests, always operates in the service of "the greatest *servility* to the law, and *docility*" (129). It operates, as Nietzsche might say, in the service of those particular memories "burned" into one's head by society's "*mnemotechnics*" of pain.

Self-overcoming, on the other hand, is about moving beyond one's socially constructed Self through an/Other self-construction. It's about, according to Nietzsche's Zarathustra, *creating* a new nobility for oneself, a nobility that does "not look backward but ahead!" (*Thus Spoke* 203–4). Those self-creators, those artists of the noble do not "have to establish their happiness artificially by examining their enemies, or to persuade themselves, *deceive* themselves, that they [are] happy (as all men of *ressentiment* are in the habit of doing)" (*Genealogy* 38). Most of us, however, do indeed establish our happiness by constructing an "evil enemy" (39). Zarathustra tells his followers that turning his gaze from "the now to the past" always turns up the same thing: "fragments and limbs and dreadful accidents—but no human beings" (138). What Zarathustra finds "most unendurable" is "the now and the past on earth" (*Thus Spoke* 138). Because the will "cannot will backwards," it is "powerless against what has been done" (139), powerless against a past that it cannot get back to, cannot *set straight*. "That time does not run backwards," Zarathustra says, "that is [our] wrath; 'that which was' is the name of a stone [we] cannot move" (139). From this powerless position, the will reflects over the "already gone by" that is its gatekeeper, sees its own and others' suffering, and desires justice, desires to *punish*.

The "will's ill will against time and its 'It was,'" Nietzsche defines as revenge or *ressentiment*. S/he who is imprisoned by *ressentiment*, unable to move "that which was," moves *other* "stones out of wrath and displeasure, and [s/he] wreaks revenge on whatever does not feel wrath and displeasure as [s/he] does" (140). For "where there is suffering," Zarathustra says, "one has always wanted punishment, too" (140). But "punishment" is only "what revenge calls itself; with a hypocritical lie, it creates a good conscience for itself" (140). Denied what Nietzsche calls "a true reaction," because they cannot will backwards, those ravaged by *ressentiment* and "bad conscience" "compensate themselves with an imaginary revenge" (*Genealogy* 36). Here's Nietzsche on *ressentiment*:

> While every noble morality develops from a triumphant affirmation of itself, slave morality from the outset says No to what is "outside," what is "different," what is "not itself"; and *this* No is its creative deed. This

inversion of the value-positing eye—this *need* to direct one's view outward instead of back to oneself—is of the essence of *ressentiment*: in
order to exist, slave morality always first needs a hostile external world;
it needs, physiologically speaking, external stimuli in order to act at
all—its action is fundamentally a reaction. (*Genealogy* 36–37).

Deleuze, in *Nietzsche and Philosophy*, notes that there are certain
movements that are "only able to exist through reactive forces and their
victory. There are things which can only be said, thought or felt, values
which can only be believed, if one is animated by reactive forces" (86).
Those pragmatic feminisms that will not "have done" with the past are
manifestations of *ressentiment*. Animated by reactive forces, they proceed
with memory burned in and the "value-positing eye" directed outward.
But a re-action against the past in the "now" cannot/will not move the
stone called "It was"; there is no redemption in revenge. And there is no
future in it—revenge is a fight with the past that, in demanding our
concentration, sends us tumbling into the future without any
anticipation of it.

Zarathustra says that for humankind to be "redeemed from revenge"
would be the "bridge to the highest hope and a rainbow after long
storms" (Nietzsche, *Thus Spoke* 99). The *Übermensch*, the Trans-human,
is one who finds such redemption by actively forgetting the boundaries
defined by a metaphysics of presence and, therefore, releasing her ill will
from its "No!" to the passage of time and freeing it for a "Yes!" that affirms transiency and takes responsibility for its own thrownness. Here's
Zarathustra: "To redeem those who lived in the past and to recreate all
'it was' to a 'thus I willed it'—that alone should I call redemption" (139).
"The will," Zarathustra says, "is a creator. All 'it was' is a fragment, a
riddle, a dreadful accident—until the creative will says to it, 'But thus I
willed it'" (141). Affirmatively forgetting the logocentric thought-barriers
burned-in by his social coding, he overcomes his Self by attempting to
will backwards, to re-create all "it was" into a "thus I willed it." In this
way, he redeems his past and so himself; not by punishing others but by,
as Heidegger might say, affirming his "ownmost being-guilty."

Zarathustra recognizes his Self as a *moment*, a flickering signifier,
rather than an enduring subject moving through progressive evolutions.
The *Übermensch* engages an active forgetting that allows it to recreate its
past as a way of projecting itself into the future. Heidegger, too, suggests

that the future does not come later than the past any more than the past comes earlier than the present. Rather, the past is constructed in a "moment of vision" with an eye on the future (*Being and Time* 376).[63] Like Nietzsche, Heidegger suggests that the present is no more than a flicker in time, which manifests itself as the result of the constant production and reproduction of a past comporting itself toward its future potentialities. As a moment, a flickering signifier, one might recreate one's past so as to project oneself into the future in new terms. If both the future and the past lead out from the gateway of the present moment, then to temporalize oneself is to affirm one's capacity to recreate the past (what one has been) at *every moment* as one pro-. · · · · · · · · · ·-jects oneself into the future.

What Zarathustra wants for the hunchback, for instance, is not that he be freed from his Situation or that anyone be made to *pay* for it. Rather, it is that the hunchback comport himself toward himself, as Heidegger would say, with "anticipatory resoluteness," that he take over his own thrownness and proclaim his "ownmost Being-guilty"—that he exclaim, in other words, from within his own horrendous Situation, a hearty "Thus I willed it." In such an exclamation, Dasein determines that its Situation is its own: its own responsibility, its own creation. In taking over one's own thrownness, one "releases" oneself from one's thrown basis to one's Self *as* basis (*Being and Time* 330). And from here, another sensibility becomes possible, a sensibility that is incapable, as Nietzsche says, "of taking one's enemies, one's accidents, even one's own misdeeds seriously for very long—that is the sign of strong, full natures in whom there is an excess of the power to form, to mold, to recuperate and to *forget*" (*Genealogy* 39).

A justice that *begins* here, with the notion that "everything is dischargeable, everything must be discharged," Nietzsche says, "ends by winking and letting those incapable of discharging their debt go free: it ends as does every good thing on earth, by *overcoming* itself" (*Genealogy* 72–73). Nietzsche doesn't get any better than this . . . any more profound than this:

> It is not unthinkable that society might attain such a *consciousness of power* that it could allow itself the noblest luxury possible to it—letting those who harm it go *unpunished*. "What are my parasites to me?"

it might say. "May they live and prosper: I am strong enough for that!"
... This self-overcoming of justice: one knows the beautiful name it
has given itself—*mercy*; it goes without saying that mercy remains the
privilege of the most powerful man, or better, his—beyond the law.
(72–73, my emphasis)

It's important to remember that Nietzsche is offering an ethics rather
than a politics—or, rather, he is offering an *ethical* politics, *a politics of
the self(s)*. He's describing a way to the *Übermensch*, to the Trans-human
condition. To get *there* from *here*, it will be necessary to forget, to dis-
charge, to let go. A feminist politics, operating as a resistance to closure—
of self, of situation, of time—would do well to begin here: to dis-
charge the debt,
> to have mercy,
>> to *have done*
>>> with the past.

Parody as Politics

Butler's destabilization of the "metaphysics of substance" is also a form
of affirmative forgetting, which
is anything but apolitical.[64] Re-
counting Michel Foucault's descriptions of the state's (successful)
attempt to compel prisoners'
"bodies to signify the prohibitive law as their very essence, style, and
necessity," Butler notes that even outside the penitentiary, "bodies are
produced which signify that law on and through the body" (*Gender
Trouble* 134). The "soul" is not an illusion, Foucault says, and neither,
Butler adds, is it "imprisoned by or within the body, as some Christian
imagery would suggest" (135). Rather, Butler says: "The figure of the
interior soul understood as 'within' the body is signified through its inscription on the body" (135). The soul, Foucault says, "exists, it has a
reality, it is produced permanently around, on, within, the body by the
functioning of a power that is exercised on those that are punished. ...
the soul is the prison of the body" (Foucault, *Discipline and Punish* 29–

Tricksters or fakes, assistants or "toons,"
they are the exemplars of the coming community.

—Agamben, *Coming Community*

30; Butler, *Gender Trouble* 135). This redescription of "interpsychic processes in terms of the surface politics of the body," Butler says, "implies a corollary redescription of gender" as phantasmatically produced through prohibitions, through absences. (135). In *Bodies That Matter*, Butler admits that it also implies a corollary redescription of race, able-bodiedness, and a host of other sites which operate in the production of abject bodies (48, 181).

Make no mistake, Butler warns in *Gender Trouble*, "coherence," that is, *solidification* of identity "is desired, wished for, idealized," not only by the "state" but by its subjects. Braidotti was correct: we do *desire* female subjecthood. But, and this is what Braidotti misses and Butler gets, "this idealization is an *effect* of a corporeal signification" that has been, as Nietzsche says, "burned" into our consciousness/memories. What Butler spotlights, after Nietzsche, is that even these "corporealities" are *significations*, performances that we have forgotten are performances and in which we have come to believe. They operate, Butler says, as "border control that differentiates inner

> from
> outer,
> and so
> institutes
> the
> 'integrity'
> of the
> subject"

(*Gender Trouble* 136). They operate as devices of *clOsure*, closure of gender, of race, of subjects, of the body politic, etc. A *feminist politics* that would operate as a critical unworking, an affirmative unraveling will have found a site for its resistance to closure here, in a performance of Self that is unfaithful to its supposed solidity, a performance that leakssss and has no end in ssssight.

Butler calls for a parody of the superimposed "integrity" of the subject, a parody that flies into *pastiche* to reveal that so-called integrity as "an imitation without an origin." She calls for theatricalization of identity as a "perpetual displacement" of the "origin," a perpetual re-turning to "a fluidity of identities" (138)—to, in Žižekian terms, "the place of the hole." [65] And, though Fredric Jameson suggests that parody-turned-*pastiche* is "parody that has lost its humor," Butler, in a re-cogitation of the scene, suggests that it is precisely the "loss of the sense of 'the normal,'" or the "original" that sparks "the occasion for laughter" (138).

When the "normal" or the "original" is "revealed to be a copy, and an inevitably failed one, an ideal that no one *can* embody" (Butler, *Gender Trouble* 139), affirmative laughter bursts out, shattering the official roadblocks and opening to/revealing excess. And we say Yes to that opening not to be "deviant" but to be *ethical*. The ethical experience, as Agamben puts it, "is the experience of being (one's own) potentiality, of being (one's own) possibility—exposing, that is, in every form one's own amorphousness and in every act one's own inactuality" (44). Affirmative laugher invites the ethical experience.

Butler picks up this thread again in *The Psychic Life of Power*, where she suggests that if there is "an elsewhere" where the law of identity does not "monopolize the terms of existence," but where, also, we do not deny "our complicity in the law that we oppose," it would be the result of "a different kind of turn, one that, enabled by the law, turns away from the law, resisting its lure of identity, an agency that outruns and counters the conditions of its emergence" (130). This "turn," she says, would demand "a willingness *not to be*—a critical desubjectification—in order to oppose the law as less powerful than it seems." It would demand a determination to perpetually re/cognize that "being" will remain "unexhausted by any particular interpellation" (131). Interpellation's failure to solidify the fluidity that we are undermines the "capacity of the subject to 'be' in a self-identical sense." But—and don't miss this—it is also this failure that opens a path to futurity. Butler's call is to point perpetually to that failure, to expose it constantly by overperforming the excess that "we" are.

"Practices of parody," because they challenge the distinction between "a privileged and naturalized gender configuration and one that appears as derived, phantasmatic, and mimetic—a failed copy as it were" (Butler, *Gender Trouble* 146), expose us to our finitude. A politics of parody, would resist closure, and, among other things, "have the effect of proliferating gender configurations, destabilizing substantive identity, and depriving the naturalizing narra-

> [W]e might read "being" as precisely the potentiality that remains unexhausted by any particular interpellation. Such a failure of interpellation may well undermine the capacity of the subject to "be" in a self-identical sense, but it may also mark the path toward a more open, even more ethical, kind of being, one of or for the future.
>
> —Butler, *Psychic Life of Power*

tives of compulsory heterosexuality of their central protagonists: 'man' and 'woman'" (146). This *feminist* politics would, in other words, have the effect of inviting the *ego* to laugh its Self "to death" (Sloterdijk 144). And it is there, at that instant, in that flash of destabilization, that resistance will have been *affirmative*, and *nonpositively* affirmative because it will have occurred in the shattering of the either/or choice. This *feminist politics* will not only have been beyond the *ressentimental* urge, but it will have become, as Ronell hoped, a "feminism that is joyous, relentless, outrageous, libidinally charged" ("Interview" 127).

This is a feminism that anticipates laughing itself out of a job. Luce Irigaray, for instance, suggests that laughter is the first form of "liberation" from a secular oppression (*This Sex*); Hélène Cixous calls for laughter because it can "break up the truth" ("Laugh") and "knock the wind out of the codes" ("Castration"); Julia Kristeva celebrates a laughter that can transgress rigid semiotic boundaries ("Postmodernism?"); and Butler applauds the "explosive laughter" that jolts us into the recognition that so-called copies have never had a metalinguistic original (*Gender Trouble*). These "feminists" are *good* laughers. Their muse is Thalia, the muse of comedy, because they know that laughter *releases* the "feminine," "desire-in-language" from its binary bondage. They are willing to laugh and to be laughed, to take the chance of losing consciousness and *forgetting*, if only for an instant, about the old battle. And it is here, in the space of this affirmative forgetting, that an/other politics and an/other feminism gets underway, a *feminist politics* that breaks up the Phallocratic Order by breaking up *at* it. And *this* will have taken us a long way toward

thinking

the

unthought . . .

4

A RHETORIC OF LAUGHTER FOR COMPOSITION PEDAGOGY

What our beginning students need to learn is to extend themselves, by successive approximations, into the common places, set phrases, rituals and gestures, habits of mind, tricks of persuasion, obligatory conclusions and necessary connections that determine the "what might be said" and constitute knowledge within the various branches of our academic community.
— David Bartholomae, "Inventing the University"

This is a great discovery, education is politics! After that, when a teacher discovers that he or she is a politician, too, the teacher has to ask, What kind of politics am I doing in the classroom? That is, In favor of whom am I being a teacher?
— Paulo Freire, *A Pedagogy for Liberation*

In 1988, Jim Berlin's "Rhetoric and Ideology in the Writing Class" noted that a "rhetoric can never be innocent, can never be a disinterested arbiter of the ideological claims of others because it is always already serving certain ideological claims" (477). Berlin's article exposed the extent to which politics is always already driving any/every rhetoric of composition and its corresponding pedagogy, the extent to which power/ knowledge in the classroom is ideologically saturated. In fact, education itself, Gregory L. Ulmer reminds us, "is fully inscribed within the logic of Late Capitalism, enjoying the patronage of multinational corporations and any other entity with funds" ("The Spirit Hand" 138). There is no pure knowledge. Even the teaching of composition, as Berlin suggests, is the teaching of a world view: it assumes and then propagates a particular relationship among the writer, the reader, language, and "reality," and from there it peddles assumptions about what is, what ought to be, and what can be changed. *This is a seriously political business.*

If pedagogies devoted to current-traditional rhetorics of composition (CTR) have been masquerading as apolitical for decades, radical pedagogies (including, for instance, critical and feminist pedagogies) have been out to demask them, and by so doing, to help students overcome some aspect of false consciousness. These pedagogies strive to uncover the violent and exclusionary political assumptions that CTR's approaches to composition pedagogy uncritically propagate, assumptions with regard to race, class, gender, and sexual orientation. Similarly, if traditional composition pedagogies labor under what John Schilb calls the "ethos of service,"[1] a conviction that they exist to support *real* society (and its economic structure) and the *real* disciplines, radical pedagogies aim for an almost full reversal of that ethos. What radical pedagogies are after, in other words, is a composition course that refuses to serve the state and its social-economic apparatus.

And yet, interestingly enough, radical pedagogies have also been accused of putting composition courses into the service of their left-wing politics. Maxine Hairston, for instance, laments the rise of this "new model" of classroom pedagogy (radical pedagogy), calling it a "regressive model" and offering the following justifications: radical pedagogies put "dogma before diversity, politics before craft, ideology before critical thinking, and social goals of the teacher before the educational needs of the student" (23). This critique reveals more about Hairston, of course, than the "new model" she's attacking: (a) she views writing as a *craft*; (b) she believes teaching it as a craft is apolitical; and (c) she believes there is nothing political in *her version* of "the educational needs of the student." Oh yes . . . Hairston gives us a good peek at her own motivations and assumptions here. And yet, let's not allow that to overwhelm an important point: composition courses, to the left and to the right, do indeed typically operate as prosthetic extensions of political agendas. If traditional composition pedagogies use writing instruction to perpetuate the existing political and economic structure, radical composition pedagogies use it to foster the subjects of their Grand March against that structure.

We will make no attempt here to navigate, à la Hairston, a path out of politicized pedagogy.[2] We will, however, attempt to locate a composition pedagogy that has eXscripted itself from *oppositional* politics. We'll be on the lookout for a pedagogy that embraces the feminist politics we defined in the last chapter: we will hope to locate a composition pedagogy that would be *feminist* inasmuch as it would ex/scribe itself from phallogocentric ordering systems. This feminist composition pedagogy would be devoted to a political *désoeuvrement*, an affirmative resistance to textual/sexual closure. This feminist composition pedagogy would place itself in the service of a libidinalized writing rather than the other way around.

To get there from here, it will be necessary, however, first to take a critical look at what already goes by the name "feminist pedagogy" in composition studies: inasmuch as feminist composition pedagogy, as we know it, has a tendency to re-mystify pedagogical power and to perpetuate oppositional politics, it will not have been an answer for us. We won't trek with a feminist pedagogy that simply in/scribes a new method on an old aim. In the name of liberal education's prime directive, which we will call E^3—Enlightenment, Empowerment, and Emancipation—feminist composition pedagogies often attempt to use the authority inherent in the pedagogical position as a means towards what they consider a worthwhile end. Rather than producing the unquestioning "productive citizens" that traditional pedagogies aim to produce, feminist pedagogies hope to produce critical feminist subjects, revolutionary feminists armed for the Grand March of women's liberation.

Although this certainly looks more ethical at first glance, it is not at all unproblematic. The point that needs to be made before we move on is that this aim makes feminist pedagogies as reactionary as the mainstream feminist politics they proffer; it makes them reactions to other reactions. Indeed, as Shoshana Felman has suggested, "Every pedagogy has historically emerged as a critique of pedagogy" (24). Feminist composition pedagogies typically offer themselves as alternatives, but they do so by inscribing themselves within a set of existing assumptions, within an already (phal)logocentric ordering system and its pedagogical imperative. In short, they enter the fight; they therefore assume the rules of that fight and end up protecting and perpetuating rather than dethroning the assumptions of the political and economic structures they mean to oppose. Feminist pedagogies, in this sense, operate as a symptom of, rather than a cure for, a much larger cultural/pedagogical problem.

Michel Foucault addresses the slipperiness of this problem in *Discipline and Punish*, arguing that the transition from public torture to carceral detentions did not evidence a break from torturous methods of discipline; rather, the transition evidenced the *perfection* of the techniques of domination and a newly acquired ability to conceal relations of power. In the concealing, Foucault suggests, in the masquerading as more humane, they became all the more nasty. Similarly, radical pedagogies, including feminist pedagogies, often camouflage pedagogical violence in their move from one mode of "normalization" to another. Even so-called emancipatory pedagogical techniques function within a disciplinary matrix of power, a covert carceral system, that aims to create *useful* subjects for particular political agendas. Inasmuch as these pedagogies are pledged at some level to the grand narrative of emancipation and to the mobilization of the Grand March, they participate in the carceral network they so desperately hope to transcend.[3]

This chapter hopes to expose what often gets masked in current feminist approaches to pedagogy: that is, their/our own recourses to pedagogical tyranny. Much feminist composition pedagogy promotes itself as the proprietor of a "safe place" and focuses attention on decentered authority, nurturance, and affective connection. This approach to feminist pedagogy, however, may be no less violent and no more capable of E^3 than the harsh and sexist "banking system of education" it aims to supplant. A brief critique of some common feminist pedagogical moves in composition studies will satisfy this minor aim of chapter 4.

The major aim of this chapter will be to question the unquestioned pedagogical imperative that founds the educational impulse. Foucault's description of the penitentiary imperative is, again, instructive. He notes that a reintroduction of the principles of the "penitentiary technique" is always offered as a solution to the prison's "perpetual failure," that the prison has invariably been "offered as its own remedy" (*Discipline* 268). Here, we'll suggest that a reintroduction of the principles of the "pedagogical technique" has been offered continuously in answer to the failure of pedagogy. Pedagogy continues to be "offered as its own remedy" by a field that is often blinded by what Victor J. Vitanza calls "pedagogy hope" ("Three Countertheses" 161) and what Lynn Worsham calls "the will to pedagogy" ("Writing Against" 96). Worsham notes that this pedagogical imperative—which is a *political* imperative—is "at the heart of a discipline requiring every theory of writing to translate into a pedagogical practice or at least some specific advice for teachers" (96). Vitanza observes that we tend to "hope for improved modes of production (a set of *techné*) to create an improved product" ("Three Countertheses" 161) but that that much hope is too much hope.

It may be time to stop offering *more* pedagogy or *altered* pedagogy in answer to the failure of pedagogy. The pedagogical imperative has been responsible for perpetuating a subtle reign of terror in universities and schoolhouses, and it may be time to call the whole sordid affair into question. Here we will not attempt to inscribe yet another pedagogy into the pedagogical scene. We will hope, rather, to EXscribe ourselves, to locate a postpedagogy, a pedagogy that would be other/wise. We will cross the "feminist politics" we redefined in the last chapter with the serious pedagogical imperative that runs amok in the uni-versity system in order to get at what we will call a *pedagogy of laughter* for composition studies. This approach to composition pedagogy will have operated as a critical unworking of pedagogical violence, a perpetual unraveling of what is called composition, and a continual and affirmative resistance to identity poly-ticking—both the right's and the left's. In short, a pedagogy of laughter will have kept things broken up and brrrreaking up in the composition classroom.

FEMINIST COMPOSITION PEDAGOGIES— IN (THEIR) BRIEF(S)

Success, according to the phallo-logic of the so-called masculine economy, both requires and affords power, and this little detail places feminists, who are out to challenge phallic domination, in a precarious position: it seems that one can effectively undo authority only from a position *of* authority, a position that appears to trap feminists within the very phallic economy they aim to subvert. In order to "empower" students, the female pedagogue must first assume the power of the pedagogical position herself and then succeed in passing that power on/off. She is trapped in this acute double-bind: either she refuses power and so has none to *give* or she assumes power and so plays the phallocratic game. The problem is hardly a new one. "As mothers," note Margo Culley et al., "we are expected to nurture; as professionals, we are required to compete. . . . [T]he role of nurturer and intellectual have been separated not just by gender, but by function" (12). The *female* feminist pedagogue is faced with a particularly difficult power negotiation.

One by now common negotiation tactic is to try to steer clear of the trap altogether by embracing both sides of the equation, by activating a *powerful* nurturance, a *politics* of nurturance in which the combination of nurturance and intelligence creates a productive "confusion" in the classroom (13). Feminist pedagogy itself, Nancy Schniedewind suggests, is about encouraging the "feminist values of community, communication, equality, and mutual nurturance" (171).[4] Schniedewind even suggests that such an atmosphere might be promoted, in part, by building "festive procedures" into the run of the course. "Festive procedures," she says, "are community builders. Refreshments during breaks of long classes, a potluck dinner on occasion, and the integration of poetry and songs into the course, all catalyze energy and build solidarity" (172).[5] The pedagogue in such a course performs the role of the social lubricant, the instigator of "participatory decision-making" and "cooperative goal-structuring" (173–74).

Culley and the other authors of "The Politics of Nurturance" argue that assuming the role of authoritative-nurturer in the classroom may make it possible for teachers and female students to "empower each other to become mutually whole and autonomous. . . . [T]he feminist classroom may become the place where the cultural split between mother and father may be healed." These authors offer a concise explication of the goals for which this pedagogy aims:

> The feminist classroom is the place to use what we know as women to appropriate and transform, totally, a domain which has been men's. . . . Let us welcome the intrusion/infusion of emotionality—love, rage, anxiety, eroticism—into intellect as a step toward healing the fragmentation capitalism and patriarchy have demanded from us. . . . [F]or all its irrational dimensions, the demand for nurturance and support is finally a rational one, and we must dare to embody and empower the vision of a supportive and nurturant community of women. (19)

The political importance of this vision is eloquently put: "From this experimental here and now, we can begin to elaborate a new feminist epistemology, and to foster and encourage the subjects of that feminist transformation" (13).

In the field of composition studies, specifically, these approaches to feminist pedagogy have operated in conjunction with certain collaboration-consensus oriented critical pedagogies, defining a fundamental distinction between "bad" authority and "good" authority: calling feminist pedagogues to assume the role of the "nurturing mother" rather than the "authoritative father" (Flynn 423), proponents of this powerful nurturance hope to "overthrow" phallic domination in the composition classroom. Playing what Marilyn Cooper and Michael Holzman have called the part of the "benign authority" (156) and exercising "good" power or "authority *with*" (as opposed to authority *over*), these pedagogues encourage what Catherine Lamb, echoing Schniedewind, has called a classroom of "cooperation, collaboration, shared leadership, and integration of the cognitive and the affective" (11). The feminist composition pedagogue functions, according to Sally Miller Gearhart, as the "co-creator and co-sustainer" of human interaction (200) and as guardian against conflict, competition, and hierarchy in the classroom. Which also means that s/he functions as Bouncer, as Border Patrol charged with securing the boundaries of the "womb-like" (Gearhart 199) matrix.

There is a strong contention among feminist composition pedagogues that argumentation and conflict foster a hostile classroom environment and should not be practiced in any feminist curriculum.[6] Gearhart, for instance, defines a difference between "male chauvinist" interaction (which is argument) and dialogic (which she says is feminist), and she is after the latter. Though there are also many feminists in composition studies who insist that conflict/argument is necessary in the classroom, they tend to redefine it in terms of mediation and to refashion it as a step in the direction of consensus. Lamb, for example, who does indeed invite conflict into the feminist classroom, says the ultimate goal of the feminist pedagogue is to urge a "mediation" and a "resolution to the conflict that is fair to both sides" (11). She champions what she calls "maternal thinking" and invites conflict into the classroom so that the teacher-mother might help to re*solve* it, so that s/he might help bring it to an end. Here, the pedagogue functions as mediator, arbiter, and/but also as Bouncer, since mediators determine what gets a hearing and what does not.

Susan Jarratt makes a thorough and insightful case for conflict in the writing classroom, calling for a feminist composition pedagogy "designed to confront and explore the uneven power relations resulting from [gender, race, and class] differences" ("Feminism and Composition" 113). Unlike Lamb, Jarratt is highly suspicious—for all kinds of reasons—of the turn toward "maternal thinking" in the feminist classroom: anticipating a "positive response to teacher as mother," Jarratt notes, "naively ignores the deep ambivalence toward and repression of the mother in our culture" (113).[7] There is no reason to expect the *mother* to be less the [m]Other inside the classroom than out. And yet, though Jarratt, following Kathleen Weiler, suggests that conflict should not be avoided in a feminist classroom, she does argue that it ought to be "negotiated" and "transformed" (119). Jarratt notes that any classroom is, by definition, a site for conflict and not a safe space, and she argues against the drive for consensus motivating so many expressionist strategies. But interestingly, Jarratt's stake in conflict is based on the sophistic hope that it is "through recognition of and argument over differences" that conflict can "be resolved into *homonoia*, like-mindedness" (114).[8] Don't miss this: following Weiler, Jarratt hopes that admitting conflict into the classroom might be the "starting point" for a kind of consciousness-raising for students and teachers "through which the inequalities generating those conflicts can be acknowledged and transformed" (*Rereading* 114). Jarratt invites conflict in so that it might ultimately *bring itself to an end* ("Feminism and Composition" 119).

Jarratt's negotiation with conflict turns on a shift from *physis* to *nomos*: she hopes to make the classroom a "middle space" in which students who would oppose "speech with speech" might become, "[even] in this hierarchical society, a class of equals" (*Rereading* 40; Jarratt is reading Jean-Pierre Vernant). The transformation/negotiation for which she calls puts its money on social construction and the capacity of the social body to construct a better reality by allowing conflict to emerge so that it might be re/solved through hermeneutical understanding. As Jarratt, quoting Mario Untersteiner, suggests, this faith in *nomos* is a bet on "the human capacity to 'fix the main headings of reality' by means of a 'humanizing essence'" (42).

Even when conflict is admitted into these feminist classrooms, then, it's typically admitted *to be soothed or transformed*; it is invited in as a means to a *predetermined* end. The end goal, as suggested in "The Politics of Nurturance," is to "foster and encourage the subjects of [a] feminist transformation." In the feminist composition classroom, Jarratt notes, "feminism and rhetoric become allies in contention with the forces of oppression troubling us all" ("Feminism and Composition" 121). The ultimate goal is compelling: to end oppression. The means to that end is troubling: placing rhetoric and composition into the service of particular feminist visions. If traditional composition courses are designed to serve the state and its existing economic structure by fostering subjects who will take their places within that structure, feminist composition courses serve feminist politics and foster the subjects of a "feminist transformation."

THE PHARCE OF THE PHALLIC PHEMININE—
A CRITIQUE, IN BRIEF(S)

I should begin by noting that these pedagogical performances are, a good bit of the time, *my* pedagogical performances; driving this critique are the concerns that haunt me even as I continue to inhabit these problematic subject positions in the classroom. I am haunted by the sneaking suspicion that these/my feminist pedagogies, for all their nurturance and/or "negotiation" with conflict, remain as much a function of the phallic *ph*antasy as does traditional, authoritarian pedagogy. Does-

"What's Love Got to Do with It?"
—Tina Turner

"Love Hurts" (ooo-ooo, love hurts)
—Heart

n't the desire to homogenize differences and/or to transform conflict into enlightened "like-mindedness" expose a nostalgia for Oneness, for the Proper, for the very phallic standard feminist pedagogy intends to displace? Shouldn't any writing classroom that strives for "rational consensus" and/or "hermeneutical understanding" spark some serious suspicion?

Looking for "common ground" involves no radical reworking of terms, no attending to the exscribed; both the pedagogy that bans argumentative discourse for the sake of harmony and the pedagogy that calls on argumentative discourse to challenge the differences that prevent harmony operate on the hope that finally the battle will have been won/ One, finally we will have understood each other, finally we will have found common ground. It makes me nervous. After all, as Vitanza never stops reminding us, "Commonplaces have an insidious way of only fostering the dominant discourse; commonplaces are in no way revolutionary" ("Three Countertheses" 151–52). How could they be? To think the Unthought, to speak the Unspeakable, one necessarily would have to begin elsewhere, from the realm of the unfamiliar, the "indecent," the "imund." One would have to be willing to take off from an ec/topia of all common places. One would have to begin, then, by listening more rigorously, by tuning in past the frequency regulators.[9]

It also seems enormously problematic to draw an easy distinction between *good* authority and *bad* authority, between the nurturer and the authoritarian. This is a tricky business, is it not? After all, "the teacher-mother" is no politically neutral nurturer—s/he admits to advancing a specific agenda in the classroom. Again, I'm suspicious: suspicious of a Mother who assumes the role of Master, but especially of a Master who drapes herself in the facade of "feminine nurturance," a facade that successfully remystifies pedagogical tyranny. To be sure, the realm of the Proper in her/my classroom undergoes a significant shift: it demands interconnection over separation, collaboration over competition, and, ultimately, harmony over conflict. And yet, the game is the same the same the ssssssssssssssssssssssssame old thing.

Pedagogical domination gets camouflaged but not challenged in the powerful nurturer's classroom, which continues to function within an oppressive disciplinary matrix, a covert carceral system designed to "foster and encourage the [useful] subjects of [a] feminist transformation" (Culley et al. 19). Though the boundaries of the proper in this classroom do shift, they do not blur. There is finally no letting up of what Cixous calls the "masculine urge to judge, diagnose, digest, name" ("Castration" 51). The job of the pedagogue is to bring and keep student language/thought within the lines of the new legitimacy.

same thing
same thing
same thing

No doubt about it: the Proper is continually erected and protected in this approach to "feminist" pedagogy, and it is erected and protected by the *Mother*, a not-at-all "benign" authority figure *par excellence* (albeit incognito). S/he represents what Kathryn Morgan has called the "bearded mother" (Gore 68) and what Freud has dubbed the "Phallic Mother." S/he is the Mother endowed with the power of the *Ph*ather, the "feminine" erected by the "masculine": she is the "*ph*eminine." Under the guise of the "Good Mother," this pedagogue *lovingly* nurtures her students into Proper (politically correct) ways of knowing, thinking, and problem-solving. The nourishment the Mother offers is not free-flowing nor freely given; it is as paralyzing, as fixating, as solidifying as the Father's Law.[10] The Mother plays and requires the students to play the game of the Father: erecting the big (Proper) (re)solution.

The Mother is no closer to a "feminine" space than the father—she is a creation, a function of the same structures of power, the same "scepter of sovereignty" (Keuls 2). It is, after all, as Michelle Ballif reminds us, "the Mother's voice that first introduces the child to the Symbolic: it is the Mother's voice and hands that first territorialize the child's body" ("Mothers in the Classroom" 11). Indeed, inasmuch as the figure of the Mother perpetuates, as Ballif observes, "the family structure, *ad nauseam*, that very family structure which creates misogynist men and submissive women," She is up to her eyebrows in phallogocentrism. And the idealization of the Mother, Ballif argues, could easily be read as "another example of the conservative backlash *against women*" (16, my emphasis).

The Mother's phallogocentrism actually may be even more potent than the Father's since, as Foucault reminds us, "power is tolerable only on the condition that it masks a substantial part of itself. Its success is proportional to its ability to hide its own mechanisms" (*History of Sexuality* 86). Power—the Phallus—is not ever where we expect it to be. If, as Lacan argues, the phallus "can play its role only when veiled" ("Signification of the Phallus" 288), Kristeva may be right when she suggests that the Phallic Mother is even more dangerous than the Primitive Father precisely because . . . her phallus is *always* veiled. The Mother—but, significantly, this is also true of the *Mediator*—retains her authority precisely through her ability to conceal
                    the fact
          that she
      has it.

The oppressive structure upon which both "nurturing" *and* "negotiating" pedagogical strategies depend can be glimpsed in the following passage, by Jarratt:

> In the polyphony of voices, not all will or should sound equally. Ira Shor, using Freire, explains how the teacher, even while creating a "loving matrix" for dialogue, may sometimes need to take on an adversarial role against an abusive student or to voice an unrepresented view in the dialogue (*Critical* 95, 102). As [Toril] Moi asks, "What dogmatism says that it is *never* feminist to speak with authority?" ("Feminism and Composition" 119)

The point here is not that the teacher ought never take on an adversarial role or that it's not important for the pedagogue to try to keep a single voice from dominating the conversation. But it does seem that those ground rules ought also apply to the pedagogue herself, who may find "abusive" precisely those voices that refuse to mimic her own.

Notice that it's acceptable to become *blatantly* authoritarian at precisely the moment when a student refuses the teacher-mother's hail. Nurturing and/or "negotiation" operate(s) in these feminist composition classrooms with a very particular end in mind, and when "power-with" (mediation) doesn't get it, "power-over" is Plan B. These feminist classrooms are set up as "safe spaces" or democratic "common spaces"— spaces in which "abusive" students will be challenged. But let's listen carefully to what that suggests: Whenever what Jane Gallop calls the "woman-to-woman" model of feminist pedagogy ("Teacher's Breasts" 81) gets disturbed by a male student (or a female student who resists), the feminist classroom becomes a mirror site for the very "banking system" of education it aims to supplant. Here, the authoritative *feminist* pedagogue steps in to assure that the class will socially construct the *correct* truth(s), or those truths deemed correct by the pedagogue facilitating this "democratic" interaction.

The question, then, becomes: For whom, exactly, is this safe space *safe?* And/or for whom does this "common space" become equalizing? Clearly, the answer is not For *all* students, *all* women, or even *all* feminists. Apparently, this space is safe and/or equalizing only for those willing to operate within the lines of the "new feminist epistemology" elaborated by the feminist pedagogue. Jarratt, for instance, is not interested in "removing the teacher from the center of the classroom—away from the authoritative position as the source of knowledge." That, she says, is a "postmodern move" that ends up "affirming the voice of a white, middle- or upper-middle-class student," which makes the teacher complicit in a racist, sexist, and classist American culture ("Feminism and Composition" 109). And Jarratt's argument is compelling—it's a potent warning against letting a pomo sensibility hurl us back to a prefeminist starting point. But the bottom line here is this: The teacher remains *the undisputed head cheese* of this feminist composition classroom. And difference is celebrated only inasmuch as it can be brought into line with whatever style of "feminist transformation" this subject (who is) supposed to know envisions. This is the phallic model for the classroom par excellence—and this I-write has been a proponent of it more times than she cares to admit.[11]

The Pedagogue in Drag— Performing the *Sujet Supposé Savoir*

These/our feminist pedagogies fail in their prime directive, E^3, precisely inasmuch as they fail to provide a space for thinking the unthought. They fail because they are enchanted by the pedagogical imperative

> As soon as the subject supposed to know exists somewhere . . . there is transference.
> —Lacan, *Four Fundamental Concepts*

("pedagogy hope"), which trusts, as Worsham observes, that pedagogy can be engaged as a "*concrete* political practice" ("Writing Against Writing" 96, my emphasis). The will to pedagogy is a will to truth-in-political-pedagogy, and the prime directive is forestalled precisely at the moment when radical pedagogies, of any flavor, begin to believe that they can *teach* that truth: E^3 becomes impossible as soon as the teacher her/himself begins to

       suppose

          s/he

            knows.

Lamb's critique of Clara Juncker's "Writing (with) Cixous" is a case in point.[12] She applauds Juncker's attempts to make the writing classroom a site of critique of what Juncker calls "the fantasy of a central, idealized subject and the phallus as signifier of power and authority"

(Juncker 425; Lamb 12). She also notes, in favor of Juncker's approach, that "if this order is dislocated, students may be able to find their own voices on the margins" (12). Similarly, by reading "material sufficiently outrageous," she says, students "are more likely to empathize with otherness, whether 'radically, politically, sexually, herstorically'" (12). But Lamb finds Juncker ultimately unacceptable because her writing theories do not translate into an operator's manual for feminist teachers. Let's let Lamb speak for herself:

> My concerns with Juncker's essay are theoretical and practical. . . . *[A]fter the disruptions, then what?* I can imagine an essay written this way that is every bit as combative as the masculinist discourse we are seeking to supplant. Further, *how can students take these forms and use them in other classes or in the world of work?* If we are serious about the feminist project of transforming the curriculum and even affecting the way students think, write, and act once they leave us, we need an approach to teaching composition that is more broadly based and accessible to our students. (12–13, my emphasis)

The pedagogical imperative demands that every theory be immediately translatable into workable classroom practice for the pedagogue, that is, to use Lacan's definition, into a "concerted human action . . . which places man in a position to treat the real by the symbolic" (*Four Fundamental Concepts* 6). Lamb finds Juncker's essay unacceptable precisely because Lamb can discern no "concerted human action" that can be derived from it *for* the feminist March *in* the writing classroom.

Vitanza, on the other hand, calls for a "moratorium on attempting to turn theory into praxis/pedagogy," on turning all theory into "*applied theory*" ("Three Countertheses" 160, my emphasis). Why? Because, he says, "(critical) theory paradoxically can, but *cannot*, be employed to critique and to found theoretical praxis. Theory has become, for the field of composition, the will to *unified* theory . . . it has become 'theory hope'" (160, my emphasis). "Pedagogy hope" is a function of "theory hope," the hope that we-pedagogues might finally get the story straight, might finally land on a pedagogical *techné* that will pump out the *right kind* of student-subjects (161) [!] By now our original suspicions have developed some significant muscle tone—it's time to bust a move.

We'll be on the lookout not for *more* pedagogy—for, it cannot "fix" itself—but for what Vitanza calls *post*pedagogy: a postpedagogical pedagogy that operates, like Lyotard's avant-garde art, "without criteria." We will be after a *feminist* composition pedagogy [un]founded on an *ethical* politics, on a politics that risks losing the *polis* (class) as it turns its "value-positing eye" back on itself. Many feminist composition pedagogies are not suspicious enough of the pedagogical position or the pedagogical imperative; and, therefore, they have not transformed pedagogy. They have not offered an exscription from but rather an/other inscription of pedagogical tyranny . . . a move from one mode of normalization to another. This will no longer have been enough for us. Any pedagogy that becomes too serious about passing off its truths and fostering the subjects for its own Grand March is a pedagogy in need of *a good displacing ssssssssnort*. No doubt about it, it is time for a genuine critique of pedagogy *qua* pedagogy. It will be necessary to discover what is laughable in pedagogy if we hope to evoke a *pedagogy that can laugh* . . .

SUPPOSING WE DON'T KNOW— TURNING TEACHING "ARSE UPWARDS"

In book VII of Lacan's seminars, Lacan discusses a dream one of his patients had in which someone attending the seminar "cried out concerning [Lacan], 'But why doesn't he tell the truth about truth?'" Lacan's answer to the dreamer's question is significant for us: He says, "haven't you noticed that in wanting to tell it—something that is the chief preoccupation of those who are called metaphysicians—it often happens that not much truth is left?" Lacan continues:

> That's what is so risky about such a pretension. It is a pretension that so easily lands us at the level of a certain knavery. And isn't there also a certain "knavery," a metaphysical "knavery," when one of our modern treatises on metaphysics, under the guise about the truth of truth, lets a great many things by which truly ought not be let by? (184)

There it is, again: the non-truth of truth. Like "woman," the subject "supposed to know"—here, Lacan himself—knows that he does not know; that is, he does not believe in what he knows. Lacan leaves little

It almost looks as if analysis were the third of those "impossible" professions in which one can be sure beforehand of achieving unsatisfying results. The other two, which have been known much longer, are education [pedagogy] and government [politics].

—Freud, "Analysis Terminable and Interminable"

room for speculation on this point: the subject *supposed* to know ought not begin to *believe* s/he knows. In fact, Lacan blames those pedagogues who *do* begin to believe in their own performance for reducing teaching to a "functional apprenticeship" (*Ecrits* 144; translated in Felman 23). This is pedagogical tyranny: using the pedagogical position to foster particular kinds of subjects or student-citizens, either to take their place in the economic/political system or in the Grand March against it. Once the pedagogue begins to believe that s/he knows the truth and proceeds to pass that truth on/off, teaching is reduced to a "functional apprenticeship," even as "truth" is disrobed and paraded unabashedly as *Truth* (*Aletheia*). What's at stake is the excess, the noise/static that gets "let by" (silenced) in the name of a reproduceable practice.

Without prepackaged knowledge to disseminate to students, pedagogy *qua* pedagogy is, as Freud suggests, quite "impossible" ("Analysis Terminable and Interminable" 248). And yet, Shoshana Felman calls Freud, the Father of Psychoanalysis, one of "humanity's great teachers" (21). Lacan also makes Felman's top three list—the other is Socrates. Why? Because Freud and/but especially Lacan, like Socrates, know that they *do not know.* But if the best teachers are those who know that they do not know, what might pedagogy be? Or, more to the point: What are we-teachers supposed to be *doing* in the classroom? If not teaching-as-knowledge-passing or teaching as subject-producing, then what? If it is impossible to teach, as Freud has suggested, then "What," we ask with Felman, "can the impossibility of teaching teach us?" (22).

Or, rather, "What," as Lacan himself asks, "*is the order of truth that our praxis engenders?*" (*Four Fundamental Concepts* 263, his emphasis). "Has that which our praxis engenders the right to map out for itself necessities," he continues, "even contradictory ones, from the standpoint of truth?" In the next

[I]n the most private feelings of each psycho-analyst, imposture looms overhead—as a contained, excluded, ambiguous presence against which the psycho-analyst barricades himself with a number of ceremonies, forms and rituals.

—Lacan, *Four Fundamental Concepts*

sentence, Lacan restates his own question, and we begin to get a sense of what is at play in this line of thought. He asks, "*[H]ow can we be sure we are not imposters?*" (263). And that does seem to be the question, after all; we hope not to be seen as faking it. But Lacan's answer to himself turns the question on its head: We can be sure that we are always already imposters/impostures.

The subject position the teacher occupies calls for a performance without essence, a "ceremony" that evokes but does not/cannot re/present. Here's Lacan on the training of analysts:

> It is clear, in the experience of all those who have passed through this training, that in the *absence of adequate criteria*, something that is of the order of *ceremony* is put in their place and—since for the psycho-analyst there is no beyond, no substantial beyond, by which to justify his conviction that he is qualified to exercise his function—the substitution, in this instance, can be interpreted in only one way—as a *simulation*. (*Four Fundamental Concepts* 230, my emphasis)

Indeed, Lacan continues, "no psycho-analyst can claim to represent, in however slight a way, a corpus of absolute knowledge" (232). As a matter of fact, he says, "even the most stupid analyst" (233, my emphasis) is often capable of pulling off the performance of "the subject supposed to know." The pedagogical position, in Lacanian psychoanalysis, is an impersonation for an effect rather than a re/present/ation of reality. The "function of language" in analysis "is not to inform but to evoke," he says, and the question of the "correctness" of interpretation moves "into the background" (*Ecrits* 86–87).

But before we are tempted to think that the pedagogue *merely* performs someone who knows, before we think of it as *just* a performance/impersonation, it will help to recall Donna Haraway's caution: simulation is "a *much more potent* field of operations" than so-called "reality" ("Manifesto" 205). Lacan suggests much the same thing in book VII of the Seminars, when he notes that, though "we know that God is dead," it hasn't stopped the impact of His field of operation. Indeed, "the next step," Lacan says, "is that God himself doesn't know that [he is dead]. And one may suppose that he never will know it because he has always been dead" (184).

He's here
He's gone
He's *back*

Lacan elaborates this idea somewhat in *The Four Fundamental Concepts* by drawing a loose analogy between religion and psychoanalysis as they relate vis-à-vis science. When "enlightenment man" called religion's bluff in the eighteenth century and labeled it a "fundamental imposture," he wasn't suspicious enough of his own reductivism. "It is not enough," Lacan says, "to overcome superstition . . . for its effects in the human being to be attenuated" (264). When the scientific impulse, which seeks solid ground, *a priori*, declares religion an "imposture," Lacan notes, it does so without problematizing the very notion of foundations. If "impersonation"[13] is all we have, if truth doesn't get any truer than *that*, our notions of what it is to be an imposter will have to be redefined. To say that the psychoanalyst is performing a role, embracing ceremony over essence, is not to say that psychoanalysis is ineffective or that the psychoanalyst is not "qualified."

Something similar can be said of the pedagogue: to note that the pedagogue, playing the *sujet supposé savoir*, is an imposter turns the pedagogical imperative "arse upward,"[14] but it does not suggest that the pedagogue is unqualified or that nothing is happening in the classroom. It only suggests that something *else* is happening, an/*Other* something: it is not, could not be, *true* knowledge—universal nor socially constructed—that is being passed here, in the pedagogical situation.

"THE *SUJET SUPPOSITAIRE*"—
PEDAGOGICAL INSERTIONS AND INTRUSIONS

"Words are trapped in all corporeal images that captivate the subject; they make the hysteric 'pregnant,' be identified with the object of *penis-neid*, represent the flood of urine of urethral ambition or the retained faeces of avaricious *jouissance*." There. We have hit bottom.

—Ronell (reading Lacan's *Ecrits*), "The *Sujet Suppositaire*"

I promised the patient [Wolf Man] a complete recovery of his intestinal activity, and by means of this promise made his incredulity manifest. I then had the satisfaction of seeing his doubt dwindle away, as in the course of the work his bowel began, like a hysterically affected organ, to "join the conversation," and in a few weeks time recovered its normal functions.

—Freud, *Three Case Histories*

What the teacher, who does not know what s/he k*n*ows, passes in the classroom is *her own desire* as s/he attempts to find the articulation of what s/he knows in the student-Other. It is not that the operation (performance) of the "subject supposed to know" isn't effective for the pedagogical imperative; it is that it could not be *more effective* . . . more malevolent, or more intrusive. Avital Ronell compares the *sujet supposé savoir* in the pedagogical situation to a glycerin suppository: both insert their desire into a "virginal space" of "originary innocence" in order to make something particular happen in the formation of the Other ("*Sujet*" 106). Lacan makes the point clearly enough in "The Function and Field of Speech and Language in Psychoanalysis":

> But if I call the person to whom I am speaking by whatever name I choose to give him, I intimate to him the subjective function that he will take on again in order to reply to me, even if it is to repudiate this function. Henceforth the decisive function of my own reply appears, and this function is not, as has been said, simply to be received by the subject as acceptance or rejection of his discourse, but really to recognize him or abolish him as a subject. Such is the nature of the analyst's [or pedagogue's] responsibility whenever he intervenes by means of speech. (86–87)

In other words, Lacan says, "not only is every spoken intervention received by the subject [student] in terms of his structure, but the intervention takes on a structuring function in him in proportion to its form." Inasmuch as "language solidifies into body," the *sujet supposé savoir* acts also as the *sujet suppositaire*, making "glycerinic insertions into the subject [student] who thereby receives his structuring" (Ronell, "*Sujet*" 108). Here we note, with Ronell, and only half in jest, the etymological link between the Sphinx and the sphincter. huh oh. The pedagogue, playing the one who knows, launches "a suppository movement" into her students' subjectivity, the success of which is then determined and evaluated by way of an examination of the student-subjects' productions/ excretions: "How do I get an A in this class?" You become moldable, you accept my desire without a fight, and you manage to articulate well my desire once I have made my deposit (in you).

As soon as there is a subject supposed to know, there is forced subjectification, "a partial parceling out of the [student] subject," Ronell observes, "the robotization and militarization" (117) of the Other. To be a good student is to be/come a beautiful mirror for the teacher. The pedagogue who encourages students to suppose s/he knows, to suppose that s/he can tell the truth about truth, makes them an implicit promise: that they too will know if they will only listen carefully and do what s/he asks. The illusion of the *sujet supposé savoir* is imperative to pedagogy hope, and the enormity of its power to mold students into certain types of subjects, to take "on a structuring function" inside them, ought not be underestimated. A horrifically constipated Wolf Man, for instance, listened carefully to Freud, believed he knew, believed his promise, and was *cured*. That is, his bowels almost immediately began to "join the conversation" . . . on the basis of that *promise* (Freud, *Three Case Histories* 265). This is a powerful illusion; it launches what Ronell calls a "suppository torpedo" (122) into the student in order to make something specific happen: a cure is effected when the student embraces and manifests the desire of the teacher. The pedagogical imperative cannot want more than this; and/but what can one expect, after all, from a situation that takes off from a merely *supposable* subject ?

IN THE NAME OF WRITING:
(DE)COMPOS(T)ING THE
PROSTHETIC COMPOSITION COURSE

We-teachers of composition, of course, launch our own torpedoes of desire, aimed directly into our students and designed to *make something happen*, something that will affect their structural formation and, therefore, their productions/excretions. We do it in the name of "literacy." What is usually being passed (off) for truth/knowledge in the composition classroom is a set of "teachable practices," codifications of language and writing that are teachable and that support a flavorful assortment of identity politics. Composition/writing is used and abused to promote this identity here or that one over there. Indeed, composition courses have historically figured as prostheses, as "basics courses" designed to complete a very particular service for the university and/or society's economic structure itself. Radical pedagogies have attacked this setup, for obvious reasons. Donald Morton and Mas'ud Zavarzadeh, for instance, argue that service-oriented writing courses not only pump out social dupes ("literate" citizens) ready to hop into the existing oppressive power-structure but also participate in the backlash against posthumanist thought. In fact, they insist that "[t]he courses most privileged by the humanists are mostly courses in 'writing,' whether technical writing and composition ('basic skills') or 'creative writing'" ("Theory" 15).

Not only the state but also parents and students, more often than not, demand that universities be in the business of preparing citizens to "take their rightful place" in the "free economy" (14). And this post-Fordist "free economy," as Berlin has noted, demands excellent communications skills. The "technological compression of time and space," he says, has made "rapid means of communication and transportation" not a luxury but a requirement, and if students-cum-workers aim to compete in this economy, they must be *armed* with what the state tends to think of as *basic writing skills* ("Postmodernism" 49). "Literacy." Writing is reduced in these classrooms to a codifiable set of practices to be memorized and utilized by the speaking/writing subject in order to make him/her more marketable. A mechanics of solids freezes the movement of writing and then calls it *teachable*.

Morton and Zavarzadeh suggest that humanities programs scramble to comply with state, student, and parental demands by developing "a carefully planned and packaged series of writing and skills courses that will secure the student the job he 'deserves'" (14). But this service-oriented view of composition studies is, of course, far from neutral. Education itself, as Lester Faigley points out, is no longer about "promoting social equality"; it's about churning out "a 'trained capability' adequate to compete with those of Germany and Japan and a host of new economic rivals" (51–52). Composition studies is called to perform a major role in producing this "trained capability"—it is charged with pumping out *literate* citizens. But "the ideal of literacy as a means for achieving social equality," Faigley notes, has been replaced with "a cynical acknowledgment of education as part of the machinery for sorting people into categories of winners and losers" (52).

Composition studies also manages perpetually to reinstate the humanist subject and, in the name of *the competitive edge*, fend off the economically disastrous potential of what we have been calling the post-humanist paradox: we both make and/but are (more so) made by history. Here's Morton and Zavarzadeh's accusation:

> Writing courses (in fact, the entire "freshman English program") have become the last bastion of defense of traditional humanism against radical (post)modern critical theory. At a time when theory has questioned the grounds of conventional literary training, writing courses have been enthusiastically embraced by humanists as happily beyond the contestation of theory: they are firmly grounded in the "self" of the writer-student and also self-evidently useful. Regardless of their specific model and method, most writing courses are based on the notion of the subject as a rational, coherent individual who, at times, is present to himself. The writer-student, in other words, is assumed to have direct access to the "raw materials" of writing through his sensations, perceptions, and cognitions. (*Texts for Change* 15)

This double-edged charge—that writing programs are designed both to guard over humanism's slumber and to produce "agents" to perpetuate the existing economic structure—is a serious one. And over the last few decades, radical approaches to composition pedagogy have attempted to redirect the aims of composition instruction by exposing the political dimension of traditional rhetorics of composing and their pedagogical techniques. Feminist pedagogy has offered one of the most outspoken critiques of service-oriented composition courses, which necessarily remystify and renaturalize masculinist discourses, learning styles, and thinking processes.

And yet, writing is obviously not dismissed from its tour of duty in radical composition pedagogies. As we noted above, composition is colonized in feminist classrooms, too, for the purpose of particular political aims. Lamb's reaction against leaving language/writing deconstructed illustrates the problem—for her and for others, feminist composition pedagogy is about reterritorializing writing, strapping it into the service of "the" feminist March. Furthermore, radical pedagogy is as guilty as traditional pedagogy of launching *humanist* "torpedoes." Morton and Zavarzadeh's accusation is a case of projection, par excellence. Their project centers around their faith that human beings can be taught to reason correctly through a critical approach to pedagogy, and that is a *humanist* hope.[15] If traditional composition pedagogies prostitute writing for the

sake of the status quo, radical composition pedagogies have a tendency
to prostitute it for the sake of revolution.

But there is another way to approach composition courses. What if
we put ourselves into the service of writing rather than the other way
around? Hairston makes an interesting point when she argues that
"writing courses, especially required freshman courses, should not be *for*
anything or *about* anything other than writing itself" (22). Though it is
unlikely that she would approve of our interpretation of this passage, the
temptation is too much to resist: What if "writing itself" were to get its
say in a college composition course? What if we invited into the
composition classroom a *language on*
                   the
                        LOOOOSE?

Killing It Softly:
"Undertaking" Writing-as-Meaning-Making

Obsessed and entranced, narcissistic, private, unable to achieve transference,
the writer often resembles the addict. This is why every serious war on drugs
comes from a community that is at some level of consciousness also hostile
to the genuine writer, the figure of drifter/dissident, which it threatens to
expel.

—Ronell, *Crack Wars*

In the preface to *Finitude's Score*, Ronell announces that she is "writing
for writing because it died" (xiii). In a posthumanist, postfoundational
era, she says, there is a real sense
that "writing has been obsolesced,
divested." And writing, as a har-
nessing of language for the making-manifest of "reality," most certainly did die; the possibility of
re/presentation went out the window along with its support-system: God
and Man. But then, if writing died, what are we doing when we teach
composition, when we "teach" students how to *use* language? Going
through the fantasy? Mourning?[16] Might as well face it, we-teachers of
composition are employed to work and work over *the dead.* In this
post-almost-everything era, we fulfill the function of linguistic under-

> I am writing for writing because it died.
> This is why, at least in part, writing is
> necessarily bound up with mourning.
> —Ronell, *Finitude's Score*

taker: we are charged, as Ronell says, with coming up with "what to do with the remainders of writing" (xiii). We are also hailed into the position of security guard, hired to protect citizen-subjects, the university system, and the state itself from a language separated from meaning-making, from a language on the looooooooose.

And yet, we often fulfill our duty without quite grasping what it entails. Language has yet to become enough of a problem for many of even the most radical composition pedagogies. Composition courses often dutifully direct attention away from language's tendency to go organic, and they do so under the banner of the Good, in the name of education's three Es, each of which would be severely problematized in the face of a nonrepresentational language. It seems quite understandable that the state would have a long history of language-phobia; indeed, the war on language was in effect long before the war on drugs, and these wars have run surprisingly parallel courses. Perhaps that is because literature has been treated as a drug in the juridical system.[17] "The horizon of drugs," Ronell notes, "is the same as that of literature: they share the same line, depending upon similar technologies and sometimes suffering analogous crackdowns before the law. They shoot up fictions, disjuncting a whole regime of consciousness" (*Crack Wars* 78).[18]

Both the war on language and the war on drugs have been waged in the name of *freedom*: the freedom of the citizen-subject, as Ronell says, "to be protected from the condition of enslavement" that both (bad) drugs and (bad) literature "are said unavoidably to produce" (*Crack Wars* 55). Language, after all, is a dangerous (dis)possession. And writing is analogous to drugging inasmuch as both offer a "mode of departing," a mode of "desocialization," but "without the assurance of arriving anywhere" (106; see also Cixous, *Three Steps* 65). Writing, Cixous tells us, is about "letting everything go" ("Coming to Writing" 40) about "learning to die" (*Three Steps* 10), about "seek[ing] out the shattered, the multiple I" ("Coming to Writing" 40). Writing, like drugging, operates as a transgression of borders; both blast open a passage to the excess, the improper, the unaccountable, the overflow. And they drop us off there, for a moment, "where the excluded live" (*Three Steps* 108). They drop us, Cixous says, "beyond the good side of the law, the proper, the world of order" (119), and the "cops of the signifier" *cannot have that*.

Enter the service-oriented composition course: it does for language what the pharmacy/drugstore does for narcotics. Ronell observes that "[t]he drug store figures a legalized reproach to uncontrolled or street drugs but at the same time argues for the necessity of a certain drug culture." Indeed, she points out, "there is no culture without a drug culture, even if this is to be sublimated to pharmaceuticals" (*Crack Wars* 96). Similarly, composition courses often operate as control centers, mediating between the subject and a rowdy body of language, which threatens the subject's autonomy. Like the drugstore, the composition classroom functions as a neutral zone, positioning itself between the subject and the "drug" so that the object of desire/study will not be free to take possession of the subject. Both the drugstore and the prosthetic composition course are on the side of "truth," the "scientific impulse." They intervene to keep the creatures of simulacrum in line; it is, once again, a matter of *dosage*. One of the questions determining the particular rhetoric of composing that will be proffered in any composition course (be it CTR, cognitive, expressive, feminist, or social-epistemic) is this: *How much interaction between the drug (language) and the addict (student writer) will produce the desired result, the desired kind of citizen-subject-author?* What's at stake here is not only freedom; it is also and more so "reality."

In "The Rhetoric of Drugs," Derrida asks, "What do we hold against the drug addict?" His answer: Something that we don't hold against the smoker or the alcoholic:

> that he cuts himself off from the world, in exile from reality, far from objective reality and the real life of the city and the community; that he escapes into a world of simulacrum and fiction. We disapprove of his taste for something like hallucinations. . . . [W]e cannot abide the fact that his is a pleasure taken in an experience without truth. (7)

When language operates representationally, that is, when writing can be viewed as a making-manifest of reality, it is believed to produce "safe text," to operate on the side of "truth," and it affirms the capacity of academic programs, liberal and conservative, to attain their versions of E^3. When representation is suspended, reality is at risk. Bad literary drugs are those that, at some point, offer a representational hesitation. *these are the drugs that blow your mind* Writing is most threatening to reality and to "community," Ronell notes, when "it stops representing, that is, when it ceases veiling itself with the excess that we commonly call *meaning*" (*Crack Wars* 57).

Writing is most threatening when it stops testifying to *homo seriosus's* *"Serious Premises,"* when it interrupts the meaning-making machine and, in the instant of that interruption, opens the possibility for an/Other hearing, a hearing of that which has been drowned out by the workings of the machine itself. It is in the moment of this hearing of the previously UNheard, in the activation of an interruption that exposes the rustlings of finitude, that community—our being-in-common—presents itself. Finitude is exposed in the instant that the myth of common-being is interrupted by the excess it attempts to silence. But the job of the typical composition course is to perpetuate that myth . . . for the sake of society . . . Reality . . . Truth. For the sake of *knowledge*.

> When a voice, or music, is suddenly interrupted, one hears just at that instant something else, a mixture of various silences and noises that had been covered over by the sound, but in this something else one hears again the voice or the music that has become in a way the voice or the music of its own interruption: a kind of echo, but one that does not repeat that of which it is the reverberation.
>
> —Nancy, *Inoperative Community*

One of Generation X's most telling slogans, "Image is everything!" comes into focus here: the question of any piece of writing's licit or illicit label comes down to its fashion statement, "the way [it] dresses up the wound of its non-being when it goes out into the world" (Ronell, *Crack Wars* 57). "The court," Ronell says, "keeps a close watch on creatures of simulacrum." What it takes to slip by the surveillance systems is a *veil of meaning*. The "pleasure and play of fiction," Derrida says, "(now still as with Plato) are not in themselves condemned unless they are inauthentic and devoid of truth" ("Rhetoric of Drugs" 8; also Ronell, *Crack Wars* 102).

Literature courses tend to come equipped with that representational safeguard: the language studied in literature courses has, more often than not, been dressed up with meaning by a series of academic essays and review articles. "Literature has to be seen wearing something external to itself," Ronell notes, "it cannot simply circulate its non-being, and almost any article will do" (*Crack Wars* 57). But in composition courses, there is no such prefabbed safeguard against the linguistic abyss that is so threatening to the university and its prime directive, E^3. The safeguard must be built into it by putting writing into the service of something else, some greater aim or grander goal than writing itself. What gets protected in the prosthetic composition course is the economy of the Same, as Irigaray calls it; what gets *ex*cluded is that which this economy makes unhearable, unthinkable. What gets silenced is any thinking, as Cixous puts it, of "what is not-the-same" ("Sorties" 86). And the whole show is dependent upon the pedagogue, the teacher who knows and shows the way.

WRITING RE-VIVED: BEYOND THE "WHITE TERROR OF TRUTH"

But if we admit that the teacher does not know, that s/he *cannot know*, a world of other possibilities opens up for the pedagogical situation in composition studies. What would happen if writing were dismissed from its representational servitude, if, that is, *we put ourselves in the service of writing* rather than the other way around? What would happen if a composition course were to let writing have its say?[19] If it were to serve nothing but writing? Not writing "for" another purpose, not writing as mastery, but writing *for writing's sake?* Writing as a pressing of the limits of discourse? Not a writing that stabilizes identities but one that b-l-o-w-s minds? A writing that puts finitude into play and unceremoniously shatters what Cixous calls "the eggshell [that] we are" (*Three Steps* 63)? A writing that costs us a myth . . . but then grants us [a] life?

Such a course could not be more subversive of the educational system and of every liberal and/or conservative political agenda. On the other hand, such a course would have an easy affinity with the redefinition of feminist politics we outlined in chapter 3: it would devote itself to a critical unworking of reactionism, an affirmative unraveling of pre-established truth/knowledge in a radical resistance to closure/totality. In devoting itself to the Laughter in language, such a course would invite a thinking of the Unthought. It would invite an exposition of our finitude, the very thing that makes community possible. Now we're getting where we want to be/come.

Writing as Dissimulation

> In the beginning, there can only be dying, the abyss, the first laugh.
>
> After that, you don't know. It's life that decides. It's terrible power of invention, which surpasses us. . . . Write! What? Take to the wind, take to writing, form one body with the letters. Live! Risk: those who risk nothing gain nothing, risk and you no longer risk anything.
>
> In the beginning, there is an end. Don't be afraid: it's your death that's dying. Then: all the beginnings.
>
> When you have come to the end, only then can Beginning come to you.
>
> —Cixous, "Coming to Writing"

No doubt about it, the composition course for which Hairston (unwittingly) called, the course devoted to "writing itself," would be a dangerous one. Language is not benevolent when it's unleashed. In fact, Foucault calls it "malevolent," carrying a "slight suspicion of ill will and 'malice'" ("Nietzsche, Freud, and Marx" 65). Lyotard says it operates as a "red cruelty of singularities" (*Libidinal Economy* 241). This language will not hold still, will not submit to any prescribed normativism—when forced there, it will overflow, it will leakleakleak. Foucault says this language is so "excessive and of so little density that it is fated to extend itself to infinity without ever acquiring the weight that might immobilize it" ("Language" 65).

And yet, it ought not be assumed that language-*leashed* is any more benevolent. In fact, language forced into representational servitude appears in all instances to be the most terrifying option. When we build a hermeneutic around semiology, around the belief in "the absolute existence of signs," Foucault says, we do give "up the violence, the incompleteness, the infinity of interpretations" inherent in a language on the loose. However, what we get in its place, he says, is a "reign of *terror* where the mark rules" (67). Lyotard calls it the "white terror of truth" (*Libidinal Economy* 241), in which the play of language is immobilized and discourse "becomes a unity and a totality" (243) designed *for* something. Systematic exclusions are born here, in this space designed specifically to block out the Unthought, to keep it unthinkable; in this space designed specifically to hush the roaring Laughter-in-language. All avenues of what Ronell calls our "indecent" history can be traced back to this starting point, not only to our belief in but also to our dedicated protection of the white terror of truthhhh.

A composition course devoted to *writing only* would be in the position to work against this terror. It would play another game with language, a game, Lyotard says, that "would not seek to paralyze" interpretation or stabilize the ego. This game would "seek powerlessness [*impouvoir*]; it would let the plugging-in of its uncertain border with that of its client body [the reader] take place in aleatory fashion, without bothering to try to control it" (255). This game, in other words, would not be governed by the "cops of the signifier." It would also not be about instruction or information exchange—it would hope for "communication" but communication *as* the exposition of finitude.

There would be no supposition, in this writing-for-writing course, that signs, as Lyotard puts it, "transport messages that are communicable in principle" (51). The "overriding passion" of the "white terror of truth" is to demand clarity for the sake of *understanding*. But in this course, we would be after something else: we would "hope, rather, to be set in motion" (51), to be brushed by "singularities," "unprecedented things," the unthought (255). The demand for clarity brings out what Deleuze and Guattari call "the General in you" (*A Thousand Plateaus* 25). But in a composition course out to serve writing only, it would be necessary to receive such a demand "in terror"; Lyotard says the best we can do is ffffleeeeeeeeeeeeeeeeeeeeeeeeeeeeeeeeeeeeeeeeeeeeeeeeeeeeeeeee

> [This communication] would be a bottle thrown into the sea, but without desperation, without ultima verba, without its launch being a last attempt to signal and communicate a message entrusted to it. There would be no message in our bottle; only a few energies, whose transmission and transformation was left out and was desired to be unpredictable. Because we believe in forces, we do not force our client [reader] to pair up with our discursive model. Do we even have a model?
>
> —Lyotard, *Libidinal Economy*

·

·

·

from it, as it is "the first imprint of power on the libidinal band" (*Libidinal Economy* 258), the first move toward systematic exclusion.

This course would invite students to engage in what Ronell calls a "genuine" writing (*Crack Wars* 106), a "writing for no one" and "to no address," without a grand "purpose" or "point" (107). (Notice that she doesn't say: without any purposes or points.) This is, without a doubt,

scat
scat
scat

the most "vulnerable type of writing," and it "belongs," Ronell notes, "to the registers of a 'feminine' writing in the sense that it is neither phallically aimed nor referentially anchored, but *scattered like cinders*" (107, my emphasis). Here's Ronell:

> At no point a prescriptive language or pharmacological ordinance, it is rather a *writing on the loose*, running around without a proper route, even dispensing with the formalities of signing. The impropriety of such writing—which returns only to haunt itself, refusing to bond with community or affirm its health and value—consistently reflects a situation of depropriation, a loss of the proper. (107)

This writing refuses to weave another thread into the myths of community [common-being] upon which the ideal of "good writing" is usually built. This writing instead works at the weave, yanking, pulling, ripping . . . exposing the infinite finitude that the rhetorics of "the social" and "the individual" attempt to cover over. The "genuine text," Cixous observes, is the place where "writing give[s] into itself" (*Three Steps* 100). This writing will not have been at the service of any proper authority, any regime of power.

But, and this is important, though it is *to no one in particular*, this writing will have been written *for the sake* of others; not to give or address anything *to* others but to expose the limit—"*not the limit of communication, but the limit upon which communication takes place*" (Nancy, *Inoperative* 67, emphasis in original). This is not to say that messages will not or ought not be passed in writing. Of course, of course. They are being passed [off] here. (Whether they are being "received" is quite another question.) But it is to say that a genuine writing is "the act that obeys the sole necessity of exposing the limit" (67). Writing is the singular gesture of touching that limit and so of *reaching for others*. Anyone who writes, as Nancy notes, "for the same, for himself, or for the anonymity of the crowd is not a writer" (66). Writing: attending to inscription's exscriptions. It follows that there is a precious little bit of *writing* going on in comp classes today, where students are commanded to "know" their audience and their (lone) purpose, where they are rewarded for grounding their inscriptions in "common places" (the same), for pretending to have mastered something, and for perpetuating the myths of community and identity via the strategies of clarity and linear presentation—for *effacing* inscription's exscriptions.

To let writing have its say is to acknowledge that "we are incapable of guaranteeing the link between our words, our deeds, our looks, and our pulsional sweeps" (Lyotard, *Libidinal Economy* 258). There can be no guarantee of clarity if there is no ego in charge of the play of language, no General demanding closure. The white terror of truth presumes his majesty the ego is on duty, *a priori*, and that he carries out that duty *responsibly*, under the banner of the Good. But, Lyotard says, "if we are sure of anything, it is that this operation (of exclusion) is a sham, that no-one produces incandescences and that they belong to no-one, that they have effects but no causes" (258). "We always," Cixous notes, "have the belief and the illusion that we are the ones writing . . . clearly this isn't true." We are taken (over) by writing in the way we are taken (over) by dreams. Writing "has us, carries us, and at a given moment, it drops us . . ." (*Three Steps* 98). "What we call texts," Cixous says, "escape us as the dream escapes us on waking" (98). We are not at the wheel of either one—we are the passengers, "riding a crazy text" (100). "Coming to writing" demands a certain giving (in), a certain passivity, a "passivity beyond passivity," as Ronell puts it, not the opposite of "activity," but "a space of repose and reflection . . . that would let the Other come" ("Activist" 300). Or cum. Don't miss the significance of this double entendre: "Coming to writing" is about allowing writing to *come to you* and to *cum through you*; coming *to* writing is cumming *for* writing, offering oneself up to its force. The whole affair of/with writing is about an orgasmic release of that which *wants to be said*, or rather *exposed* (cf. Cixous, "Coming to Writing" 52).

> Make rhizomes, not roots, never plant! Don't sow, grow offshoots!
> —Deleuze and Guattari, *A Thousand Plateaus*

Coming to writing requires, therefore, a certain "slowness," the slowness Cixous attributes to Clarice Lispector, which attends to the "living space, the betweenus"—or, in other terms, the "gathering" (Heidegger), the "you shares me" (Nancy)—of language (Cixous, "Clarice Lispector" 62). The epistemological attitude has forgotten the value of this space. "We no longer know how to receive," Cixous observes, we no longer take the time "to think the littlest thing according to its living mode." Our approach is murderous. We arrogantly attempt to conduct the flow of language, stuffing it into our prefabbed grids. For the sake of identity; for the sake of meaning-making; for the sake of "teachability." But it's time, Cixous says, to "save the approach that opens and leaves space for *the other*" (62). It's time to remember how to "'see,' before sight," to "hear before comprehension, to keep the space of waiting open" (62). It's time to hesitate rigorously in the face of our own hyper-re-activity, our own refusal to *reach toward the Other*.

A writing-for-writing course would not limit itself to "teaching" students to pretend to *conduct* language; it would not be reigned in by the hopelessly naive conception of "literacy" for which service-oriented composition courses were conceived. It would, rather, be about inviting the affirmative decision to "*let everything go*" (Lyotard, *Libidinal Economy* 259), to let loose the writing in you and watch it move, feel its brilliance crack your shell, blow your mind. It would be about inviting students to become-anonymous-conducting-machines, "not in order to stop the effects" but to allow them to flow into "new metamorphoses, in order to exhaust their metamorphic potential [*puissance*], the force [*puissance*] of effects that travels through us" (258). It would not be about founding an/other identity, solidifying the ego, but about watching this writing interrupt the myth of stable identity, about allowing the Laughter-in-language to laugh the notion of an ego-ideal *to death*. What this course would invite, then, would be an interruption of mythation and so . . . a celebration of finitude and an exposition of community.

The Teacher Supposed (Not) to Know: Performing a Pedagogy of Laughter

It is imperative to recognize the distinction between the white terror of truth and the "red cruelty of singularities." The former is about power, acquiring it and enforcing it—the pedagogical position is heaped in exactly this. The latter is about force, a violent force that cannot be possessed and that *breaks up/cracks up* (!) as it flows. The former territorializes; it only ever de-territorializes in order to re-territorialize (to move from *this* pedagogy to that *better* one). Red cruelties, on the other hand, are not constructive. Lyotard says they "consist entirely in non-construction, non-edification (uselessness), in sweeping away defences, in opening up routes, meanings, minds." This red cruelty, he says, "leaves fresh scars, just like a bulldozer." And, inasmuch as it sweeps away (radically sheds), it also "destroy[s] instantiated appropriations, powers" (261). A pedagogy in the service of red cruelties, that is, in the service of a libidinalized language, is a pedagogy in the service of *breaking up*: it is, in that sense, a pedagogy of laughter.

This pedagogy would protect no/thing. All instantiated appropriations—including the ones favored by the pedagogue assigned to "teach" this writing-for-writing course—would be fair game. What this pedagogue would have to know, then, is precisely that s/he does not/cannot *kno*w. If the typical pedagogical situation turns, like Lacanian psychoanalysis, on the illusion of the subject supposed to know, a pedagogy of laughter would turn on its demystification of that illusion. If the very best we can do in the service of writing-only is to become-anonymous-conducting-machines, it is time to admit that even the composition pedagogue cannot be a master of language or, therefore, of the truth it creates. The "masterful grasp" is a *masterful illusion*.

And a pedagogy of laughter would not be content to proffer the illusion: the ideal of the *sujet supposé savoir* would have to go. Pedagogical authority, of course, is intricately connected to the ideal of the teacher-as-knower, so to jettison the latter puts the former in a precarious situation—this is problematic. And/but, this problematic situation itself can run a line of flight for us. As Jane Gallop suggests, "To speak without authority is nothing new; the disenfranchised have always so spoken" (*Reading Lacan* 21). It is the ambiguity of the situation—to speak as an authority who has no authority—that may offer us the most.

A pedagogy of laughter would mimic phallic authority in the classroom in a way that would pervert its authenticity; authority would find itself enacted as a pedagogical performance—a farce or pastiche—informed by the notion that we cannot be masters of a language that *commands us*. Authority would not be renounced; rather, it would be performed in a way that would expose its illusoriness:

> Simply to refuse authority does not challenge the category distinction between phallic authority and castrated other, between "subject presumed to know" and subject not in command. One can effectively undo authority only from the position of authority, in a way that exposes the illusions of the position without renouncing it, so as to permeate the position itself with the connotations of its illusoriness.
>
> —Gallop, *Reading Lacan*

it would become *laughable*. It would be enacted, but it would not/
could not be seized. Gallop, following Irigaray, has suggested that this
type of mimicry is an infidelity, like marital infidelity, that "hollows [the
institution] out, ruins it, from within" (*Daughter's* 48). But "ruin" is too
harsh a term here. Authority in this classroom would get mercilessly
teased, parodied, pastiched, so that the distinction between the "castrated
other" and the subject presumed to know would seem less and less
distinct.

A pedagogy of laughter would recognize no politically correct position. It would not be a pedagogy of privilege flipping but pedagogy as
affirmative purgative: a pharmakon for spitting up the Proper and
its rationalism, a vomiting of vomiting itself. It would answer Cixous's
call for a "disgorging," a metaphorical "throwing up" of the "basic structures of property relations" ("Castration" 54) to free us for an excessive
affirmation beyond the false clarity of the either/or choice. It would make
a place for a heterogenous relation that would not only celebrate differences but would multiply them to the extent that they are no longer
capable of being named, classified, or purified. It would multiply them,
then, in a way that exscribes them from phallogocentric orderings. This
would be *feminist pedagogy at its best*.

Writing for Writing—
The Writer as Laugh(t)er

> [Writing is w]here we hope we will not be afraid of understanding the in-
> comprehensible, facing the invisible, hearing the inaudible, thinking the
> unthinkable, which is of course: thinking. Thinking is trying to think the
> unthinkable; thinking the thinkable is not worth the effort. Painting is
> trying to paint what you cannot paint and writing is trying to write what
> you cannot know before you have written.
>
> —Cixous, *Three Steps on the Ladder of Writing*

The role of the writer in this dangerous classroom space, where there is
no possibility of seizing phallic authority or mastering language, would
undergo a radical transformation. And the rhetorics of writing here
would invite that transformation—writing would be discussed other/
wise. The assignments in this class, for instance, would not ask students
to promote a single thesis, progress through a focused argument, or come

to a (necessarily premature) conclusion. They would not, that is, ask students to *im*pose themselves without *ex*posing themselves; writing involves risk—if they sign up for the class, they sign up for exposure, and not the comforting exposure of some tidy "inner self" but an exposure that will blast that illusion of (self-)unity to smithereens.

These assignments would not ask students to listen and think *for a moment* only so that they might then *stop* listening and thinking in order, clearly and cleanly—as if they write from the genre of genres—to wrap things up. Such assignments are not about *writing*; as soon as one turns one's attention to them, one is "no longer writing, no longer reading, no longer thinking, no longer communicating" (Nancy, "Myth Interrupted" 68). In this course, writing assignments would ask students to keep listening rather than to decide. Or even to decide but with heroic tentativeness—decisions would not signal an end to listening but only a momentary pause. These assignments would ask students not to "conclude" but to find a way to keep the communication going beyond their own text. They would not be about "exposition" or "argumentation" but about "trying out questions,"[20] pressing the limits of discourse, making unusual links, pointing to the limit, the betweeenus space. Listening, as Krista Ratcliffe has observed, gets the shaft in most comp courses, but (or perhaps *because*) it is listening that calls a writer toward the other. In this course, writing would operate as a function of perpetual listening, a constant straining toward and attending to the other, and not so much in order to under/stand as to bear constant witness to understanding's *withdrawal*, to embrace the fact that there is the Unhearable.

Of course, all of this implies the perturbing intervention of rhetoric. In this class, rhetoric would not be drained of its vitality, as it is when it is put into the service of the tiny aims of "comp." Indeed, this class demands a rhetoric on steroids, rhetoric as the intricate and continuous examination of the way language is working to produce what functions as truth—in any piece of discourse. This rhetoric would work alongside a "genuine writing," forcing a writer constantly to double back on herself and her "texts," to crack them open again to expose her own assumptions, to reveal inconsistencies, motivations, contradictions, limitations, incantations . . . In this class, students would be invited to disrupt their own positions, to contradict themselves, to expose all that must be hidden and excluded in the precious name of clarity.[21]

The demand for clarity is tied tightly to the assumption that the writer is a unified subject, an authentic Selfhood. This course, which would make no such presumption, would instead invite a writing that exposes the "polyethoi" (Vitanza) as such. Here, the entire range of the "polyphony of voices"—within and among students—would be invited in. The pedagogue in this course would make a space for even "abusive" conceptions of the other; to shush them, in a course like this one, would be to grant them immunity, to protect them from the bulldozer. This pedagogue would instead encourage the exposition and then the intricate teasing through of such conceptions. Rhetorical analysis would substitute for prohibition, demanding the careful and self-reflexive examination of the many emissions flowing from the one who is *never* [but] One, the perpetual analysis of what Irigaray calls "the specular make-up of discourse, that is, the self-reflecting (stratifiable) organization of the subject in that discourse" (*This Sex* 80). Students would be required, then, to be constantly on the lookout for what each of their various and incompatible discourses is making of them (the "good" the "bad" and the "ugly") . . . and to become aware of the multiplicity of subject positions they occupy—or, rather, that *occupy them*.

So, is there a text in this class? Yes, yes, yes. There are texts—a wild proliferation of texts, written and then written *on*, overloaded: palimpsests bursting at the seams, pushing the edge of the page, exhausted, messy, running over, zooming in several directions at once. *Réécriture*: not simply writing again to perfect what had been written previously (comp's "rewriting") but writing again and again, responding in every possible way to the call that writing never stops placing. *Réécriture*: writing's responsibility—not to "answer" a question but to respond to the call of the exscribed, to "muddy [inscription's] pages with added lines to the point of the utter confusion of signs and of writings . . . fulfill[ing] its original unreadability, crumpling it into the shapeless exhaustion of a [writer's] cramp" (Nancy, "Exscription" 322–23). Writing, in this class, would be on the loose, but it would never be released from its responsibil- E ity *to itself*, from its duty to respond perpetually to its *own* x call.

Deleuze and Guattari's c comparison of trees and rhizomes is helpful here. The e "aborescent" metaphor pretends that thought is system- s atic, hierarchical (branches of

knowledge), and grounded in
borescent models, by defini-
sion, clean distinctions. The
other hand, suggests that
it is never, they say, "a bi-
(*Anti-Oedipus* 39). A rhizome
taneously; it has no "begin-
the middle, between things,
Thousand Plateaus 25). It is
structured: it's "flat." Rhi-
other kind of analogy for
mand "a General" (17) to
writing is a writing for the
cation of the "characteristics

Reveals Itself As Truth
Nietzsche

firm foundations (roots). Ar-
tion, demand clarity, preci-
rhizomatic metaphor, on the
thought is heterogeneous:
univocalized, linearized one"
grows in all directions simul-
ning or end; it is always in
interbeing, *intermezzo*" (*A*
not unified or hierarchically
zomes, therefore, offer an-
writing, one that doesn't de-
regulate the flow. Rhizomatic
polyethoi. Here's their expli-
of a rhizome":

> [U]nlike trees or their
> any point to any other
> necessarily linked to traits
> brings into play very differ-
> even nonsign states. . . .
> but of dimensions, or rath-
> has neither beginning nor

T r u t h
Nietzsche

> roots, the rhizome connects
> point, and its traits are not
> of the same nature; it
> ent regimes of signs, and
> It is composed not of units
> er *directions in motion*. It
> end, but always a middle
>
> (*milieu*) from which it grows and which it overspills. . . . [T]he
> rhizome is an acentered, nonhierarchical, nonsignifying system without
> a General and without an organizing memory or central automaton,
> defined solely by a circulation of states. (*A Thousand Plateaus* 21)

The rhizomatic metaphor, when associated with writing, evokes a
paratactic linking-(non)system. If tree metaphors demand hypotactic
linkage and a road map with a charted course—beginning, middle, and
end—rhizomatic metaphors emphasize movement without criteria. The
emphasis is not on the origin or the destination but on the *going*, on the
motion itself. Through what Deleuze and Guattari call the "logic of the
AND" (the coordinating conjunctions of parataxis), writing in rhizomatic fashion becomes a libidinalized writing that "sweeps one way *and*
the other way, a stream without beginning or end that undermines its
banks and picks up speed in the middle" (*A Thousand Plateaus* 25). This
writing cannot be "defined by what it says, even less by what makes it a

signifying thing," they note. Rather, this writing is defined "by what causes it to move, to flow, and to explode—desire" (*Anti-Oedipus* 133). And there it is: a writer in this space would put her/himself(s) into the service of *desire in language*, into the service of finitude: writing would respond to its own call, which is the call of community, Being-in-common.

In an insightful 1993 MLA presentation called "Spaces for Resistance in Feminist Classrooms," Jarratt suggests that we might invite students to work with this desire in language by running what she calls a "black-market economy" in the writing classroom. Through this economy, students would be invited to explore the *excesses* in their language that can't be contained by the strictures and structures of the "old economy" (4). They would be invited to engage "forms of writing that set aside coherence, linear narrative, and conventions of classical realism as they inform academic writing." Jarratt suggests that pedagogues might be able to cut under-the-table "deals" with their students to focus on the excess, on what "clarity" sheers off, on what, we might say, is *laughable* and *laughing* in the language. Jarratt attempts, in other words, to find a way to validate the work that gets produced by *accident*:

> Here's an example: A student drops a word, writes a brilliant fragment in a journal, a daily assignment, a part of the paper that doesn't fit. I say, This is really interesting. Why don't you go with this? . . . The student says, Will it count? . . . And I say, Well . . . it doesn't really fit an assignment, but . . . [w]e'll cut a deal, a special deal. [But] You, the teacher, can't announce this as your plan, your intent to the whole class without falling back into the old economy. (6)

This is a leap in a good direction, and its momentum can only carry us further. What if we promoted a postpedagogical pedagogy in which this "blackmarket" economy operated as more than an exception? We wouldn't want a classroom in which the "blackmarket" became the "old economy," the status quo—Jarratt's warning is an important one. But we would be after a classroom in which the economy is *always* dark, shifting, erupting, out of order; in which there is no safe place to rest or to catch one's breath.[22] We wouldn't want the inscription of another Truth but an exscription from the arena of Truth. Writers in this writing-for-writing course would be encouraged to be severely suspicious of any seemingly serious or transparent communication, to point up the irrepressible dark side of their own discourse, and to violate linearity and the Law of Noncontradiction in what Worsham calls the "discursive equivalent of laughter" ("Writing Against Writing" 89). Writers, in this space, would be writers-cum-laughers.

[**Another Excursus: Writing The (Techno-)Body.**

What ought not go without note here is that the writing-for-writing course for which we've been calling is already flickering on the virtual horizon,

computers in composition
computers and composition
computers in/and composition

and it has spawned a revolution in composition instruction, a revolution that *breaks up* [at] some of the longest-lived "truths" of our profession. When writing and modern technology lean in and perform the handshake of connection, it sends traditional notions of composition instruction sssssspinning out of control. And, as we have already indicated, there is no turning back. We are not free to "just say no." We've been beaming out signals again, saying Yes before we got the chance to just say No.

Simply jacking into the Internet offers a great deal to what we already do in composition classrooms. One click of the mouse significantly upgrades our capacity for researching, peer-reviewing, and rewriting. However, we would do well to remember Heidegger's warning: we're in deep shit at the moment we begin to "regard [technology] as something neutral" ("Question" 4). When we take a full hit of new technologies in the composition classroom, we allow them to bring us into Being and invite them to redefine what pedagogy, knowledge, and composition can be. We're not talking about a face-lift for composition instruction; we're talking about a radical rrrr-u-p-t-u-r-e in what we thought was possible.

When we called for student-centered classrooms and enthusiastically rearranged the classroom furniture into cozy circles, most of us had no idea what was coming. here it comes Consider, for instance, what happens to pedagogical authority in a MOO, a Multi-User Domain, where the teacher's voice manifests itself as one line of text scrolling across the screen among many, with no special space allocation or privilege. Consider what happens to knowledge when the gatekeepers of its sacred borders can't seem to cover their territory fast enough or to get a word in edgewise. Learning in a MOO looks a lot like it does in Geoffrey Sirc's A&P parking lot: messy and out of control.[23] The cybergogue may strategically lay out class time, assign traditional essays, and "@shout" or hold up "big signs" to get everyone's attention. But in the end, s/he will not have been capable of commanding this classroom while it is in session. S/he will not have been capable of holding the floor, running the discussion, or protecting the process of mythation from interruption. In fact, in the virtual classroom, whether or not the teacher *thinks s/he knows* is irrelevant—the cybergogue's performance necessarily will have been one of interruption and demystification/demythification, one in which the illusion of the subject supposed to know cr-r-racks up.

And what happens to composition itself when texts go blatantly hyper-active, as they do in a MOO, on the Web, and in other hyper-textual spaces? Hypertexts spotlight something about language that our humanist impulses and pedagogical imperatives try like hell to forget: that language won't sit still, that it won't denote without also disseminating, and that we cannot control it. It is easier to command back a sneeze than it is to master the unruly body of language through the "technology of composition." Foucault t[r]ipped us off to this long ago, noting that "writing unfolds like a game that invariably goes beyond its own rules and transgresses its limits." He called then for the demystification of the author-function and described writing as "a space into which the writing subject constantly disappears" ("What Is" 142). To a certain degree, the Web, Multi-User Domains [MUDs, MOOs, MUSHs, etc.], and hypertext authoring programs are answering that call, emptying the author-slot and taking writing and writing instruction into a new era.

MOO-writing, in particular, exposes and challenges the mythic legitimacy of the "writer," pulling back the veil of authority by spotlighting the one who writes *as* a (piece of) writing (*itself*). Writing in a MOO—but this is also the case for *any* writing—is not the product of "the author" or "the hero," is not even the product of "the poet" or "the thinker," but is simply the exposition of "a singular voice" (Nancy, "Myth Interrupted" 70)—a finitude, a *polyethoi* who has been written and is perpetually being rewritten. MOO-writing, by explicitly exposing its own *illegitimate, unauthorized* state, suggests the illegitimate, unauthorized state of *any* writing. Similarly, when electronic texts go hypertextual, flaunting their embeddedness and explicitly inviting excavation, they signal the embedded state of *every* text: *all texts—pulp and electric— are always already hypertextual.* There is no text that's not hypertext. This is what the goals of clarity and linear progression hope to contain. This is the excess that the prosthetic composition course is designed to hush.[24]

But it's time to cut the shit: A wired classroom full of netheads who are happily addicted to technology is not at all comparable to a traditional classroom of technophobes who don't yet know that they are cyborgs. The "world" is ssShiftinggg. The drug we are beginning to push in the composition classroom will no doubt effect a fundamental change in our field, a gestalt turn roughly equivalent to a Copernican revolution. And this ride is not equipped with an emergency brake.

Hold on . . .

        hesitate • • •

            this road has not been paved

To those who still think they can *use* technology in the writing classroom to *empower* students, Cynthia Haynes issues a polite wake-up call: "[V]irtual spaces," she reminds us, "disrupt power relations, technify pathos, and morph identity" ("prosthetic_rhetorics" 84). The alliance between computers and composition fffforces the posthumanist paradox into the writing classroom. The argument for empowerment, Haynes notes, tactfully, seems at best "misguided." Here's Haynes:

> Using computers in composition pedagogy feels like a prosthesis that either compensates for a lack of control or frustrates when we can't control it. What we experience, then, is a psychological phantom pain associated with a threat to the self. ("Loss" 5)

A *phantom* pain. A *laceration*, not of the *Self* but of the "fabric of identity" that the rhetorics/myths of the Self have woven for more than a century. And/but, still .

              .

        . YOUCH! .

           .

         . Buckle up for a wild ride. Because, as

Haynes notes, "neither the fugitive nor the fortress mentality will stave off the electronic revolution" (9). The question is what we think we have to lose. If we think it's *writing,* Haynes invites us to "teleport to a MOO to see a community where *everything is writing,* or surf the World Wide Web and download all the text you want" ("Loss" 9–10). And if it is the Self we are hoping to protect, to hold together, to continue to revive, well . . . we're already too late for *that . . . ●*]

Forget Empowerment— Becoming-Imperceptible

In his essay "The Subject in Discourse," John Clifford asks a simple and yet "perplexing" question: "What do we teachers of composition hope to accomplish?" Do we hope, he asks, only to fulfill our "contractual obligations" by focusing on "syntactic clarity," and other skills "highly valued in business, industry, and government; or do we dare encourage oppositional thinkers, social activists, and resistant readers and writers?" His concern is whether composition teachers can be "politically responsible in traditional institutions" (38). He ends up suggesting that we-teachers not only can but *must* be "politically responsible," that our role is to help "students to read and write and think in ways that both resist domination and exploitation and encourage self-consciousness about who they are and can be in the social world" (51). Teachers, then, must be in the business of *em-powering* their students, but for Clifford, empowerment is not so much about making students more marketable as it is about liberating them from the false consciousness that drives big business, government, etc.

This seems an admirable goal. It is necessary, however, to remain suspicious of any pedagogical imperative that does not admit that the solidification of identity ("self-consciousness" about who one *is*) functions as a manifestation of "domination and exploitation." Clifford's question arises from a reductive dichotomy: The job of the pedagogue, he suggests, *either* is to use the composition classroom to mold students into "productive citizens" *or* to use it to mold students into political activists. He determines that we might accomplish the former even as we focus on the latter. Both options, however, turn on the question of *power;*

that is, both claim to empower the student in one way or the other. What both options have in common is a humanist impulse: Power always *belongs to Some/One*; it is always *an ego's power* (Lyotard, *Libidinal Economy* 261). The pedagogue placed in Clifford's di/lemma is forced to make a choice *for power*, either way, for both *assuming* power(/knowledge) and then for passing it on. This is a humanist equation offering only humanist solutions, and we choose not to be trapped in it. In fact . . . *llllet's get out of here!*

> We-writing-teachers are not after power. We are after the chance to experience the *force* that runs through language—what Cixous calls the "rhythm that laughs you" ("Laugh" 885)—and to offer students the chance to experience it.

Is the dance true? One will always be able to say so. But that is not where its force [puissance] lies.
— Lyotard, *Libidinal Economy*

We could not care less about molding egos or stabilizing identities—not through authoritarianism nor through nurturance: a ride on the finite rhythm that laughs language and technology and human-Being will do anything but stabilize. The force of writing works, Lyotard observes, "towards the eradication of all subjectivity" (*Libidinal Economy* 261). The writing in our writing-for-writing course would ceaselessly expose "composition" as a fraud and consequently "render impossible a certain type of foundation, utterance, and literary and communitarian fulfillment: in short, a[n oppositional] politics" (Nancy, "Myth Interrupted" 69). A composition pedagogy that actually devoted itself to *writing*, to making a space for students to *be written* by an unstable, laughing language, would be our choice. Door number three: genuine writing, writing as an exposition of finitude. If there is a place that "is not economically or politically indebted to all the vileness

"Political" would mean a community ordering itself to the unworking of its communication . . . a community consciously undergoing the experience of its sharing. To attain such a signification of the "political" . . . implies being already engaged in the community, that is to say, undergoing . . . the experience of community as communication: it implies writing. We must not stop writing, or letting the singular outline of being-in-common expose itself.
—Nancy, *Inoperative Community*

and compromise," a place that "is not obliged to reproduce the system," Cixous says, *that is writing* ("Sorties" 72, my emphasis). "If there is a somewhere else that can escape the infernal repetition," she continues, "it lies in that direction, where *it* writes itself, where *it* dreams, where *it* invents new worlds."

But this pedagogy of laughter, again, makes no claims to be apolitical. It only pledges its allegiance to an/other politics, an ethical and *feminist* politics, determined to fold back on itself, to laugh at itself laughing, to tune its ears to the rustle of finitude. This pedagogy is not interested in molding stable egos, but it is interested in fostering the writers of its own agenda. The difference, however, is significant: A pedagogy of laughter does not encourage students to Become-Human/ist or to Become-Social/ist; it does not, in other words, hail them as actors *per se*. Rather, this pedagogy encourages students to Become-Woman, to Become-Imperceptible,[25] to Become-Anonymous-Conducting-Machine; it invites them to hesitate, to strain to hear the noise, the static that gets drowned out by the booming call of the One. It invites them to Become *Legion*, to grow off-shoots, to do their morning mirror-check in a house of (multiply-hinged) mirrors. They ask: "Where am I?" And after this course, they answer: "Here . . .

    and here . . .

    and here . . .

    and here . . ."

The students in this class would be invited to be/come border-runners, to tremble at the edge of "every aspect and form of [their] definition," and to imagine, with Cixous, "the birth of borders" (*Three Steps* 130–31). They would be invited to enjoy their own identity-overflow, to laugh in the face of identity poly-ticks, to find joy in the realization that they land somewhere outside "the good side of the law," the "proper," "the world of order" (117). They would be invited to join Cixous in recognizing that "joy is imund," and that "it is not unclean. . . . Joy is out-of-the-world" (117). This pedagogy would invite students to take a full hit of language, to Be-on-language without censorship, without *protection*. It would invite them to shed their inherited need to fix meaning and erect solutions; it would offer them a not-at-all safe space to test the boundaries of the Proper and, perhaps, to begin to think precisely what formal education aims to make un thinkable.

Serving nothing but writing, a pedagogy of laughter would invite students to strain toward the Unhearable, to be made and simultaneously unmade by a language on the loose; it would invite them to be/come laughers who *get* laughed, to embrace incommensurabilities, to listen for the noise/static without needing to silence it. With a nod to Fleetwood Mac, this pedagogy would say: "Go your own way." But it would do so with no warm fuzzies or illusions of peacefulness. As Lyotard notes, to say "let each go his own way," is not "a prayer for non-violence, it is violence itself. Stop confusing violence with the white terror" (*Libidinal Economy* 261)—de(con)struction with devastation. This pedagogy would not be interested in creating a safe space. It would not be interested in protecting categories, borders, genders, or genres. It would, rather, offer students the chance to write, to be written, to follow "the writing" in them "like a painter draws: in flashes" (Cixous, *Three Steps* 156). It would offer them chance to "trip out" on/with "the imund text" (156), a text that will *blow their minds* and, in the process, blow up the "order of things." • • •

A(NOTHER) POST-SCRIPT ON
LAUGHTER AND FUTURITY

Whereas the common man takes this span of being with such gloomy seriousness, those on their journey to immortality knew how to treat it with Olympian laughter . . .

—Nietzsche, *Philosophy and Truth*

There can be no doubt about it, the deaths of God and Man have left us abandoned in the "world"—if that term, *world*, can still be used with any significance at all. The "foundations" on which we have attempted to construct meaning—about living, about dying—have crumbled, broken up. We have been abandoned to a free-fall. But the aim of this project has not been to dis-cover an-other toehold, to discover another way to stop the fall. Rather, the call issued here is for an *abandonment* to this abandonment, for a giving of oneself up to it affirmatively. Abandonment is, after all, what we share; the only commonality among we-singularities is our finitude: that we are infinitely singular and all alone *together*. To abandon oneself to abandonment in, for instance, a fffffit of laughter, is to experience the very limits of finitude, the place where singular beings touch, irrepressibly. Such experiences propel us, in a flash, beyond the fascist within and expose us to an/other community, without essence or telos, a community that always already *is*, that always already *shares*, that always already operates on an ethic of care for the Other *beyond the transcendental one*.

Inevitably, the tendency will be to judge this work across a pre-fabbed list of criteria: "Does it offer a solution or just criticize?" "Does it propose a workable plan of action or a feasible classroom practice?" "Is it politically, ethically, and academically responsible?"

254

Etcetera

•

•

•

But this work could not be less interested in ful-
filling such traditional expectations. It prefers to challenge the assumptions upon which such expectations are based; it hopes to question the
usual questions, to open a space for other questions to be posed. This
work will not help anyone "gain time." It attempts only to open
an/Other sensibility . . . an/Other "logic," an/Other "sense," an/Other
way of thinking about *being-with-one-another-in-the-world*. Not through
the reinscription of community, not through the creation of new myths.
But through the exposure of what those myths exscribe, through tiny
interruptions that could give community back to us . . . sans the "myth
of community," in indiscriminate flashes.

About Mis-readings and DIS-missings:
"Mis/readings" of this text are both inevitable and invited—after all,
what else is there? Every reading is a *mis*reading. But it's also necessary to
note that all [mis]readings are not equal. Some readings engage a text rigorously and with good faith, teasing through it with a careful consideration of all its possibilisms, its lines, its rides. Readers who engage a text
in this way (Heidegger might call it reading-with) expect and long to be
set in motion. Other readings, however, are the offspring of bad faith;
they offer an excuse to *dis*-miss a text up front, to not work through it
carefully, to avoid what it has to say. These readings shield the reader
from what *might have been read*. It seems unavoidable that this book frequently will be the object of bad-faithed readings, [mis]readings that will
have led to [mis]dismissings.

Some, for instance, will dismiss this work by arguing that its abstract
theorizing has nothing to do with "real life," that it doesn't empower or
enlighten the "real people" who attend our classes and/or walk our
streets. This work, some will say, is too abstract to bring about the finite
"revolution" for which it calls.

But what wants to be remembered here is that abstract notions have
already carved up "the world" for us; the most outlandish abstractions
are already responsible for motivating and justifying some of the most

frightening atrocities imaginable. Ethnic cleansing. Slavery. Rape. Genocide/Genus-cide/Gyno-cide. Is there anything more abstract than "race," "sex," or "class"? The category distinctions that support these very *real* persecutions have been *abstractly determined already.*

> One has to enter areas that are not covered by the insurance of "political correctness." One has to posit theories that appear unacceptable or problematic—it takes the courage of indecency to figure out why things have been so massively defeated.
>
> —Ronell, "Interview"

And any genuine "revolution" will have to venture there, into the zones of the "abstract," to provoke a radical rupture in what goes by the name "reality." This work aims for a revaluation of previously determined distinctions, for a dis/ruption of the border zones that make those distinctions thinkable; it aims for an/other, indecent "reasoning" that hopes to perturb and pervert "the system" to such an extent that we might find a line of flight from its drama.

At the same time, however, it ought to be noted that from the start this book has been driven by a certain kind of full-steam-ahead *empiricism.* It has been inspired and motivated by the failure of rational philosophies (which continue to ground this/our field of study), by the failure of their unified abstractions to ac/count for the overflowing multiplicities that surround us, that *are* us. This book began with glimpses of what

> [The rational philosopher] starts with abstractions such as the One, the Whole, the Subject, and [then] looks for the process by which they are embodied in a world which they make conform to their requirements. . . . Even if it means undergoing a terrible crisis each time that one sees rational unity or totality turning into their opposites, or the subject generating monstrosities.
>
> —Deleuze, *Dialogues*

gets left out, of what gets silenced by those abstractions. It began with the desire to attend to the material other who is perpetually erased via species-genus analytics and via the myths of "community" that support it. This book actually began, very personally, during a long conversation with my brother, the loving and brilliant recovering drug addict who may never "fit in" because he wears the numerous badges of "one" who *belongs* "out." This book began after witnessing, in an in-your-face manner, the ways in which inscriptions of communal mythology necessarily create a zone of exclusion as well, a "population erased from view."

It's in the name of that zone of exclusion that this work puts a call through to the Unthought, asking it to amplify itself—not to come clean but to announce itself *as* unpresentable, and so to challenge the limits of the/our knowable, to catapult us out of "the world" and into the Uncanny, where the exscribed play. "The only book worth writing," Cixous says, "is the one we don't have the courage or the strength to write. The book that hurts us (we who are writing), that makes us tremble, redden, bleed" (*Three Steps* 32). The only book worth writing is the one that refuses to stabilize identities and strives to *break them up*, the one that strains toward the Unhearable and tries to *crank it up*. Why write? To attend to the call of the exscribed. Same goes for reading: if it is to be worth it, we-readers will have to be willing to venture into a text unshielded, to dive in alone, to sever our links to the already-known, to the already-written.[1] One has to risk one's Self, let everything go. Without this risk, one goes nowhere. One relearns over and over again what one already knows: one thinks the thinkable, hears the hearable, speaks the speakable. One risks nothing and gains nothing.

This work also will be dismissed by those who fear that it will take something away from them, those who will read the call to "let everything go" as a grabbing away of some-thing they've got. But "an approach—to anything whatsoever," as Clarice Lispector puts it, "must traverse even the very opposite of what is being approached" (v). Only readers who understand that will recognize that this present work takes nothing away from anyone, that it *could not* take anything away. If it does not move you, if it offers you nothing new, soon you will be on your way, bored perhaps, but otherwise unaffected. If it, at times, breaks with your habits of thought, shatters your *topoi*, hurls you into foreign countries; if it manages, that is, to cost you your "world," it also will have opened for you another: Other worlds are always waiting impatiently in the wings. And finally, even if you guard your Self(s), your world(s), your life(s)—you will walk away with them intact. Any way you slice it, you will have been robbed of no/thing.

And lastly (though there will have been other dis/miss/als), this work will be dismissed by those who will read it uncritically and ungenerously as a leap into nihilism. Despite everything that has been said here about nonpositive affirmation, this work will have been heard by right and left

ears as a celebration of the No/Thing, of absence. What those who tune
in with their *third* ears will manage to pick up, however, is that the affirmation for which this project calls requires a *double negative*: a No to
presence and/but *also a No to absence*. A genuine affirmation says No to
nihilism in both its positive and its negative manifestations; it says no to
the positivity of the negative and to the negativity of the positive.[2] The
negative and the positive are caught in a closed circuit of signification,
each acquiring meaning and value through its negation of the other. It
will take a *double negative*, a No to both sides of the circuit, to break out
of what Derrida calls this "fabric of meaning" and to break *into* a nonpositive affirmation.

What's at stake in breaking out/in—in breaking ^{up}—is not an/other
landing site but the liberation/mobilization of what Deleuze has called
"another way of feeling: another sensibility" (*Nietzsche* 94). If this project
issues an invitation to laugh with the Laughter that shatters "all the familiar landmarks of [our] thought" (Foucault, *Order of Things* xv), it does
so in the name of the Unthought. *The stakes are high.* What is at stake
here is the potential for an ethics of decision that strains to hear the noise,
that hopes not to systematically exclude through solidification but to
resist closure through an affirmation of fluidity fluidity fluidity. What's at
stake in this celebration of destruction, this irreverent call to laughter, is
nothing short of .   .   .   .   .

.

.

the
FUTURE
●
●
●
●
●
●

NOTES

BIBLIOGRAPHY

INDEX

Notes

Preambulatory Emissions

1. In the preface to *The Differend: Phrases in Dispute*, Jean-François Lyotard notes that these days "we" often operate on the notion that "success comes from gaining time"; "reflection" is "thrust aside" today because it seems a "waste of time," because it gets us nowhere fast, because it offers us no "profit margin." Philosophy (or, what we might call *post*-philosophy—slow reflection), Lyotard notes, has to defend itself these days against two major adversaries: "on its outside, the genre of economic discourse (exchange, capital); on its inside, the genre of academic discourse (mastery)." Many who will pick up this book will lose interest when they realize that it offers no helpful pedagogical tips or quick political fixes . . . when they realize that reading it will not help them *gain time*. Those who continue reading past that realization are those to whom I-write, those interested less in mastery and quick fixes than in explosive dispersions and ethical revaluations. This book will not help "us" (we teachers of rhetoric/composition) do better what we've *always done*. It will question what we've been doing, problematize our assumptions, complicate what many wish to simplify.

2. It is typically assumed that technology is a tool, an invention that simply helps us do better what we've always done, teach what we've always taught. But the "question concerning technology" deserves to be reopened; we will attempt to do that here.

3. I'm thinking of Richard Rorty's suggestion in *Contingency, Irony, and Solidarity* that "speaking differently, rather than arguing well, is the chief instrument of cultural change" (7). This text interests itself in redescriptions. It's not interested in suggesting better ways to do what we've been doing; it's interested in redescribing to such an extent that other possibilities show up for us.

4. I always loved this passage in Cixous's "The Author in Truth":

> And to think that we spend precious months of our existence trying to give "proofs," falling into the trap of critical interpellation, allowing ourselves to be

261

led before the critical tribunal, where we are told: "Give us proof, explain to us what 'feminine writing' or 'sexual difference' is." I should retort: "A flute for proof—*I am alive*." (157)

5.   Vitanza's *Negation, Subjectivity, and the History of Rhetoric*, as well as his numerous articles on writing histories/hysteries of rhetoric, devote themselves to what he has called, variously, "*dissoi-paralogoi*," "anti-body rhetoric," "third sophistic rhetoric," and "libidinalized rhetoric."

6.   Third sophistics interest themselves not just in the supplement, the dirty underside that holds the logocentric (binary) system intact, but also in the nonsequential and uncountable *third* that overflows and upsets any dichotomy, in the harassing other that the epistemological impulse aims to excrete. Third sophistics set their scanners to "static," to the "noise" that must be silenced or appropriated for the sake of meaning-making. Third sophistics move beyond the *disso-logoi*, the privilege-flippings of negative deconstruction, and into what Vitanza has called *dissoi-paralogoi*, affirmative deconstructions that point to the excess flying around, to the leftover that's busily shattering the border zones of thought.

7.   See, for instance, Jim Porter's "Developing a Postmodern Ethics of Rhetoric and Composition" and John Schilb's "The History of Rhetoric and the Rhetoric of History."

8.   Gilles Deleuze and Felix Guattari suggest that "the book itself is a little machine" (*A Thousand Plateaus* 4) that ceaselessly plugs itself into other little machines in order to "work." Here's Deleuze and Guattari:

> We have been criticized for overquoting literary authors. But when one writes, the only question is which other machine the literary machine can be plugged into, *must* be plugged into in order to work. (4)

We'll be out to plug this little machine into as many others as possible, be they literary, theoretical, and/or musical.

9.   I have borrowed this term from Jean-Luc Nancy, who makes it a title for one of his chapters in *The Birth to Presence*. Here's Nancy:

> The exscribed is exscribed from the very first word, not as an "inexpressible" or as an "uninscribable" but, on the contrary, as writing's opening, within itself, to itself, to its own inscription as the infinite discharge of meaning—in all the senses in which we must understand expression. Writing, reading, I exscribe the "thing itself"—"existence," the "real"—which *is* only when it is exscribed, and whose *being* alone is what is at stake in inscription. By inscribing significations, we exscribe the presence of what withdraws from all significations, being itself (life, passion, matter . . .). The being of existence is not unpresentable: it presents itself exscribed. (338–39)

10.   This is Nancy again, describing an exscribing writing. See *The Birth to Presence*, 340.

11. This book is not *anti*-reason. Certainly, the language game of logic has a place in this text . . . but it is not consistently privileged; it makes its debut as *one language game among many*. To judge all other language games and thinking styles across One so-called standard is to perpetuate the very order of privilege we hope to problematize. Those interested in perpetuating the reign of reason tend to refer to any other thinking style as "*ir*rational," but here we will not take "reason" to be our reference point, our ground zero across which to judge all other ways of thinking/writing/reading. See note 12, below.

12. I'm working out of Lyotard's *The Differend* again. Specifically, I'm thinking about his discussion of signs and silences, in which he calls for historians ([re]writers of History) to begin lending "an ear to what is not presentable under the rules of knowledge." He continues:

> Every reality entails this exigency insofar as it entails possible unknown senses. Auschwitz is the most real of realities in this respect. Its name marks the confines wherein historical knowledge sees its competence impugned. [But] it does not follow that one falls into non-sense. The alternative is not: *either* the signification that learning [science] establishes *or* absurdity. (57–58, my emphasis)

There are Other ways of knowing, other significations, other ways of *making sense*. Here, we will have been after a liberation of these *Other* ways.

13. In *A Thousand Plateaus*, Gilles Deleuze and Felix Guattari discuss three basic types of lines that constitute the subject of a rhizomatic analysis. The first is a molar line that represses differences as it constructs fixed identities by way of oppositional hierarchies (self/other, male/female, white/black, good/evil, etc.). The second is a molecular movement away from Oneness, which disrupts its linearity and its cohesiveness, "as when 'cracks' occur in the facade of one's identity, or when," Best and Kellner suggest, "one begins *cracking up*" (!) (100, my emphasis). Lastly, there are lines of flight, of "deterritorialized intensities" (Deleuze and Guattari, *A Thousand Plateaus* 32) where, Best and Kellner say, "cracks becomes [*sic*] ruptures and the subject is shattered in the process of becoming multiple" (100).

14. Thanks to Michelle Ballif for this phrase (this turn of a trope) and for this idea. For an innovative take on linguistic seduction, see Ballif's *Seduction, Sophistry, and the Woman with the Rhetorical Figure*, forthcoming from Southern Illinois UP in this series.

15. I'm alluding to Jean-François Lyotard's discussion, in a notice to Hegel in *The Differend*, about the ways in which totalizing patterns of thought, from Plato on, led us straight to Auschwitz. Lyotard says: though "we wanted the progress of the mind," what we got was the mind's "shit" (91).

1   PHYSIOLOGICAL LAUGHTER

1.   See, for instance, *Fatal Strategies*, where Baudrillard suggests that the subject may as well give up its attempt to dominate the object; it has never been successful. Also, see his essay "Fatal Strategies," in *Selected Writings*, where he says that "things have found a way to elude the dialectic of meaning, a dialectic which bored them" (185).

2.   I'm alluding to Jean-François Lyotard's pagan pragmatics here. In *Just Gaming*, "Second Day," Lyotard discusses the pragmatic/political differences between a monotheistic God and the pagan gods (19–43).

3.   I capitalize Laughter here and throughout this work when I refer to a Laughter that is not human. When we speak of *this* Laughter, of *kairotic* Laughter, we speak of a force, a rhythm beyond human control. Human laughter is not *kairotic* Laughter, but human laughter can, and occasionally does, call into the force of *kairotic* Laughter with a wild and affirmative invitation. This kind of human laughter will be discussed later in this chapter as a political-cum-ethical response to the posthumanist paradox.

4.   Typically, *physis* implies divine *order*, the way things are by "nature," and *nomos* refers to local order, local customs/conventions and the laws they support. The former is metalinguistic, the latter is linguistic, socially constituted, a work of Man—the supposed measure of all things. *Physis*, in this book, however, will align itself with what Nietzsche called the "great sweep of life," which has, he says, "shown itself to be on the side of the most unscrupulous polytropoi" (*Gay Science* 282). *Physis*, then, in this context, will refer to that *un*civil and wildly excessive space outside of our conventions and category restrictions. *Nomos* will refer to those rational restrictions, which are imposed by human beings in an effort to assert control over what Heidegger called the "storm" of Being.

5.   References to the "divine" and "mysticism" ought not be misread in Miller as nods to any kind of metaphysical presence. Here, they refer simply to that for which human reason cannot account. Not God but EXCESS. Similarly, Miller's suggestion that *kairos* controls the speaker is not a suggestion that *kairos* is a godlike, teleological force. That human beings operate as functions of other functions does not necessarily indicate that some-Thing is willingly and consciously pulling the/our strings. Put simply, that we are often puppets doesn't necessarily indicate that there is a puppeteer. This was Nietzsche's point: it is our grammatical structure that leads us to believe there must be a doer for every deed.

6.   I use the generic masculine here because the subject, for Descartes and Kant, is, without exception, male.

7.   The continued lullaby is evidenced in rhetoric and composition, for instance, in the after-rustlings of those who have scrambled to *save* the humanist subject somehow, whether it be by "rescuing" or "discerning" it, so that this subject might continue to act and get on with the old liberatory programs (but also pogroms). These after-rustlings are continual reminders that we remain deep in the throes of the double slumber. In the midst of the hype about the "death of man," or "the author," or "the subject," we respond simply by transferring our desire for mastery onto a subjected subject.

8.   Obviously, if I were to point to all the instances of the so-called *generic* masculine in my sources, I'd be spending more time *sic*[k]ing than writing. Therefore, this *sic*[k]-fit will be my last explicit indulgence.

9.   I will explicitly discuss the political potential of this work in chapters 3 and 4. Those chapters will be applications (to politics and pedagogy) of the rhetoric of laughter that will be worked through in the first two chapters and the major excursus of this project.

10.   Two things: first, thanks to Cynthia Haynes for the phrase "negatively projected hologram." And, second, none of this is to say that *politics* is no longer possible; *homo seriosus's* troubles are transferable only to a certain (humanist) approach to politics. It will be necessary for a "polyethoi" to engage [in] a politics that would Be Other/Wise, a posthumanist politics, perhaps, that would have no *end* in/as/to sight/site/cite. See, for instance, the end of Butler's *Bodies That Matter*, where she suggests that because we are made by the very laws we hope to battle politically, politics can neither be a matter of intentional production nor "pure" subversion. Performativity, Butler asserts, means being implicated in what one opposes and forging ahead anyway, recognizing that "[t]he incalculable effects of action are as much a part of their subversive promise as those we plan in advance" (241).

Deleuze and Guattari's call for rhizomatics and schizo-analysis, Lyotard's call for "paratactics" and "pagan pragmatics," and Victor Vitanza's call for "just drifting," for instance, are other examples of political tactics that need not (*ought not*) have an end in sight. For this group, it is necessary, rather, that politics have only moments, instants in sight. Furthermore, "the deconstruction of identity," Butler says, "is not the deconstruction of politics; rather it establishes as political the very terms through which identity is articulated" (*Gender Trouble* 148). And it is from here that we might reconfigure the possibilities for a posthumanist "agency" and a postidentity "politics"-cum-ethics that will have promoted a "community" with neither the glue of sub/stance nor of a fascistic "project." This will be our goal in chapters 3 and 4.

11.   I'm using the term "man" here unproblematically and in the gendered sense in reference to the subject because I believe the subject of the human sciences is inherently rather than incidentally a masculine construct.

12. But see Lyotard's *Libidinal Economy* for an/other look at Marx as a "hermaphrodite," that is, as a conflicted subject who is *both* an ideologue and a cynic: he works to transcend false consciousness but is haunted by the recurring realization that it cannot be transcended.

13. Žižek, it should be noted, doesn't like this laughter, as his term for it suggests. He says that it occupies a critical distance from the workings of things, which makes it only and always a *cynical* laugh.

14. Kundera's notion of Devil laughter makes no explicit distinction between it and what I will call "giving laughter." Even my own distinction is, to be sure, a slippery one, as the two laughters work together and blend into each other. What Kundera calls Devil laughter actually embraces both forms of laughter I'm attempting to describe. For Kundera, we laugh when things are suddenly deprived of their "putative meaning." "Initially, therefore," he says, "laughter is the province of the Devil. It has a certain malice to it (things have turned out differently from the way they tried to seem) [Devil's laughter], but a certain beneficent relief as well (things are looser than they seemed, we have greater latitude in living with them, their gravity does not oppress us) [giving laughter]" (*Book of Laughter and Forgetting* 61).

15. I'm thinking here of Burke's outrageous treaties on the "Demonic Trinity"—a parody of the Holy Trinity that consists of excretions of the body's privy parts: excrement, urine, and erotic ejaculations (*Grammar of Motives* 300–303; *Language as Symbolic Action* 340).

16. I'm referring to the following reference made by Aristotle in the *Rhetoric*: "Gorgias rightly said that one should spoil the opponent's seriousness with laughter and their laughter with seriousness" (*On Rhetoric* 3.18). Nietzsche says almost the same thing in *The Gay Science* when he says: "Come let us kill the spirit of gravity" with comedy. Vitanza's attention to this notion in his article entitled "What's 'at Stake' in the Gorgian Fragment on Seriousness/Laughter," in *PRE/TEXT* 10.1–2 (1989): 107–14, has been enormously helpful to me in this book.

17. The street-gang model comes to mind, whose initiation techniques often include demand for some proof of allegiance in the form of a random violent act against someone *outside* the gang.

18. It is, however, important to note here that in *Discours, Figure* (Paris: Klincksieck, 1971), just a year before Deleuze and Guattari's *Anti-Oedipus* and three years before his own *Libidinal Economy*, Lyotard suggests that the subject *enters into* desire through castration/lack. Deleuze and Guattari attack him for this in *Anti-Oedipus*, suggesting that it's an "idea originating in bad conscience rather than the unconscious" (294). And by *Libidinal Economy*, as this quote suggests, Lyotard appears to agree, at least in this section of the book.

19. It ought to be made explicit here that we are drawing a critical distinction between unproblematically forgetting ("just forgetting") and forgetting *justly, affirmatively.* In her discussion about Desert Storm and the Vietnam Syndrome, Ronell, for instance, asks, "How can cure depend upon uncomplicated forgetting—unless it issued from a Nietzschean injunction which our sorry-assed political body would be incapable of assimilating? Even this would require some understanding of what it was we were supposed to forget" ("Activist" 296). And this will have been an important point: we are not dismissing the significance of countermemory here. Countermemory will have been our starting point, our springboard.

2   DISCURSIVE LAUGHTER

1. Samuel Ijsseling devotes a chapter and a chapter title to this very question in *Rhetoric and Philosophy in Conflict: An Historical Survey.* He is playing off the same question (posed in other terms) asked by Nietzsche, Heidegger, and Lacan—it is a question about the substance of the subject who "speaks."

2. Offered, for example, by Ferdinand de Saussure (*Course in General*), Martin Heidegger ("Language"), Jacques Lacan (*Ecrits* 280), Michel Foucault (*Language, Counter-Memory, Practice*), Jacques Derrida (*Of Grammatology; Dissemination;* "Differance" 145), Judith Butler (*Gender Trouble; Bodies That Matter*), and Jean-François Lyotard (*Just Gaming* 38), etc.

3. See Leo Tolstoy, *What Then Must We Do?* Trans. Aylmer Maude. London: Oxford UP, 1960.

4. Fredric Jameson has offered this translation of Nietzsche in an epigraph to his *The Prison-House of Language.* Walter Kaufmann and R. J. Hollingdale, however, offer a different translation in their edition of Nietzsche's *Will to Power.* The passage in question is aphorism #522, p. 283 in that edition; or, in Schlecta's classic edition, *Werke,* it is on p. 862 of the third volume (p. 454 in the four-volume edition). The latter source, in the original German, reads: "Wir hoeren auf zu denken, wenn wir es nicht in dem sprachlichen Zuange tun wollen, . . ."

Here's Kaufmann and Hollingdale's translation: "We cease to think when we refuse to do so under the *constraint* of language" (my emphasis). And here's Jameson's translation of the same sentence: "We have to cease to think if we refuse to do it in the *prison-house of language*" (my emphasis). Driven by our own shameless motivations, we will go with Jameson's translation.

5. In *Being and Time,* Heidegger establishes a clear distinction between "willing and wishing" and "urge and addiction" (238). Ronell's discussion of

Being-on-drugs takes off from and/but also overflows this distinction. Willing, in Heidegger's ontology, is only *authentic* if it is not "tranquilized" by addiction. While addiction "does not rule out a high degree of diligence in one's concern," he says, it does "tactically alter" the potential for that willing (239). In other words, it turns one's "hankering" to only "what is 'there'" in the "actual world" (238). Here's Heidegger:

> In hankering, Being-already-alongside . . . takes priority. The "ahead-of-itself-Being-already-in . . ." is correspondingly modified. Dasein's hankering as it falls makes manifest its addiction to becoming "lived by" whatever world it is in. . . . Being-ahead-of-oneself has lost itself in a "just-always-already-alongside." (238)

Because you can only be addicted, as Ronell says, to "what is available," it "traps you in a circle without futurity" (*Crack Wars* 42). To suggest that Dasein is stuck in the mode of "just-always-already-alongside" is, as Ronell says, an ontological way of suggesting that someone is "going nowhere fast," that someone has been "sped up only to fall behind" (42). Ronell, however, challenges Heidegger's distinction between Being-authentically and Being-on-drugs. This excursus attempts to open connections between our project and this challenge.

6.   Don't miss the significance of this: the question of who/what is doing the calling no less than haunted Heidegger's ontology and Freud's ego-psychology. Whether it is the "call of conscience" or the "superego" that beams out signals for a "hit" of language (or any other drug), our notions of Being authentically are severely problematized.

7.   It's important to note that Althusser's antihumanist turn is also a *structuralist* turn. Structuralism will be discussed later in this chapter, but before proceeding further, it is necessary to say that structuralism will not have been an acceptable turn out of humanism—it simply moves the certainty from the subject to the structure that constitutes it. Either way, excess is rejected, excluded, silenced. We use Althusser here for his insights into the call of subjectivity, but we, along with Vitanza, reject his rigid structuralism. Here's Vitanza, from "An After/word":

> If I reject humanism, I also cannot trek with Althusser's *turn* (i.e., his particular tactic) away from humanism; he finally achieves it at too high a price. Which is structuralism. (His is a turn, therefore, that I cannot leave unstoned.) . . . Structuralism is a paranoid's (not a para/noyance's) vision. (230–31)

8.   See Bernstein 14.

9.   Both Heidegger and de Man frequently have been dismissed as thinkers because of their involvement with National Socialism. However, easy dismissal seems both a naive and an irresponsible tack with regard to these two path-breaking (post)philosophers. It seems important, rather, to read them all

the more *carefully*, to listen closely to what kind of Being-in-the-world they're promoting.

10. *Dissoi Paralogoi* is Vitanza's neologism, first used in "Critical Sub/Versions."

11. It seems important to head off right away a potentially disastrous mis/reading of this term. *Ecriture féminine* is not only "women's writing." Hélène Cixous, following Derrida, uses deconstruction to explode binary oppositions to facilitate the releasing of a "new" writing that she says would "steal" and "fly," that would steal idioms from theoretical discourse and reinscribe them so as to make them fly out of the logocentric structure. Derrida steals the term *écriture* from the theoretical lexicon and makes it fly in the face of the structure that that lexicon supports. And Cixous, very much in the Derridean countertradition of the trickster, *steals* the Derridean notion of "*écriture*" ("writing-as-feminine-locus") and turns it into "*écriture féminine*." This engages a very subtle distinction: "the feminine," though a postgendered space, remains, for Cixous, a space that females have an easier access to than males precisely because of their gender coding. (See, especially, "Sorties," in *Newly Born Woman*.)

Nevertheless, Cixous ("Laugh") and Julia Kristeva ("Women's Time") explicitly and Irigaray (*This Sex*) implicitly suggest that males are not incapable of creating that "writing said to be feminine." (Here, I disagree with Diana Fuss, who says in *Essentially Speaking* that *l'écriture féminine* is a sophisticated expression of essentialism.) This writing cannot be theorized, interpreted, mastered. It eludes our will-to-theorize, and that's what makes it revolutionary and "feminine." Interpretation, the will-to-knowledge (Nietzsche), is the coping stone of scientific and philosophic discourse, but it is also the murder of play, of differences, of the "feminine." *L'écriture féminine* refuses to be interpreted, codified; to sail in its waters means to allow oneself to *Be* differently, to think differently, to "become Woman"—whether the sailor be male or female. So there is men's writing and there is women's writing; and then there is *l'écriture féminine*. The "feminine" of *l'écriture féminine* is a postgendered feminine, a third position, beyond the male/female binary.

12. Vitanza's relentless(ly) "light manipulations" have earned him the reputation of being the "bad boy of rhetoric," and I know of no better example in the field of rhet/comp of one who is out to laugh with the Laughter in language. Vitanza's texts pull back the discursive facade to expose, as its "foundation," a wild and unmasterable language on the loose.

13. It is important to note the incredible resistance Vitanza has faced in the still terribly *philosophical* field of rhetoric. Here is George Kennedy on Vitanza's "Critical Sub/Versions":

Vitanzan Vitalism is a form of *letteraturizzazione*, a kind of linguistic herpes that comes and goes, privileging the *ecrible* over the *lisible*, expression over analysis. Note its fondness for figures of speech. The major question [!], not faced by Vitanza, though Gerard Genette tried to grapple with it in *Figures*, is how we translate some awareness of the antibody of rhetoric into teaching composition. (231)

What Kennedy calls the "major question" is certainly an interested one: he is invested, philosophically so, in making *language* teachable, in *mastering* it, codifying it. But Vitanza's "theatricks" expose the naivete of such an investment. Language is on the loose, and Vitanza's "vitalism" exposes its uncontrollable break outs/ups. Suppose we asked an/other question entirely and called *it* the "major question"? What if we asked: What can a re/cognition of the antibody rhetoric teach us about what we're trying to teach in composition classes? How might we reconfigure the teaching of composition so as to make a space for this re/cognition? These are the questions driving this present work, and in the last chapter, they are the questions with which we will deal.

14. In the second section of chapter 3, we will take up this notion that we are "called" by our own finite being.

15. Obviously, for Heidegger, this unethical territory involves his acceptance of the rectorship and his flirtation with National Socialism. Heidegger's ethics, including the distinction it makes between the call of the "they" and the call of one's ownmost authenticity, may not have been suspicious enough of the multiplicitous nature of *any* call. It may not have provided for a distinction to be drawn between the call of conscience and the call of the Storm Trooper—when he tried, presumably in good faith, to answer the former, he connected with the latter. (See Ronell's *Telephone Book* for an intense examination of this.)

When I mention Freud's unethical territory, I'm referring to his disregard—but I mean to the level of torture—for his patients (Emma Eckstein as example, par excellence). In his effort to be true to the call of a *structure*, of a theory, and to the proponent of that theory (Fleiss), he sacrificed Emma. He sacrificed Emma-the-human-being, for instance, in order to be true to Emma-the-statistic, Emma-the-symptom . . . of Fleiss's unorthodox notions about the connection between psychosis and nasal cavities. For a good peek into this horrific scene, see Jeffrey Masson's *Assault on Truth*.

EXCURSUS—BEING-HARD/WIRED

1. For an interesting reexamination of the term "interpellation," see pp. 49–52 of Donna Haraway's *Modest Witness@Second_Millennium.FemaleMan© _Meets_OncoMouse*™.

2.   It is not necessarily the "drug," in other words, that is the problem for Heidegger. It is, rather, the addictive *structure*, already in place, through which addiction becomes addicted.

3.   It probably doesn't need to be noted that this seemingly bodiless war actually wracked up quite a few bodies. And not just so-called enemy bodies, either. All our high-tech equipment didn't prevent "our side" from accidentally blowing away its own soldiers in what is paradoxically termed "friendly fire"; it also wasn't able to warn our soldiers about the hazardous gases they were breathing in. In fact, bodies were such an unacceptable topic in the rhetoric of this war that when vets began falling ill from those gases, the "powers that be" continued for some time to *lie lie lie*, to insist that U.S. soldiers had not been exposed to any such gases, to keep the topic of bodies and death out of the discourse on Desert Storm.

4.   It is necessary, perhaps, to comment once more on Heidegger's flirtation with National Socialism. It may be that Heidegger's hope, his faith that a distinction can be maintained between the "call of conscience" and a(ny) call from the "they," led him into a trap with the Nazis. That is, Heidegger's posthumanist approach was limited by his unwavering belief in the capacity to Be-*authentically*. And if language was admitted into the authentic scheme of things in Heideggerian ontology, other "drugs" were not. Therefore, Heidegger's "metaphysics" perpetuated, in some sense, the humanist distinction between Being-*authentically* and Being-*on-something*. Even Heidegger, then, found himself temporarily seduced by that particular intersection of humanism and technology.

5.   Thanks to Cynthia Haynes for pointing this out to me and for being my RL "knowbot" in all things VR.

6.   This, by the way, is no futuristic dream/nightmare—indeed, even a cursory Net Search on "Agents" yields a hefty return. Agent software is now available for a reasonable price from any number of independent companies. Most new computers come with agent software already installed. Testing is well underway for soft-bots that, as Sherry Turkle notes in *Life on the Screen*, "collaborate with their human users and, through producing off-spring, they continue to improve." And it gets better. Turkle continues:

> In other projects, the agents collaborate with each other in order to learn: "My agent talks to your agent." An agent for sorting electronic mail is trained to consult its peers (other software agents) when faced with an unfamiliar situation. Over time, the agents learn to trust each other, just as users learn to trust the agents. (99)

7.   Turkle notes that plenty of users are already worried about the social and legal implications of these software agents. They want to know up front if they could "be held responsible for their agent's actions and transactions" (100).

Some also want to know "who owns the immense stores of information about their habits that their agents might come to possess?" Others worried about the possibility of agents working for "rival corporations" that might "be programmed to give you very good advice for a time, until your agent came to rely on him. Then, just at a critical moment, after you had delegated a lot of responsibility to your agent who was depending on the double agent, the unfriendly agent would be able to hurt you badly" (100). These are not unfounded concerns.

    8.   This is an allusion to Jean-François Lyotard's refrain in the "Presentation" section of *The Differend*: "Is it happening?" (79).

3   A RHETORIC OF LAUGHTER FOR FEMINIST POLITICS

    1.   See Victor Vitanza and Diane Davis's "Logocentrism" entry in Teresa Enos's *Encyclopedia of Rhetoric*, New York: Garland Publishers, 1996.

    2.   It seems necessary to blush openly at this reductive label: "mainstream feminist politics." What this term will hope to evoke (for it cannot re/present anything) is any oppositional politics engaged *in the name of feminism and/or a category "women."* It hopes to evoke a host of pragmatic (mostly American) feminist political endeavors (there are, of course, other kinds of American "feminisms"), including those operating under other reductive labels, such as radical, eco-, spiritual, and liberal feminisms. What is at issue here is not the overwhelmingly diverse manifestations of (American) "feminist politics" but rather the feminist impulse to the political *over* the ethical—a pointing outward rather than inward. What is at issue is a political imperative that demands a particular type of "action": action commensurable with the Enlightenment's dream of "liberation." Ethics is here subordinated to and *derived from* the political imperative. This project is interested in investigating an/other politics, an ethical politics that takes its cue from a Nietzschean revaluation of all values, a pointing inward first.

    3.   For the record, I would not call this approach "postmodern." It appears, rather, to be a metaphysical after-spasm, a retroactive foundationalism that is *modern*, through and through.

    4.   But this is way too easy. It's not that "emancipation" is abandoned in "ludic" postmodernism; it is, rather, like other key Enlightenment terms (e.g., "subject," "agency," "foundation," etc.), radically redefined and redescribed so as to occupy a (nomadic) space in a postmodern world. It remains a goal—but a goal of a different kind.

    5.   "Radical feminisms" are often an exception because they tend to be interested in female privilege rather than equality.

6.   See the first chapter of Susan Hekman's *Gender and Knowledge* for a detailed account of this link.

7.   But this ought not be confused with neoconservatism. Nor ought it be conflated with timidity or cowardice. "Let's get out of here!" ("Laugh" 885) is not in any sense equal to the refrain that runs through Monty Python's *Holy Grail*: "Run away!" Cixous's call is to resoluteness, a bold flying straight in the face of phallogocentric orderings with the aim of bursting through and *out*. Lines of flight/escape are not for fearful retreats but for momentary anticipatory advances.

8.   It seems important to note that celebrating a third way(ve) does not necessarily challenge the continuing value of other way(ve)s. We are after a both/ and approach here. In fact, third wav(er)ing would be unthinkable without the work of first and second waves, as their negative deconstructions bust loose the encrusted site of privilege to unconceal an/Other (third) way. Strategic essential-isms—sometimes in the form of antipluralist feminist political strategies—are dangerous but can nevertheless be of inestimable value as negative deconstruc-tions. As (post)feminists, we *cannot not* want what the work of first and second wavers are after.

9.   The issue here is not that anyone ever mis/takes the word for the thing, the word "tree" for a tree. The issue is one of signification. The nursery rhyme about sticks and stones, for instance, propagates an unfortunate dichotomy be-tween "real" violence and "just words." It is not true that "names will never hurt me." Names, in fact, will *create* me, who I can be and what I can do. As Giorgio Agamben puts it: "Even if we can completely distinguish a shoe from the term 'shoe,' it is still much more difficult to distinguish a shoe from its being-called-(shoe), from its being-in-language" (73). To a large extent, you *are* what you're called . . . as much as you are what you *eat*. Linguistic representation is a serious business.

10.   Susan Hekman has taken Gilligan's notion of "*the* moral voice" into a postmodern arena in her book *Moral Voices, Moral Selves*. Her generous inter-pretation of Gilligan's work and its implications explode the male/female binary in ways that Gilligan very likely never imagined. *The* moral voice, through Hek-man's explication, becomes moral voices, and an entire world opens up at the site of that newly inscribed plurality. This is an excellent example of the ways in which negative deconstructions invite postoppositional thought.

11.   I want to acknowledge that it does an enormous disservice to the wide-ranging differences among feminist activities to lump them in this way. When I use these reductive labels (radical, spiritual, eco-), it is with the recognition that there is as much diversity *within* what gets called, for instance, "radical femi-nism" as there is *between*, say, "radical" and "spiritual" feminisms. As usual,

identity terms cannot/will not cover their territory fully enough. When these terms are used here, they are used with much wincing and squirming on my part.

12. See, for instance, Susan Faludi's *Backlash: The Undeclared War Against American Women*. New York: Doubleday, 1991.

13. For a brilliant reading of *SCUM* across the Bobbitt Bobbing, see Melissa D. Deem's "From Bobbitt to SCUM: Re-memberment, Scatological Rhetorics, and Feminist Strategies in the United States." Suggesting that the "contemporary appeal of the *SCUM Manifesto*" ought not be "surprising given the place of women and violence in the 1990s," Deem notes that SCUM "taps into a collective rage which resonates today with a new generation of women who encounter it for the first time." "Women," she observes, "have finally caught up to *SCUM*." And Deem quotes Ruby Rich to make her point: "The '90s is the decade of the Riot Grrrls, the Lesbian Avengers, Thelma and Louise, the Aileen Wournos case, and Lorena Bobbitt (the woman who cut off her husband's penis). There's something intensely contemporary about Solanas, not just in her act but in her text as well" (see Deem 521).

14. See Butler, *Bodies That Matter*, pp. 167 and 181–82, for a good discussion of both claims.

15. The problem, of course, is that of simple reversal. In a call for exscription from phallogocentrism in *This Sex*, Luce Irigaray also offers some applause for those feminisms busy deconstructing the phallocratic machine from the inside. Here's Irigaray:

> But we do not escape so easily from reversal. We do not escape, in particular, by thinking we can dispense with a rigorous interpretation of phallogocentrism. There is no simple manageable way to leap to the outside of phallogocentrism, nor any possible way to situate oneself there, that would result from the simple fact of being a woman. (163)

What is of importance to us here is that we are after more than what Baudrillard calls the "phallic fable reversed," even if we get there *only* through the rupture created in the play of that reversal.

16. Woman, according to Freud and Lacan, wants to HAVE the phallus but can't ("penis envy"). And to make mat(t)ers worse, a perverse twist in the castration complex lands her in the unenviable position of functioning AS the phallus, of BEING the phallus. According to psychoanalytic theory, she wants to own it but can only ever Be it. For a more thorough rereading of the Bobbitt affair across the notion of a postfeminist perspective, see my "Breaking Up at Phallocracy: Post-Feminism's Chortling Hammer."

17. I can't resist mentioning the fact that John Wayne Bobbitt ended up a porn star(lett). He and the "Bobbitt Girls" have traveled the country doing

strip bars and even did low-budget porn flicks that offer an up-close and personal glimpse of phallic-power reattached. Perhaps still more stunning is the hot demand for a peek at his "Franken-penis," a scanned photograph of which quickly became obtainable over the WWW.

18. This seems to me to be precisely where Camille Paglia misses the proverbial boat. She recognizes that men's violence against women is a fundamental problem, primal—she recognizes it perhaps more clearly than those feminists who refuse to talk with her. But because she doesn't deconstruct that "primal" scene, because she never unpacks what calls itself "the natural," she doesn't consider the *conditions of its possibility*. Rather than challenge the phallogocentric structures of thought that have produced what goes by the name "nature," she opts to call those very structures to the rescue. She argues that "society" is our only hope against the violent forces of "nature," that it is a "system of inherited forms" designed to reduce "our humiliating passivity to nature" (1). We can't change nature; men's violence against women is natural; therefore, we need society to intercede. "The foulmouthed roughneck," she says, "is produced not by society's sexism but by society's absence" (16). Again: "Rape is a mode of natural aggression that can be controlled only by the social contract" (23).

Here, we'll agree with Paglia that it is naive to believe that changing a few laws will change "nature." No amount of litigation now will alter what she calls the "sexual expression of the will-to-power" (no comment on this most un-Nietzschean use of a Nietzschean term), no amount of legislation will change the "natural" impulse toward violence against women. In fact, for an intricate examination of the latest violent backlash against that kind of legislation, what Naomi Wolf has called men's declaration of "war against the war against men," see Michelle Ballif's "Mothers in the Classroom." However, our job here is to recognize that the so-called natural is already a function of a particular phallogocentric system of thought. What calls itself "nature" has always already been constructed by the Father's Law.

19. But why is this "suspicious"? Of *course* the concept of "the subject," the stable, solid, masculine organizing principle, will begin to collapse when "marginalized" groups start demanding their share of the pie. There's not enough pie to go around; that was always already the problem.

20. The notion that postmodernism "abandons" the subject seems particularly wrong-headed; the subject has perhaps *never* gotten so much attention as it does in postmodern theories, where it is certainly problematized but hardly forgotten.

21. This claim strikes me as, well, outrageous. Braidotti seems to suggest that there are "natural" desires, desires that are not *given* to us by our social coding and identity struggles. And she may be correct that an *unconscious* desire

itself is constitutive of who we "are." But the *objet petit autres*, the stand-ins with which we hope to fulfill that desire, are not. Desire desires only itself, say Deleuze and Guattari; the potential stand-ins are always already given to us by our society and our culture. We are taught what to want. And the feminist desire for a powerful female subject position is no exception. "Reactive" is *precisely* the mode of this desire—had there been no sexist subject un/covered, there would be no longing for a *female* subject to even out the score.

22. See "Foucault on Power: A Theory for Women?" in Linda J. Nicholson's *Feminism/Postmodernism*, pp. 163–64.

23. Many have been interested in *linking* feminism and postmodernism, too, of course. A partial list would include Susan Hekman's *Gender and Knowledge* and *Moral Voices, Moral Selves*; Kathy Ferguson's *The Feminist Case Against Bureaucracy*; Nancy Fraser and Linda Nicholson's "Social Criticism Without a Philosophy"; C. Owens's "The Discourse of Others"; and Nicholson's *Feminism/Postmodernism*. It's interesting, however, that the latter is a collection of essays, only two of which actually work at *integrating* a notion of feminism and postmodernism (Donna Haraway's and Judith Butler's). Every other essay in the collection fights against postmodernism in one way or another.

24. But note that according to our definitions, Ebert's "resistance postmodernism" is not post/modern at all; it's modern.

25. It's not only that this "revolution" has brought about a medicalization of women's bodies that has left them, perhaps more than ever, under the control of men's scrutiny. It is also, maybe more importantly, that the so-called "sexual revolution" didn't suspend the traditional moral values that had already disenfranchised women. In fact, today the backlash against the *attempt* to suspend them is at an all-time high. The option remains the same: Lady or Slut? Or, because women's bodies continue to be defined across their re/productive function and their property value, the option could be between illegal and legal prostitution (marriage).

26. This is not a call for "passivity" as it is typically defined; it is, rather, a call for a passivity *beyond* passivity, a radical redefinition of the "passive" that would locate it outside the humanist dichotomy, which makes it the dirty underside of the "active."

27. Here's Nietzsche on trusting the "voice of conscience": "But why do you listen to the voice of your conscience? And what gives you the right to consider such a judgment true and infallible? For this faith—is there no conscience? A conscience behind your 'conscience'? Your judgment 'this is right' has a prehistory in your instincts, likes, dislikes, experiences, lack of experiences. 'How did it originate there?' you must ask, and then also: 'What is it that impels me to listen to it?'" He goes on to suggest that "the firmness of your moral judg-

ment could be the evidence of your personal abjectness, of impersonality; your 'moral strength' might have its source in your stubbornness—or in your inability to envisage new ideals" (*Gay Science* 263–64).

28. The last chapter of Jean-Luc Nancy's *The Inoperative Community*, "Of Divine Places" also explores this kind of politics. Heidegger's "What Are Poets For?" in which he traces the "tracks of the dead gods," appears to be at least one of Nancy's inspirations.

29. In her portion of *Dialogues* (with Gilles Deleuze), Claire Parnet puts it nicely:

> It's wrong to say that the binary machine exists only for reasons of convenience. It is said that "the base 2" is the easiest. But in fact the binary machine is an important component of the apparatuses of power. So many dichotomies will be established that there will be enough for everyone to be pinned to the wall, sunk in a hole. Even the divergences of deviancy will be measured according to the degree of binary choice; you are neither white nor black, Arab then? Or half-breed? You are neither man nor woman, transvestite then? This is the white wall/black hole system. (21)

30. For another clever unpacking of Freud's phallogocentrism, see Dana Heller's "Housebreaking Freud," where she notes that "Freud is compelled time and time again to return to the patriarchal family romance as the origin of human experience, an investment suggesting that psychoanalytic theory may itself constitute the grandest family romance of modernity" (24).

31. In other words, the performance gets confused and confusing. Is the drag queen simply a male on the inside (essentially) performing a female on the outside (fashion-wise)? Or is s/he, rather, "essentially" a female trapped in the outer shell (body) of a male . . . who happens to be dressed in women's clothes? The significance of the confusion here lies in the realization that *both* the male and the female, *both* the masculine and the feminine roles are being *performed*. "Essence" is a performance, a construction of appearance. A deconstruction of cause and effect occurs in Butler's examination of drag queens: appearance is exposed as the cause of essence rather than the other way around. I can't help but cite Nietzsche's comment in book 1 of *The Gay Science*: "what could I say about any essence except to name the attributes of its appearance!" (116).

32. In *Bodies That Matter*, Butler appears to have changed her mind about multiplying sexualities, suggesting that such a proliferation would create an even bigger problem with negotiation among them than we have currently. She continues, however, to call for a pluralistic rather than a binaristic world view.

33. It may be necessary, once again, to distinguish affirmative forgetting from unproblematic forgetting. If the latter is an embarrassed covering-over of the past, the former is a life-affirming *shedding* in anticipation of a new future. Here's Nietzsche:

> To close the doors and windows of consciousness for a time; to remain undis-
> turbed by the noise and struggle of our underworld of utility organs working
> with and against one another; a little quietness, a little *tabula rasa* of the con-
> sciousness, to make room for new things [the *un*thinkable] . . . that is the pur-
> pose of active forgetfulness . . . there could be no happiness, no cheerfulness,
> no hope, no pride, no *present*, without forgetfulness. (*Genealogy of Morals*
> 57–58)

Indeed, Nietzsche compares those in whom this "apparatus" of forgetfulness is
"out of order" with those suffering from indigestion: he says they are "dyspeptic"
and "cannot 'have done' with anything" (57–58). The human animal, Nietzsche
says, "*needs* to be forgetful"; forgetfulness is a sign of "robust health," a spring
cleaning that makes way for Being-Toward-Futurity. But in those cases in which
"promises are made," human-Being has opted for the "opposing faculty, a memory" (57–58). Significantly, however, this option is never totally one's own.

Nietzsche notes that society creates "a memory for the human animal." Society "impress[es] something on this partly obtuse, partly flighty mind, attuned
only to the passing moment, in such a way that it will stay there." Through a
"*mnemotechnics*" of *pain*, through techniques of punishment built into social
norms and moral values, particular memories are *etched* in—Nietzsche says
"burned in" (60–62). And this *burning in*, Nietzsche notes, has been quite effective in rendering certain ideas "inextinguishable, ever-present, unforgettable,
'fixed.'" He says that "ascetic procedures and modes of life are means of freeing
these ideas from the competition of all other ideas, so as to make them 'unforgettable'" (60–62). These are "memories" not only of "history," of past wrongs
and grievances, but also of stable selfhoods, of stable gender-identities, of particular (logocentric) setups and privilegings within those setups.

What is important here is that the "individual" is not the autonomous
author of these memories: they are not the memories of an experience *qua* experience for the individual her/himself(s). (Even individual "histories" are interpreted through a metaphysics of presence that has been *burned in*.) And yet,
these memories are what hold the "individual" together. Nietzsche says that to
think the unthinkable—to effect a revaluation of all values—it will be necessary
to resist this socialization of memory, to become capable of *letting memory go*.

34. The vomiting/purging metaphor has been used by a number of others.
In *Bodies That Matter*, Butler, writing with Julia Kristeva's *Powers of Horror*,
notes that "the speaking 'I,' is constituted by the force of exclusion and abjection" (3). Butler suggests that "the boundary of the body as well as the distinction between internal [me] and external [not me] is established through the
ejection and transvaluation of something originally part of identity into a defiling otherness" (*Gender Trouble* 133). Lynn Worsham has also used this meta-

phor in her "Eating History, Purging Memory, Killing Rhetoric." In each case, vomiting has been associated with the impulse to create and then separate one's Self from the abject realm. But most recently and in an/other vein, Victor Vitanza has used this metaphor affirmatively, suggesting that vomiting can be a denegation of negation, a *just*-vomiting. In his "Taking A-Count" and "An After/word," Vitanza discusses vomiting as the expulsion of expulsion itself. That is, for Vitanza, vomiting operates as a double negative: the purging of the impulse to purge. Vomiting, then, becomes an affirmation of excess. I would associate Nietzsche with *this* take on vomiting.

35. Gayatri Spivak notes that the "quotation marks indicate a catachrestical setting apart." When "truth" or "woman" appear in quotation marks, they indicate catachreses that have "no *adequate* literal referent" ("Feminism" 211).

36. See Jean-Luc Nancy's "Shattered Love" for an exploration of this idea.

37. It is necessary to note that Spivak nevertheless, after a good-faithed negotiation with the texts of both Nietzsche and Derrida, still comes to the conclusion that "putting the *name* of woman on" the space between truth and the non-truth of truth "misfires for feminism" (117; see also Teresa de Lauretis's *Technologies of Gender* 31–50). And Spivak makes a compelling case. To come to this conclusion, however, she must make an appeal to strategic essentialism (118) and make the drive for "anti-sexism" the *a priori* basis for her essay (117). We hope here, however, to allow an/other "feminism" to emerge precisely through the use of this naming. We hope to get past the logocentric politics of an "*anti-*" anything, to get past the fight. I go with the name "woman" here because it seems necessary to inhabit it differently, to reopen the signification of this term and stretch its signifying potential, as Butler might say. To leave it closed up and off seems to me a particularly antirhetorical approach that may leave us with less to lose but also leaves us with no/thing to gain. Butler's reopening and s-t-r-e-t-c-h-i-n-g of the term "queer" has, I think, set a respectable precedent for this move. I discuss the decision to keep the name "woman" in the excursus that follows.

38. Baudrillard suggests that the attempts by radical, eco-, and spiritual feminists to locate a female origin or superiority is an attempt to retrofit the phallus onto the female. He considers this a futile and wrong-headed project.

39. This is Walter Kaufmann's paraphrasing of the *Oxford Classical Dictionary*'s definition of "Baubô," which appears in his footnote on p. 38 of *Gay Science*. Kaufmann also notes that Baubô was originally a "personification of the female genitals." What's important for us here is the phallogocentric choice, both the *Oxford Dictionary*'s and Kaufmann's, to re/present Baubô as a demon rather than as a goddess. For a detailed and cogent rethinking of this move, see Luanne Frank's "Uncovering the Exhibitionist Goddesses I: 'The Metamorphoses of Baubô.'"

40. Here's Cixous:

Flying is woman's gesture—flying in language and making it fly. . . . It's no accident that *voler* has a double meaning . . . women take after birds and robbers just as robbers take after birds. They go by, fly the coop, take pleasure in jumbling the order of space, in disorienting it, in changing around the furniture, dislocating things and values, breaking them all up, emptying structures and turning propriety upside down.

What woman hasn't flown/stolen? Who hasn't felt, dreamt, performed the gesture that jams sociality? Who hasn't crumbled, held up to ridicule, the bar of separation? Who hasn't inscribed with her body the differential, punctured the system of couples and oppositions? ("Laugh" 887)

41. In other words, it is easier, according to Cixous, for women to become-"woman" than it is for men to become-"woman" because the gender socialization most women have gone through leaves them closer to fluidity. "It is much harder," she says, "for man to let the other come through him" (*Newly Born* 85).

42. See Maurice Blanchot's *The Unavowable Community* and Jean-Luc Nancy's *The Inoperative Community* for an intense unpacking of this French term—which is experienced as much more than the opposite of *working*. When I say "woman" can name a space of "*productive* indecision," I am suggesting a "production" that is, nevertheless, a *désoeuvrement*—an *active* unworking, an *active* pause. "Might as well face it," Ronell says in *Crack Wars*, "some hesitations are rigorous" (58).

43. Humanism tends to operate on an "if we build it, they will come" mentality: if we can *make* a place for "community" to happen (a common goal), the "people" *will commune*—those who won't will be expelled or thrown in the gulag.

44. Even those who assume "women" are culturally constructed tend to assume, Butler says, that the female subject "is vested with an agency, usually figured as the capacity for reflexive meditation, that remains intact regardless of its cultural embeddedness. On such a model, 'culture' and 'discourse' *mire* the subject, but do not constitute that subject" (*Gender Trouble* 143).

45. This, of course, is highly problematic. Coalitional groups aim to be postidentity affiliations—in *theory*. In practice, as Butler points out in *Gender Trouble*, they fall short of this aim.

46. In *Bodies That Matter*, Butler offers a potent example of what gets sacrificed to the bulldozer of consensus when feminist politics is taken as a meta-narrative. Butler points to three radically different "radical feminists," bell hooks, Marilyn Frye, and Janice Raymond, who find a little space of common ground in their criticisms of the productions of gay male drag; they argue that these are misogynistic performances that are degrading and offensive to women. Butler spotlights what gets subsumed under the blinders of a feminist politics

driven to protect the category "women": that this is a homophobic (!) critique that makes male homosexuality *about* women, about a "failure in the heterosexual machinery" (127), which it, incidentally, upholds by taking this position. (This is a perfect example of feminism holding the hand that holds it down.) Butler, ever ready to expose the ways in which we "do it without knowing we're doing it," adds that the reversal of such a position would make lesbianism a matter of misandry (hating men).

47. "Immanence" is defined by Christopher Fynsk in the forward of Nancy's *The Inoperative Community* as "the self-presence of individuals to one another in and by their community" (xv). Re-presentation, even self re-presentation, would demand this immanence, which, Nancy says, has nothing to do with our Being.

48. See Patricia Bizzell's "The Prospect of Rhetorical Agency," where she argues that the pomo subject would be too decentered to be able to share anything. In contradistinction to Bizzell, we will suggest here that finite beings are always already sharing.

49. What can be shared, however, in the exposition of our finitude, is the very *realization* that it cannot be shared. The difference between singularities, in other words, is part of what they share in-common.

50. It should be noted that Nancy's terminology is thoroughly Heideggerian, even if Nancy takes that vocabulary beyond where Heidegger would have gone.

51. The question of who or what is doing the calling no less than haunts Heidegger's ontology and Freud's ego-psychology. But both the "call of conscience" and the "superego" posit this punitive voice as one that gets us on the line ahead of time, that "holds sway over us like an unconditional prescription" (Ronell, *Dictations* xvii). And in each case, it turns out to be *us*, to be what Deleuze and Guattari would call the "general" in us, that is placing the call. We answer and are answerable to *ourselves*.

52. As Heidegger puts it, "In Dasein's everydayness the agency through which most things come about is one of which we must say that 'it was no one'" (164–65).

53. Heidegger's ethics, particularly the distinction it draws between the call of the "they" and the call of one's ownmost authenticity, may not have been suspicious enough of the multiplicitous nature of *any* call. Assuming that he is able to differentiate between *the* call of conscience and *the* call of the Storm Trooper, Heidegger strained toward the former and/but connected with the latter. His own ontology of Being, that is, may have led him into a trap with the Nazis. (See Ronell's *Telephone Book* for an intense examination of this problem.)

Nietzsche, on the other hand, explicitly asked: "But why do you listen to the voice of your conscience? And what gives you the right to consider such a judgment true and infallible? For this faith—is their no conscience?" (*Gay Science* 263).

54. See Nancy's *The Inoperative Community*, p. 158, note 24.

55. For a brilliant and intricate teasing through of Heidegger's avoidance of the question of the Other, see Christopher Fynsk, "The Self and Its Witness: On Heidegger's *Being and Time*."

56. This is Cixous's term. See *Three Steps on the Ladder of Writing*.

57. See, for instance, *On Nietzsche*, where Bataille says: "When communication—the sweetness of intimate communication—is cut off by death, separation, or misunderstanding, I feel a less familiar sweetness, a sweetness that's sobbing within me—and this is laceration" (54).

58. All kinds of examples pop to mind. Feminist movements have been exclusionary from their inception, excluding on the basis of race, class, sexual orientation, able-bodiedness, etc.

59. I first developed this idea in an online essay called "Laughter; or, Chortling into the Storm." It's in the first issue of *PRE/TEXT: Electra(Lite)*. Ed. Victor J. Vitanza and Cynthia Haynes, at http://www.utdallas.edu/pretext/PT1.1/PT1.html.

60. I can't resist suggesting what perhaps needs no suggestion here: that to "become who we are" (à la Nietzsche), it will be necessary to become what we have defined as "woman," to become-woman, the pause of indecision. This is the "feminine" that has not been thought, the unthought behind thought.

61. Nancy, it should be noted, radically redescribes freedom. This is not the Enlightenment's unproblematized "liberation." Freedom, here, has nothing to do with emancipation in its modern sense. In his foreword to Nancy's *The Inoperative Community*, Christopher Fynsk describes Nancy's notion of freedom as "a name for ecstasis." Because Being's character is "necessarily multiple, differential," then "the articulation of Being is always singular[;] Being cannot be One, and it cannot be thought simply as a gathering or collecting." Freedom is experienced in the "singularity of the self that knows itself as an opening to alterity." Freedom, then, "is the exposure of thought to the fact [Heidegger would say the "facticity"—the that-it-isness] of Being, *that there are beings* (and not nothing)" (xii–xiii). Here, freedom has nothing to do with politics as such. It has more to do with ethics: it is experienced as a gestalt switch in the midst of an *inward* glance.

62. Vitanza's "Concerning a Postclassical Ethos" details out this re/turn to ethics over politics, or rather, ethics *before* politics. Here's Vitanza:

> I favor "ethics" over "politics" only initially so as eventually to re(dis)cover the social-parapolitical in the individual, which will allow for a "paraethics." . . .

[A] non-oppressive politics is impossible unless and until there is a "paraethical politics"—by which I mean a condition* for a politics informed by (free-flowing) "desires," by which, in turn, I mean that these desires have not already been *pre*formed (or controlled through homogenization) [Nietzsche: "burned in"] by socialist or capitalistic codings or by present-day "political ethics." (395)

And yet, Vitanza freely admits (as did Nietzsche) that it may be too hopeful to assume that this re/turn to [para]ethics will have actually led into a "non-oppressive politics." It may not be possible, as a group, to get beyond preformed desires/codings. Rather, Vitanza is suggesting that to *begin* with a political imperative that has *not* considered the social-in-the-individual is to *begin* with an oppressive imperative. Therefore: back to ethics, anyway. Here's Vitanza's follow-up:

But then, let me express some doubt again and suggest that such a "politics" may not be possible. . . . It may very well be (as Louis Althusser would say) an impossibility, for to be a Subject is to be inevitably "hailed" or "interpellated" by the Ideological State Apparatus. . . . Which then leaves—for me—only schizo/nomadic ethics (radical heterogeneity) in ever perverse forms of "resistance" and "disruption" or in my form of "hysterical neo-anarchism." (395)

63. Here's Heidegger on this *moment*: "When resolute, Dasein has brought itself back from falling, and has done so precisely in order to be more authentically 'there' in the 'moment of vision,' as regards the Situation which has been disclosed" (328). Heidegger's "moment of vision" is roughly analogous to Nietzsche's "midday sun"; they both refer to that moment in which past, future, and present are *constructed*—Heidegger calls these temporalities, respectively, "facticity" (past), "falling" (present), and "existence" (future).

64. It is political in the very sense of the term this chapter hopes to enact; it is political Other/Wise, in a posthumanist, postphallocratic way.

65. For my explanation of Žižek's terminology, see chapter 1.

4   A RHETORIC OF LAUGHTER FOR COMPOSITION PEDAGOGY

1.   See Schilb's "Cultural Studies, Postmodernism, and Composition," in *Contending with Words*, where he suggests that an "ethos of service" motivates composition instruction "to this day: a belief that it exists only to serve the 'real' disciplines, which are best served where composition focuses on student's 'basic skills'" (178).

2.   Though, to be sure, we will have called into question the inherent tyranny of the pedagogical position, the intimate connection between discipline and totalitarianism.

3.   "Emancipation" gets redefined by radical pedagogy, but it does not get questioned as a goal. If traditional pedagogy hopes to emancipate students by making them useful subjects, by making them capable, in other words, of assuming their rightful place in the existing economic system; radical pedagogies hope to emancipate students by making them capable of critiquing that existing economic system and by arming them with a belief in transformative politics.

4.   This is, of course, controversial. Schniedewind has laid claim to these goals as if they were inherently feminist, but composition studies has, throughout its histories, promoted these goals without reference to feminism or, for that matter, any sense of the gender problem. On the other hand, we will offer Schniedewind temporary passage here. And we will do it with a nod of thanks to Jan Swearingen, who once suggested that whether these goals ought to be considered "feminist" or not is not the issue—the issue is that *they have come to be discussed* as gendered goals.

5.   Schniedewind, then, offers us an example of a humanist approach to community. This is a prime instance of the notion that humanity is in charge of making/building community.

6.   Gearhart, Flynn, and Joyce Trebilcot, for instance, insist that any attempt to persuade anyone else, to change anyone's mind about anything, is an act of violence. On the other hand, Susan Jarratt and Catherine Lamb, for instance, suggest that persuasion and persuasive writing are necessary in the feminist composition classroom—without them, offending voices cannot be counterbalanced, difference is silenced (again), and women are left doubly castrated.

7.   For a clever and intricate unpacking of this issue, see Michelle Ballif's "Mothers in the Classroom: Composing Masculinity via Fetal Pedagogies." Forthcoming in *PRE/TEXT*.

8.   It's important to note more directly here that Susan Jarratt is highly critical of "nurturing mother" approaches to feminist pedagogy. In fact, her in-depth critique of those approaches has been enormously helpful to me in my work. It was her presentation on this issue at the University of Texas at Arlington's Cultural Theory Symposium in 1992 that originally sparked my own interest in it. Jarratt also offers an intense critique of "consensus" as a goal for feminist pedagogy. She argues, against Carol Stranger, that when students are encouraged to come to a consensus, it will probably be the women—culturally coded to seek compromise—who end up once again conceding their voices ("Feminism and Composition" 113). She is not after—indeed, she is deeply suspicious of—the kind of mediation and resolution for which Lamb calls. And yet, Jarratt remains interested in a very specific transformative politics and in fostering the (feminist) subjects for that politics in the composition classroom.

I think—my respect for her work and her insights notwithstanding—that this is where our intellectual and feminist paths part.

9. But pedagogy itself depends upon the regulators. Any pedagogy *qua* pedagogy must territorialize (appropriate) and/or silence that which hangs out in the fluid middle-muddle of even the *dissoi-logoi*—it must do so to accomplish the task of "teaching" something in particular. And therein lies the problem with even radical pedagogical strategies: what even these/our feminist pedagogies end up teaching is a greater capacity to shut down the Other in the name of the Self-Same.

10. The allusion here is to Irigaray's "And the One Doesn't Stir Without the Other," where the Mother feeds the child excessively, and the child finds herself immobilized. It is the mother's social duty to map out (territorialize) the child's libidinal flow, to restrict it and thus make it possible to control—the child's first step into the symbolic is prompted by a mother's shove.

11. I owe a note of thanks to Tim Richardson, a graduate student at Old Dominion University who took my seminar on *écriture féminine*. Tim taught me my own lesson one day just after the semester had ended when he noted that the constant protestations of one hyperrational student in the class had been an interesting phenomenon. I sighed heavily and said that I had found the interruptions "frustrating." Tim raised an eyebrow, smiled at me, and said: "Oh, I thought they were a *good* thing?" Ooof. Indeed. It's not easy to wish for an interruption in the illusion of common-being or to affirm a wild *différance* that insists on interrupting one's own little celebrations of difference. It's not easy, but it will have been necessary.

12. It should be noted that Juncker's article is every bit as devoted to the pedagogical imperative as Lamb's. Juncker domesticates Cixous to an embarrassing extent, demanding from *écriture féminine* a list of practical applications for the writing classroom. See Lynn Worsham's "Writing Against Writing" for a thorough critique of Juncker's appropriation.

13. "Im-personation" is the term Jane Gallop uses to indicate a distinction "between impersonation in the restricted, traditional sense and a generalized impersonation" ("Im-Personation" 15). The former presumes a subject who precedes the performance and decides to "play a role." The latter, on the other hand, does not presume such a "volitional subject," recognizing that the subject is a function of the "role," an effect. Im-personation, then, indicates the kind of performative politics Butler promotes. As we noted in chapter 2, this performative politics blurs the distinction between constructivism and determinism—the constraints of language become, for Butler, the condition of possibility for performance. Performance is not, could not be, the "function of an originating will" (*Bodies That Matter* 13).

I suppose I should also mention here, while we're interrupting ourselves, that it is not politically unproblematic to align oneself with any aspect of Jane Gallop's pedagogical style, one that ended up getting her accused of sexual harassment. But it seems necessary here to look beyond one pedagogue's particular performance to what the notion of pedagogue drag itself suggests. That pedagogue drag, like any other drag, indicates a performance "without essence," an inhabiting that is itself *constructive*, attests to the importance of examining carefully the specifics of that performance.

14. See Avital Ronell's "The *Sujet Suppositaire*: Freud, And/Or the Obsessional Neurotic Style (Maybe)," in *Finitude's Score*.

15. I should note that I suggested this to Donald Morton himself when he spoke at the University of Texas at Arlington in December 1994. He did not agree.

16. I'm thinking of the demands of the mourning process as they manifest themselves, for instance, in the need to view a body—drained of life, with its orifices sewn or wired shut, and its skin shellacked for that "peaceful look"—in order to convince ourselves that it is dead or to camouflage death in an attempt to make it look more . . . lifelike.

17. It's important to remember that the fight is not with all literature or all drugs but only with *bad* literature and *bad* drugs. When in doubt, litigation determines the value of the literary work, which emerges as licit (literature) or illicit (pornography/smut).

18. See Derrida's "The Rhetoric of Drugs," where he puts it this way:

> Let us consider literature, in a fairly strict sense, distinguishing it, at least in Europe, from poetry and belles lettres, as a modern phenomenon (dating from the sixteenth or seventeenth century.) Well then, is it not thus contemporaneous with a certain European drug addiction? (9)

19. It may be necessary to draw a distinction here between this writing for writing's sake and what is commonly called "expressive writing." The latter, as it is defined and employed by such advocates as Donald M. Murray (*Write to Learn*, 1984), William Coles (*The Plural I*, 1978), and Peter Elbow (*Writing Without Teachers*, 1973), is interested in self-discovery, in dis/covering the unconscious selfhood through an unleashing of creative expression. It is interested in liberating the individual and his/her unique voice, as Elbow suggests when he argues that helping students "get control over their words" makes them "less helpless, both personally and politically" (vii). The writer in an expressive writing course, Murray says, "is on a search for himself [*sic*]" (4). Berlin, in "Rhetoric and Ideology," notes that the "underlying conviction of expressionists is that when individuals are spared the distorting effects of a repressive social order, their privately determined truths will correspond to the privately determined

truths of all others: my best and deepest vision supports the same universal and external laws as everyone else's best and deepest vision" (486).

Expressionist rhetorics of composing make the author an agent and foster an insidious foundationalism. To the question "who speaks?" they answer, with the ideologue, "man speaks." Vitanza notes that this approach "founds a humanist philosophy and educational system" ("Three Countertheses" 156). It fosters the illusion of a solid, stable ego-identity, which it believes can be known through its linguistic expression. This is definitely not what we will be after here. Putting ourselves in the service of *writing itself* is not about discovering our inner voice or our authentic selfhood. It is about allowing the force of language to make and unmake us, simultaneously and perpetually. It is about becoming capable, as Vitanza says, of "just drift[ing]" (151) with the rhythm that laughs us. It's about paying homage to the self(s) as a "polyethoi" and celebrating our incapacity to master the rowdy body of language. This is not about dis/covering a hidden selfhood through our use of language but about celebrating *how language makes use of us*, its tendency to construct us, perpetually, and in rhizomatic fashion. It's about writing as the exposition of finitude.

20. See p. 24 of Philippe Lacoue-Labarthe's "Talks," where he attempts to open the lines of communication with Jean-François Lyotard through "essay," through "a way of trying questions," of testing them to see if they work. "A way, above all," he says "of remaining 'just,' of respecting that extremely fragile thing that is the justness of a relationship. It is necessary to talk," he says, "but one must not force anything, twist, or handle anything roughly" (24). To do so, he notes, would be "a catastrophe." In this address, Lacoue-Labarthe strains beyond reactive posturing and toward an "affirmative differend," a version that "talks and negotiates," one that "listens and articulates itself responsively rather than reactively" (Ronell, "Differends" 262). The affirmative *differénd* is interested not in litigation or in resolution but in establishing the conditions for *co*legitimacy. There is a real hesitation in Lacoue-Labarthe's address, a real determination to postpone judgment.

This is what our assignments would encourage—a perpetual listening. Not a tuning in so that they might then finally and for good *finish* listening and *conclude* but a trying out of questions that would invite *the listening to go on*. The drive would not be for closure but for a perpetual hearing. Any decision issued forth from a genuine/generous listening will have been under no illusion of totality. It will not have performed itself as the final word but as one defining moment in the perpetual discussion, always tentative and up for more "negotiation," always interested in keeping the question open. Judgments that arise out of *this* listening will follow the rules of Homer's Contest—they will never have been final; the matter will never have been settled.

21. For a provocative argument against the demand for clarity in the writing class, see two essays by Roxanne D. Mountford. One was published: "Let Them Experiment: Accommodating Diverse Discourse Practices in Large-Scale Writing Assessment." The other was a conference paper in which she performed what the published piece could not perform (and still be published): "Clarity Is Political: Assigning and Evaluating Experimental Writing."

22. At the 1997 French Feminism Conference at Texas Tech University, I gave a paper that was extracted from this chapter, and Toril Moi was in the audience. Her first question to me was: What would keep this new "flowing, feminine writing" from becoming the status quo? What's to stop the presses from pumping out "how to" books for writing the perfect "imund" text? What's to stop us from turning this writing into as prescribed a writing as that which you challenge? This point is well-taken; and I believe it is the same point Jarratt is making here.

But my reply was and is that one cannot *teach* anyone how to write the "imund text." As soon as there is a standard, a template, a "how to" book—this kind of writing will already be *gone*. It's avant-garde art in that sense. It pushes the limits of thinking, pushes further and further, never stops pushing. You'll never find it again where you last saw it. As soon as you manage to track down its rules, they already will have changed. This kind of writing *can't be taught*. But, and here's the important part, it can be *learned*. The "teacher" in this writing-for-writing course, the "teacher" who does not "know" and cannot "teach," has no choice but to take on another function in the classroom. It is necessary that s/he become a writing facilitator, one who makes a space within the pedagogical situation for that which is unprecedented, for that which s/he will never have been able to prepare herself, for what could never be expected. No textbook could cover this kind of writing, and no teacher-training course could possibly prepare the pedagogue for what her students will have learned while taking its ride.

23. See Sirc's brilliant essay: "Writing Classroom as A & P Parking Lot."

24. It's not nothing that Victor J. Vitanza's blatantly hypertextual writing style continues to *irritate* many of his colleagues to no end. Way before electronic hypertexts hit the rhetoric and composition scene, Vitanza's work in pulp was performing what was to come. Interestingly, he is continuously mis/taken for being apolitical because, both on-line and in print, he allows the hyperactive element in language to expose itself in his writing, because he doesn't strive to cleanse his writing of its hyperactivity. But what we're suggesting here is that this kind of writing is vigorously political, political other/wise, because it exposes the rustle of finitude.

25. See pp. 232–309 in Deleuze and Guattari's *A Thousand Plateaus*.

A(NOTHER) POST-SCRIPT ON LAUGHTER AND FUTURITY

1. Here's Cixous, from *Three Steps on the Ladder of Writing*: "Whoever wants to write must be able to reach this lightening region that takes your breath away, where you instantaneously feel at sea and where the moorings are severed with the already-written, the already-known" (59).

2. "To the famous positivity of the negative," Deleuze says, "Nietzsche opposes his own discovery: the negativity of the positive" (*Nietzsche* 180).

WORKS CITED

Abbeele, Georges Van Den. Introduction. *Community at Loose Ends*. Ed. Miami Theory Collective. Minneapolis: U of Minnesota P, 1991. ix–xxvi.

Agacinski, Sylviane. "Another Experience of the Question, or Experiencing the Question Other-Wise." Cadava, Connor, and Nancy 9–23.

Agamben, Giorgio. *The Coming Community*. Trans. Michael Hardt. Minneapolis: U of Minnesota P, 1993.

Alcoff, Linda. "Cultural Feminism Versus Poststructuralism: The Identity Crisis in Feminist Theory." *Signs* 13 (Spring 1988): 405–36.

Althusser, Louis. "Freud and Lacan." Althusser, *Lenin and Philosophy* 195–219.

———. "Ideology and Ideological State Apparatuses." Althusser, *Lenin and Philosophy* 127–86.

———. *Lenin and Philosophy and Other Essays*. Trans. Ben Brewster. New York: Monthly Review, 1971.

Aristotle. *On Rhetoric*. Trans. George A. Kennedy. New York: Oxford UP, 1991.

Ballif, Michelle. "Mothers in the Classroom: Composing Masculinity via Fetal Pedagogies." *PRE/TEXT: A Journal of Rhetorical Theory*, forthcoming.

———. *Seduction, Sophistry, and the Woman with the Rhetorical Figure*. Carbondale: Southern Illinois UP, forthcoming.

Barlow, John. "Life in the Data Cloud: Scratching Your Eyes Back In." Interview with Jaron Lanier. *Mondo 2000* (Summer 1990): 2–50.

Bartholomae, David. "Inventing the University." *When a Writer Can't Write: Studies in Writer's Block and Other Composing Problems*. Ed. Mike Rose. New York: Guilford, 1985. 134–65.

Bataille, Georges. *The Accursed Share: An Essay on General Economy*. Vol. 1: *Consumption*. Trans. Robert Hurley. New York: Zone, 1991.

———. *The Accursed Share: An Essay on General Economy*. Vol. 2: *The History of Eroticism*. Vol. 3: *Sovereignty*. Trans. Robert Hurley. New York: Zone, 1993.

———. *Guilty.* Trans. Bruce Boone. Venice, CA: Lapis, 1988.

———. *On Nietzsche.* Trans. Bruce Boone. New York: Paragon, 1992.

Baudrillard, Jean. "Fatal Strategies." Baudrillard, *Selected Writings* 185–206.

———. *Fatal Strategies.* Trans. Philip Beitchman and W.G.J. Niesluchowski. Ed. Jim Fleming. New York: Semiotext(e), Columbia UP, 1990.

———. *Forget Foucault.* New York: Semiotext(e), 1987.

———. *Jean Baudrillard: Selected Writings.* Ed. Mark Poster. Stanford: Stanford UP, 1988.

———. *Seduction.* Trans. Brian Singer. New York: St. Martin's, 1990.

———. *Simulations.* Trans. Paul Ross, Paul Patton, and Philip Beitchman. New York: Semiotext(e), 1983.

Belenky, Mary Field, et al. *Women's Ways of Knowing: The Development of Self, Voice, and Mind.* New York: Basic, 1986.

Benhabib, Seyla. "Feminism and Postmodernism: An Uneasy Alliance." *Feminist Contentions: A Philosophical Exchange.* By Seyla Benhabib, Judith Butler, Drucilla Cornell, and Nancy Fraser. New York: Routledge, 1995. 17–34.

Benhabib, Seyla, and Drucilla Cornell. *Feminism as Critique: Essays on the Politics of Gender in Late Capitalist Societies.* Minneapolis: U of Minnesota P, 1987.

Benveniste, Emile. *Problems in General Linguistics.* Trans. Mary Elizabeth Meek. Coral Gables: U of Miami P, 1971.

Berkun, Scott. "Agent of Change: Interview with Pattie Maes." *WIRED* 3.4 (April 1995): 117.

Berlin, James. "Postmodernism, the College Curriculum, and Composition." *Composition in Context.* Ed. Ross Winterowd and Vincent Gillespie. Carbondale: Southern Illinois UP, 1994. 46–61.

———. "Rhetoric and Ideology in the Writing Class." *College English* 50.5 (September 1988): 477–94.

Bernstein, Michael. "On Foucault." *University Press: An International Quarterly Review of Books* 13 (1984): 14.

Best, Steven, and Douglas Kellner. *Postmodern Theory: Critical Interrogations.* New York: Guilford, 1991.

Bizzell, Patricia. "The Prospect of Rhetorical Agency." *Making and Unmaking the Prospects of Rhetoric.* Ed. Theresa Enos and Richard McNabb. Mahwah, NJ: Erlbaum, 1997. 37–43.

Blanchot, Maurice. *The Unavowable Community.* Trans. Pierre Joris. Barrytown, NY: Station Hill, 1988.

Bordo, Susan. "Feminism, Postmodernism, and Gender-Scepticism." Nicholson 133–56.

———. *Flight to Objectivity: Essays on Cartesianism and Culture.* Albany: State U of New York P, 1987.

Braidotti, Rosi. "Toward a New Nomadism: Feminist Deleuzian Tracks; or, Metaphysics and Metabolism." *Gilles Deleuze and the Theater of Philosophy.* Ed. Constantin V. Boundas and Dorothea Olkowski. New York: Routledge, 1994. 157–86.

Brossard, Nicole. "Only a Body to Measure Reality." *Journal of Commonwealth Literature* 31.2 (1996).

Brown, Norman O. *Life Against Death.* Middletown, CT: Wesleyan UP, 1959.

Burke, Kenneth. *A Grammar of Motives.* Berkeley: U of California P, 1945.

———. *Language as Symbolic Action: Essays on Life, Literature, and Method.* Berkeley: U of California P, 1968.

———. "The Rhetorical Situation." *Communication: Ethical and Moral Issues.* Ed. Lee Thayer. New York: Gordon and Breach, 1973. 263–76.

———. *A Rhetoric of Motives.* Berkeley: U of California P, 1969.

Butler, Judith. *Bodies That Matter: On the Discursive Limits of "Sex."* New York: Routledge, 1993.

———. "Contingent Foundations: Feminism and the Question of 'Postmodernism.'" Butler and Scott 3–21.

———. *Excitable Speech: A Politics of the Performative.* New York: Routledge, 1997.

———. *Gender Trouble: Feminism and the Subversion of Identity.* New York: Routledge, 1990.

———. *The Psychic Life of Power: Theories in Subjection.* Stanford: Stanford UP, 1997.

Butler, Judith, and Joan W. Scott, eds. *Feminists Theorize the Political.* New York: Routledge, 1992.

Cadava, Eduardo. "Toward an Ethics of Decision." *Diacritics* 24.4 (Winter 1994): 4–29.

Cadava, Eduardo, Peter Connor, and Jean-Luc Nancy, eds. *Who Comes After the Subject?* New York: Routledge, 1991.

Carpenter, Edmund. *Oh, What a Blow That Phantom Gave Me!* New York: Holt, 1972.

Chisholm, Dianne. "Violence Against Violence Against Women." *The Last Sex: Feminism and Outlaw Bodies.* Ed. Arthur and Marilouise Kroker. New York: St. Martin's, 1993. 28–66.

Chodorow, Nancy. *Reproduction of Mothering: Psychoanalysis and the Sociology of Gender.* Berkeley: U of California P, 1978.

Cixous, Hélène. "The Author in Truth." Cixous, "Coming to Writing" 136–81.

———. "Castration or Decapitation?" Trans. Annette Kuhn. *Signs* 7.11 (1981): 41–55.

———. "Clarice Lispector: The Approach." Cixous, *Coming to Writing* 59–77.

———. "Coming to Writing." Cixous, *Coming to Writing* 1–58.

———. *"Coming to Writing" and Other Essays.* Ed. Deborah Jenson. Cambridge: Harvard UP, 1991.

———. *"La*—The (Feminine)." *The Hélène Cixous Reader.* Ed. Susan Sellers. New York: Routledge, 1994. 59–67.

———. "The Laugh of the Medusa." Trans. Keith Cohen and Paula Cohen. *Signs* 1.4 (1976): 875–93.

———. "Sorties: Out and Out: Attacks/Ways Out/Forays." Cixous and Clément 63–132.

———. *Three Steps on the Ladder of Writing.* New York: Columbia UP, 1993.

Cixous, Hélène, and Catherine Clément. *The Newly Born Woman.* Trans. Betsy Wing. Vol. 24 of *Theory and History of Literature.* Minneapolis: U of Minnesota P, 1975.

Clifford, John. "The Subject in Discourse." Harkin and Schilb 38–51.

Conley, Verena Andermatt, ed. *Rethinking Technologies.* Minneapolis: U of Minnesota P, 1993.

Cooper, Marilyn, and Michael Holzman. *Writing as Social Action.* Portsmouth: Boynton, 1989.

Culler, Jonathon. *On Deconstruction: Theory and Criticism after Structuralism.* New York: Cornell UP, 1982.

Culley, Margo, et al. "The Politics of Nurturance." *Gendered Subjects: The Dynamics of Feminist Teaching.* Ed. Margo Culley and Catherine Portuges. Boston: Routledge, 1985. 11–20.

Davis, D. Diane. "Breaking Up [at] Phallocracy: Post-Feminism's Chortling Hammer." *Rhetoric Review* 14.1 (Fall 1995): 126–40.

———. "Laughter; Or, Chortling into the Storm." *PRE/TEXT Electra (Lite)*: 1.1 (1997). http://www.utdallas.edu/pretext/PT1.1/PT1.html

Deem, Melissa D. "From Bobbit to SCUM: Re-memberment, Scatological Rhetorics, and Feminist Strategies in the United States." *Public Culture* 8 (1996): 511–37.

Deleuze, Gilles. *Nietzsche and Philosophy.* 1962. Trans. Hugh Tomlinson. New York: Columbia UP, 1983.

Deleuze, Gilles, and Felix Guattari. *Anti-Oedipus: Capitalism and Schizophrenia.* Trans. Robert Hurley, Mark Seem, and Helen R. Lane. Minneapolis: U of Minnesota P, 1983.

———. *A Thousand Plateaus: Capitalism and Schizophrenia.* Trans. Brian Massumi. Minneapolis: U of Minnesota P, 1987.

Deleuze, Gilles, and Claire Parnet. *Dialogues.* Paris: Flammarion, 1977.

Derrida, Jacques. "Cogito and the History of Madness." Derrida, *Writing and Difference* 3–30.

———. "Differance." Derrida, *Speech and Phenomena* 129–60.

———. *Dissemination.* Trans. Barbara Johnson. Chicago: U of Chicago P, 1981.

———. "'Eating Well,' or the Calculation of the Subject: An Interview with Jacques Derrida" (with Jean-Luc Nancy). Cadava, Connor, and Nancy 96–119.

———. "Freud and the Scene of Writing." Derrida, *Writing and Difference* 196–231.

———. "From Restricted to General Economy: A Hegelianism Without Reserve." Derrida, *Writing and Difference* 252–77.

———. *Of Grammatology.* Trans. Gayatri Chakravorty Spivak. Baltimore: Johns Hopkins UP, 1976.

———. "The Rhetoric of Drugs: An Interview." *Differences* 5.1 (1993): 1–24.

———. *Speech and Phenomena: And Other Essays on Husserl's Theory of Signs.* Trans. David B. Allison. Evanston: Northwestern UP, 1973.

———. *Spurs: Nietzsche's Styles.* Chicago: U of Chicago P, 1978.

———. "Structure, Sign, and Play." Derrida, *Writing and Difference* 278–95.

———. *Writing and Difference.* Trans. Alan Bass. Chicago: U of Chicago P, 1978.

Diprose, Rosalyn. "Nietzsche and the Pathos of Distance." *Nietzsche, Feminism, and Political Theory.* Ed. Paul Patton. London: Routledge, 1993. 1–26.

Di Stefano, Christine. "Dilemmas of Difference: Feminism, Modernity, and Postmodernism." Nicholson 63–82.

Dworkin, Andrea. "Terror, Torture and Resistance." Keynote speech. Women and Mental Health Conference—Women in a Violent Society. Canadian Mental Health Assoc., May 1991. *Canadian Woman Studies/Les cahiers de la femme* (Special Issue: "Violence Against Women: Strategies for Change") 12 (Fall 1991): 37–42.

Ebert, Teresa L. *Ludic Feminism and After: Postmodernism, Desire, and Labor in Late Capitalism.* Ann Arbor: U of Michigan P, 1996.

———. "Ludic Feminism, the Body, Performance, and Labor: Bringing Materialism Back into Feminist Cultural Studies." *Cultural Critique* (Winter 1992–93): 5–50.

Ecker, Gisela. *Feminist Aesthetics.* Trans. Harriet Anderson. Boston: Beacon, 1986.

Eisler, Riane. *The Chalice and the Blade: Our History, Our Future.* San Francisco: Harper, 1986.

Elbow, Peter. *Writing Without Teachers.* New York: Oxford UP, 1973.

Elshtain, Jean Bethke. *Public Man, Private Woman*. Princeton: Princeton UP, 1981.

Endres, Bill. "A Short Discourse." Unpublished poem. 1996.

Faigley, Lester. *Fragments of Rationality: Postmodernity and the Subject of Composition*. Pittsburgh: U of Pittsburgh P, 1992.

Fausto-Sterling, Anne. "The Five Sexes: Why Male and Female Are Not Enough." *Sciences* (March–April 1993): 20–25.

Felman, Shoshana. "Psychoanalysis and Education: Teaching Terminable and Interminable." *Yale French Studies* 63 (1982): 21–44.

Ferguson, Kathy. *The Feminist Case Against Bureaucracy*. Philadelphia: Temple UP, 1984.

Feyerabend, Paul. *Against Method*. New York: Verso, 1988.

Flax, Jane. *Thinking Fragments: Psychoanalysis, Feminism and Postmodernism in the Contemporary West*. Berkeley: U of California P, 1990.

Flynn, Elizabeth A. "Composing as a Woman." *CCC* 39.4 (December 1988): 423–35.

Foucault, Michel. *Discipline and Punish: The Birth of the Prison*. Trans. Robert Hurley. New York: Vintage, 1990.

——. *The History of Sexuality: An Introduction*. Vol. 1. Trans. Robert Hurley. New York: Vintage, 1990.

——. *Language, Counter-Memory, Practice: Selected Essays and Interviews*. Ed. Donald F. Bouchard. Trans. Donald F. Bouchard and Sherry Simon. Ithaca: Cornell UP, 1969.

——. "Language to Infinity." Foucault, *Language* 53–67.

——. *Madness and Civilization*. New York: Vintage, 1973.

——. "Nietzsche, Freud, and Marx." *Transforming the Hermeneutic Context: From Nietzsche to Nancy*. Ed. Gayle L. Ormiston and Alan D. Schrift. Albany: State U of New York P, 1990. 59–67.

——. *The Order of Things: An Archaeology of the Human Sciences*. New York: Vintage, 1973.

——. Preface. *Anti-Oedipus: Capitalism and Schizophrenia*. By Gilles Deleuze and Felix Guattari. Minneapolis: U of Minnesota P, 1983. xi–xiv.

——. "Preface to Transgression." Foucault, *Language* 29–52.

——. "What Is an Author?" *Textual Strategies: Perspectives in Post-Structuralist Criticism*. Ed. J.V. Harari. Ithaca: Cornell UP, 1979. 141–60.

Frank, Francine, and Frank Ashen. *Language and the Sexes*. Albany: State U of New York P, 1983.

Frank, Luanne T. "Uncovering the Exhibitionist Goddesses I: 'The Metamorphoses of Baubô.'" *Rhetoric Society of America 1990 National Conference*

Proceedings. Ed. Victor J. Vitanza and Michelle Ballif. Arlington: Rhetoric Society of America, 1990. 243–70.

Fraser, Nancy, and Linda Nicholson. "Social Criticism Without Philosophy: An Encounter Between Feminism and Postmodernism." *The Institution of Philosophy: A Discipline in Crisis?* Ed. Avner Cohen and Marcelo Desca. Totowa, NJ: Rowman, 1988.

Freire, Paulo. *Pedagogy of the Oppressed.* Trans. Myra Bergman Ramos. New York: Continuum, 1990.

Freud, Sigmund. "Analysis Terminable and Interminable." Freud, *Standard Edition*, vol. 23. 209–53.

———. *The Ego and the Id.* Freud, *Standard Edition*, vol. 19. 1–66.

———. *The Standard Edition of Complete Psychological Works.* Trans. James Strachey. Ed. James Strachey and Anna Freud. 24 vols. London: Hogarth, 1953–74.

———. *Three Case Histories.* Ed. Philip Rieff. New York: Macmillan, 1963.

Fynsk, Christopher. Foreword. *The Inoperable Community.* By Jean-Luc Nancy. Minneapolis: U of Minnesota P, 1991. vii–xxxv.

———. "The Self and Its Witness: On Heidegger's *Being and Time*." *Boundary 2* 10.3 (Spring 1982: 185–207.

Gadon, Elinor W. *The Once and Future Goddess: A Symbol for Our Time.* New York: Harper, 1989.

Gallop, Jane. *The Daughter's Seduction: Feminism and Psychoanalysis.* Ithaca: Cornell UP, 1982.

———. *Feminist Accused of Sexual Harassment.* Durham, NC: Duke UP, 1997.

———, ed. "Im-Personation: A Reading in the Guise of an Introduction." Gallop, *Pedagogy* 1–18.

———. *Pedagogy: The Question of Impersonation.* Bloomington: Indiana UP, 1995.

———. *Reading Lacan.* Ithaca: Cornell UP, 1985.

———. "The Teacher's Breasts." Gallop, *Pedagogy* 79–89.

Gearhart, Sally Miller. "The Womanization of Rhetoric." *Women's Studies International Quarterly* 2 (1979): 195–201.

Gilligan, Carol. *In a Different Voice: Psychological Theory and Women's Development.* Cambridge: Harvard UP, 1982.

Gore, Jennifer. *The Struggle for Pedagogies: Critical Feminist Discourses as Regimes of Truth.* New York: Routledge, 1993.

Gorgias. *Encomium of Hellen.* Sprague 50–54.

Hairston, Maxine. "Diversity, Ideology, and Teaching Writing." *CCC* 43 (May 1992): 179–93.

Haraway, Donna. "The Actors Are Cyborg, Nature Is a Coyote, and the Geography Is Elsewhere: Postscript to 'Cyborgs at Large.'" Penley and Ross 21–26.

———. *"Ecce Homo*, Ain't (Ar'n't) I a Woman, and Inappropriate/d Others: The Human in a Post-Humanist Landscape." Butler and Scott 86–100.

———. "A Manifesto for Cyborgs: Science, Technology, and Socialist Feminism in the 1980s." Nicholson 190–233.

———. *Modest Witness@Second Millennium. The Female Man©_Meets_ OncoMouse™: Feminism and Technoscience*. New York: Routledge, 1997.

Harding, Sandra. "Feminism, Science, and the Anti-Enlightenment Critiques." Nicholson 83–106.

Harkin, Pattie, and John Schilb, eds. *Contending with Words: Composition and Rhetoric in a Postmodern Age*. New York: MLA, 1991.

Hartsock, Nancy. "Foucault on Power: A Theory for Women?" Nicholson 157–75.

Haynes, Cynthia. "Loss, Prosthetics, and the Rhetoric of Technology." CCCC Convention. March 1995.

———. "prosthetic_rhetorics@writing.loss.technology." *Literacy Theory in the Age of the Internet*. Ed. Todd Taylor and Irene Ward. New York: Columbia UP, 1998. 79–92.

Heidegger, Martin. *Being and Time*. New York: Harper, 1962.

———. *Early Greek Thinking: The Dawn of Western Philosophy*. Trans. David Ferrell Krell and Frank A. Capuzzi. San Francisco: Harper, 1984.

———. *An Introduction to Metaphysics*. New Haven: Yale UP, 1959.

———. "Language." Heidegger, *Poetry* 189–210.

———. *On the Way to Language*. Trans. Peter D. Hertz. New York: Harper, 1971.

———. *Poetry, Language, Thought*. Trans. Albert Hofstadter. New York: Harper, 1971.

———. "The Question Concerning Technology." *The Question Concerning Technology and Other Essays*. Trans. Albert Hofstadter. New York: Harper, 1971.

———. "What Are Poets For?" Heidegger, *Poetry* 89–142.

Hekman, Susan J. *Gender and Knowledge: Elements of a Postmodern Feminism*. Boston: Northeastern UP, 1990.

———. *Moral Voices, Moral Selves: Carol Gilligan and Feminist Moral Theory*. Oxford: Polity, 1995.

Heller, Dana. "Housebreaking Freud." *Family Plots: The De-Oedipalization of Popular Culture*. Philadelphia: U of Pennsylvania P, 1995.

Herder, Johann Gottfried. "Essay on the Origin of Language." Trans. Alexander

Gode. *On the Origin of Language: Jean-Jacques Rousseau.* Ed. John H. Moran. New York: Unger, 1966.

hooks, bell. *Yearning: Race, Gender, and Cultural Politics.* Boston: South End, 1990.

Irigaray, Luce. "And the One Doesn't Speak Without the Other." Trans. Hélène Vivienne Wenzel. *Signs* 7.1 (1981): 60–67.

———. *This Sex Which Is Not One.* Trans. Catherine Porter with Carolyn Burke. Ithaca: Cornell UP, 1977.

———. "When Our Lips Speak Together." Irigaray, *This Sex* 205–18.

Jameson, Fredric. *The Prison-House of Language: A Critical Account of Structuralism and Russian Formalism.* Princeton: Princeton UP, 1972.

Jardine, Alice A. *Gynesis: Configurations of Woman and Modernity.* Ithaca: Cornell UP, 1985.

Jarratt, Susan C. "Feminism and Composition: The Case for Conflict." Harkin and Schilb 105–23.

———. *Rereading the Sophists: Classical Rhetoric Refigured.* Carbondale: Southern Illinois UP, 1991.

———. "Spaces for Resistance in Feminist Classrooms." MLA Convention. December 1993.

Juncker, Clara. "Writing (with) Cixous." *College English* 50 (1988): 424–35.

Kennedy, George. "Some Reflections on Neomodernism." *Rhetoric Review* 6.2 (1988): 230–33.

Keuls, Eva. *The Reign of the Phallus: Sexual Politics in Ancient Greece.* New York: Harper, 1985.

Kofman, Sarah. "Nietzsche and the Obscurity of Heraclitus." *Diacritics* 17.3 (1987): 39–55.

Kristeva, Julia. "Postmodernism?" *Romanticism, Modernism, Postmodernism.* Ed. Harry R. Garvin. Lewisburg: Bucknell UP, 1980. 136–41.

———. *The Powers of Horror: An Essay on Abjection.* Trans. Leon S. Roudiez. New York: Columbia UP, 1982.

Kundera, Milan. *The Book of Laughter and Forgetting.* Trans. Michael Heim. New York: Penguin, 1986.

———. *Immortality.* Trans. Peter Kussi. New York: Grove Weidenfeld, 1991.

———. *The Joke.* Trans. David Hamblyn and Oliver Stallybrass. New York: Coward-McCann, 1969.

———. *The Unbearable Lightness of Being.* Trans. Michael Henry Heim. New York: Harper, 1984.

Lacan, Jacques. *Ecrits: A Selection.* Trans. Alan Sheridan. New York: Norton, 1977.

———. *The Four Fundamental Concepts of Psychoanalysis.* Ed. Jacques-Alain

Miller. Trans. Alan Sheridan. New York: Norton, 1981.

———. "The Function and Field of Speech and Language in Psychoanalysis." Lacan, *Ecrits* 30–113.

———. *The Seminar of Jacques Lacan: Book II, The Ego in Freud's Theory and in the Technique of Psychoanalysis 1954–1955*. Ed. Jacques-Alain Miller. Trans. Sylvana Tomaselli. New York: Norton, 1991.

———. *The Seminar of Jacques Lacan: Book VII, The Ethics of Psychoanalysis 1959–1960*. Ed. Jacques-Alain Miller. Trans. Dennis Porter. New York: Norton, 1992.

———. "The Signification of the Phallus." Lacan, *Ecrits* 281–91.

Lacoue-Labarthe, Philippe. "Talks." *Diacritics: A Review of Contemporary Criticism* 14.3 (Fall 1984): 24–35.

Lakoff, Robin. *Language and Women's Place*. New York: Harper, 1975.

Lamb, Catherine E. "Beyond Argument in Feminist Composition." *CCC* 42 (February 1991): 11–24.

Lanham, Richard. *The Motives of Eloquence*. New Haven: Yale UP, 1986.

de Lauretis, Teresa. *Technologies of Gender*. Bloomington: Indiana UP, 1987.

Lerner, Gerda. *The Creation of Patriarchy*. New York: Oxford UP, 1986.

Lévi-Strauss, Claude. *The Savage Mind*. Chicago: U of Chicago P, 1966.

———. *Structural Anthropology*. Trans. Claire Jacabson and Brooke Grundfest Schoepf. Garden City, NY: Doubleday, 1967.

Lispector, Clarice. *The Passion According to G.H.* Minneapolis: U of Minnesota P, 1988.

Lotman, Juri. *The Structure of the Artistic Text*. Trans. Ronald Vroon and Gail Vroon. Ann Arbor: U of Michigan P, 1977.

Lovibond, Sabina. "Feminism and Postmodernism." *New Left Review* 78 (November–December 1989): 5–28.

Lyotard, Jean-François. "A l'insu (Unbeknownst)." Miami Theory Collective 42–48.

———. *The Differend: Phrases in Dispute*. Trans. Georges Van Den Abbeele. Minneapolis: U of Minnesota P, 1988.

———. "Lessons in Paganism." *The Lyotard Reader*. Ed. Andrew Benjamin. Oxford: Basil Blackwell, 1989. 122–54.

———. *Libidinal Economy*. Trans. Iain Hamilton Grant. Bloomington: Indiana UP, 1993.

———. *The Postmodern Condition: A Report on Knowledge*. Trans. Geoff Bennington and Brian Massumi. Minneapolis: U of Minnesota P, 1984.

Lyotard, Jean-François, and Jean-Loup Thebaud. *Just Gaming*. Trans. Wlad Godzich. Minneapolis: U of Minnesota P, 1985.

Masson, Jeffrey Moussaieff. *Assault on Truth: Freud's Suppression of the Seduction*

Theory. New York: Harper, 1992.

McCracken, Grant. "A Call to Arms for Women?" *Toronto Globe and Mail*, 16 December 1991. A16.

Miami Theory Collective, ed. *Community at Loose Ends*. Minneapolis: U of Minnesota P, 1991.

Miller, Bernard A. "Heidegger and the Gorgian Kairos." *Visions of Rhetoric*. Ed. Charles W. Kneupper. Arlington, TX: RSA, 1987.

Moi, Toril. *Sexual/Textual Politics: Feminist Literary Theory*. London: Netheun, 1985.

Morton, Donald, and Mas'ud Zavarzadeh. *Texts for Change: Theory/Pedagogy/Politics*. Chicago: U of Illinois P, 1991.

———. "Theory/Pedagogy/Politics: The Crisis of 'The Subject' in the Humanities." Morton and Zavarzadeh 1–32.

Mountford, Roxanne. "'Clarity' Is Political: Assigning and Evaluating Experimental Writing." NCTE Summer Conference. Colgate University, Hamilton, NY. August 1995.

———. "Let Them Experiment: Accommodating Diverse Discourse Practices in Large-Scale Writing Assessment." *Evaluating Writing*, 2d ed. Ed. Charles Cooper and Lee Odell. Urbana, IL: NCTE, forthcoming.

Mountford, Roxanne, and Nedra Reynolds. "Rhetoric and Graduate Studies: Teaching in a Postmodern Age." *Rhetoric Review* 15.1 (Fall 1996): 192–214.

Nancy, Jean-Luc. *The Birth to Presence*. Trans. Brian Holmes et al. Stanford: Stanford UP, 1993.

———. "Exscription." Nancy, *Birth to Presence* 319–40.

———. *The Inoperative Community*. Ed. Peter Connor. Trans. Peter Connor, Lisa Garbus, Michael Holland, and Simona Sawhney. Minneapolis: U of Minnesota P, 1991.

———. Introduction. Cadava, Connor, and Nancy 1–8.

———. "Myth Interrupted." Nancy, *The Inoperative Community* 43–70.

———. "On Being-in-Common." Miami Theory Collective 1–12.

———. "Shattered Love." Nancy, *The Inoperative Community* 82–109.

———. "Speaking Without Being Able To." Nancy, *Birth to Presence* 310–18.

———. "War, Law, Sovereignty—Techné." Conley 28–58.

Neel, Jasper. *Plato, Derrida, and Writing*. Carbondale: Southern Illinois UP, 1988.

Nicholson, Linda J., ed. *Feminism/Postmodernism*. New York: Routledge, 1990.

Nietzsche, Friedrich. *Beyond Good and Evil*. 1886. Trans. R.J. Hollingdale. New York: Viking, 1972.

———. "Dialogue." Nietzsche, *Gay Science* 41.

———. *The Gay Science*. Trans. Walter Kaufmann. New York: Vintage, 1974.

———. *On the Genealogy of Morals* (1887) and *Ecce Homo* (1888). Trans. Walter Kaufmann and R.J. Hollingsdale. New York: Random, 1967.

———. *Philosophy and Truth: Selections from Nietzsche's Notebooks of the Early 1870s*. Ed. and trans. Daniel Breazeale. New Jersey: Humanities P International, 1993.

———. *Thus Spoke Zarathustra: A Book for None and All*. Trans. Walter Kaufmann. New York: Penguin, 1978.

———. *Untimely Meditations*. Trans. R.J. Hollingdale. New York: Cambridge UP, 1983.

———. *Will to Power*. Trans. Walter Kaufmann. New York: Vintage, 1968.

"Octolog." *Rhetoric Review* 7.1 (Fall 1988): 5–49.

Owens, Craig. "The Discourse of Others: Feminists and Postmodernism." *The Anti-Aesthetic: Essays on Postmodern Culture*. Ed. Hal Foster. Port Townsend, WA: Bay, 1983. 57–82.

Pagels, Elaine. *The Gnostic Gospels*. New York: Vintage, 1981.

Paglia, Camille. *Sexual Personae: Art and Decadence from Nefertiti to Emily Dickinson*. New York: Vintage, 1991.

Pefanis, Julian. *Heterology and the Postmodern: Bataille, Baudrillard, and Lyotard*. Durham: Duke UP, 1991.

Penley, Constance, and Andrew Ross, eds. *Technoculture*. Minneapolis: U of Minnesota P, 1991.

Plato. *Phaedrus*. *The Collected Dialogues of Plato*. Trans. R. Hackforth. Ed. Edith Hamilton and Huntington Cairns. Princeton: Princeton UP, 1961. 475–525.

Poynton, Cate. *Language and Gender: Making the Difference*. Oxford: Oxford UP, 1989.

Ratcliffe, Krista. "A Rhetorical Listening: A Strategy for Complicating Gender with Ethnicity." Forthcoming in *CCC* December 1999.

Regis, Ed. *Great Mambo Chicken and the Transhuman Condition: Science Slightly over the Edge*. Reading, MA: Addison-Wesley, 1990.

Ronell, Avital. "Activist Supplement: Papers on the Gulf War." Ronell, *Finitude's Score* 293–304.

———. *Crack Wars: Literature, Addiction, Mania*. Lincoln: U of Nebraska P, 1992.

———. *Dictations: On Haunted Writing*. Lincoln: U of Nebraska P, 1993.

———. "The Differends of Man." Ronell, *Finitude's Score* 255–68.

———. *Finitude's Score: Essays for the End of the Millennium*. Lincoln: U of Nebraska P, 1994.

———. "Interview with Avital Ronell." Interviewed by Andrea Juno. *Re/search:*

Angry Women no. 13. San Francisco: Research Publications, 1991. 127–53.

———. "Namely, Eckerman." Ronell, *Finitude's Score* 159–82.

———. "The *Sujet Suppositaire*: Freud, And/Or, the Obsessional Neurotic Style (Maybe)." Ronell, *Finitude's Score* 105–28.

———. "Support Our Tropes: Reading Desert Storm." Ronell, *Finitude's Score* 269–92.

———. *The Telephone Book: Technology, Schizophrenia, Electric Speech*. Lincoln: U of Nebraska P, 1989.

———. "The Uninterrogated Question of Stupidity." *Differences* 8.2 (Summer 1996): 1–19.

———. "The Worst Neighborhoods of the Real: Philosophy-Telephone-Contamination." Ronell, *Finitude's Score* 219–36.

Rorty, Richard. *Contingency, Irony, and Solidarity*. New York: Cambridge UP, 1989.

Saussure, Ferdinand de. *Course in General Linguistics*. Trans. Wade Baskin. New York: McGraw-Hill, 1966.

Schilb, John. "Cultural Studies, Postmodernism, and Composition." Harkin and Schilb 173–88.

Schniedewind, Nancy. "Feminist Values: Guidelines for Teaching Methodology in Women's Studies." *Freire for the Classroom: A Sourcebook for Liberatory Teaching*. Ed. Ira Shor. Portsmouth: Boynton, 1987. 170–79.

Serres, Michel. *Hermes*. Ed. Josué V. Harari and David F. Bell. Baltimore: Johns Hopkins UP, 1982.

Shor, Ira. *Critical Teaching and Everyday Life*. Boston: South End, 1980.

Shor, Ira, and Paulo Freire. *A Pedagogy for Liberation: Dialogues on Transforming Education*. Westport, CT: Bergin, 1987.

Showalter, Elaine. "Feminist Criticism in the Wilderness." *Critical Inquiry* 8.1 (1981): 179–205.

Silverman, Kaja. *The Subject of Semiotics*. New York: Oxford UP, 1983.

Simon, Roger. "Empowerment as a Pedagogy of Possibility." *Language Arts* 64.4 (1987): 370–82.

Sirc, Geoffrey. "Writing Classroom as A&P Parking Lot." *PRE/TEXT* 14.1–2 (Spring–Summer 1993): 27–70.

Sloterdijk, Peter. *Critique of Cynical Reason*. Foreword by Andreas Huyssen. Minneapolis: U of Minnesota P, 1987.

Solanas, Valerie. *The SCUM [Society for Cutting Up Men] Manifesto*. New York: Olympia P, 1967/8.

Spivak, Gayatri Chakravorty. "Feminism and Deconstruction, Again: Negotiating with Unacknowledged Masculism." *Between Feminism and Psychoanalysis*. Ed. Teresa Brennen. London: Routledge, 1989. 206–23.

———. Translator's Preface. *Of Grammatology*. By Jacques Derrida. Baltimore: Johns Hopkins UP, 1974. ix–xxxvii.

Sprague, Rosamund Kent, ed. *The Older Sophists*. Columbia: U of South Carolina P, 1972.

Starhawk. "Feminist, Earth-based Spirituality and Ecofeminism." *Healing the Wounds: The Promise of Ecofeminism*. Ed. Judith Plant. Philadelphia: New Society, 1989. 173–85.

Stone, Merlin. *When God Was a Woman*. New York: Dorset, 1976.

Taylor, Mark C. *Nots*. Chicago: U of Chicago P, 1993.

Turkle, Sherry. *Life on the Screen: Identity in the Age of the Internet*. New York: Simon, 1995.

Ulmer, Gregory L. "The Spirit Hand: On the Index of Pedagogy and Propaganda." Morton and Zavarzadeh 136–51.

Untersteiner, Mario. *The Sophists*. Oxford: Basil Blackwell, 1954.

Virilio, Paul. *Speed and Politics: An Essay on Dromology*. Trans. Mark Polizzotti. New York: Semiotexte, 1986.

———. "The Third Interval: A Critical Transition." Conley 3–12.

Vitanza, Victor J. "An After/word: Preparing to Meet the Faces that 'We' Will Have Met." Vitanza, *Writing Histories* 217–57.

———. "Concerning a Post-Classical Ethos as Para/Rhetorical Ethics, the 'Selphs,' and the Excluded Third." *Ethos: New Essays in Rhetorical and Critical Theory*. Ed. James S. Baumlin and Tita French Baumlin. Dallas: Southern Methodist UP, 1994. 389–431.

———. "Critical Sub/Versions of the Historiographies of Rhetorics; or the Rhetorics of the Histories of Rhetorics: Traditional, Revisionary, and Sub/Versive." *PRE/TEXT* 8.1–2 (1987): 63–125.

———. *Negation, Subjectivity, and the History of Rhetoric*. New York: State U of New York UP, 1997.

———. "On Negation—and Yet Affirmation—in Dis/respect to Critical Theory." Unpublished paper.

———. "'Some More' Notes, Toward a 'Third' Sophistic." *Argumentation* 5 (1991): 117–39.

———. "Some Rudiments of Histories of Rhetorics and Rhetorics of Histories." *Rethinking the History of Rhetoric*. Ed. Takis Poulakos. San Francisco: Westview, 1993. 193–239.

———. "Taking A-Count of a (Future-Anterior) History of Rhetoric as 'Libidinialized Marxism' (A PM Pastiche)." In Vitanza, *Writing Histories* 180–216.

———. "Three Countertheses: Or, A Critical In(ter)vention into Composition Theories and Pedagogies." Harkin and Schilb 139–72.

————. "Threes." *Composition in Context: Essays in Honor of Donald C. Stewart.* Ed. W. Ross Winterowd and Vincent Gillespie. Carbondale: Southern Illinois UP, 1994. 196–218.

————. "What's 'at Stake' in the Gorgian Fragment On Seriousness/Laughter." *PRE/TEXT* 10.1–2 (1989): 107–14.

————, ed. *Writing Histories of Rhetoric.* Carbondale: Southern Illinois UP, 1994.

Vitanza, Victor J., and Diane (Mowery) Davis. "Logocentrism." *Encyclopedia of Rhetoric and Composition: Communication from Ancient Times to the Information Age.* Ed. Theresa Enos. New York: Garland, 1996. 408–9.

Whalen, John. "Super Searcher: Cybarian Reva Basch is the Ultimate Intelligent Agent." *WIRED* 3.05 (May 1995): 153.

Wittgenstein, Ludwig. *Philosophical Investigations.* Trans. G. E. M. Anscomb. Oxford: Basil, 1953.

Worsham, Lynn. "Eating History, Purging Memory, Killing Rhetoric." Vitanza, *Writing Histories* 139–55.

————. "Writing Against Writing: The Predicament of Ecriture Féminine in Composition Studies." Harkin and Schilb 82–104.

Young, Iris M. "Humanism, Gynocentrism, and Feminist Politics." *Women's Studies International Forum* 8 (1985): 173–83.

Zavarzadeh, Mas'ud, and Donald Morton. *Theory as Resistance: Politics and Culture after (Post)Structuralism.* New York: Guilford, 1994.

Žižek, Slovoj. *The Sublime Object of Ideology.* London: Verso, 1989.

————. *Tarrying with the Negative: Kant, Hegel, and the Critique of Ideology.* Durham: Duke UP, 1993.

INDEX

D. Diane Davis is an assistant professor of rhetoric at the University of Iowa. Her current research and teaching interests include rhetoric and writing theory, posthumanist approaches to community, and issues in postmodern politics.